NEW YORK THEATRE GUIDE

NEW YORK THEATRE GUIDE

by Chuck Lawliss

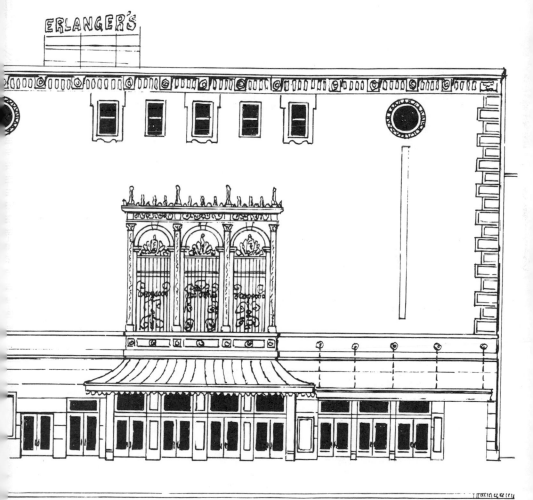

The Rutledge Press
New York, New York

Acknowledgments

Many people were helpful in the preparation of this guide. I particularly want to thank my research associate, Fred Plotkin, and the researchers: Richard Hurst, Vimi Vaidya, David Halpren, George Wieser, Jr., Margaret Kaufman, and Rolf Mann. The maps represent the skill of Tony Reid. Also Harvey Sabinson of the League of New York Theatres and Producers, Dr. Mary Henderson of the Museum of the City of New York, Louis Rachow, librarian at The Players, the staff of the Library of Performing Arts at Lincoln Center, Richard H. Brown, and my friends and agents, George and Olga Wieser.

Edited by: Christy Polk
Designed by: Allan Mogel
Front Photo: Mel Di Giacomo

The Anthony Dumas drawings courtesy of the Theatre Collection, Museum of the City of New York

Published by The Rutledge Press
A Division of W. H. Smith Publishers Inc.
112 Madison Avenue
New York, New York 10016

First Printing 1981
Printed in the United States of America

Library of Congress Cataloging in Publication Data

Lawliss, Chuck.
   New York theatre guide.

   Includes index.
   1. Theaters—New York (N.Y.)—Handbooks, manuals, etc.   2. New York (N.Y.)—Theaters—Handbooks, manuals, etc.   3. New York (N.Y.)—Nightclubs, dance halls, etc.—Handbooks, manuals, etc.
I. Title.
PN2277.N5L3   792'.097471   81-10547
                                      AACR2

ISBN 0-8317-6498-8 Pbk.

This book is for three lovely daughters—Lisa, Lucy, and Laura—who share their father's love of the theatre.

Foreword

I first appeared on the stage when I was five years old, playing Pease-blossom in *A Midsummer Night's Dream,* and I first appeared on Broadway when I was nine. Mr. Lew Fields hired me for his production of *Old Dutch,* a Victor Herbert operetta. Mr. Fields was in the show and so was Vernon Castle. It ran for 88 performances. There's a photograph of me from that show. I'm almost lost in a coat that practically reaches my ankles.

A few years later I was touring the country with John Drew. I was nineteen when I played with William Gillette in Barrie's *Dear Brutus.* Then dear Alfred Lunt and I were in Booth Tarkington's *Clarence.* You can understand when I say it's hard to remember when the theatre wasn't my life. I've done so many wonderful plays with so many wonderful people.

The theatre was different then, before movies became so big and before television brought professional entertainment into our homes. If you wanted to be entertained in those days, you went to the theatre. Some of the shows were a little silly by today's standards but Eugene O'Neill hadn't arrived yet to show us all what American theatre could be.

In my life in the theatre, one thing has never changed. Every few years some seemingly intelligent, well-informed person in the theatre announces that Broadway is dying and soon will be gone. Yet somehow Broadway just goes marching on. You've probably heard people refer to Broadway as "the incredible invalid". It's incredible, all right, but if Broadway is an invalid we should all be such invalids.

The *New York Theatre Guide* is a testimony to the health of the theatre today. So many talented people doing so many great things. I find it very reassuring. Of course, it is also a memory book for me, full of names and places that were important parts of my life. It's nice to remember the good old days. It's even nicer to be part of the good new days.

I found things in the book I didn't know—interesting things and useful things. So I think it's fair to say that the book can be helpful to anyone who loves the theatre, whether you are seeing your first Broadway show or are a veteran trouper like me.

Helen Hayes

Contents

INTRODUCTION

No one who is not intimately involved with theatre in New York can appreciate its size, diversity, and sheer quality. At the time this was written there were only 40 new movies and 32 revivals playing in the city while there were 183 different theatrical productions. *New York* magazine counts 99 movie houses in Manhattan; I know of more than twice as many legitimate theatres.

The 42 Broadway theatres are the most visible; hence the Broadway area is known as the theatre district. Yet there are more theatres in Greenwich Village and SoHo. Manhattan is dotted with legitimate theatres from the Battery to the Cloisters. Some are in former manufacturing lofts; others in church community centers. But make no mistake: These lofts and church community centers and the converted garages and all the rest are presenting first-class professional theatre.

If that sounds like an overstatement, consider this. *A Chorus Line* came from Joseph Papp's Astor Place complex; *Ain't Misbehavin'* from the Manhattan Theatre Club; *The Elephant Man* from St. Peter's Church theatre at Citicorp Center; *Gemini* from a workshop production at Playwrights Horizons; *The Best Little Whorehouse in Texas* from Entermedia. *Annie, Children of a Lesser God, Evita, Morning's at Seven,* and *To Grandmother's House We Go,* all are products of non-Broadway theatres. You could have seen Linda Ronstadt, Kevin Kline, and George Rose do *The Pirates of Penzance* at the Delacorte Theater in Central Park—free.

Whatever sort of theatre you seek, chances are it's being performed right now somewhere in the city: Shakespeare, Strindberg, Ibsen, Chekhov, Molière, O'Neill, Odets; theatre in Spanish, Yiddish, French, Korean; mime, puppets, children's theatre, labor theatre, avant-garde conceptual theatre, improvisational theatre, theatre of the absurd. It's all here in this wondrous city.

You can pay $35 for an orchestra seat to *42nd Street;* $14.50 (less on a subscription series) to see Nicol Williams in John Osborne's *Inadmissible Evidence* at Chelsea's Roundabout/Stage One, or $3 to see the Potter's Field Theatre Company do *Twelfth Night.* And all can be memorable.

Many think of theatre as elitist, yet more than 1,500,000 people attend the theatres listed in this guide *every month.* And that's more each month than the *season* attendance of the Yankees or any other New York athletic team. The state department of commerce recently conducted a survey of tourists and found that "seeing a Broadway show" was given as the number one reason for visiting the city. Hardly elitist at all.

What is the special appeal of the theatre? The demise of the theatre has been predicted many times. Radio was going to kill the theatre. Then the movies were. Certainly television would do it, the experts said. It was predicted theatre would go the way of vaudeville. But here it is, healthier than it has been in half a century. Why?

Part of the answer lies in the special nature of theatre. It is man's oldest intellectual entertainment. Theatre of a sort predates writing. Theatre has been an integral part of every civilization, every culture this planet has known. Perhaps the roots just go too deep for theatre to die easily.

Probably it is the live nature of theatre, too. There is an excitement, an electricity, a something that actors and an audience generate in the theatre that can't be projected on a screen or beamed through a cathode-ray tube. People are rediscovering the pleasure of live entertainment. Something in our subconscious must be telling us, *"It is happening in front of us right now and it will never happen exactly this way again. Ever."* I enjoy the movies and I enjoy television, but neither has ever given me the physical sensation that theatre so often can—the tingling that goes up my back and neck. Movies and television have given me much pleasure, but I've never felt the urge to jump to my feet and clap until my hands hurt.

And theatre thrives because of the superbly talented people it attracts. The actors and actresses aren't all doing eight shows a week in the hopes it will get them into the movies or a television series. Ask Henry Fonda or George C. Scott. Or Katharine Hepburn or Lauren Bacall. Nor is it money. One hit single could earn Linda Ronstadt more than she will make in the run of *The Pirates of Penzance*. No, it is the lure of the demanding craft of acting on the stage with no retakes or editing or doubles to make things easier for you. Jim Dale has to walk that tightrope every night, and every night the audience repays him in coin he treasures more than money.

It is not an exaggeration to say that there is more talent at work in the theatre in New York now—playwrights, producers, composers, directors, choreographers, stage and lighting and costume designers as well as performers—more here now than there ever has been, any time, any place.

There is so much good theatre here now that, one might say, a guide is needed. Some compendium of who's doing what, where, how to get there, what to expect when you do get there, and a lot of other items that theatregoers will find useful or interesting.

First off, every theatre of interest in the city and the surrounding area is listed with all pertinent information, an indication of the sort of productions to be seen there, and a bit of its history. (A nagging fear persists that some worthy theatres have been inadvertently overlooked, as much of the material here has never been researched and assembled before. I apologize if this is the case and hope to correct my omissions in subsequent editions.)

The theatres are grouped by area; each area has a map locating the theatres, restaurants, parking, and other places of interest. The maps also show accessibility by public transportation.

Restaurants are included because it's a rare evening at the theatre that doesn't include drinks and dinner or supper in some combination. Eating out is part of the theatre experience and each one makes the other more enjoyable.

A representational sampling of night spots—jazz spots, comic workshops, and the like—is included for they, too, can enhance the theatre experience. They are secondary, though, and have been measured against one standard: How much do they add to the pleasure of going to the theatre? To the degree that they do, one, two, or three stars appear by their names. Here I make no apology for omissions. To be exhaustive would make the guide unwieldy, not to mention that the tail would seem to be wagging the dog.

Finally, the listings contain the best sources in the city for books on the theatre, posters, original cast albums, memorabilia, and other artifacts for theatregoers, and, where pertinent, places of interest near the theatres, particularly in less frequented parts of the city.

The appendix is a potpourri of things I have always wished were available in one place: complete lists of the recipients of theatrical awards; the longest-running Broadway and Off Broadway productions; theatre terms; birthplaces and birthdates of leading actors and actresses and when they first appeared on the New York stage; some suggestions on how to get more out of theatregoing; and tips on how to stretch your theatre dollar when buying tickets.

I know this book will save you time, disappointment, and money. But I hope it will do more. I hope it will help you to broaden your theatre experience, to see more and different productions, to be a better audience. For a good audience is essential to good theatre.

HOW TO USE THIS GUIDE

This guide contains nearly 700 listings of theatres, restaurants, nightspots, shops, where to buy things of interest to theatregoers, other places of special interest, information on parking and public transportation, and a host of other things that should inform or entertain anyone who loves the theatre. But information loses much of its value if it's not presented in a useful way. I've attempted to do just that, and a few words of explanation are in order.

The key to the guide is the maps. The book is divided into geographical sections and each section has a map that locates the theatres in the area, parking, restaurants, other places of interest, and public transportation. If you know what area a theatre is in, turn to the map for the section and see where it is and what's nearby. If you're unsure of the area, check the index. There are a few areas where there isn't sufficient theatre activity to warrant a map. Then the how-to-get-there information is included at the end of the theatre listing.

The hard-core information is at the top of each theatre listing: box office phone number and hours, whether it accepts credit cards, size and seating details, whether it's air conditioned and accessible to the handicapped. The description tells what you might expect when you go there, or, in the case of the Broadway theatres, some of the theatre's history. There's a special section for producing groups that have no permanent home, again, to suggest what you might expect from their productions.

Restaurants and nightspots are handled in the same manner as the theatres. They are shown on the maps, and appear in the index. Essential information on price ranges, hours, and specialties is given in the individual listings.

There's a special section in the back that's a theatregoers's buying guide. These places are shown on the appropriate maps and are cross-indexed.

The restaurants and nightspots listed are described as *Inexpensive, Moderate,* or *Expensive. Inexpensive* denotes a place where the average check should not exceed $12 per person, exclusive of liquor, wine, and tip; *Moderate,* between $12 and $22; and *Expensive,* from $22 up. When a place is listed as *Inexpensive to Moderate,* or *Moderate to Expensive* it means either there is a prix fixe dinner in the lower of the two categories, or that there is a range of entree prices to encompass both categories. Hours are noted only when a restaurant closes too early for after-theatre dining. Unless otherwise noted, they are open daily. No star indicates that the restaurant is fair, * indicates good, ** very good, and *** superb.

In the listings, the following abbreviations are used:
AE - American Express
CB - Carte Blanche
DC - Diners Club
MC - Master Charge
V   - Visa
TDF- Theatre Development Fund
AC - Air Conditioning

BROADWAY

Broadway I

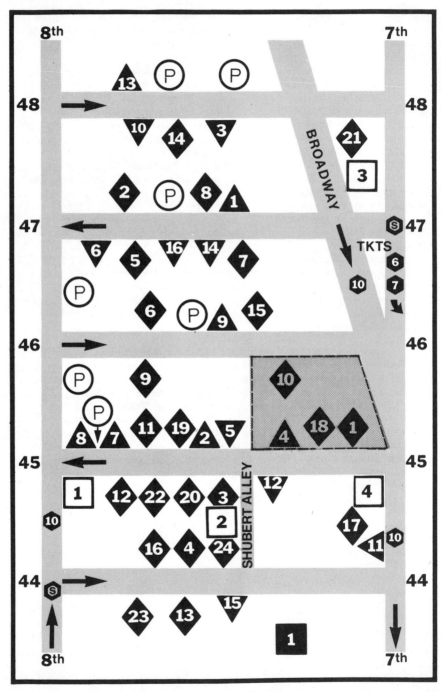

♦ Broadway Theatres

1. Bijou / 209 West 45
2. Biltmore / 261 West 47
3. Booth / 222 West 45
4. Broadhurst / 235 West 44
5. Brooks Atkinson / 256 West 47
6. Century / 235 West 46
7. Edison / 240 West 47
8. Ethel Barrymore / 243 West 47
9. 46th Street / 226 West 46
10. Helen Hayes / 210 West 46
11. Imperial / 249 West 45
12. John Golden / 252 West 45
13. Little Theatre / 240 West 44
14. Longacre / 230 West 48
15. Lunt-Fontanne / 205 West 46
16. Majestic / 245 West 44
17. Minskoff / 1515 Broadway
18. Morosco / 217 West 45
19. Music Box / 239 West 45
20. Plymouth / 236 West 45
21. Princess / 200 West 48
22. Royale / 242 West 45
23. St. James / 246 West 44
24. Shubert / 235 West 44

■ Other Theatres

1. CAP (Center for the Acting Process) / 276 West 43

▲ Restaurants

1. Alfie's / 225 West 47
2. Barrymore's / 247 West 45
3. Bernard's / 218 West 48
4. Café Ziegfeld / 227 West 45
5. Charlies' / 263 West 45
6. Delsomma / 266 West 47
7. Footlight / 259 West 45
8. Frankie and Johnnie's / 269 West 45
9. Kenny's Steak Pub / 221 West 46
10. Le Alpi / 234 West 48
11. Leo Lindy's / 1515 Broadway
12. Ma Bell's / 218 West 45
13. Mama Leone's / 239 West 48
14. Pierre au Tunnel / 250 West 47
15. Sardi's / 234 West 44
16. Spindletop / 254 West 47

□ Other Attractions

1. Broadway Posters / 252 West 45
2. One Shubert Alley / 1 Shubert Alley
3. Theatrebooks / 1576 Broadway
4. Theatre Museum in the Theatre District / Minskoff Theatre Arcade / 1515 Broadway

⑰ Bus Numbers

Ⓢ Subway Stations

Ⓟ Parking

→ One-way Street

⇄ Two-way Street

▭ Site of Portman Hotel

Broadway II

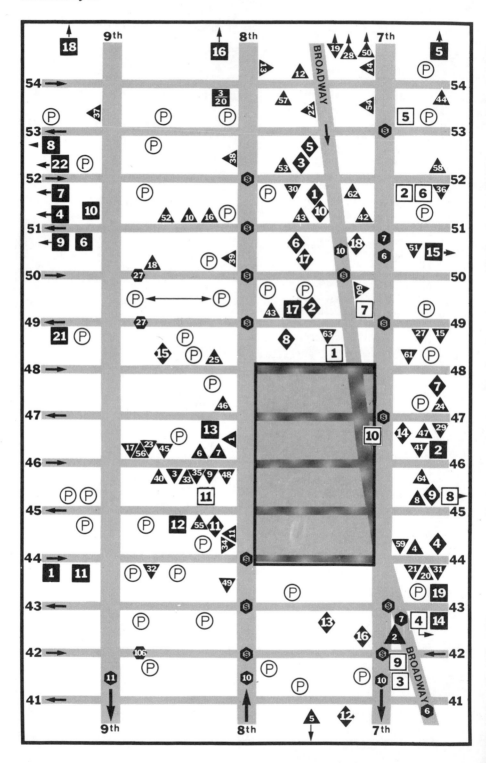

◆ Broadway Theatres

1. Alvin/250 West 52
2. Ambassador/215 West 49
3. ANTA/245 West 52
4. Belasco/111 West 44
5. Broadway/1681 Broadway
6. Circle in the Square/1633 Broadway
7. Cort/138 West 48
8. Eugene O'Neill/230 West 49
9. Lyceum/149 West 45
10. Mark Hellinger/237 West 51
11. Martin Beck/302 West 45
12. Nederlander/208 West 41
13. New Apollo/234 West 43
14. Palace/1564 Broadway
15. Playhouse/359 West 48
16. Rialto/1481 Broadway
17. Uris/1633 Broadway
18. Winter Garden/1634 Broadway

■ Other Theatres

1. Actors Studio/432 West 44
2. American Place Theatre/111 West 46
3. American Theatre of Actors/314 West 54
4. The Apple Corps/601 West 51
5. City Center/131 West 55
6. The Cubiculo/414 West 51
7. Ensemble Studio Theatre/549 West 52
8. Interart Theatre/549 West 52
9. Irish Rebel Theatre/553 West 51
10. Network Theatre/754 Ninth
11. The New Dramatists/424 West 44
12. No Smoking Playhouse/354 West 45
13. Puerto Rican Travelling Theatre Company/304 West 47
14. Quaigh Theatre—Hotel Diplomat/108 West 43
15. Radio City Music Hall/1280 Sixth
16. Royal Court Repertory/301 West 55
17. St. Malachy's Theatrespace/239 West 49
18. Theatre Four/424 West 55
19. Town Hall/123 West 43
20. Veterans Ensemble Theatrespace/314 West 54
21. WestSide Mainstage I & II/424 West 49

▲ Restaurants:

1. Acropolis/767 Eighth
2. Act One/One Times Square
3. A la Fourchette/342 West 46
4. Algonquin/59 West 44
5. Artist & Writers/213 West 40
6. Barbetta/321 West 46
7. Broadway Joe Steak House/315 West 46
8. Cabana Carioca/123 West 45
9. Café de France/330 West 46
10. Café des Sports/329 West 51
11. Call Back/709 Eighth
12. Capri/261 West 54
13. ¡Caramba!/918 Eighth
14. Carnegie Delicatessen/854 Seventh
15. Ceylon India Inn/148 West 49
16. Cheshire Cheese/319 West 51
17. Chez Cardinale/347 West 46
18. Chez Napoleon/365 West 50
19. Chez Raymond/240 West 56
20. Chilie's/142 West 44
21. China Bowl/152 West 44
22. China Song/1705 Broadway
23. Chuck Howard/355 West 46
24. Dish of Salt/133 West 47
25. Du Midi/311 West 48
26. El Tenapa/304 West 46
27. Farm Food/142 West 49
28. Fuji/238 West 56
29. Fundador/146 West 47
30. Gallagher's/228 West 52
31. Ho Shin/120 West 44
32. The Improvisation/358 West 44
33. Jack's Epicure/344 West 46
34. Jim Downey's/705 Eighth
35. Joe Allen/326 West 46
36. Joe's Pier 52/144 West 52
37. K. C. Place/807 Ninth
38. King Crab/871 Eighth
39. La Grillade/845 Eighth
40. Le Chambertin/348 West 46
41. Le Vert Galant/109 West 46
42. Les Pyrenees/251 West 51
43. Marta's of Bergen Street/249 West 49
44. Mickey's Cabaret Restaurant/44 West 54
45. Mildred Pierce/345 West 46
46. Molfetas/307 West 47
47. Molly Bloom's/150 West 47
48. Nick and Guido/322 West 46
49. Pantheon/689 Eighth
50. Patsy's/236 West 56
51. Rainbow Room/30 Rockefeller Plaza
52. René Pujol/321 West 51
53. Roseland/239 West 52
54. Stage Delicatessen/834 Seventh
55. Ted Hook's Backstage/318 West 45
56. Ted Hook's Onstage/349 West 46
57. Thai Palace/261 West 54
58. "21" Club/21 West 52
59. Un Deux Trois/123 West 44
60. Un Rinion Argentino/1626 Broadway
61. Vesuvio/163 West 48
62. Victor's Cafe 52/236 West 52
63. Wally's/224 West 49
64. Xochitl/146 West 46

□ Other Attractions

1. Colony Record Center/1619 Broadway
2. The Drama Bookshop/150 West 52
3. Hotalings News Agency/One Times Square
4. Music Masters/25 West 43
5. Park South Gallery/885 Seventh
6. Props and Practicals/150 West 52
7. Sam Goody/235 West 49
8. Samuel French, Inc./25 West 45
9. Songwriters Hall of Fame/One Times Square
10. TKTS/Duffy Square
11. Triton Gallery/323 West 45

🅱 Bus Numbers

🅂 Subway Stations

Ⓟ Parking

➡ One-way Street

⇄ Two-way Street

For Shaded Area see Broadway I Map

15

In the past seven years the attendance on Broadway has just about doubled. At the halfway mark in the 1980–81 season, attendance was up 24 percent. The League of New York Theatres and Producers was estimating a season's total attendance of 11,500,000, close to the all-time record set in 1927–28 when 12,000,000 persons saw Broadway shows.

There is no one reason why this is so. The half-price TKTS booth in Duffy Square helped; so did the convenience of buying by phone and credit card. But these are hardly innovations. Some point to the number of successful musicals, others to the high number of tourists in the city. And all note that this phenomenon has occurred despite sharply rising ticket prices.

Orchestra seats to *42nd Street* are $35 at all evening performances, a new high for musicals. Orchestra seats to *Amadeus* are $30, a new high for plays. Both have been selling out, night after night. By comparison, when *A Chorus Line* opened on Broadway in 1976, the top ticket price was $16.50.

Some producers venture the opinion that in times of adversity people are more interested in going out and having a good time. But the previous heyday of Broadway was the Roaring Twenties, hardly a time of adversity.

In the late 1920s there were 63 Broadway theatres. That, of course, was before the real impact of movies and television was felt. Nearly 10 years ago, Brooks Atkinson, in his excellent book *Broadway,* suggested that perhaps 10 theatres should be adequate to meet Broadway's needs. There now are 42 Broadway theatres and the talk is of more, not fewer. In 1927, there were 30 musicals running simultaneously on Broadway; when this was written, there were 20.

Whatever the reason, Broadway is healthy. Theatre is healthy. There has been a corresponding growth in what theatre professionals call "the road"—the cities with theatres that book national companies of Broadway productions. Two years ago, the road had grown to the point where more people saw a Broadway show on the road than did on Broadway.

When we were preparing this guide, we immediately noticed that the overwhelming majority of theatre companies in the city were less than 10 years old. In fact, 10 years ago there might not have been a clear need for a guide such as this.

Throughout the guide you will find references to Broadway, Off Broadway and Off-Off Broadway. This is as good a place as any to note the distinctions between them.

Broadway theatres are the big theatres in the 41st to 53rd Street–Sixth to Eighth Avenue theatre district—with some exceptions. The Vivian Beaumont and the New York State Theatre at Lincoln Center are considered Broadway houses. The Rialto, the Princess, and the Bijou are hardly big theatres, and some Off and Off-Off Broadway theatres are within the theatre district. The real distinction is that all Broadway theatres are members of the League of New York Theatres and Producers. Also important is that only shows produced in member theatres are eligible for the Tony Awards.

Off Broadway refers to the approximately 25 theatres where regular productions are presented, either by producers who rent the theatres or by production groups associated with the theatres. The Provincetown Playhouse, Circle in the Square Downtown, and the Entermedia are examples of the first; the Circle Repertory, Manhattan Theatre Club, and the Phoenix are examples of the second. At most of the Off Broadway theatres, the top ticket price will be about $15 to $18, much less when a subscription series is offered.

Off-Off Broadway is the profusion of small theatres, lofts, church auditoriums, etc., that usually present showcase productions. Through an agreement with Equity, actors are paid less than scale so that they may have the opportunity to "showcase" their talent. The showcase runs are limited, although some move up to extended runs under a different union agreement. The usual Off-Off Broadway ticket price is $3 to $5. Most Off-Off Broadway shows perform Thursday through Sundays.

To assume that these distinctions are reflective of the talent involved would be to make a major error. Hits and misses can come at any level for a variety of reasons, to be sure. However, to dismiss, say, Off-Off Broadway as amateurish is to deprive yourself of some of the most exciting theatre on any stage.

For that reason, these labels have been avoided in the guide except where necessary or helpful. To break up New York theatre into categories is to miss the fact that it functions as an entity. Not only do the various levels need and support one another in a myriad of ways; collectively they have made the entire renaissance here possible.

THE PORTMAN HOTEL

For more than seven years now, an unbuilt building has been casting a long shadow on Broadway. The Portman Hotel, a proposed 50-story, ultra-modern luxury hostelry would front Times Square between 45th and 46th streets, and, proponents say, the $261.5 million project would create a lot of jobs during and after construction, and give impetus to the revitalization of the Broadway area. Mayor Koch also estimates that the hotel would generate some $200 million in tax revenues during its first 10 years of operation. Besides city hall, the League of New York Theatres and Producers is squarely behind the Portman.

Where, then, is the rub? Who do Actors' Equity, Joseph Papp, and Clive Barnes, to name a few, oppose the Portman? Two reasons: To build the Portman three theatres must be demolished—the Helen Hayes, the Bijou, and the Morosco—not to mention the moderately priced Hotel Piccadilly and the attractive Café Ziegfeld; and a key, early part of the project's financing is a $22.5 million HUD grant that, critics say, could be better used either to improve existing theatres or creating low-income housing.

Partly mitigating the loss of the theatres is a new 1,500 seat theatre to be built into the Portman and named the New Helen Hayes. The League says that more 42nd Street theatres can be reconverted to legitimate houses to more than make up the rest of the loss. Foul! cry the critics. The theatre needs intimate houses like the Helen Hayes and the Morosco, not new 1,500-seaters. Foul! cry the producers. Big houses are needed because rising production costs need big houses to show a profit at current ticket prices.

What's going to happen? I say take the Portman and give odds; the muscle is behind it and there's too much money at stake. As this was written, a demolition contract had just been signed to raze the area by October, 1981. With full financing not yet in place, this brought a new concern—three theatres gone, with no hotel, no new theatre, nothing, perhaps, but an unneeded new parking lot.

WARNING!
If you see a small crowd gathered on Broadway, chances are that there's a three-card monte game going on. It looks simple: Three cards are dealt face down on a cardboard box; you guess which one is the black suit. Guess right, and you double your money. If you do win the first time, you're being set up for a bigger bet. If you see someone else win more than once, he's a shill. It's a can't-win proposition and a disgrace to the area.

BROADWAY THEATRES

ALVIN

250 West 52nd Street

Owner: The Nederlanders
Box Office: 757-8646
Box Office Hours: Wednesday–Saturday, 10 a.m.–8 p.m.; Sunday, 12 noon–7 p.m.; Monday–Tuesday, 10 a.m.–7 p.m.
Credit Cards: AE, MC, V   CHARGIT
Group Sales: 398-8383
Total Seating: 1,334 (Orchestra, 683; Boxes, 24; Mezzanine, 190; Balcony, 437; Standing room, 18)
Stage Type: Proscenium stage
AC
Handicapped: Semi-accessible

The Alvin is an acronymic name for the two producers who built the theatre to showcase musical comedy, Alex Aarons and Vinton Freedley. It opened on November 22, 1927, with a smash hit: the Gershwin brothers' *Funny Face,* starring Fred and Adele Astaire. Ethel Merman made her Broadway debut here in the Gershwins' *Girl Crazy,* and followed with the Cole Porter hits, *Anything Goes* with William Gaxton and Victor Moore, and *Red, Hot and Blue!* with Jimmy Durante and Bob Hope. George M. Cohan returned to the stage here to star as Franklin D. Roosevelt in *I'd Rather Be Right.* Another 1930s hit was Rodgers and Hart's *The Boys from Syracuse.* During the 1930s, CBS acquired the Alvin and used it from time to time as a radio playhouse. In the 1940s, Gertrude Lawrence and Danny Kaye sizzled in *Lady in the Dark* by Moss Hart, Kurt Weill, and Ira Gershwin. Alfred Lunt and Lynn Fontanne shone in *There Shall Be No Night* (featuring the young Montgomery Clift), which was awarded a Pulitzer Prize. Ethel Merman was back in Cole Porter's *Something for the Boys.* Ingrid Bergman starred in *Joan of Lorraine;* Maurice Evans, in *Man and Superman;* and the decade closed with one of the Alvin's biggest hits, Henry Fonda in *Mister Roberts,* which ran from 1948 to 1951. Then came Claude Rains in *Darkness at Noon;* Shirley Booth in *A Tree Grows in Brooklyn;* Mary Martin and Charles Boyer in *Kind Sir; House of Flowers;* Andy Griffith in the hit *No Time for Sergeants;* and Henry Fonda again in *Point of No Return.* The 1960s were a memorable decade here: Lucille Ball in *Wildcat,* Zero Mostel in *A Funny Thing Happened on the Way to the Forum,* Bea Lillie and Tammy Grimes in *High Spirit,* the Broadway debut of Liza Minnelli in *Flora, the Red Menace.* Among the musicals came Tom Stoppard's *Rosencrantz and Guildenstern Are Dead* and the Howard Sackler Pulitzer Prize winner, *The Great White Hope* with James Earl Jones and Jane Alexander. Three hits dominated the 1970s: Stephen Sondheim's *Company,* which won seven Tony Awards, and two from the Goodspeed Opera House in Connecticut, *Shenandoah* with John Cullum, and the smash hit *Annie,* which opened in April, 1977, and was still playing to sellout houses when this was written.

Area codes are 212 unless otherwise noted.

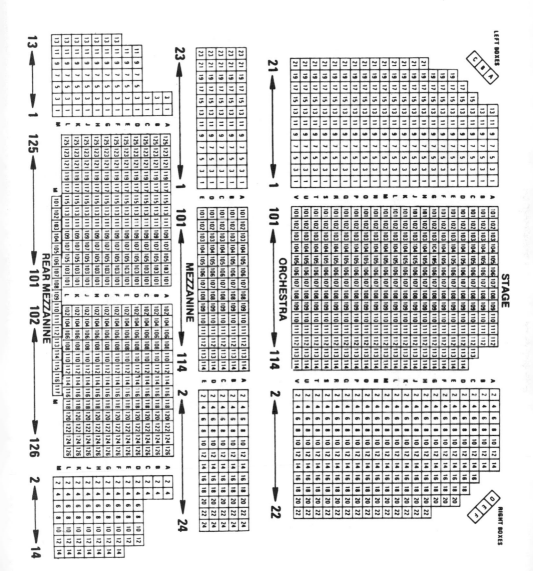

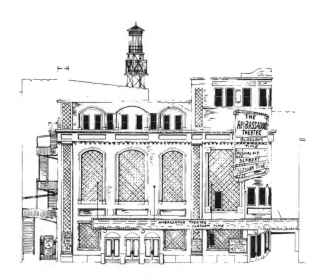

AMBASSADOR

215 West 49th Street

Owner: The Shubert Organization
Box Office: 541-6490
Box Office Hours: Monday–Saturday, 10 a.m.–8:30 p.m.; Sunday, 10 a.m.–6 p.m., if performance
Credit Cards: AE, DC, MC, V TELECHARGE Personal checks
Group Sales: Shubert Group Sales (944-4100)
Total Seating: 1,125 (Orchestra, 602; Mezzanine, 515; Boxes, 8; Standing room, 30)
Stage Type: Proscenium stage
AC
Handicapped: No access

The Ambassador has had a checkered career, switching from legitimate theatre to motion-picture house to radio and television studio several times between 1935 and 1955, when the Shuberts repurchased the theatre they had built and restored it to legitimacy. Good sites for theatres were running out when the Ambassador was built in 1921, so the architect had to design it to run diagonally for maximum site utilization. It opened February 11 of that year with *The Rose Girl* and its early hits included *Blossom Time; The Lady in Ermine; The Great Gatsby; Springtime for Henry;* the Abbey Theatre Players in *Juno and the Paycock; The Straw Hat Review* (which launched the careers of Imogene Coca, Alfred Drake, and Danny Kaye); and *School for Brides.* In 1959, *The Gang's All Here* starred E. G. Marshall, Melvyn Douglas, and Arthur Hill. Joseph Cotten and Patricia Medina took *Calculated Risks* in 1962. In 1967, four plays by Robert Anderson were presented with Eileen Heckart, George Grizzard, Martin Balsam, and Melinda Dillon. Judy Carne starred in a revival of *The Boy Friend* in 1970. *Ain't Supposed to Die a Natural Death* was here in 1971, and Jim Dale in *Scapino* was a big hit in 1974. Recently, Linda Hopkins starred in *Me and Bessie;* Billy Dee Williams, in *I Have a Dream;* and Estelle Parsons, in *Miss Margarida's Way.* The musical revue *Eubie* was followed by Bob Fosse's smash hit *Dancin',* still in residence in spring 1981.

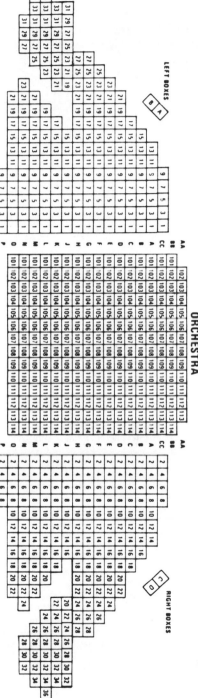

STAGE

ORCHESTRA

LEFT BOXES

RIGHT BOXES

FRONT MEZZANINE

REAR MEZZANINE

Front Mezzanine row AA overhangs Orchestra row H

Front Mezzanine row AA overhangs Orchestra row H

ANTA

245 West 52nd Street

Owner: ANTA
Box Office: 246-6270
Box Office Hours: Monday–Saturday, 10 a.m.–8:30 p.m.; Sunday, 12 noon–3 p.m., if performance
Credit Cards: AE, MC, V CHARGIT Personal checks for mail order
Group Sales: Through box office
Total Seating: 1,177 (Orchestra, 720; Loge, 175; Balcony, 282)
Stage Type: Proscenium stage
AC
Handicapped: Semi-accessible

This theatre was built for the Theatre Guild, which had been working at the old Garrick. Named the Guild, it opened April 13, 1925, with a production of *Caesar and Cleopatra* and the good wishes of President Calvin Coolidge, who threw a switch in Washington, D.C., to light the stage. Mary C. Henderson writes in her excellent book *The City and the Theatre* that for a variety of reasons the theatre was unpopular with both actors and audiences and a number of the Theatre Guild's productions opened at other theatres. In 1943, the theatre was leased as a radio playhouse. ANTA (American National Theatre and Academy) bought the house in 1950. Productions that decade included *Twentieth Century* with Gloria Swanson and José Ferrer, *Desire under the Elms,* and a revival of Thornton Wilder's *The Skin of Our Teeth* starring Mary Martin and Helen Hayes. Pat Hingle and Christopher Plummer starred with Raymond Massey in *J.B.,* Archibald MacLeish's drama based on the Book of Job. From 1961 to 1963, the ANTA was home to Robert Bolt's *A Man for All Seasons* with Paul Scofield as Sir Thomas More. Later Pat Hingle was back with Rip Torn and Diana Sands in James Baldwin's *Blues for Mister Charlie.* Ms. Sands returned in 1964 to star with Alan Alda in *The Owl and the Pussycat.* Henry Fonda came in 1968 to play the stage manager in a revival of *Our Town,* and, in 1969, the Pulitzer Prize winner *No Place to Be Somebody* came here from Off Broadway. In 1970, James Stewart teamed up with Helen Hayes in a revival of *Harvey,* and the American Shakespeare Theatre presented *Othello* starring Moses Gunn. Elizabeth Ashley headed the cast of a successful revival of *Cat on a Hot Tin Roof.* Recent productions: *Heartaches of a Pussycat;* Tom Stoppard's *Night and Day,* starring Maggie Smith; Derek Jacobi in *The Suicide;* and, from London, the musical *David Copperfield.*

Log row A overhangs Orchestra row L

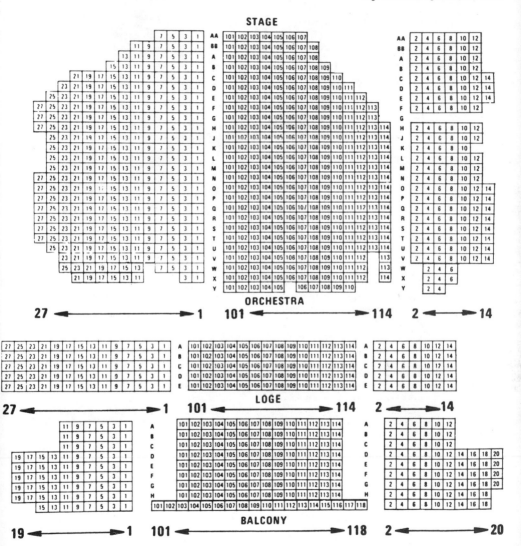

STAGE

ORCHESTRA

27 ← → 1   101 ← → 114   2 ← → 14

LOGE

27 ← → 1   101 ← → 114   2 ← → 14

BALCONY

19 ← → 1   101 ← → 118   2 ← → 20

23

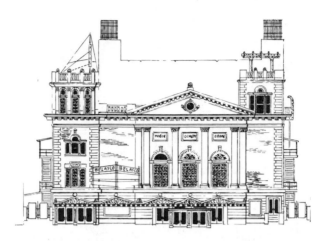

BELASCO

111 West 44th Street

Owner: The Shubert Organization
Box Office: 354-4490
Box Office Hours: Monday–Saturday, 10 a.m.–8:30 p.m.; Sunday, 10 a.m.–6 p.m., if performance
Credit Cards: AE, DC, MC, V TELECHARGE Personal checks
Group Sales: Shubert Group Sales (944-4100)
Total Seating: 1,018 (Orchestra, 532; Mezzanine, 285; Balcony, 201)
Stage Type: Proscenium stage
AC
Handicapped: Semi-accessible

David Belasco built this theatre to house his productions and incorporate his ideas of what a theatre should be. Originally named the Stuyvesant when it opened in 1907 (with *A Grand Army Man*), it had an elevator stage, and an apartment for Mr. Belasco upstairs. Belasco, who dressed like a clergyman but did not always behave like one, renamed the theatre the Belasco in 1910, and it remained his until his death in 1931. Belasco was a playwright as well as an entrepreneur and among his works produced here were *Madame Butterfly* and *The Girl of the Golden West*. In the 1930s, such realistic dramas as Sidney Kingsley's *Dead End,* Clifford Odets's *Golden Boy* and *The Gentle People* were presented here. John Barrymore's abortive comeback in *My Dear Children* opened the 1940s, followed by *Dark Eyes, Home of the Brave, Me and Molly,* and *The Madwoman of Chaillot.* The theatre was leased several times in this period: to Katharine Cornell, who presented Thornton Wilder's *Lucrece* and Sidney Howard's *Alien Corn;* to the Group Theater, who presented Odets's *Awake and Sing!* In the early 1950s, NBC used the Belasco as a radio playhouse. After it was returned to legitimate production, Josephine Hull starred in *The Solid Gold Cadillac* and Noel Coward starred in his own *Nude with Violin.* In the 1960s, Tad Mosel's *All the Way Home* won the Pulitzer Prize; Eva Le Gallienne presented her productions of *The Seagull* and *The Crucible;* Sam Levene starred in *The Last Analysis* and Nicol Williamson in *Inadmissible Evidence.* Other plays of the decade included *The Killing of Sister George, Does a Tiger Wear a Necktie?,* and *Oh! Calcutta!.* In 1975, came *The Rocky Horror Show.* On a more serious note, Colleen Dewhurst starred in *An Almost Perfect Person.* Herschel Bernardi was here briefly in *The Goodbye People,* as were Uta Hagen and Charles Nelson Reilly in *Hide and Seek.* At this writing, *Ain't Misbehavin'* had moved here for an extended run.

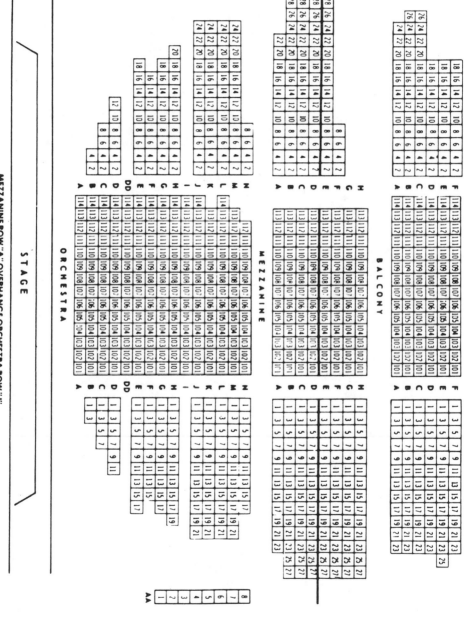

STAGE

MEZZANINE ROW "A" OVERHANGS ORCHESTRA ROW "J"
BALCONY ROW "A" OVERHANGS MEZZANINE ROW "C"

ORCHESTRA

MEZZANINE

BALCONY

25

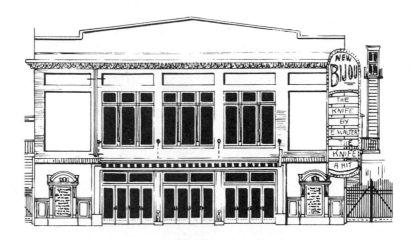

BIJOU

209 West 45th Street

Operator: Arthur Shaftman International Ltd.
Box Office: 221-8500
Box Office Hours: Monday–Saturday, 11:30 a.m.–8:30 p.m.; Sunday, 11:30 a.m.–3 p.m., if performance
Credit Cards: AE, MC, V   CHARGIT   Personal checks
Group Sales: Through box office and theatre party agents
Total Seating: 365 (Orchestra, 293; Balcony, 72; Standing room, 20)
Stage Type: Proscenium stage
AC
Handicapped: Semi-accessible

The Bijou Theatre opened April 12, 1917, with *The Knife.* It was not as successful as the other Shubert theatres but had some early successes: a long run of *Springtime for Henry,* the first Broadway appearance of Tallulah Bankhead in 1918, and Helen Hayes in a 1926 revival of *What Every Woman Knows.* During the Depression, at different times the theatre was closed or used as a movie house. It returned as a legitimate house in 1957 with the Broadway premiere of Eugene O'Neill's *A Moon for the Misbegotten.* This second life didn't last long, though, and it became the D. W. Griffith movie theatre in 1962. The following year it was again sold and renamed the ToHo, showing only Japanese films. In 1973, it was refurbished again and opened as a legitimate theatre under its original name. Some of the productions seen here since include the long-running *Mummenschanz,* Shelley Berman's one-man show, a Kurt Weill cabaret, and *Shakespeare's Cabaret.*

STAGE

ORCHESTRA

Row	Seats		Row	Seats
B	108 107 106 105 104 103 102 101		B	2 4 6 8
C	109 108 107 106 105 104 103 102 101		C	2 4 6 8
D	110 109 108 107 106 105 104 103 102 101		D	2 4 6 8
E	110 109 108 107 106 105 104 103 102 101		E	2 4 6 8
F	111 110 109 108 107 106 105 104 103 102 101		F	2 4 6 8
G	112 111 110 109 108 107 106 105 104 103 102 101		G	2 4 6 8
H	112 111 110 109 108 107 106 105 104 103 102 101		H	2 4 6 8
J	113 112 111 110 109 108 107 106 105 104 103 102 101		J	2 4 6
K	114 113 112 111 110 109 108 107 106 105 104 103 102 101		K	2 4 6 8
L	114 113 112 111 110 109 108 107 106 105 104 103 102 101		L	2 4 6 8
M	114 113 112 111 110 109 108 107 106 105 104 103 102 101		M	2 4 6 8
N	114 113 112 111 110 109 108 107 106 105 104 103 102 101		N	2 4 6 8
O	114 113 112 111 110 109 108 107 106 105 104 103 102 101		O	2 4 6 8
P	114 113 112 111 110 109 108 107 106 105 104 103 102 101		P	2 4 6 8
Q	114 113 112 111 110 109 108 107 106 105 104 103 102 101		Q	2 4 6 8
R	114 113 112 111 110 109 108 107 106 105 104 103 102 101		R	2 4 6 8
S	114 113 112 111 110 109 108 107 106 105 104 103 102 101		S	2 4 6 8
T	114 113 112 111 110 109 106 105 104 103 102 101		T	4 6 8

114 ◄———————————► 101   ◄—►8

MEZZANINE

Row	Seats		Row	Seats
A	114 113 112 111 110 109 108 107 106 105 104 103 102 101		A	2 4 6 8 10
B	112 111 110 109 108 107 106 105 104 103 102 101		B	2 4 6 8 10
C	113 112 111 110 109 108 107 106 105 104 103 102 101		C	2 4 6 8 10
D	113 112 111 110 109 108 107 106 105 104 103 102 101		D	2 4 6 8 10

114 ◄———————————► 101   2 ◄———► 10

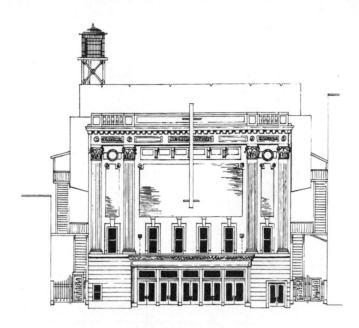

BILTMORE

261 West 47th Street

Owner: David Cogan; Operator: Biltmore Nederlander Corp.
Box Office: 582-5340
Box Office Hours: Monday–Saturday, 10 a.m.–8:30 p.m.; Sunday, 10 a.m.–6 p.m., if performance
Credit Cards: AE, DC, MC, V   CHARGIT   TDF Vouchers   Personal checks
Group Sales: Theatre Party Associates (564-5180)
Total Seating: 948 (Orchestra, 520; Balcony, 428; Standing room, 18)
Stage Type: Proscenium stage
AC
Handicapped: No access

Easy Come, Easy Go opened the Biltmore on December 7, 1925, but the most unforgettable event came in the early 1930s when the police raided Mae West's *Pleasure Man* on its second night, arrested the cast, and closed the show. The management quickly booked Claudette Colbert in *Tin Pan Alley* to improve the house's image. The Biltmore was the first of six theatres built by the Chanin Brothers in the Broadway area, and they lost them all in the Depression. The Federal Theater Project made its home here in the mid-1930s presenting free "living newspaper" productions that tackled tough issues of the day. In 1936, *Brother Rat* was a hit here; *My Sister Eileen* was another in 1940. Warner Brothers bought the Biltmore in the late 1930s to house George Abbott productions. CBS leased it for 10 years in 1952; the first production after the lights went on again was *Take Her, She's Mine* with Art Carney and Elizabeth Ashley. In 1963, Ms. Ashley starred with Robert Redford in *Barefoot in the Park*. Dyan Cannon and Martin Milner starred in 1967's *The Ninety Day Mistress,* and Joe Orton's comedy *Loot* came here from London the next year. One of the Biltmore's highlights was *Hair*'s arrival from Off Broadway on April 29, 1968, making stars of Diane Keaton and Melba Moore. More recent productions include Jules Feiffer's *Knock, Knock,* Barry Bostwick in the musical comedy *The Robber Bridegroom,* Lily Tomlin's one-woman show *Appearing Nitely,* Peter Allen's *Up in One,* Claudette Colbert and Rex Harrison in *The Kingfisher,* and, early this year, the regal Eva Le Gallienne and Kim Hunter in *To Grandmother's House We Go.*

STAGE

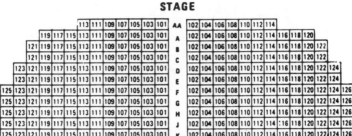

ORCHESTRA

127 ⟵⟶ 101   102 ⟵⟶ 128

MEZZANINE

9 ⟵⟶ 1   121 ⟵⟶ 101   102 ⟵⟶ 122   2 ⟵⟶ 10

BALCONY

129 ⟵⟶ 101   102 ⟵⟶ 130

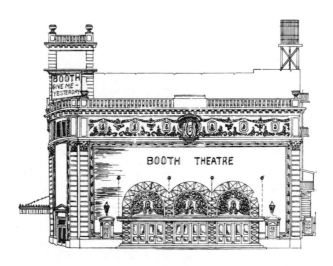

BOOTH

222 West 45th Street

Owner: The Shubert Organization
Box Office: 246-5969
Box Office Hours: Monday–Saturday, 10 a.m.–8:30 p.m.; Sunday, 12 noon–6 p.m., if performance
Credit Cards: AE, DC, MC, V TELECHARGE Personal checks
Group Sales: Shubert Group Sales (944-4100)
Total Seating: 783 (Orchestra, 515; Mezzanine, 252; Boxes, 16; Standing room, 25)
Stage Type: Proscenium stage
AC
Handicapped: Semi-accessible

This handsome theatre at the north end of Shubert Alley was named for Edwin Booth, the greatest actor of his time, and has been the scene of many distinguished plays since it opened October 16, 1913, with *The Great Adventure.* Booth Tarkington's *Seventeen* was an early hit. Kaufman and Hart's *You Can't Take It with You* won the Pulitzer Prize in 1936; William Saroyan's *The Time of Your Life* won in 1939. In 1950, Shirley Booth and Sidney Blackmer illuminated William Inge's *Come Back, Little Sheba.* Other important productions included Cornelia Otis Skinner's one-woman *Paris '90;* Bea Lillie in *An Evening with Bea Lillie;* Gore Vidal's *Visit to a Small Planet; Two for the Seesaw; The Tenth Man;* and *A Shot in the Dark,* with Julie Harris and Walter Matthau. In the 1960s, Tammy Grimes, Edward Woodward, and George Segal did *Rattle of a Simple Man;* Mike Nichols directed Eli Wallach, Anne Jackson, and Alan Arkin in *Luv;* James Patterson won a Tony in Harold Pinter's *The Birthday Party* as did Blythe Danner co-starring in *Butterflies Are Free* with Eileen Heckart. In 1972, *That Championship Season* came here from the Public Theater to win the Pulitzer Prize. Murray Schisgal's farce *All Over Town* opened in 1974 with Cleavon Little. *Very Good Eddie* came from the Goodspeed Opera House in Connecticut, and another hit came from the Public Theater: *For Colored Girls Who Have Considered Suicide . . . .* Another Tony winner was here in 1981: Bernard Pommerance's *The Elephant Man.*

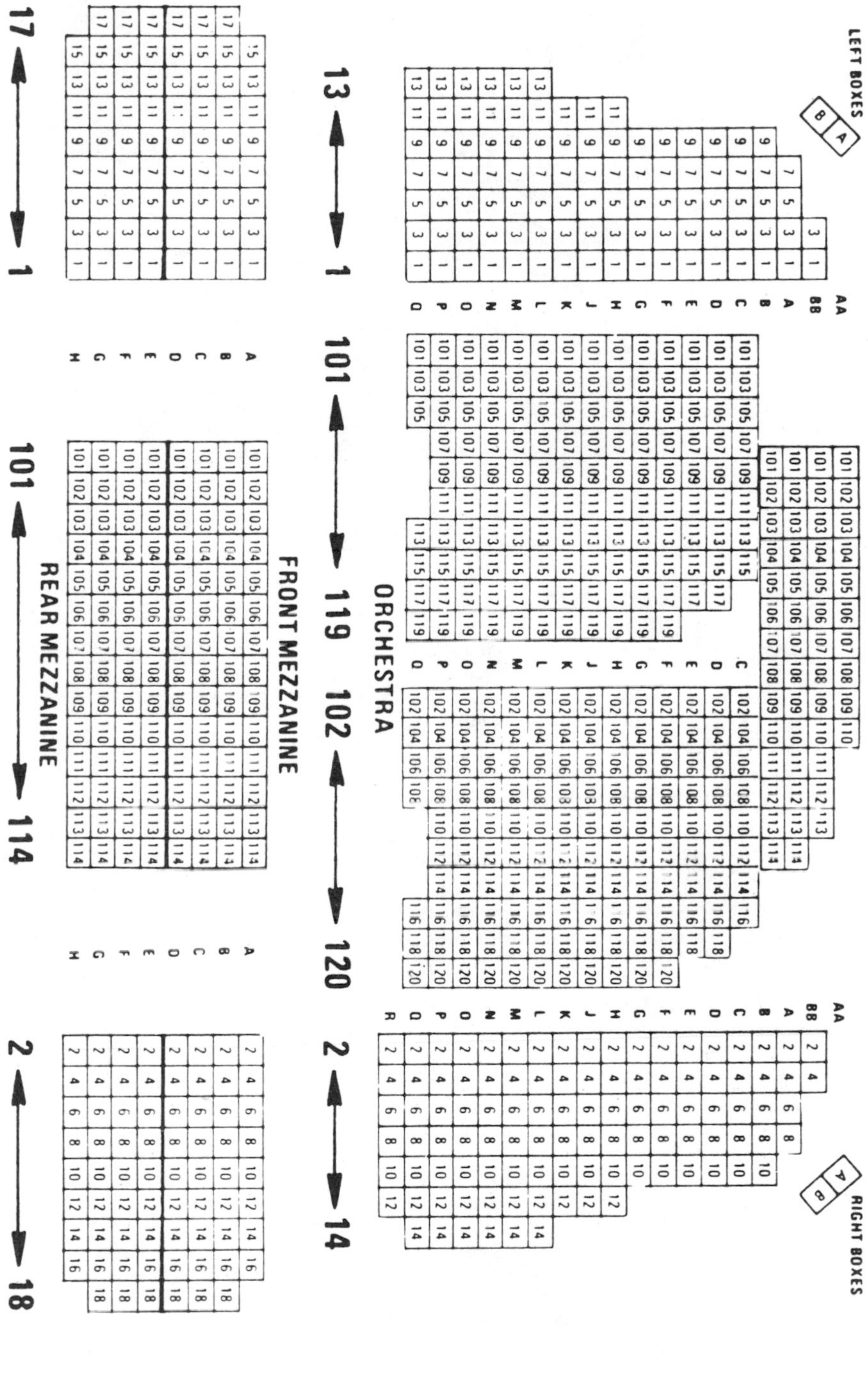

STAGE

ORCHESTRA

LEFT BOXES

RIGHT BOXES

FRONT MEZZANINE

REAR MEZZANINE

BROADHURST

235 West 44th Street

Owner: The Shubert Organization
Box Office: 247-0472
Box Office Hours: Monday–Saturday, 10 a.m.–8:30 p.m.; Sunday, 12 noon–6 p.m., if performance
Credit Cards: AE, DC, MC, V TELECHARGE Personal checks
Group Sales: Shubert Group Sales (944-4100)
Total Seating: 1,155 (Orchestra, 702; Mezzanine, 429; Boxes, 24; Standing room, 34)
Stage Type: Proscenium stage
AC
Handicapped: Semi-accessible

The Broadhurst with its strange array of balconies and fire escapes was named for playwright George Broadhurst and opened on September 27, 1917, with Shaw's *Misalliance.* Bert Lahr sang "You're the Cream in My Coffee" here in *Hold Everything.* In 1932, Ben Hecht and Charles MacArthur's *Twentieth Century* was a hit, and the next year the Group Theatre's produced Sidney Kingsley's *Men in White* which was later awarded the Pulitzer Prize. Also in the 1930s was *The Petrified Forest* with Leslie Howard and Humphrey Bogart in the tough-guy role that started him on his way to Hollywood fame, and Helen Hayes and Vincent Price in *Victoria Regina.* Productions in the 1940s included Ed Wynn's *Boys and Girls Together;* Agatha Christie's *Ten Little Indians;* and *Follow the Girls.* The 1950s here saw Olivia de Haviland in *Romeo and Juliet;* Rosalind Russell in *Auntie Mame; The World of Suzie Wong;* and another Pulitzer Prize winner, *Fiorello,* with Tom Bosley. The 1960s opened with Elaine Stritch in Noel Coward's *Sail Away;* followed by *Oh What a Lovely War; Half a Sixpence;* and in 1966 the smash hit *Cabaret,* with Joel Grey, Jill Haworth, Lotte Lenya, and Jack Gilford, winning eight Tony Awards. After *Cabaret* moved came Jules Feiffer's *Little Murders,* and, in 1967, Eugene O'Neill's *More Stately Mansions* with Ingrid Bergman, Colleen Dewhurst, and Arthur Hill. Woody Allen wrote and starred here in *Play It Again, Sam.* In the past decade, the Broadhurst has housed Neil Simon's *The Sunshine Boys; Sherlock Holmes,* Katharine Hepburn in *A Matter of Gravity;* George C. Scott in *Sly Fox;* and Bob Fosse's smash hit, *Dancin'.* As this was written, Peter Shaffer's *Amadeus* had settled in for a long run.

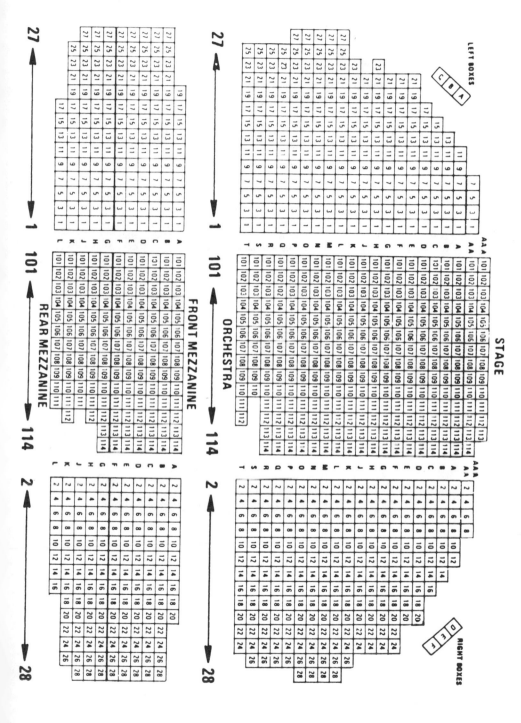

STAGE

LEFT BOXES

C B A

RIGHT BOXES

D E F

ORCHESTRA

27 ← 1

27 ← 1

101 → 114

101 → 114

2 ← 28

2 ← 28

FRONT MEZZANINE

27 ← 1

101 → 114

REAR MEZZANINE

27 ← 1

101 → 114

2 ← 28

BROADWAY

1681 Broadway (53rd)

Owner: The Shubert Organization
Box Office: 247-3600
Box Office Hours: Monday–Saturday, 10 a.m.–8:30 p.m.; Sunday, 12 noon–6 p.m., if performance
Credit Cards: AE, DC, MC, V   TELECHARGE   Personal checks
Group Sales: Shubert Group Sales (944-4100)
Total Seating: 1,765 (Orchestra, 909; Mezzanine, 844; Boxes, 12)
Stage Type: Proscenium stage
AC
Handicapped: Semi-accessible

Forty-second Street has a lot of movie houses that once were legitimate theatres. The Broadway opened as a movie house in 1924 and became a legitimate theatre five years later with the revue *The New Yorkers*. Here was where Bill (Bojangles) Robinson danced in *Memphis Bound!*, and where soldiers (including Ezra Stone and Gary Merrill) performed Irving Berlin's wartime *This Is the Army*. *My Sister Eileen* and *Carmen Jones* also enjoyed long runs here in the 1940s. In the 1950s, productions included revivals of *Oklahoma!* and *Diamond Lil*, the premiere of Gian Carlo Menotti's *The Saint of Bleecker Street*, a visit from the Old Vic, and *Gypsy* with Ethel Merman. Vivien Leigh won a Tony in 1963 for her only performance in a musical, co-starring with Jean-Pierre Aumont in *Tovarich*. The 1960s saw other distinguished productions; *Baker Street* with Fritz Weaver and Martin Gabel; *The Devils* with Jason Robards and Anne Bancroft; *Annie Get Your Gun* was revived and Ethel Merman recreated her title role. The 1970s led off with Purlie and both Melba Moore and Cleavon Little won Tonys for their performances. The revival of *Candide*, with music by Leonard Bernstein, was a hit, as was the all-black revival of *Guys and Dolls*. The hit of the decade, however, opened in 1979 and was still going strong two years later—the musical *Evita*.

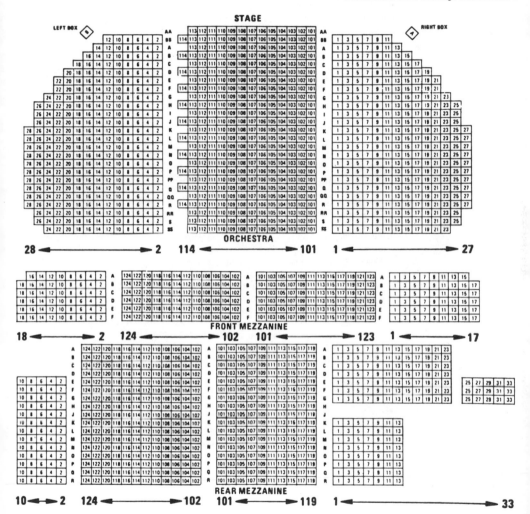

STAGE

ORCHESTRA

28 ⟵——————⟶ 2   114 ⟵——————⟶ 101   1 ⟵——————⟶ 27

FRONT MEZZANINE

18 ⟵——⟶ 2   124 ⟵——————⟶ 102   101 ⟵——————⟶ 123   1 ⟵——————⟶ 17

REAR MEZZANINE

10 ⟵—⟶ 2   124 ⟵——————⟶ 102   101 ⟵——————⟶ 119   1 ⟵——————⟶ 33

35

BROOKS ATKINSON

256 West 47th Street

Owner: The Nederlanders
Box Office: 245-3430
Box Office Hours: Monday–Saturday, 10 a.m.–8:30 p.m.; Sunday, 10 a.m.–3 p.m., if performance
Credit Cards: AE, MC, V
Group Sales: Through box office
Total Seating: 1,088 (Orchestra, 606; Mezzanine, 156; Boxes, 36; Balcony, 290; Standing Room, 30)
Stage Type: Proscenium stage
AC
Handicapped: Semi-accessible

Originally called the Mansfield, this theatre opened on Feb. 15, 1926, with Marjorie Rambeau in *The Night Duel.* Antoinette Perry, for whom the Tonys were named, then starred in *The Ladder.* Marc Connelly's Pulitzer Prize play, *Green Pastures,* opened here in 1930. Other early productions here: *In Time to Come* with Richard Gaines; *Anna Lucasta* with Hilda Simms, Frederick O'Neal, and Canada Lee; Ruth Gordon's *Years Ago* starring Fredric March; and Sartre's *Red Gloves* starring Charles Boyer. The theatre was a television playhouse from 1950 to 1960, and when it reopened as a legitimate theatre it was renamed to honor Brooks Atkinson, who had just retired after 30 years as drama critic of *The New York Times. Vintage '60,* a musical revue, was the opening production. Neil Simon's first Broadway play, *Come Blow Your Horn,* opened here. Julie Harris starred in *Ready When You Are, C.B.!,* and other comedies followed: *Love in E-Flat, A Minor Adjustment,* and *Halfway up the Tree* by Peter Ustinov. Albert Finney starred in *A Day in the Death of Joe Egg,* Renée Taylor and Joseph Bologna in *Lovers and Other Strangers,* and Dustin Hoffman in *Jimmy Shine.* Arthur Kopit's *Indians* was a 1969 success with Stacy Keach as Buffalo Bill. Maureen O'Sullivan, Louis Nye, and Martyn Green enlivened a revival of *Charley's Aunt.* In 1971, Keith Michell and Diana Rigg starred as *Abelard and Heloise;* later that year Cliff Gorman won a Tony as *Lenny.* The Negro Ensemble Company presented *The River Niger* in 1973. A revival of Steinbeck's *Of Mice and Men* starred James Earl Jones and Kevin Conway. Ellen Burstyn and Charles Grodin premiered in *Same Time, Next Year* in May, 1978, and the two-person comedy ran more than three years. Jack Lemmon did *Tribute* here, and, early in 1980, *Talley's Folly* with Judd Hirsch opened and went on to win the Pulitzer Prize. Donald Sutherland appeared in the Edward Albee adaptation of Nabokov's novel *Lolita* in spring 1981, followed by James Coco in *Wally's Cafe.*

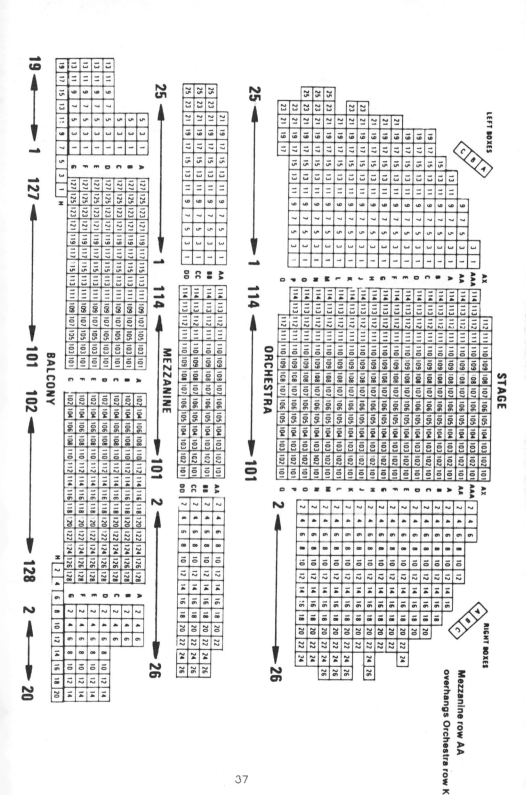

STAGE

LEFT BOXES

RIGHT BOXES

ORCHESTRA

MEZZANINE

BALCONY

Mezzanine row AA
overhangs Orchestra row K

37

CENTURY

235 West 46th Street

Owner: Jeffrey Wachtel
Box Office: 354-6644
Box Office Hours: Monday–Saturday, 10 a.m.–8 p.m.; Sunday, 10 a.m.–6 p.m., if performance
Credit Cards: AE, MC, V CHARGIT Personal checks
Group Sales: Varies with show
Total Seating: 299 (Orchestra, 299; Standing room, 20)
Stage Type: Semi-permanent proscenium stage
AC
Handicapped: Access without dignity (through hotel elevator)

If, when you arrive here, you feel as if you were entering a 1930s nightclub, you're not far wrong. From 1938 to 1951, this was Billy Rose's Diamond Horseshoe, and it still retains the Art Deco feel it once had. Since then it has been the Mayfair, then the Staircase, then the Mayfair again, before becoming the Century. A new lobby was built in 1980, and owner Jeffrey Wachtel (who bills himself in the program as "head honcho") plans to increase the orchestra by 150 during 1981. Some of the presentations here have included *On Golden Pond, The American Dance Machine, Lone Star & Private Wars, Are You Now or Have You Ever Been . . . , Banjo Dancing,* and most recently *Emlyn Williams as Charles Dickens.*

STAGE

8	6	4	2	A	101	102	103	104	105	106	107	108	109	110	111	112	113	114	115	116	A	1	3	5	7
8	6	4	2	B	101	102	103	104	105	106	107	108	109	110	111	112	113	114	115	116	B	1	3	5	7
8	6	4	2	C	101	102	103	104	105	106	107	108	109	110	111	112	113	114	115	116	C	1	3	5	7
8	6	4	2	D	101	102	103	104	105	106	107	108	109	110	111	112	113	114	115	116	D	1	3	5	7
8	6	4	2	E	101	102	103	104	105	106	107	108	109	110	111	112	113	114	115	116	E	1	3	5	7
8	6	4	2	F	101	102	103	104	105	106	107	108	109	110	111	112	113	114	115	116	F	1	3	5	7
8	6	4	2	G	101	102	103	104	105	106	107	108	109	110	111	112	113	114	115	116	G	1	3	5	7
8	6	4	2	H	101	102	103	104	105	106	107	108	109	110	111	112	113	114	115	116	H	1	3	5	7
8	6	4	2	J	101	102	103	104	105	106	107	108	109	110	111	112	113	114	115	116	J	1	3	5	7
8	6	4	2	K	101	102	103	104	105	106	107	108	109	110	111	112	113	114	115	116	K	1	3	5	7
8	6	4	2	L	101	102	103	104	105	106	107	108	109	110	111	112	113	114	115	116	L	1	3	5	7
8	6	4	2	M	101	102	103	104	105	106	107	108	109	110	111	112	113	114	115	116	M	1	3	5	7
8	6	4	2	N	101	102	103	104	105	106	107	108	109	110	111	112	113	114	115	116	N	1	3	5	7
8	6	4	2	O	101	102	103	104	105	106	107	108	109	110	111	112	113	114	115	116	O	1	3	5	7
				P	101	102	103	104	105	106	107	108	109	110	111	112	113	114	115	116	P				
				Q	101	102	103	104	105	106	107	108	109	110	111	112	113	114	115	116	Q				

8 ⟷ 2

10 ⟷ 116

1 ⟷ 7

CIRCLE IN THE SQUARE

1633 Broadway (50th, west of Broadway)

Owner: Paramount Equities; operated by Circle in the Square
Box Office: 581-0720
Box Office Hours: Monday–Saturday, 10 a.m.–8 p.m., Sunday, 10 a.m.–3 p.m.
Credit Cards: AE, DC, MC, V   CHARGIT   Personal checks (New York state only)
Group Sales: Director of audience development (581-1346)
Total Seating: 648 (Orchestra, 648; Standing room, 50)
Stage Type: Arena stage
AC
Handicapped: Access without dignity

Circle in the Square moved from the Village in 1972 to handsome new quarters below the Uris Theatre and opened with a shortened version of Eugene O'Neill's *Mourning Becomes Electra*. Under the artistic direction of Theodore Mann, the non-profit Circle is dedicated to the revival of distinguished plays and the production of significant new plays, and it is a rare pleasure to see them in this intimate setting. The productions and stars speak for themselves: 1973, Irene Papas in *Medea*, Siobhan McKenna in *Here Are Ladies*, Lillian Gish, George C. Scott, Nicol Williamson, Barnard Hughes, Elizabeth Wilson, Julie Christie, and Cathleen Nesbit in *Uncle Vanya*, Anne Jackson and Eli Wallach in *Waltz of the Toreadors*, and James Earl Jones in *The Iceman Cometh*; 1974, Murray Schisgal's *An American Millionaire*, Jim Dale in *Scapino*, Rita Moreno in *The National Health*, and Raul Julia in *Where's Charley?*; 1975, O'Neill's *All God's Chillun Got Wings*, George C. Scott, Teresa Wright, Harvey Keitel, and James Farentino in *Death of a Salesman*, Geraldine Fitzgerald in *Ah, Wilderness!*, and Maureen Stapleton in *The Glass Menagerie*; 1976, Vanessa Redgrave and Pat Hingle in *The Lady from the Sea, Pal Joey*, Mildred Dunnock in *Days in the Trees*, and Richard Chamberlain, Dorothy McGuire, and Sylvia Miles in *The Night of the Iguana*; 1977, *Romeo and Juliet, The Importance of Being Earnest*, John Wood, Mildred Dunnock, Tammy Grimes, and Victor Garber in *Tartuffe*, and Lynn Redgrave, Robert LuPone, Joseph Bova, and Philip Bosco in *Saint Joan*; 1978, Louis Jourdan in *13 Rue de l'Amour*, Kaufman and Hart's *Once in a Lifetime*, Theodore Bikel in Gogol's *The Inspector General*, and George Grizzard and Philip Bosco in *Man and Superman*; 1979, Stewart Parker's *Spokessong, Or the Common Wheel*, and Michael Weller's *Loose Ends*; 1980, *Major Barbara*, Jack Zeman's *Past Tense*, Ellis Rabb in *The Man Who Came to Dinner*, and Ibsen's *John Gabriel Borkman* with E.G. Marshall, Irene Worth, and Rosemary Murphy.

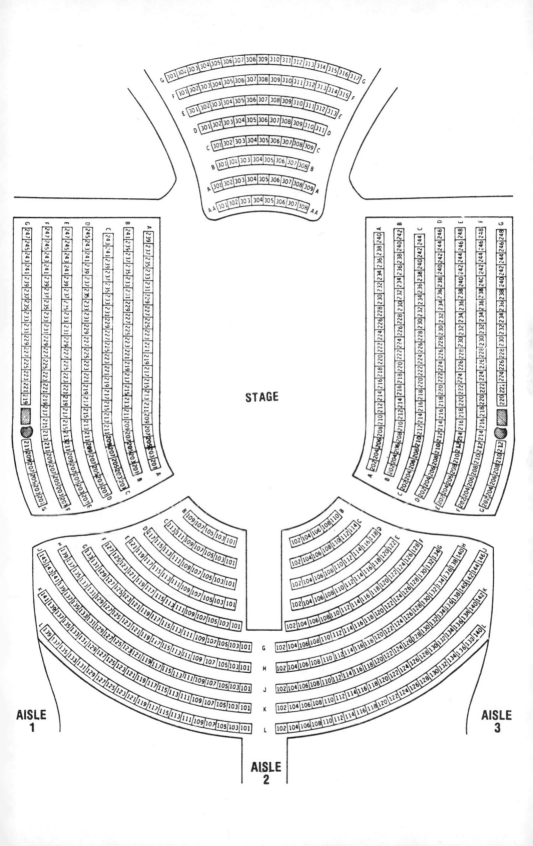

CORT

138 West 48th Street

Owner: The Shubert Organization
Box Office: 489-6392
Box Office Hours: Monday–Saturday, 10 a.m.–8:30 p.m.; Sunday, 12 noon–6 p.m., if performance
Credit Cards: AE, DC, MC, V   TELECHARGE   Personal checks
Group Sales: Shubert Group Sales (944-4100)
Total Seating: 1,089 (Orchestra, 506; Mezzanine, 264; Balcony, 283; Boxes, 36; Standing room, 20)
Stage Type: Proscenium stage
AC
Handicapped: Semi-accessible

The Cort has a reputation as a lucky house. It opened on December 20, 1912, with Laurette Taylor in *Peg o' My Heart,* which lasted two years, a phenomenal run in those days. Other early hits: Victor Herbert's *The Princess Pat,* Eva Le Gallienne and Basil Rathbone in *The Swan,* and George S. Kaufman and Mark Connelly's *Merton of the Movies. Room Service* with the Marx Brothers and *Charley's Aunt* with José Ferrer contributed to the Cort's reputation. During the war, *The Eve of Saint Mark* and *A Bell for Adano,* with Frederic March were popular attractions. In 1946, Katharine Cornell and Sir Cedric Hardwicke starred in *Antigone;* later that year Cornelia Otis Skinner was a success in *Lady Windermere's Fan.* The Cort housed two Pulitzer-Prize plays in the 1950s: *The Shrike* (1951) and *The Diary of Anne Frank* (1955); other memorable plays of that decade included *The Rainmaker, The Rope Dancers,* and *Sunrise at Campobello.* The 1960s opened with *Advise and Consent* and included *Purlie Victorious, Sunday in New York* with the young Robert Redford, *One Flew over the Cuckoo's Nest* with Kirk Douglas, and Carl Reiner's comedy, *Something Different* starring Linda Lavin, Bob Dishey, and Gabriel Dell. *The Magic Show* was the hit of the 1970s with a run of more than four years. The Cort later housed the Negro Ensemble Company's *Home,* and Glenda Jackson and Jessica Tandy in *Rose.*

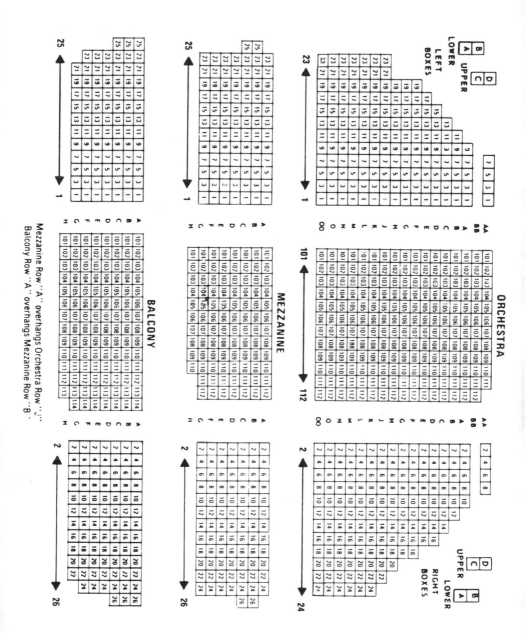

ORCHESTRA

MEZZANINE

BALCONY

LOWER LEFT BOXES

UPPER

LOWER RIGHT BOXES

UPPER

Mezzanine Row "A" overhangs Orchestra Row "J"
Balcony Row "A" overhangs Mezzanine Row "B".

EDISON

240 West 47th Street

Owner: Norman Kean
Box Office: 757-7164
Box Office Hours: Monday–Friday, 10 a.m.–8 p.m.; Saturday, 10 a.m.–10 p.m.
Credit Cards: AE, MC, V   (Telephone reservations with charge card)   Personal checks
Group Sales: Through box office
Total Seating: 499 (Orchestra, 278; Mezzanine, 68; Boxes, 36; Standing room, 14)
Stage Type: Proscenium stage
AC
Handicapped: Semi-accessible

It only seems as if *Oh! Calcutta!* has been here forever. Actually, it was the fall of 1976 when the nude musical revue moved in. It had opened at the old Eden, June 17, 1969, while this theatre was still being built. Norman Kean, owner of the Eastside Playhouse, designed the Edison to house shows that wouldn't work in large Broadway theatres. His hunch was right, for the Edison has rarely been dark since it opened with *Show Me Where the Good Times Are,* a musical roughly based on Molière's *The Imaginary Invalid.* Other productions have included a revival of the Marx brothers' classic *Room Service* starring Ron Leibman; Kurt Vonnegut's *Happy Birthday, Wanda June* with Kevin McCarthy, Marsha Mason, and William Hickey; an Israeli musical, *Only Fools Are Sad,* and the hit black musical *Don't Bother Me, I Can't Cope.* In 1974, Jon Kani and Winston Ntshona won Tonys for their starring performances in two South African plays by Athol Fugard, *Sizwe Banzi Is Dead* and *The Island.* Then came Linda Hopkins in 1975 recreating the glory of blues singer Bessie Smith in *Me and Bessie.* Then, of course, came *Oh! Calcutta!.*

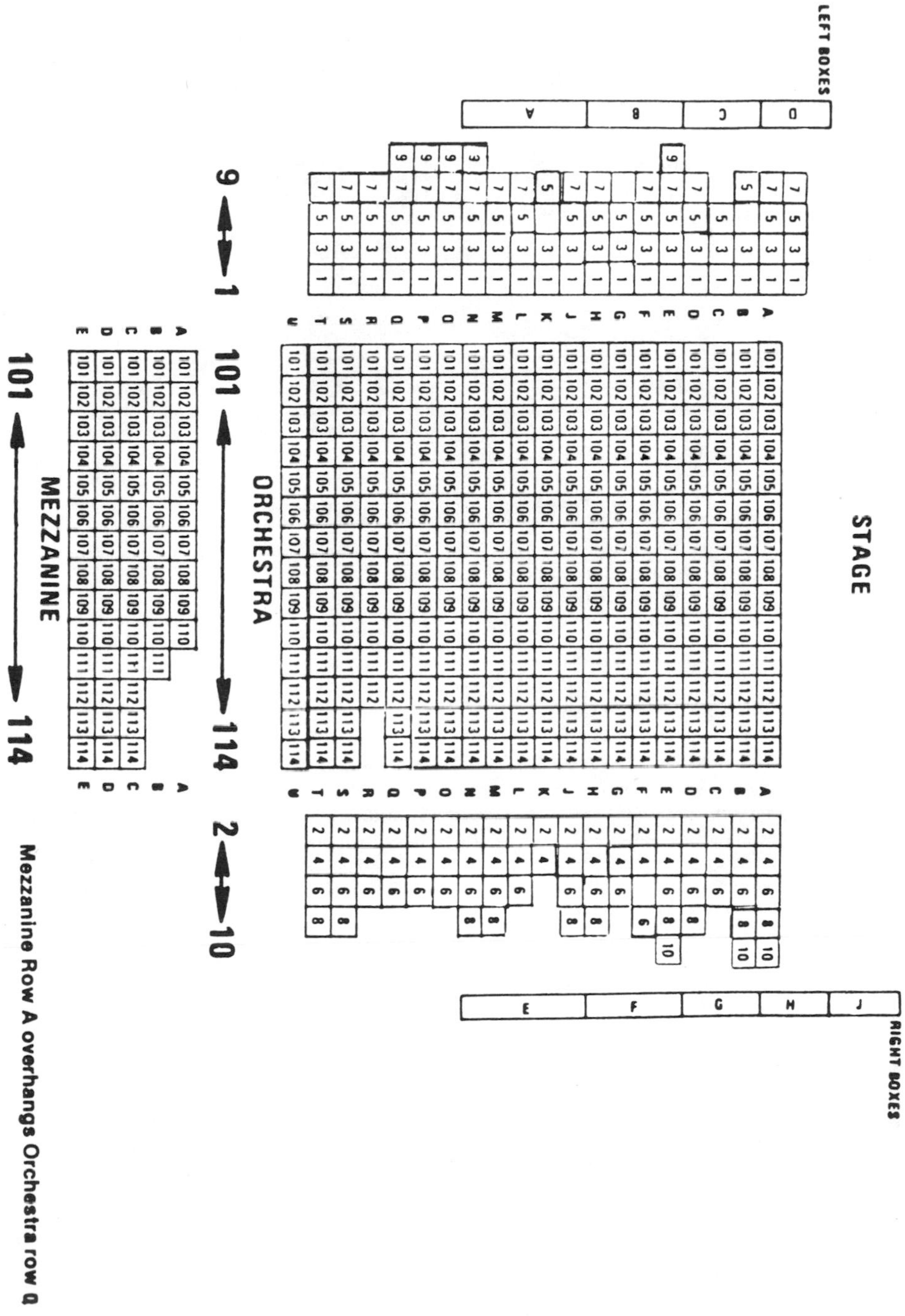

STAGE

LEFT BOXES

A
B
C
D

ORCHESTRA

101 ← → 114

9 ← → 1

2 ← → 10

MEZZANINE

101 ← → 114

101 ← → 114

RIGHT BOXES

E
F
G
H
J

Mezzanine Row A overhangs Orchestra row Q

45

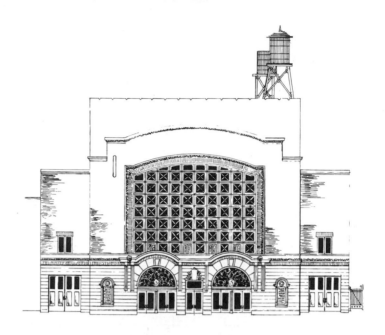

ETHEL BARRYMORE

243 West 47th Street

Owner: The Shubert Organization
Box Office: 246-0390
Box Office Hours: Monday–Saturday, 10 a.m.–8:30 p.m.; Sunday, 10 a.m.–6 p.m., if performance
Credit Cards: AE, DC, MC, V   TELECHARGE   Personal checks
Total Seating: 1,096 (Orchestra, 620; Mezzanine, 452; Boxes, 24)
Stage Type: Proscenium stage
AC
Handicapped: Semi-accessible

The Shubert brothers wanted to manage Ethel Barrymore so much that they promised to name a theatre after her if she would sign with them. She did, they did, and she opened the house on December 20, 1928, in *The Kingdom of God*. She starred here again in three plays: *The Love Duel, Scarlet Sister Mary,* and *The School for Scandal.* The first musical here was Cole Porter's *The Gay Divorcé* with Fred Astaire in 1930. Later that year, Alfred Lunt and Lynn Fontanne shone in Noel Coward's *Design for Living.* Productions in the 1930s included Clare Boothe's *The Women;* Walter Huston in *Knickerbocker Holiday;* Laurence Olivier in *No Time for Comedy;* and Paul Muni in *Key Largo.* Rodgers and Hart's *Pal Joey* was a hit in the 1940s, as was Gertrude Lawrence in *Pygmalion,* and Judith Anderson, Katharine Cornell, and Ruth Gordon in Chekhov's *Three Sisters.* The hit of the decade, however, and still holder of the house record was *A Streetcar Named Desire* with Marlon Brando, Jessica Tandy, Kim Hunter, and Karl Malden. In the 1950s came Gian Carlo Menotti's *The Consul;* Rex Harrison and Lili Palmer in *Bell, Book and Candle;* Hume Cronyn and Jessica Tandy in *The Fourposter;* Deborah Kerr in *Tea and Sympathy;* and Sidney Poitier in *A Raisin in the Sun.* In 1962, Orson Welles made a brief return to Broadway here with his production of *Moby Dick,* starring Rod Steiger. Other important productions that decade: Peter Falk as Joseph Stalin in *The Passion of Joseph D., Wait Until Dark, Black Comedy,* and Robert Ryan in the revival of *The Front Page.* The 1970s saw *Conduct Unbecoming; Ain't Supposed to Die a Natural Death;* Ingrid Bergman in GBS's *Captain Brassbound's Conversion;* Rex Harrison in *Emperor Henry IV; Travesties; American Buffalo;* and the long-running *I Love My Wife.* In spring 1981, Sam Waterson and Gilda Radner were starring in *Lunch Hour.*

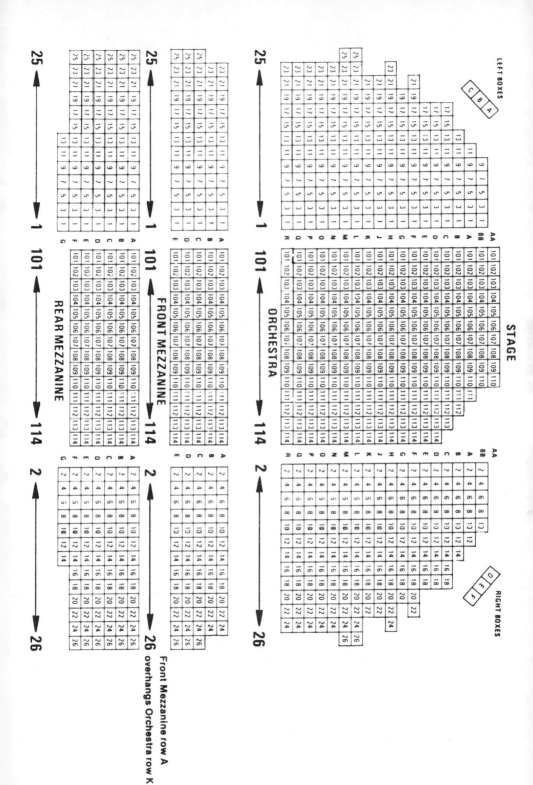

STAGE

LEFT BOXES

C B A

RIGHT BOXES

D E F

ORCHESTRA

FRONT MEZZANINE

REAR MEZZANINE

Front Mezzanine row A
overhangs Orchestra row K

47

EUGENE O'NEILL

230 West 49th Street

Owner: Nancy Enterprises, Inc.
Box Office: 246-0220
Box Office Hours: Monday–Saturday, 10 a.m.–8 p.m.; Sunday, 12 noon–3 p.m., if performance
Credit Cards: AE, MC, V ($1 service charge)
CHARGIT TELECHARGE Personal checks
Group Sales: Through box office or group sales agencies
Total Seating: 1,101 (Orchestra, 711; Mezzanine, 366; Standing room, 29)
Stage Type: Proscenium stage
AC
Handicapped: Semi-accessible

When this theatre opened November 24, 1925, with *Mayflowers* it was named the Forrest in honor of the great 19th-century American actor. From 1945 to 1959, for some reason, it was renamed the Coronet. It became the Eugene O'Neill in honor of our greatest playwright in 1959. *Tobacco Road* moved here from the Golden in September, 1934, and ran until May, 1941. Some of the outstanding presentations here have included Ed Begley and Arthur Kennedy in Arthur Miller's *All My Sons* (1947); Fredric March and Florence Eldridge in Lillian Hellman's *The Autumn Garden* (1951); Kim Hunter and Patricia Neal in Ms. Hellman's *The Children's Hour* (1952); Alfred Lunt and Lynn Fontanne in Noel Coward's *Quadrille* (1954) and *The Great Sebastians* (1956). *The Great God Brown* opened here in 1959; in 1960, George Grizzard, Sandy Dennis, and Jack Lemmon starred in *Face of a Hero*. Carol Channing followed in *Show Girl,* and in 1962 Jason Robards shone in Herb Gardner's *A Thousand Clowns*. For the past decade, the Eugene O'Neill has been a Neil Simon house—figuratively and literally: He owns it through Nancy Enterprises, Inc. James Coco in *Last of the Red Hot Lovers* (1970); *The Prisoner of Second Avenue* with Peter Falk and Lee Grant (1971); *The Good Doctor* with Christopher Plummer and Marsha Mason (1973); *God's Favorite* with Vincent Gardenia (1974), *California Suite* with George Grizzard, Tammy Grimes, Jack Weston, and Barbara Barrie (1976); *Chapter Two* moved here from the Imperial (1979); and, in 1980, *I Ought to Be in Pictures* with Ron Leibman.

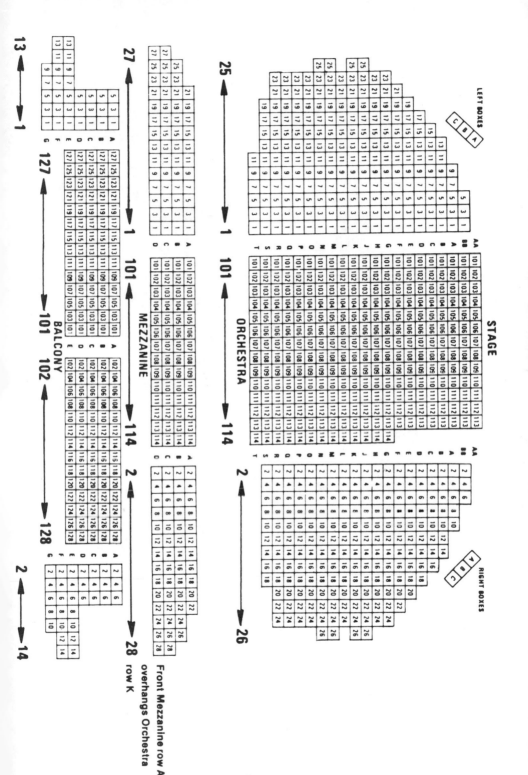

STAGE

LEFT BOXES

RIGHT BOXES

ORCHESTRA

MEZZANINE

BALCONY

Front Mezzanine row A
overhangs Orchestra
row K

49

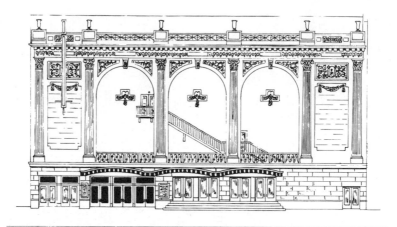

46TH STREET

226 West 46th Street

Owner: The Regency Organization Ltd.
Box Office: 246-0246
Box Office Hours: Monday–Saturday, 10 a.m.–8 p.m.; Sunday, 12 noon–6 p.m., if performance
Credit Cards: AE, MC, V CHARGIT Personal checks for future performances
Group Sales: Through box office and through theatre party agents
Total Seating: 1,342 (Orchestra, 802; Mezzanine and balcony, 540; Standing room, 36)
Stage Type: Proscenium stage
AC
Handicapped: Semi-accessible

The Chanins, movers and shakers on Broadway in the 1920s, opened their 46th Street theatre on Christmas Eve, 1925, with the *Greenwich Follies,* and it has housed mostly musicals ever since. In 1927, Zelma O'Neill made the Varsity Drag famous in *Good News; Follow Thru* in 1929 had two promising newcomers, Jack Haley and Eleanor Powell; Ginger Rogers was a hit in *Top Speed* the same year; Fannie Brice and George Jessel got the laughs in *Sweet and Low;* and, in 1935, from the Alvin came the classic *Anything Goes* with William Gaxton, Victor Moore, and, of course, Ethel Merman. Two more of her hits were here: *Du Barry Was a Lady* and *Panama Hattie.* The big hit in 1938 was *Hellzapoppin,* the success of which caused it to be moved to a larger theatre. Other big successes: Mary Martin in *One Touch of Venus; Finian's Rainbow; Guys and Dolls;* Audrey Hepburn's *Ondine;* and Gwen Verdon in *Damn Yankees, New Girl in Town,* and *Redhead.* The Pulitzer Prize musical *How to Succeed in business Without Really Trying* by Frank Loesser. In 1965, the Rodgers-Sondheim musical *Do I Hear a Waltz?* led off, followed by Mary Martin and Robert Preston in *I Do! I Do!* In 1969, it was *1776,* a Tony winner; in 1971, Ruby Keeler wowed them in the revival of *No, No, Nanette;* in 1973, *Raisin;* in 1975, Jerry Orbach and Chita Rivera and, for the fourth time here, Gwen Verdon in *Chicago.* In the summer of 1978, *The Best Little Whorehouse in Texas* moved uptown from the Entermedia and, in 1981, still was a solid hit.

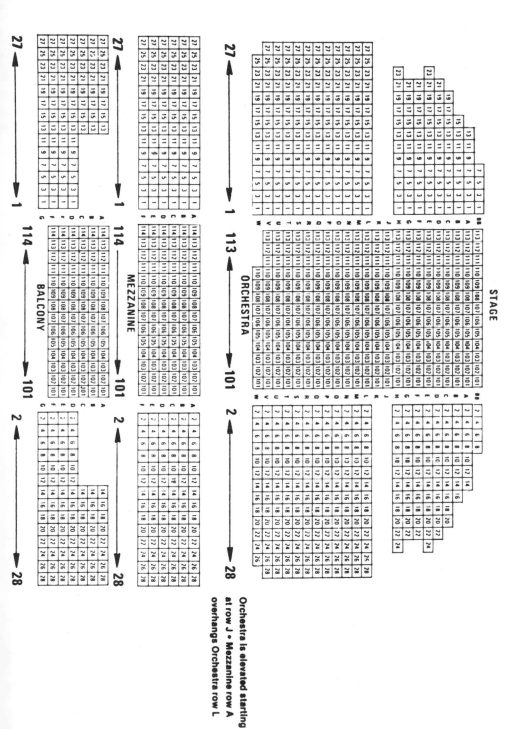

STAGE

ORCHESTRA

MEZZANINE

BALCONY

Orchestra is elevated starting
at row J • Mezzanine row A
overhangs Orchestra row L

51

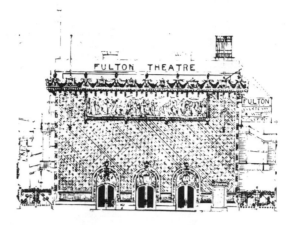

HELEN HAYES

210 West 46th Street

Owner: Lester Osterman
Box Office: 246-6380
Box Office Hours: Monday–Saturday, 10 a.m.–8 p.m.; Sunday, 2 p.m.–3 p.m.
Credit Cards: AE, MC, V
Group Sales: Varies with production
Total Seating: 1,160 (Orchestra, 612; First balcony, 298; Second balcony, 218; Mezzanine 32; Standing room, 30)
Stage Type: Proscenium stage
Handicapped: Semi-accessible

This theatre began as the Folies Bergères, Broadway's first theatre-restaurant. Shortly thereafter, it was remodeled into a legitimate theatre, renamed the Fulton, and opened on October 20, 1911, with *The Cave Man*. In 1921, *Abie's Irish Rose* premiered here but completed its record-breaking run at another theatre. Bela Lugosi thrilled the ladies in *Dracula* in 1927. George M. Cohan revived his *The Tavern* here in 1934. Leonard Stillman's *New Faces of 1934* introduced Henry Fonda to Broadway audiences. The hit *Three Men on a Horse* moved here in 1936; in 1938, Robert Morley was a hit in the title role of *Oscar Wilde*. The 1930s ended with the three-year run of *Arsenic and Old Lace*, with Josephine Hull, Jean Adair, and Boris Karloff. Montgomery Clift and Cornelia Otis Skinner starred in Lillian Hellman's *The Searchers* in 1944; Patricia Neal starred in Ms. Hellman's *Another Part of the Forest* in 1946. Gloria Swanson and José Ferrer sparkled in an ANTA revival of *Twentieth Century* in 1951. The next year saw Audrey Hepburn in *Gigi* and Tom Ewell in *The Seven Year Itch*. In 1955, the Fulton was renamed the Helen Hayes; the first production under the new name was Michael Redgrave in *Tiger at the Gates*. Perhaps the most distinguished production here was in 1956 *Long Day's Journey into Night*, with Frederic March, Florence Eldridge, Jason Robards, Jr., and Bradford Dillman. Another O'Neill play followed: *A Touch of the Poet*, starring Helen Hayes (in her only appearance to date here), Kim Stanley, Eric Portman, and Betty Field. In the 1960s came *Period of Adjustment*; Jean Kerr's *Mary, Mary* with Barbara Bel Geddes and Michael Rennie; Ms. Kerr's *Poor Richard*, starring Alan Bates and Gene Hackman; *Philadelphia, Here I Come!*; Zoe Caldwell in *The Prime of Miss Jean Brodie*; and Alec McCowan in *Hadrian VII*. In the 1970s, productions included: Jane Alexander and Jerry Orbach in *6 Rms Riv Vu*; Henry Fonda in *Clarence Darrow*; *The Royal Family*; *The Crucifer of Blood*; and the revival of *The Five O'Clock Girl*.

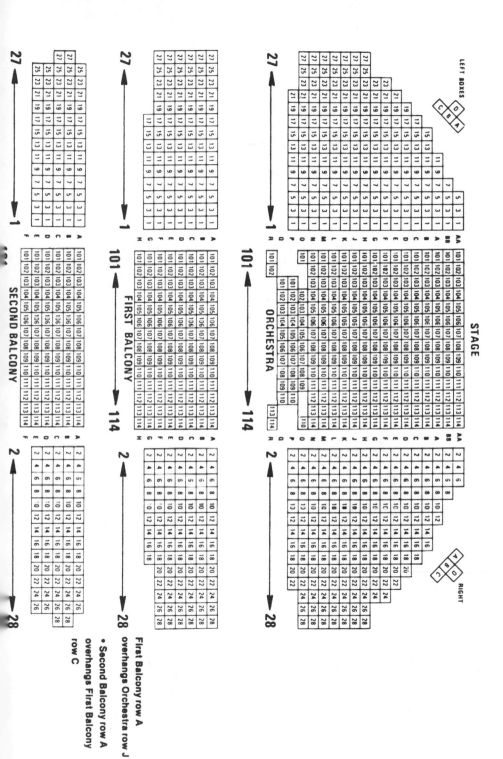

STAGE

LEFT BOXES

ORCHESTRA

FIRST BALCONY

SECOND BALCONY

RIGHT

First Balcony row A
overhangs Orchestra row J

• Second Balcony row A
overhangs First Balcony
row C

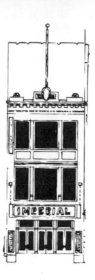

IMPERIAL

249 West 45th Street

Owner: The Shubert Organization
Box Office: 265-4311
Box Office Hours: Monday–Saturday, 10 a.m.–8:30 p.m.; Sunday, 12 noon–6 p.m., if performance
Credit Cards: AE, DC, MC, V TELECHARGE Personal checks
Group Sales: Shubert Group Sales (944-4100)
Total Seating: 1,452 (Orchestra, 755; Mezzanine, 283; Balcony, 378; Boxes, 36; Standing room, 36)
Stage Type: Proscenium stage
AC
Handicapped: Semi-accessible

This theatre has become synonomous with hit musicals. It opened on Christmas Day, 1923, with the forgettable *Mary Jane McKane*, but hit its stride the next year with *Rose Marie. Oh, Kay!* by the Brothers Gershwin was a success in 1926 with Gertrude Lawrence, as was *Sunny Days* with Jeannette MacDonald. The 1930s opened here with a revival of Victor Herbert's *Babes in Toyland.* Ed Wynn followed with *The Laugh Parade.* Clifton Webb and Patsy Kelly scored in the musical *Flying Colors.* In 1935 was *Jubilee* by Moss Hart and Cole Porter, whose score included "Begin the Beguine." Rodgers and Hart followed with *On Your Toes,* a musical that featured the revolutionary dance sequence "Slaughter on Tenth Avenue." In a complete change of pace, Leslie Howard triumphed in *Hamlet.* In the 1940s came more musical hits: *Louisiana Purchase, Leave It to Me* (Mary Martin shot to stardom in this singing "My Heart Belongs to Daddy"), and the biggest of them all, Ethel Merman in Irving Berlin's *Annie Get Your Gun.* In the 1950s the hits continued: *Jamaica* with Lena Horne, *Destry Rides Again,* and another Ethel Merman smash, *Call Me Madam. Carnival* with Anna Maria Alberghetti and Jerry Orbach led off the 1960s, followed by *Oliver,* and, in 1964, the phenomenal *Fiddler on the Roof* with the one and only Zero Mostel. *Fiddler's* 3,242 performances broke Broadway's long-run record. Herschel Bernardi came here after *Fiddler's* four-year run with the musical *Zorba.* Shelley Winters played the mother of the Marx brothers in *Minnie's Boys,* and Danny Kaye returned to the stage as Noah in *Two by Two.* The hit musical *Pippin* opened here in October, 1972, and ran until June, 1977, and made show business history as the first production to use television advertising successfully. Since then, Neil Simon has been calling the tune here: first with *Chapter Two,* starring Judd Hirsch and Anita Gillette, then with *They're Playing Our Song.*

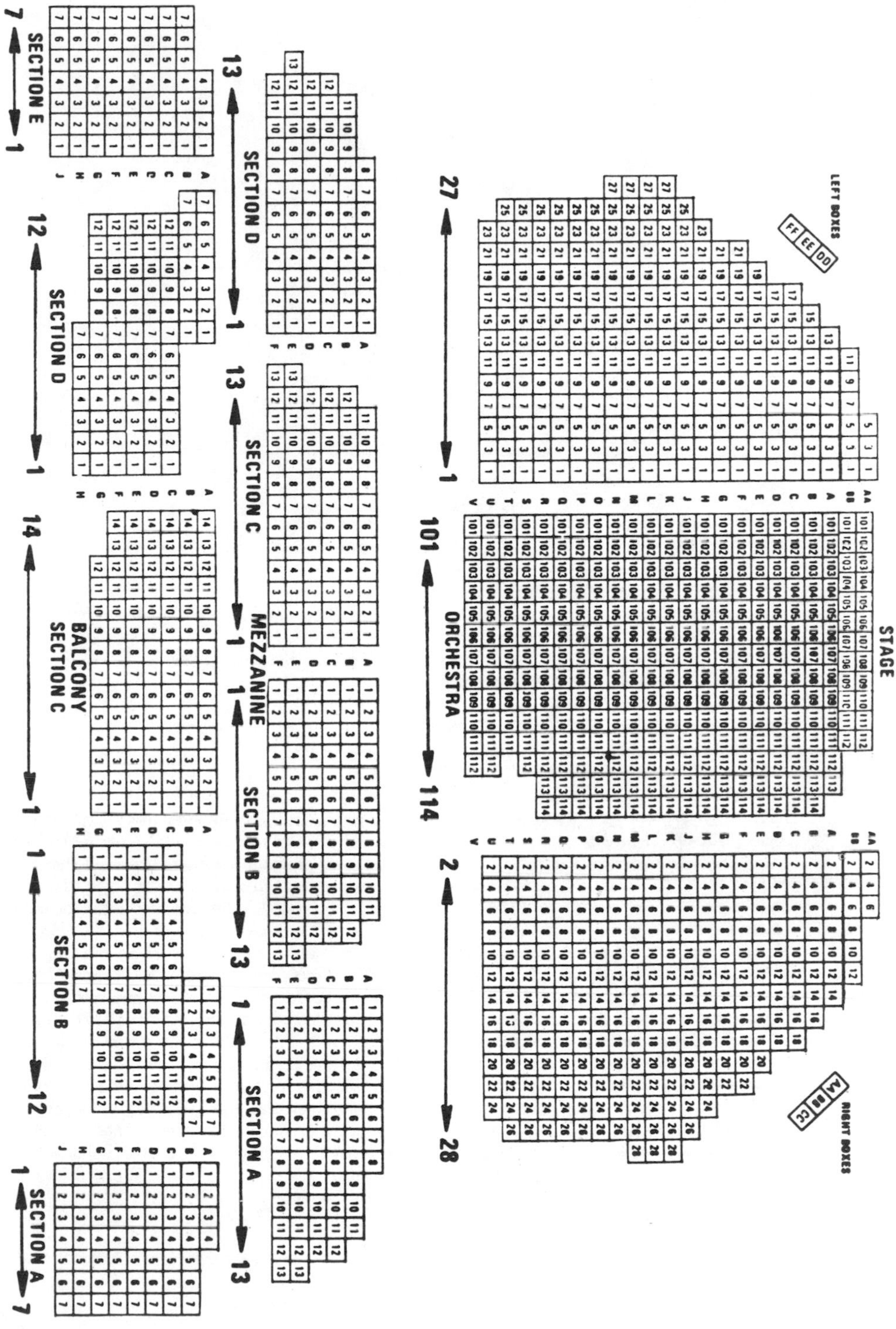

STAGE
LEFT BOXES
FF EE DD
RIGHT BOXES
AA BB CC
ORCHESTRA
27 1
101 114
2 28
MEZZANINE
SECTION D
13 1
SECTION C
13 1
SECTION B
1 13
SECTION A
1 13
BALCONY
SECTION E
7 1
SECTION D
12 1
SECTION C
14 1
SECTION B
1 12
SECTION A
1 7
Mezzanine row A overhangs Orchestra row H

JOHN GOLDEN

252 West 45th Street

Owner: The Shubert Organization
Box Office: 246-6740
Box Office Hours: Monday–Saturday, 10 a.m.–8:30 p.m.; Sunday, 10 a.m.–6 p.m., if performance
Credit Cards: AE, DC, MC, V TELECHARGE Personal checks
Group Sales: Shubert Group Sales (944-4100)
Total Seating: 805 (Orchestra, 468; Mezzanine, 337)
Stage Type: Proscenium stage
AC
Handicapped: Semi-accessible

When this theatre opened in 1927, it was named the Theatre Masque, and the owners were optimistic because it was the theatre closest to the new Eighth Avenue subway. The first production, *Puppets of Passion,* proved something less than memorable, but in 1933 came *Tobacco Road,* one of the longest-running shows of all time. Other successful shows here in the early days: Sir Cedric Hardwicke in *Shadow and Substance;* Philip Barry's *Here Come the Clowns;* and *Angel Street,* starring Leo G. Carroll, Judith Evelyn, and Vincent Price. Comedy has always found a home here: *A Party with Comden and Green* (1958); Swann and Flander's *At the Drop of a Hat* (1958); *An Evening with Mike Nichols and Elaine May* (1960); *Beyond the Fringe* with Peter Cook, Dudley Moore, Jonathan Miller, and Alan Bennett (1962); Victor Borge's *Comedy in Music* (1964); *Bob and Ray—The Two and Only* with Bob Elliott and Ray Goulding (1970); and Tom Stoppard's *Dirty Linen* (1977). Like many other Broadway theatres, it was a movie theatre in the mid-1940s. It became the John Golden in 1937 when the producer took it over from the original owners. He sold it to the Shuberts a few years later. In a serious vein, Alec McCowen starred here in 1966 in John Bowen's *After the Rain,* and recently Hume Cronyn and Jessica Tandy created the sharply edged characters of *The Gin Game.* The house record, however, was set by *Angel Street,* which opened in 1941 and ran for 1,293 performances. In spring 1981, Reneé Taylor and Joseph Bologna starred in their comedy, *It Had to Be You.*

STAGE

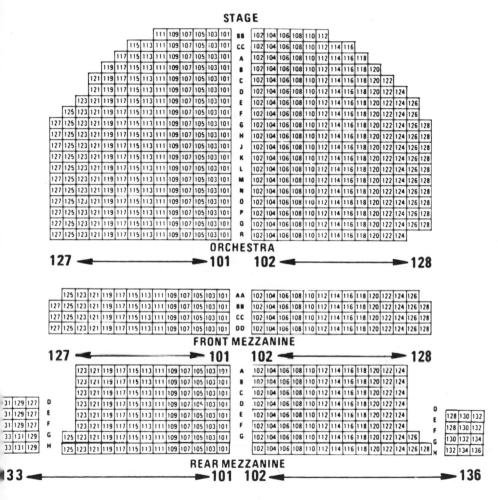

ORCHESTRA

127 ← → 101   102 ← → 128

FRONT MEZZANINE

127 ← → 101   102 ← → 128

REAR MEZZANINE

133 ← → 101   102 ← → 136

Front Mezzanine row A overhangs Orchestra row L

LITTLE THEATRE

240 West 44th Street

Owner: Little Theatre Group
Box Office: 221-6425
Box Office Hours: Monday–Saturday, 10 a.m.–8 p.m.; Sunday, 12 noon–3 p.m.
Credit Cards: MC, V CHARGIT Personal checks (10 banking days in advance)
Group Sales: Through box office
Total Seating: 499 (Orchestra, 311; Balcony, 188)
Stage Type: Proscenium stage
AC
Handicapped: No access

This theatre opened March 12, 1912, with *The Pigeon* as the Winthrop Ames. Its intention was to present small, intimate dramas that were unsuited to larger houses. Originally it had only 299 seats; it was enlarged later to 499. Thomas Mitchell starred in a 1926 comedy, Marc Connelly's *The Wisdom Tooth*. A popular revue of that era here was *The Grand Street Follies*. Rachel Crothers's 1929 comedy, *Let Us Be Gay*, was a hit. In 1931, Edward G. Robinson starred in *Mr. Samuel;* Ina Claire and Walter Slezak in Sidney Howard's 1935 *Ode To Liberty*. Other notable performances: Sir Cedric Hardwicke made his U.S. debut here in *Promise* in 1936; Cornelia Otis Skinner opened her one-woman show, *Edna His Wife*, here in 1937. For 20 years, the Little was not a legitimate theatre: the *Times* bought it, renamed it the New York Times Hall, and used it for conferences. In 1959, it became an ABC television studio. It returned to legitimacy in 1963 and a year later Paul Newman and Joanne Woodward appeared in the Actors Studio production of James Costigan's *Baby Want a Kiss*. But it was back to television for the Little in 1965, this time with Westinghouse Broadcasting: during the next 10 years the Merv Griffin and the David Frost shows were broadcast from here. The latest reincarnation was in 1974, and two years later had a hit, *The Runner Stumbles* by Milan Stitt. The best news for the Little came on May 21, 1977, however, when Albert Innaurato's *Gemini* moved here from the Circle Repertory Company.

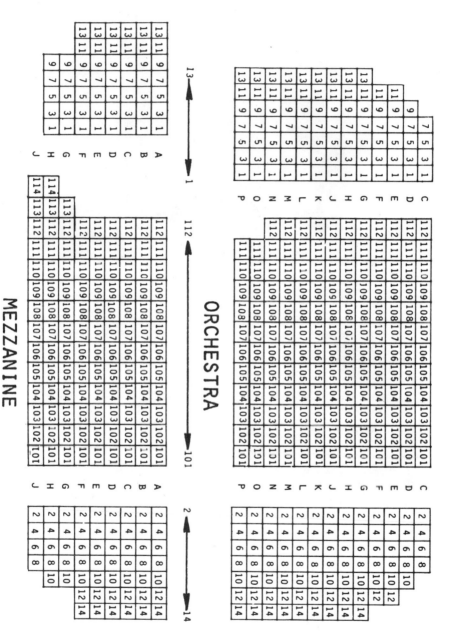

STAGE

ORCHESTRA

MEZZANINE

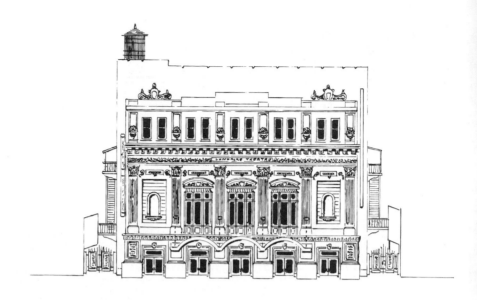

LONGACRE

230 West 48th Street

Owner: The Shubert Organization
Box Office: 246-5639
Box Office Hours: Monday–Saturday, 10 a.m.–8:30 p.m.; Sunday, 12 noon–6 p.m., if performance
Credit Cards: AE, DC, MC, V   TELECHARGE   Personal checks
Group Sales: Shubert Group Sales (944-4100)
Total Seating: 1,452 (Orchestra, 755; Mezzanine, 283; Balcony, 378; Boxes, 36; Standing room, 36)
Stage Type: Proscenium stage
AC
Handicapped: Semi-accessible

Before *The New York Times* built its tower at the south end, it was called Longacre Square, and baseball magnate and sometime theatrical producer H. H. Frazee borrowed the name when he built this theatre. It opened May 1, 1913, with *Are You a Crook?* In 1923, Miriam Hopkins starred here in the musical hit *Cobra;* three years later she starred again in *An American Tragedy.* Joan Bennett appeared with her matinee idol father Richard Bennett in *Jarnegan,* a 1928 exposé of Hollywood. In the 1930s, the Group Theatre used the Longacre for three distinguished Clifford Odets plays: *Waiting for Lefty; Till the Day I Die,* and *Paradise Lost.* Among the players were Elia Kazan and Lee J. Cobb. From 1944 to 1953, the theatre was a radio and television studio. It made a comeback with *Ladies of the Corridor* by Dorothy Parker and Arnaud d'Usseau (the cast included Edna Best, Betty Field, and the young Walter Matthau). Four Julie Harris vehicles were staged here: *Mademoiselle Colombe* (1954); *The Lark* (1955); *Little Moon of Alban* (1960); and *The Belle of Amherst* (1976). Other memorable Longacre performances: Zero Mostel in *Rhinoceros* (1961); Teresa Wright, Lillian Gish, and Hal Holbrook in Robert Anderson's *I Never Sang for My Father* (1968); Rita Moreno and Jack Weston in *The Ritz* (1975); Sir John Gielgud and Sir Ralph Richardson in Harold Pinter's *No Man's Land* (1976). Recently, the Longacre was the home of the 1978 Tony Award-winning musical *Ain't Misbehavin',* followed by the 1980 Tony Award-winning play *Children of a Lesser God.*

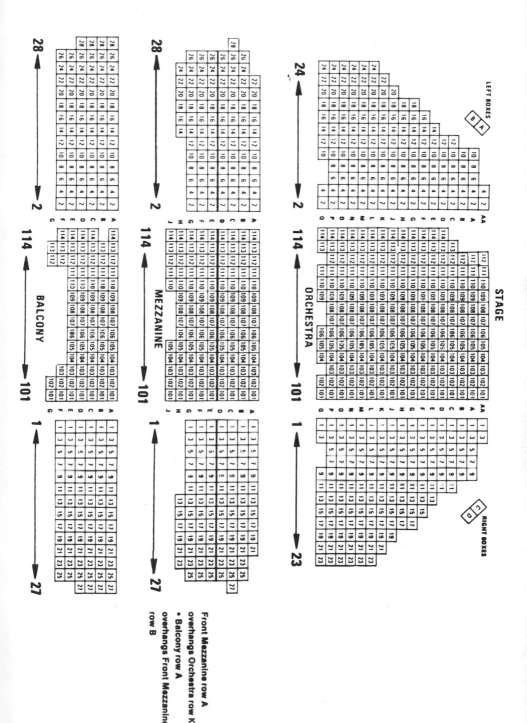

STAGE

LEFT BOXES

RIGHT BOXES

ORCHESTRA

MEZZANINE

BALCONY

Front Mezzanine row A
overhangs Orchestra row K

• Balcony row A
overhangs Front Mezzanine
row B

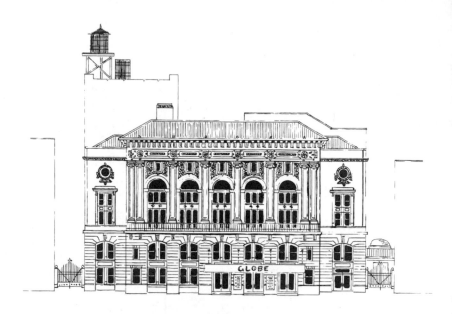

LUNT-FONTANNE

205 West 46th Street

Owner: The Nederlanders
Box Office: 586-5555
Box Office Hours: Monday–Saturday, 10 a.m.–8:30 p.m.; Sunday, 10 noon–5 p.m., if performance
Credit Cards: AE, MC, V   CHARGIT   Personal checks
Group Sales: 398-8383
Total Setting: 1,478 (Orchestra, 858; Mezzanine, 184; Balcony, 436; Standing room, 32)
Stage Type: Proscenium stage
AC
Handicapped: Semi-accessible

Charles Dillingham built this theatre and named it the Globe to house his productions. It opened with *The Old Town* on January 10, 1910. He spared no expense to make it the handsomest theatre on Broadway; he entertained stars and backers in lavish apartments in the upper stories. Came the Depression, he lost his theatre and it became a movie house until the late 1950s, when it was extensively refurbished, the entrance moved to 46th Street, and renamed to honor America's most distinguished acting couple, Alfred Lunt and Lynn Fontanne. They attended but did not act at the reopening on May 5, 1958, featuring *The Visit*. The following year, Sir John Gielgud and Margaret Leighton starred in *Much Ado about Nothing*. On November 16, 1959, *The Sound of Music* opened, starring Mary Martin and Theodore Bikel and logged 1,443 performances here. In the 1960s, Sid Caesar starred in *Little Me,* Richard Burton in *Hamlet,* Robert Preston in *Ben Franklin in Paris,* Marlene Dietrich in her one-woman show, and in 1969, another *Hamlet,* Nicol Williamson. Hal Linden and Keene Curtis won Tonys in *The Rothschilds,* which opened here in 1970. Since then, the Lunt-Fontanne has seen mostly revivals: *A Funny Thing Happened on the Way to the Forum;* Cab Calloway, Barbara McNair, and Hal Linden in *The Pajama Game;* (*The Sunshine Boys, Good Evening, Raisin,* and *My Fair Lady* transferred here for runs from other houses); Carol Channing recreated her role in *Hello, Dolly!;* and in 1979 Sandy Duncan opened in what was to become the longest run ever of the hardy perennial *Peter Pan.* The latest hit here: Duke Ellington's *Sophisticated Ladies.*

STAGE

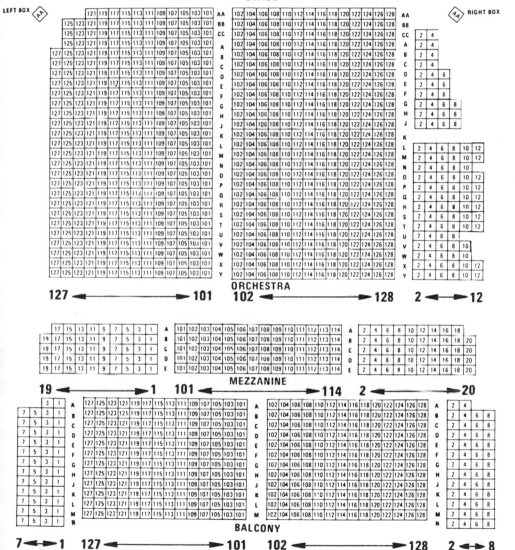

LYCEUM

149 West 45th Street

Owner: The Shubert Organization
Box Office: 582-3897
Box Office Hours: Monday–Saturday, 10 a.m.–8:30 p.m.; Sunday, 12 noon–6 p.m., if performance
Credit Cards: AE, DC, MC, V TELECHARGE Personal Checks
Group Sales: Shubert Group Sales (944-4100)
Total Seating: 928 (Orchestra, 411; Mezzanine, 297; Balcony, 210; Boxes, 20)
Stage Type: Proscenium stage
AC
Handicapped: Semi-accessible

Producer Daniel Frohman was the first to come north from 23rd Street and build in the present theatre district. His foresight was marred by two errors in judgment: He put the Lyceum on the wrong side of Broadway, and he built it for his repertory company just before repertory companies faded away. This is New York's most beautiful theatre, with its columns and mansard roof and luxurious 19th-century interior appointments. As was the practice then, Frohman built an apartment above the theatre for himself with a peephole so he could keep an eye on the stage. In 1939 and again in the 1970s, it was threatened with destruction. Now an official city landmark, the Lyceum is presumably safe. It opened November 2, 1903, with *The Proud Prince* and some of its early memorable performances included Leslie Howard in *Berkeley Square* and Ina Claire and Walter Slezak in *When We Are Married.* The 1940s saw Kaufman and Hart's *George Washington Slept Here;* Saroyan's *The Beautiful People;* Marquand's *The Late George Apley;* and Judy Holliday and Paul Douglas in *Born Yesterday.* In the 1950s were Odets's *The Country Girl; The Happiest Millionaire;* and John Osborne's explosive *Look Back in Anger.* In the late 1960s, the APA–Phoenix Repertory Company (shades of Mr. Frohman!) staged a revival of *You Can't Take It with You* and liked the Lyceum so much they made it home. Artistic director Ellis Rabb staged a number of distinguished plays with a company that included Helen Hayes, Rosemary Harris, and Donald Moffat. Since the APA–Phoenix days it has housed the 1970 Tony best play, *Borstal Boy;* Brian Bedford in *School for Wives; Your Arms Too Short to Box with God;* and Constance Cummings in *Wings.* The latest hit in this, New York's oldest legitimate theatre in continuous use, has been the revival of Paul Osborne's *Morning's at Seven,* a Tony winner for best play.

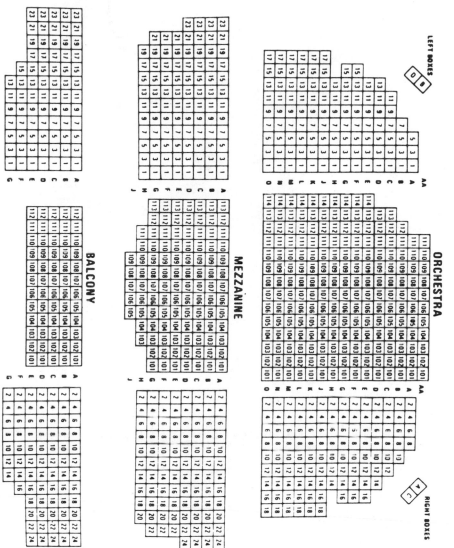

STAGE

LEFT BOXES

RIGHT BOXES

ORCHESTRA

MEZZANINE

BALCONY

Front Mezzanine row A overhangs
Orchestra row L • Balcony row A
overhangs Front Mezzanine row C

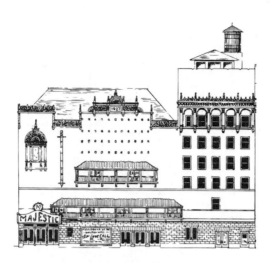

MAJESTIC

245 West 44th Street

Owner: The Shubert Organization
Box Office: 246-0730
Box Office Hours: Monday–Saturday, 10 a.m.–8:30 p.m.; Sunday, 12 noon–6 p.m., if performance
Credit Cards: AE, DC, MC, V TELECHARGE Personal checks
Group Sales: Shubert Group Sales (944-4100)
Total Seating: 1,629 (Orchestra, 895; Mezzanines, 702; Boxes, 32; Standing room, 40)
Stage Type: Proscenium stage
AC
Handicapped: Semi-accessible

The Majestic is one of Broadway's largest and most elegant houses, with a large, illuminated dome in the ceiling and an elevated orchestra floor, and it is admirably suited to musical comedies. It opened March 28, 1927, with the curiously titled *Rufus LeMaire's Affairs*, and, during the 1930s saw Gertrude Lawrence in *The International Review*, Sigmund Romberg's *Nina Rosa*, and Judy Canova, Buddy Ebsen, and Phil Silvers. In the 1940s, productions here included a revival of Gershwin's *Porgy and Bess*, *The Merry Widow*, and *Mexican Hayride*. *Carousel* opened in 1945, and the Majestic was pretty much a Rodgers and Hammerstein house for the next 10 years: *Allegro*, 1947; *South Pacific*, 1949; and *Me and Juliet*, 1953. Shirley Booth in *By the Beautiful Sea* moved here in 1954, followed with Ezio Pinza in *Fanny*, and Ethel Merman in *Happy Hunting*. Meredith Willson's super-hit, *The Music Man* opened in December, 1957, with Robert Preston and Barbara Cook; three years later was Richard Burton in *Camelot*. In 1963, Lee Remick and Angela Lansbury starred in the Laurents-Sondheim musical *Anyone Can Whistle*. *Marat/Sade* shortened its name and came here from Off Broadway early in 1967. The next success arrived in 1973 from the Shubert, Sondheim's *A Little Night Music*, and went on to win six Tonys. A winner of seven Tonys, *The Wiz* came in January, 1975. Liza Minnelli's *The Act*, was a 1977 smash. In a switch to drama, Henry Fonda and Jane Alexander starred in *First Monday in October*. Since then *Ballroom* and *I Remember Mama* have made brief stays as did a revival of Lerner and Loewe's *Brigadoon*. In April, 1981, the hit *42nd Street* moved here from the Winter Garden.

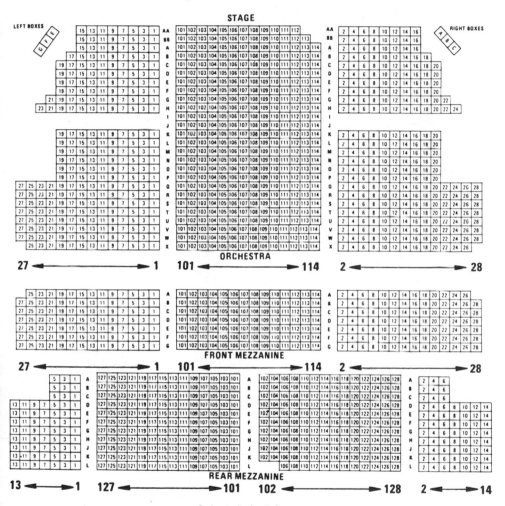

Orchestra is elevated
starting at row K
• Front Mezzanine row A
overhangs Orchestra row H

MARK HELLINGER

237 West 51st Street

Owner: The Nederlanders
Box Office: 757-7064
Box Office Hours: Monday–Saturday, 10 a.m.–8:30 p.m.; Sunday, 12 noon–6 p.m.
Credit Cards: AE, DC, MC, V   CHARGIT   Personal checks
Group Sales: 386-8383
Total Seating: 1,603 (Orchestra, 981; Balocony, 622; Standing room, 20)
Stage Type: Proscenium stage
AC
Handicapped: Semi-accessible

This theatre opened in 1930 as the Hollywood, a Warner Brothers movie palace. During the Depression, it switched from movies to plays and back again several times. The first stage production was *Calling All Stars* in December, 1934, starring Lou Holtz, Phil Baker, Martha Raye, Wills Logan, and Judy Canova. In 1936, the theatre's entrance was changed to 51st Street and it was rechristened the 51st Street Theatre. The opening production was *Sweet River*, George Abbott's musical adaptation of *Uncle Tom's Cabin* and a resounding flop. In 1941, the theatre was renamed the Hollywood and housed the Eddie Cantor hit *Banjo Eyes*. In 1949, Anthony B. Farrell bought the theatre and renamed it after the late Broadway columnist Mark Hellinger. The first production then was *All for Love* with Paul and Grace Hartman. The Hartmans returned in the 1950s in a revue, *Tickets, Please!* Other hits of the decade included *Bless You All* starring Pearl Bailey and Jules Munshin; Bert Lahr and Dolores Gray in *Two on the Aisle; Hazel Flagg; Nothing Sacred* with Helen Gallagher and Thomas Mitchell; *The Girl in Pink Tights;* and *Plain and Fancy.* Theatre history was made here on March 15, 1956, when Alan Jay Lerner and Frederick Loewe's *My Fair Lady* opened starring Rex Harrison and Julie Andrews; it played here six years. Carol Burnett and Jack Cassidy arrived in 1964 in the Betty Comden–Adolph Green musical, *Fade Out-Fade In.* Barbara Harris and John Cullum followed in the Lerner-Lane musical *On a Clear Day You Can See Forever;* Melina Mercouri starred in *Illya Darling;* and the 1960s ended with the musical comedy debut of Katharine Hepburn in *Coco.* In the 1970s came *Jesus Christ Superstar, Timbuktu!* starring Eartha Kitt, and the smash hit (still packing them in when this was written) *Sugar Babies,* starring Ann Miller and Mickey Rooney.

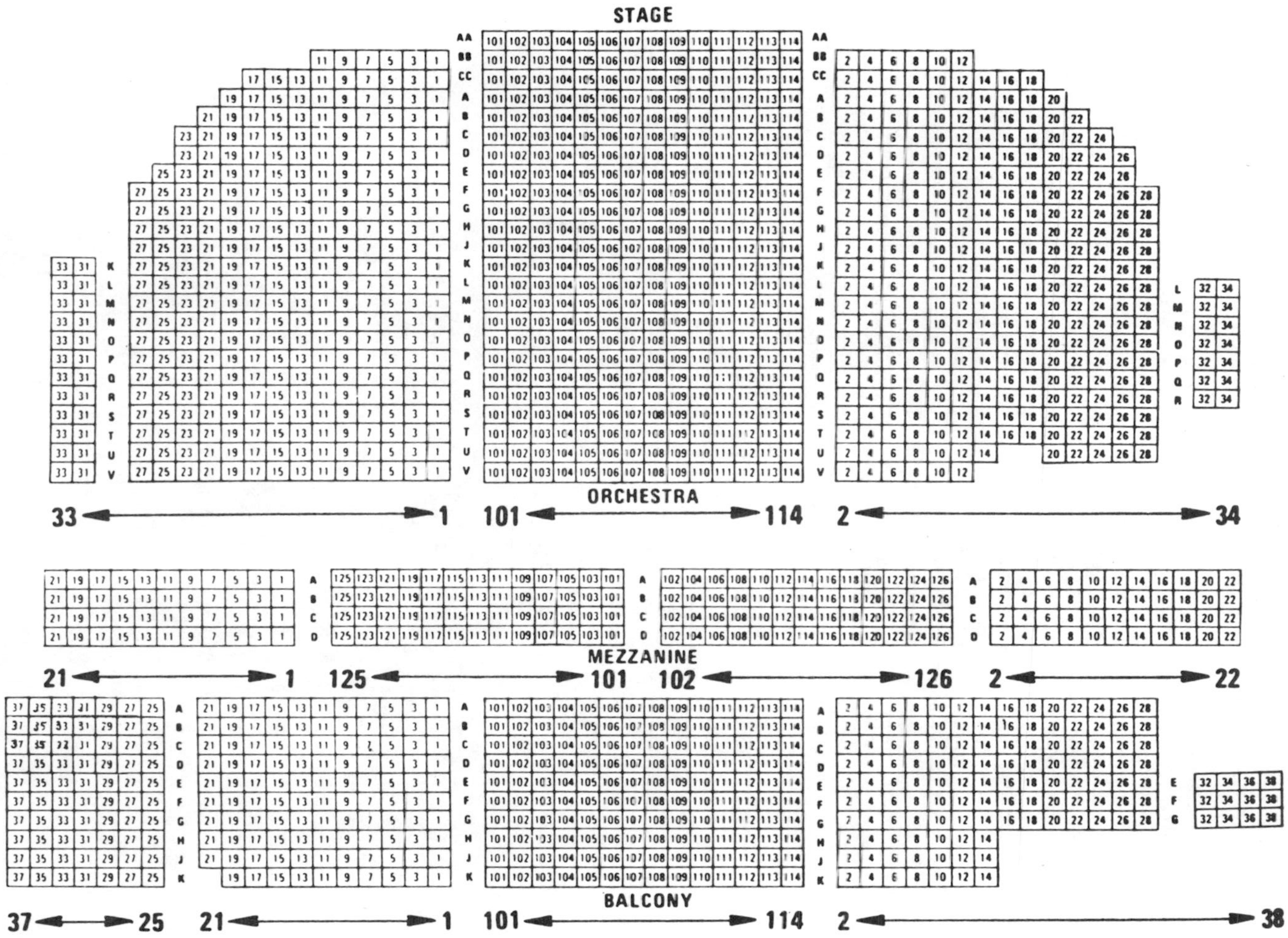

STAGE

ORCHESTRA

MEZZANINE

BALCONY

Front Mezzanine row A overhangs Orchestra row L

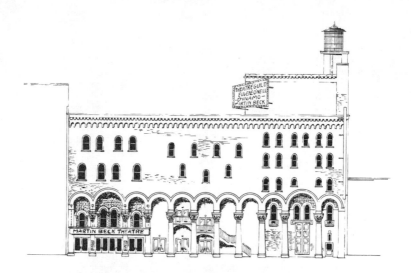

MARTIN BECK

302 West 45th Street

Owner: Jujamcyn Theatres
Box Office: 246-6363
Box Office Hours: Monday–Saturday, 10 a.m.–8 p.m.; Sunday, 12 noon–5 p.m., if performance
Credit Cards: AE, MC, V CHARGIT Personal checks
Group Sales: 298-8383
Total Seating: 1,280 (Orchestra, 666; Balcony, 614; Standing room, 10)
Stage Type: Proscenium stage
AC
Handicapped: Semi-accessible

Martin Beck, head of the old Orpheum vaudeville circuit (who also built the Palace), built this theatre west of Eighth Avenue despite predictions that theatregoers wouldn't cross the avenue. It opened November 11, 1924, with *Madame Pompadour* and remained in the Beck family until 1966. The Theatre Guild Studio used the Beck for several years, presenting Shaw's *The Apple Cart; Hotel Universe* with Ruth Gordon; and *Roar China!* The Lunts appeared in Sherwood's *Reunion in Vienna;* Katharine Cornell in *The Barretts of Wimpole Street;* and *Romeo and Juliet* with Basil Rathbone, Edith Evans, and Orson Welles, and *Saint Joan.* In the 1940s, Paul Lukas starred in Lillian Hellman's *Watch on the Rhine;* other productions included O'Neill's *The Iceman Cometh* and Tennessee Williams's *The Rose Tattoo.* The 1950s saw *The Grass Harp,* Arthur Miller's *The Crucible, The Teahouse of the August Moon,* and *Sweet Bird of Youth,* starring Geraldine Page and Paul Newman. The musical hit *Bye Bye Birdie,* starring Dick Van Dyke and Chita Rivera, opened early in the 1960s. (When this was written, the sequel *Bring Back Birdie,* with Donald O'Connor and Chita Rivera, was about to open.) In 1963, Jerome Robbins directed Anne Bancroft in Brecht's *Mother Courage and Her Children.* Colleen Dewhurst starred in Edward Albee's adaptation of Carson McCullers's *The Ballad of the Sad Café.* In 1965, the Royal Shakespeare Company presented Peter Weiss's *Marat/Sade,* starring Glenda Jackson, Ian Richardson, and Patrick Magee. Next year, Edward Albee's *A Delicate Balance* starred Hume Cronyn and Jessica Tandy. *Man of La Mancha* came to the Beck after three years at the ANTA Washington Square. Sir John Gielgud directed Albee's *All Over.* A new version of Kurt Weill and Bertolt Brecht's *Happy End* was produced. A big hit in the late 1970s was Frank Langella in the title role of *Dracula.* The Martin Beck has just been completely renovated. Most recently, Elizabeth Taylor made her triumphant broadway debut in Lillian Hellman's *The Little Foxes.*

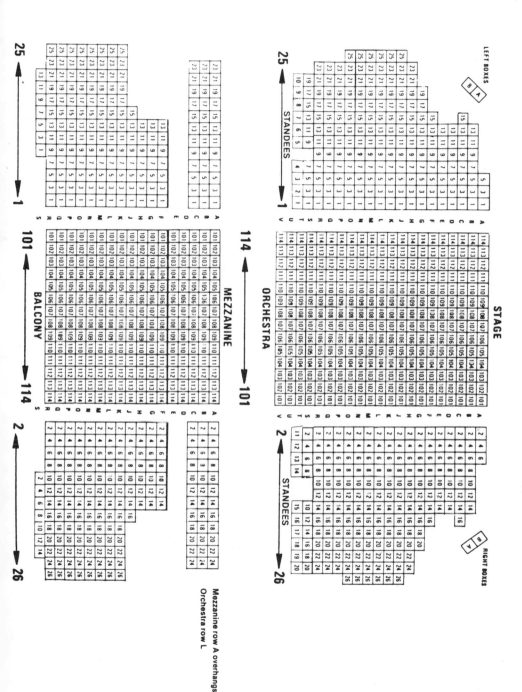

STAGE

LEFT BOXES

RIGHT BOXES

ORCHESTRA

MEZZANINE

BALCONY

STANDEES

Mezzanine row A overhangs
Orchestra row L

71

MINSKOFF

1515 Broadway (45th)

Owner: Jerry Minskoff
Operator: The Nederlanders
Box Office: 869-0550
Box Office Hours: Monday–Saturday, 10 a.m.–8:30 p.m.; Sunday, 12 noon–5 p.m.
Credit Cards: AE, MC, V   CHARGIT   Personal checks (mail order only)
Total Seating: 1,621 (Orchestra, 1,039; Balcony, 582)
Stage Type: Proscenium stage
AC
Handicapped: Full accessibility

The old Astor Hotel was an integral part of the theatre district for more than 50 years. Many actors stayed here, and the Hunt Room seemed at times like their private club. The Astor was torn down in 1968 and replaced with a 55-story office tower that includes this magnificent theatre facility. (The city zoning laws permit a building to have 20 percent more rentable space if it includes a theatre, an attractive bonus to developers.) The Minskoff, named for developer Jerry Minskoff, is second to the Metropolitan Opera at Lincoln Center in backstage space, and is the only theatre in the Broadway area fully equipped for handicapped theatregoers. It opened March 13, 1973, with a smash hit, *Irene,* starring Debbie Reynolds. Other productions here have included *King of Hearts; Got Tu Go Disco;* Bette Midler in *Clams on the Half Shell Revue;* the ill-fated *Angel,* a musical based on Thomas Wolfe's *Look Homeward Angel;* and the revival of *West Side Story.* In the spring of 1981, the Minskoff was host to the revival of Cole Porter's 1953 hit *Can-Can.*

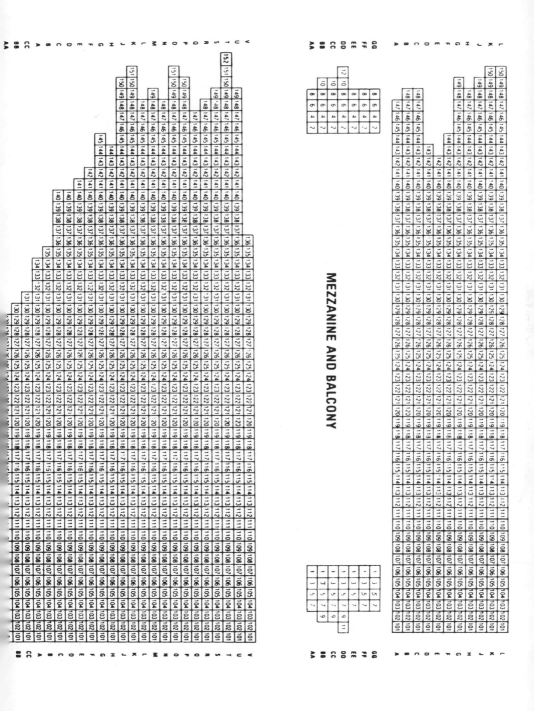

MEZZANINE AND BALCONY

73

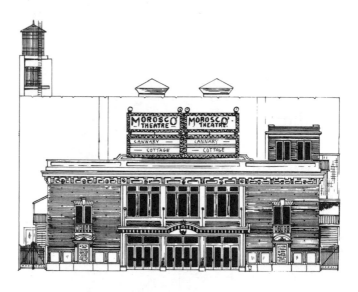

MOROSCO

217 West 45th Street

Operator: Lester Osterman
Box Office: 246-6230
Box Office Hours: Monday–Saturday, 10 a.m.–8:30 p.m.; Sunday, 12 noon–6 p.m., if performance
Credit Cards: AE, DC, MC, V   TELECHARGE   Personal checks
Group Sales: Through box office and theatre party organizations
Total Seating: 1,009 (Orchestra, 647; Balcony, 338; Boxes, 24; Standing room, 36)
Stage Type: Proscenium stage
AC
Handicapped: Semi-accessible

A wrecker's ball seems about to end the six-decade life of the Morosco to clear the site for the Portman Hotel. Playwright and theatre manager Oliver Morosco opened the house that bore his name on February 5, 1917, with a musical he wrote entitled *Canary Cottage*. The Pulitzer Prize play *Craig's Wife* and Somerset Maugham's *The Letter* were presented in the 1920s. In the 1930s, the offerings included Katharine Hepburn in *The Warrior's Husband;* George S. Kaufman and Alexander Woollcott's *The Dark Tower;* Rachael Crothers's comedy *No More Ladies* with Melvyn Douglas and Lucille Watson; *Something Gay* with Tallulah Bankhead and Walter Pidgeon; *Call It a Day* with Gladys Cooper and Philip Merivale; and George M. Cohan in *Fulton of Oak Falls*. Noel Coward's *Blithe Spirit* was the first hit of the 1940s, followed by *The Voice of the Turtle,* which ran for 1,500 performances. In 1955, Tennessee Williams's *Cat on a Hot Tin Roof* premiered; in 1957, Helen Hayes, Susan Strasberg, and Richard Burton starred in *Time Remembered*. In 1964, the Actors Studio produced *The Three Sisters*. In following years came Henry Fonda in *Generation;* Woody Allen's *Don't Drink the Water;* Arthur Miller's *The Price;* Julie Harris in her Tony Award performance in *Forty Carats;* and, in 1970, Sir John Gielgud and Sir Ralph Richardson in David Storey's *Home*. Julie Harris returned in 1971 with *And Miss Reardon Drinks a Little*. The 1970s were big years for the Morosco with Simon Gray's *Butley,* David Storey's *Changing Room,* a revival of *A Moon for the Misbegotten* starring Coleen Dewhurst and Jason Robards, *The Shadow Box,* and Anne Bancroft in *Golda*. In 1978, Hugh Leonard's *Da* went on to win Tonys for best play, best actor, best supporting actor, and best direction for Barnard Hughes, Lester Rawlings, and Melvin Bernhardt, respectively. Later productions included *The Lady from Dubuque, Billy Bishop Goes to War,* and Hugh Leonard's *A Life*.

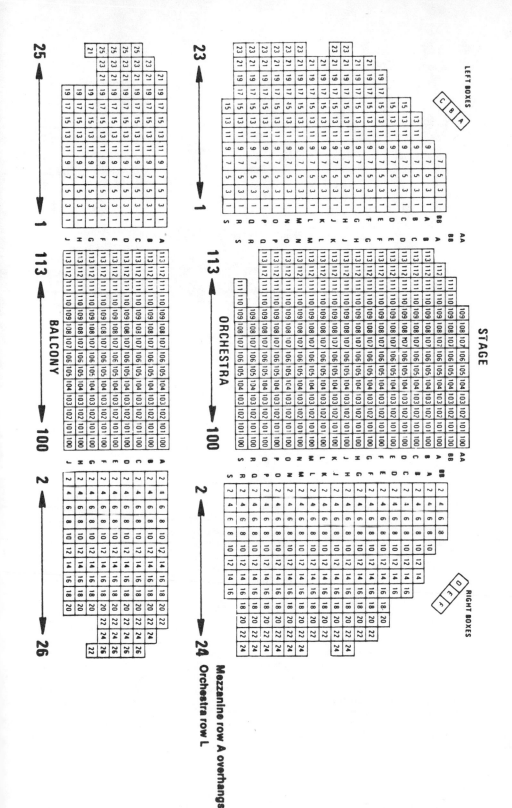

STAGE

LEFT BOXES

C B A

RIGHT BOXES

D E F

ORCHESTRA

BALCONY

Mezzanine row A overhangs
Orchestra row L

MUSIC BOX

239 West 45th Street

Owner: Norman Stone, The Shubert Organization
Box Office: 246-4636
Box Office Hours: Monday–Saturday, 10 a.m.–8:30 p.m.; Sunday, 12 noon–5 p.m.
Credit Cards: AE   CHARGIT   Personal checks
Group Sales: 398-8383
Total Seating: 1,010 (Orchestra, 539; Boxes, 16; Mezzanine, 455; Standing room, 20)
Stage Type: Proscenium stage
AC
Handicapped: Semi-accessible

Irving Berlin and his producer, Sam H. Harris, teamed up to build the Music Box to house Berlin's *Music Box Revues.* It opened September 22, 1921, with the *Music Box Review of 1921* and it has proven to be one of Broadway's most durable houses. The *Music Box Revues* continued until 1925. The first straight play here, *The Cradle Snatchers,* featured Humphrey Bogart. George Gershwin's Pulitzer Prize winner *Of Thee I Sing* opened here in December, 1931, and its success helped save the Music Box for its owners in that tough Depression year. Other 1930s productions: *Dinner at Eight; As Thousands Cheer; Merrily We Roll Along; Stage Door;* Steinbeck's *Of Mice and Men;* and *The Man Who Came to Dinner.* In the 1940s came Mike Todd's *Star and Garter* with Gypsy Rose Lee and Bobby Clark; *I Remember Mama;* Tennessee Williams's *Summer and Smoke:* and Kurt Weill and Maxwell Anderson's *Lost in the Stars.* The 1950s began with *Affairs of State;* Kim Stanley in William Inge's *Picnic;* Kim Stanley again in *Bus Stop;* William Inge again with *The Dark at the Top of the Stairs.* Claire Bloom and Rod Steiger in *Rashomon,* finishing with Brian Bedford and Jessica Tandy in Peter Shaffer's *Five Finger Exercise.* In the 1960s were *Invitation to a March;* S. J. Perelman's *The Beauty Part* with Bert Lahr, Charlotte Rae, and Alice Ghostly. The longest-running play here, *Any Wednesday* with Sandy Dennis, Don Porter, and Gene Hackman, opened in February, 1964. On a serious note, Harold Pinter's *The Homecoming* opened and won both the Tony and Drama Critics' Circle Award. Anne Jackson and George Grizzard starred in *Inquest.* Then came *Sleuth* with Anthony Quayle and Keith Baxter. Two other British works followed: Alan Ayckbourn's *Absurd Person Singular* and Trevor Griffiths's *Comedians.* In spring 1981, another thriller enjoyed a long run, Ira Levin's *Deathtrap.*

- *Theatre groups. Private dining rooms.*
- *Private parties from 10 to 300*
- *Major credit cards honored.*

254 West 47th Street ● New York, N. Y. 10036

Thank you.

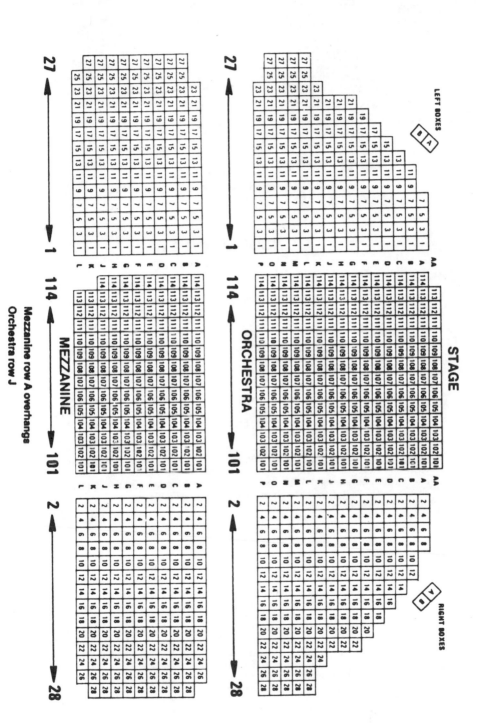

STAGE

LEFT BOXES

RIGHT BOXES

ORCHESTRA

MEZZANINE

Mezzanine row A overhangs
Orchestra row J

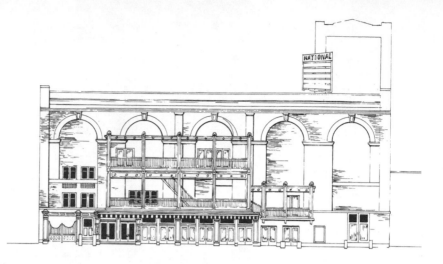

NEDERLANDER

208 West 41st Street

Owner: The Nederlanders
Box Office: 586-6150
Box Office Hours: Monday–Saturday, 10 a.m.–8:30 p.m.; Sunday, 12 noon–3 p.m., if performance
Credit Cards: AE, MC, V CHARGIT Personal checks (mail order only)
Group Sales: Through box office
Total Seating: 1,168 (Orchestra, 592; Boxes, 24; Mezzanine, 198; Balcony, 354)
Stage Type: Proscenium stage
AC
Handicapped: Semi-accessible

The only Broadway theatre now open below 42nd Street opened as the National Theatre on September 1, 1921, with Sidney Howard's *Swords.* Its history has alternated between dark periods and big hits. In the 1920s, Spencer Tracy was here in *Yellow* and Ann Harding in *The Trial of Mary Dugan.* The first big hit, however, was *Grand Hotel,* starring Eugenie Leontovich, Sam Jaffe, and Henry Hull. Other important productions of the period included *Ethan Frome,* starring Pauline Lord, Ruth Gordon, and Raymond Massey; Gertrude Lawrence and Noel Coward in *Tonight at 8:30;* Orson Welles and the Mercury Theatre in *The Shoemaker's Holiday* and *Julius Caesar;* and the one-and-only Tallulah Bankhead in Lillian Hellman's *The Little Foxes. The Corn Is Green,* starring Ethel Barrymore, opened the 1940s, followed by Maurice Evans and Judith Anderson in *Macbeth; Call Me Mister;* Judith Anderson and Sir John Gielgud in *Medea;* Carol Channing in the revue *Lend an Ear;* John Garfield and Nancy Kelly in Clifford Odets's *The Big Knife;* and in 1949 Lily Palmer, Sir Cedric Hardwicke, and Arthur Treacher in *Caesar and Cleopatra.* Katharine Cornell, Grace George, and Brian Aherne opened the 1950s with *The Constant Wife;* Margaret Sullavan and Joseph Cotten in *Sabrina Fair;* and the longest-running production in the theatre's history: Paul Muni and Ed Begley in *Inherit the Wind,* the dramatization of the Scopes monkey trial. In 1959, showman Billy Rose purchased the National, refurbished it, and renamed it the Billy Rose. It reopened in October of that year with Shaw's *Heartbreak House.* I remember the Billy Rose particularly because I was next door at the *Herald Tribune* during the long run of Edward Albee's *Who's Afraid of Virginia Woolf?,* starring Uta Hagen, Arthur Hill, George Grizzard, and Melinda Dillon. In the late 1960s, Tammy Grimes and Brian Bedford starred in a revival of *Private Lives.* Harold Pinter's *Old Times* was a hit here, and, in 1974, Brian Bedford was back with Jill Clayburgh in Tom Stoppard's *Jumpers.* After being closed during 1977, the theatre was purchased by James and Joseph Nederlander and a British company, Cooney-Marsh, refurbished, and renamed the Trafalgar. Two hits—*Whose Life Is It Anyway?* and *Betrayal*—were here before the theatre again was renamed. As the Nederlander, in honor of the late David Tobias Nederlander, it has housed *One Night Stand, Broadway Follies,* and the smash hit *Lena Horne: The Lady and Her Music.*

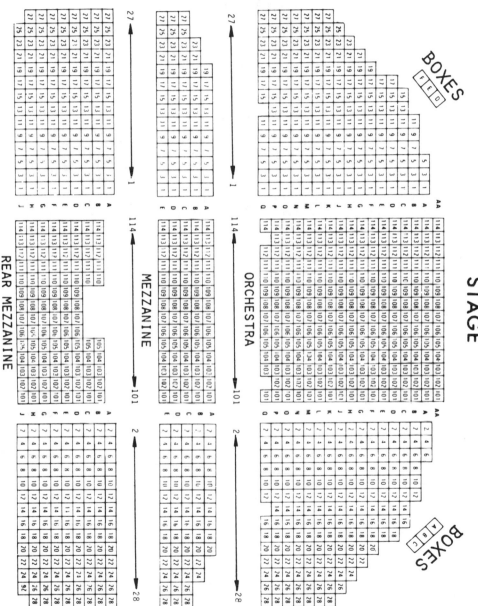

STAGE

BOXES
E | D

BOXES
A | B | C

ORCHESTRA

MEZZANINE

REAR MEZZANINE

NEW APOLLO

234 West 43rd Street

Owner: The Midtown Theatre Corp.
Box Office: 921-8558
Box Office Hours: Monday–Saturday, 10 a.m.–8:30 p.m.; Sunday, 10 a.m.–6 p.m., if performance
Credit Cards: AE, DC, MC, V   CHARGIT   Personal checks
Group Sales: Through box office
Total Seating: 1,160 (Orchestra, 655; Balcony, 505)
Stage Type: Proscenium stage
AC
Handicapped: Semi-accessible

The New Apollo is a comeback story. Originally named the Bryant, it opened in 1910 as a combination movie and vaudeville house. The Selwyns took it over in 1920 and opened it as a legitimate theatre on November 18, 1920, with *Jimmie*. In the early years, it housed such hits as W. C. Fields in *Poppy*, Ed Wynn in *Manhattan Mary,* and Lionel Barrymore in *Macbeth*. Then came six editions of the famous revue series *George White's Scandals,* shows that introduced the Charleston and the Black Bottom and had such stars as Ray Bolger, Rudy Vallee, and Ethel Merman. In 1930, Bert Lahr and Kate Smith starred in *Flying High*. A big hit in 1932 was *Take a Chance,* with Ethel Merman and Jack Haley. Times were tough, though, and the revue *Blackbirds of 1933,* with Bill (Bojangles) Robinson was the last play. The Apollo became first a movie house, a Minsky burlesque house from 1934 to 1937, then a movie house again, growing seedier and seedier. In the late 1970s, the Apollo was closed and $350,000 was spent to restore it inside and out. The entrance was changed from 42nd Street to 43rd Street, across from *The New York Times,* and it reopened February 28, 1979, with *On Golden Pond,* starring Frances Sternhagen and Tom Aldredge. *Bent* with Richard Gere followed, and, Christopher Reeve (replaced by Richard Thomas) in Lanford Wilson's comedy *Fifth of July,* which moved here from the Circle Repertory Company. The New Apollo is a handsome and welcome addition to the Broadway scene.

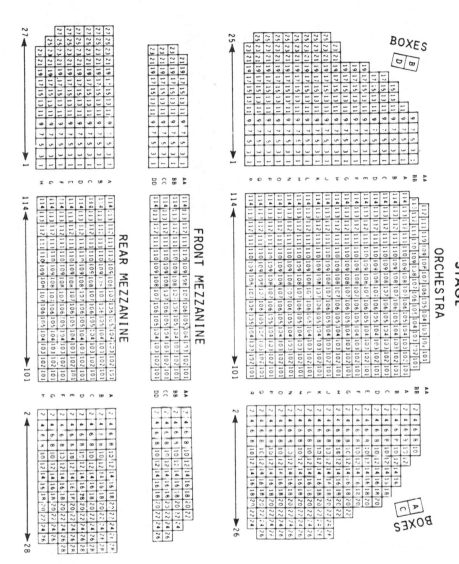

STAGE

BOXES

ORCHESTRA

BOXES

FRONT MEZZANINE

REAR MEZZANINE

Row AA of Front Mezzanine overhangs row H of Orchestra

81

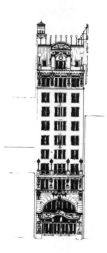

PALACE
1564 Broadway (47th)

Owner: The Nederlanders
Box Office: 757-2626
Box Office Hours: Monday–Saturday, 10 a.m.–8:30 p.m.; Sunday, 10 a.m.–3 p.m., if performance
Credit Cards: AE, MC, V
Group Sales: 398-8383
Total Seating: 1,686 (Orchestra, 807; Dress circle, 41; Front mezzanine, 248; Rear mezzanine, 160; Front balcony, 85; Rear balcony, 301; Regular boxes, 18; Balcony boxes, 26)
Stage Type: Proscenium stage
AC
Handicapped: Semi-accessible

For years, this was the "Valhalla of Vaudeville" and to play the Palace was synonymous with making it big. It opened on March 24, 1913, and it reigned as the showcase of the Keith-Albee circuit until vaudeville died in the early 1930s. Practically everyone who was anyone appeared here: Houdini, W. C. Fields, Jack Benny, Fred Astaire, Will Rogers, Sophie Tucker, even Sarah Bernhardt. (Incidentally, the Albee of Keith-Albee was the step-grandfather of playwright Edward Albee.) In the 1930s, the Palace became a movie house and remained one until it was purchased by the Nederlander brothers in 1966. Its first legitimate production was a winner: *Sweet Charity,* the Neil Simon, Cy Coleman, and Dorothy Fields musical that starred Gwen Verdon. The following year saw Judy Garland making her last New York appearance. *Henry, Sweet Henry,* a musical starring Don Ameche ran for awhile but the next Palace hit was *George M!,* starring Joel Grey as the immortal George M. Cohan. Another smash followed in 1970: *Applause,* the musical based on the movie *All About Eve.* It won four Tonys, including Best Actress for Lauren Bacall in the Margo Channing role. In the 1970s, a number of superstars came here in one-person shows: Bette Midler, Shirley MacLaine, Josephine Baker, and Diana Ross. *Cyrano,* starring Christopher Plummer in a Tony-winning performance, was followed by Carol Channing in *Lorelei* (adapted from *Gentlemen Prefer Blondes*), Richard Kiley in a revival of *Man of La Mancha,* Joel Grey in *The Grand Tour,* and the revival of *Oklahoma! Frankenstein* (a $2 million disaster early in 1981). Lauren Bacall returned in another triumph, *Woman of the Year* with Harry Guardino. Lloyd Meeker, who runs Backstage Tours, tells of taking a group from Texas here and noticing that one woman had stopped on the stage and was crying. "What's wrong?" he asked. "Nothing," she sobbed. "It's just that I've dreamed all my life of being on stage at the Palace."

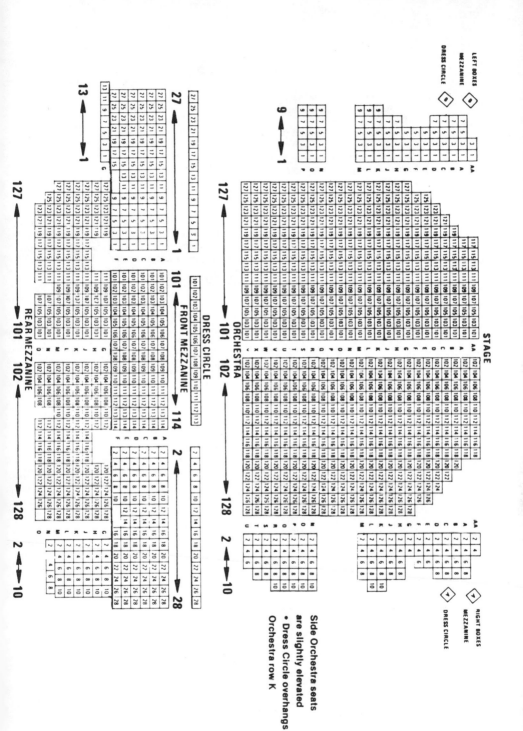

STAGE

Side Orchestra seats
are slightly elevated
• Dress Circle overhangs
Orchestra row K

83

PLAYHOUSE

359 West 48th Street

Owner: Gulf & Western
Operator: Actors Group Inc.
Box Office: 489-9237
Box Office Hours: Varies with production
Credit Cards: Varies with production
Group Sales: Varies with production
Total Seating: Upstairs, 500; Downstairs, 200
Stage Type: Open-end stages
AC
Handicapped: Upstairs: No access; Downstairs: Semi-accessible

First a Presbyterian Church and later an Albanian Orthodox Church, this building was converted to a theatre in the late 1960s at a cost of $700,000. It opened with Lanford Wilson's *Lemon Sky* on May 17, 1970. Among the productions here: *St. Mark's Gospel,* starring Alec McCowan; Arthur Miller's *The Price;* Claire Bloom in two Ibsen plays, *Hedda Gabler* and *A Doll's House;* Michael Moriarty in *G.R. Point; A Lesson from Aloes* by Arthur Fugard, starring James Earl Jones and Maria Tucci; and *It's Me, Sylvia,* with Sylvia Miles.

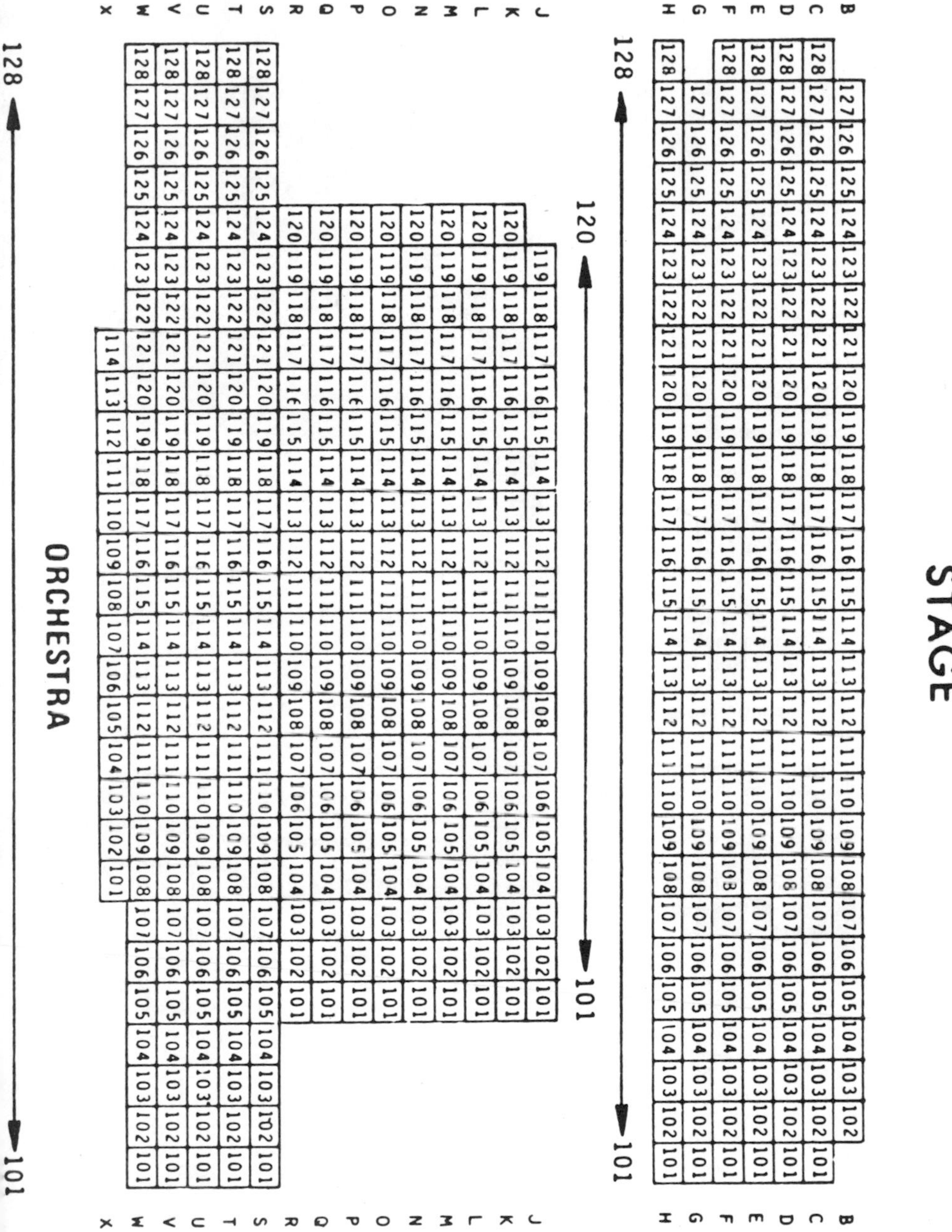
STAGE
ORCHESTRA
B C D E F G H
J K L M N O P Q R S T U V W X
128
120
101

PLYMOUTH

236 West 45th Street

Owner: The Shubert Organization
Box Office: 730-1760
Box Office Hours: Monday–Saturday, 10 a.m.–8:30 p.m.; Sunday, 12 noon–6 p.m., if performance
Credit Cards: AE, DC, MC, V   TELECHARGE   Personal checks
Group Sales: Shubert Group Sales (944-4100)
Total Setting: 1,077 (Orchestra, 660; Mezzanine, 393; Boxes, 24; Standing room, 23)
Stage Type: Proscenium stage
Handicapped: Semi-accessible

The Plymouth was built by Arthur Hopkins, a producer known for his taste, and over the years this theatre has built a reputation for housing important plays. It opened October 16, 1917, with William Gillette in *A Successful Calamity*. John Barrymore starred in *Redemption*, and, in 1919, with brother Lionel in *The Jest*. *Abe Lincoln in Illinois*, starring Raymond Massey and directed by Elmer Rice, won the Pulitzer Prize. Another Pulitzer Prize went in 1942 to Thornton Wilder's *The Skin of Our Teeth,* with Fredric March, Tallulah Bankhead, Florence Eldridge, and Montgomery Clift. The 1950s saw *Don Juan in Hell* with Charles Laughton, Agnes Moorehead, Charles Boyer, and Sir Cedric Hardwicke; *Dial M for Murder;* Michael Redgrave in *Tiger at the Gates;* Peter Ustinov's tour de force *Romanoff and Juliet;* and Charles Boyer and Claudette Colbert in *The Marriage-Go-Round*. The 1960s were equally memorable: *Irma la Douce;* Fredric March in Paddy Chayefsky's *Gideon;* Anthony Quinn and Margaret Leighton in *Tchin-Tchin;* Lillian Hellman's *My Mother, My Father and Me* with Ruth Gordon and Walter Matthau; Alec Guinness in *Dylan;* and William Hanley's *Slow Dance on the Killing Ground*. There was some comic relief in the form of three Neil Simon hits: *The Odd Couple* (Art Carney and Walter Matthau), *The Star-Spangled Girl* (Anthony Perkins and Connie Stevens); and *Plaza Suite* (Maureen Stapleton and George C. Scott). Even Neil Simon turned serious here, though, with *The Gingerbread Lady*. One of the important plays of the 1970s—*Equus* by Peter Shaffer—opened at the Plymouth. Most recently, it was home for Jane LaPoteire in *Piaf*.

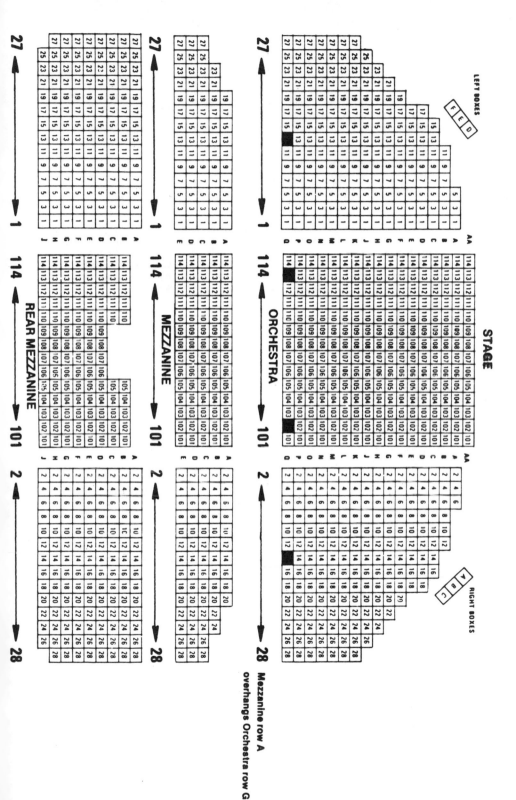

PRINCESS

200 West 48th Street

Owner: Orator Theatre Productions, Inc.
Box Office: 541-6162
Box Office Hours: Monday–Saturday, 10 a.m.–8 p.m.; Sunday, 12 noon–3 p.m., if performance
Credit Cards: Varies with production
Group Sales: Through box office
Total Seating: 499 (Standing room, 25)
Stage Type: Semi-thrust stage
AC
Handicapped: No access

This theatre has had a curious history. In 1935 it was the Cotton Club (not *the* Cotton Club—that was in Harlem). Then from 1941 to 1968 it was the Latin Quarter, Managed incidentally, by Barbara Walters's father. It was remodeled as a theatre and opened in 1979 as 22 Steps. It was renamed the Princess in 1980. No production has had much luck here, so far. Remember *Our Old Friends, Censored Scenes from King Kong, Coquelico,* and *Fearless Frank?* The future of the Princess seems doubtful, but a hit can always make a difference.

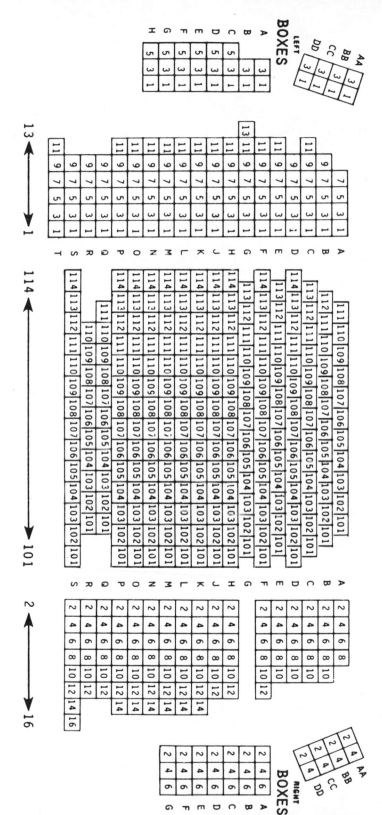

STAGE

RIALTO

1481 Broadway (43rd)

Owner: The Brandt Organization, Inc.
Box Office: 354-5236
Box Office Hours: Monday–Saturday, 11 a.m.–8 p.m.; Sunday, 12 noon–8 p.m.
Credit Cards: AE, MC, V   CHARGIT   TDF Vouchers   Personal checks
Group Sales: Through producer
Total Seating: 499
Stage Type: Semi-thrust stage
AC
Handicapped: Semi-accessible

For years this was one of the grand movie palaces at Times Square. Built in 1932, it was completely refurbished in 1980 in preparation for a new life as a legitimate theatre. All the Rialto needs now is a hit. The first production here was a revival of *Canterbury Tales,* which lasted 20 performances. The second, *Musical Chairs,* lasted 14. As this was written, *A Reel American Hero* was previewing. As a musical celebrating the Golden Age of Movies, it would seem to have found the proper setting.

Top grid

V	U	T	S	R	Q	P	O	N	M	L	K	J	H	G	F	E	D	C	B	A
13	13	13	13	13	13	13	13	13	13	13	13	13	13	13	13	13	13	13	13	13
11	11	11	11	11	11	11	11	11	11	11	11	11	11	11	11	11	11	11	11	11
9	9	9	9	9	9	9	9	9	9	9	9	9	9	9	9	9	9	9	9	9
7	7	7	7	7	7	7	7	7	7	7	7	7	7	7	7	7	7	7	7	7
5	5	5	5	5	5	5	5	5	5	5	5	5	5	5	5	5	5	5	5	5
3	3	3	3	3	3	3	3	3	3	3	3	3	3	3	3	3	3	3	3	3
1	1	1	1	1	1	1	1	1	1	1	1	1	1	1	1	1	1	1	1	1

Middle grid (row labels A B C D E F G H J K L M N O P Q R S T U V)

A	B	C	D	E	F	G	H	J	K	L	M	N	O	P	Q	R	S	T	U	V
101	101	101	101	101	101	101	101	101	101	101	101	101	101	101	101	101	101	101	101	101
102	102	102	102	102	102	102	102	102	102	102	102	102	102	102	102	102	102	102	102	102
103	103	103	103	103	103	103	103	103	103	103	103	103	103	103	103	103	103	103	103	103
104	104	104	104	104	104	104	104	104	104	104	104	104	104	104	104	104	104	104	104	104
105	105	105	105	105	105	105	105	105	105	105	105	105	105	105	105	105	105	105	105	105
106	106	106	106	106	106	106	106	106	106	106	106	106	106	106	106	106	106	106	106	106
107	107	107	107	107	107	107	107	107	107	107	107	107	107	107	107	107	107	107	107	107
108	108	108	108	108	108	108	108	108	108	108	108	108	108	108	108	108	108	108	108	108
109	109	109	109	109	109	109	109	109	109	109	109	109	109	109	109	109	109	109	109	109
110	110	110	110	110	110	110	110	110	110	110	110	110	110	110	110	110	110	110	110	110
111	111	111	111	111	111	111	111	111	111	111	111	111	111	111	111	111	111	111	111	111
112	112	112	112	112	112	112	112	112	112	112	112	112	112	112	112	112	112	112	112	112
113	113	113	113	113	113	113	113	113	113	113	113	113	113	113	113	113	113	113	113	113

Row labels below middle grid: A B C D E F G H J K L M N O P Q R S T U V

Bottom grid (row labels A B C D E F G H J K L M N O P Q R S T U V)

	A	B	C	D	E	F	G	H	J	K	L	M	N	O	P	Q	R	S	T	U	V
	2	2	2	2	2	2	2	2	2	2	2	2	2	2	2	2	2	2	2	2	2
	4	4	4	4	4	4	4	4	4	4	4	4	4	4	4	4	4	4	4	4	4
2	6	6	6	6	6	6	6	6	6	6	6	6	6	6	6	6	6	6	6	6	6
4	8	8	8	8	8	8	8	8	8	8	8	8	8	8	8	8	8	8	8	8	8
6	10	10	10	10	10	10	10	10	10	10	10	10	10	10	10	10	10	10	10	10	10
8	12	12	12	12	12	12	12	12	12	12	12	12	12	12	12	12	12	12	12	12	12
10	14	14	14	14	14	14	14	14	14	14	14	14	14	14	14	14	14	14	14	14	14

ROYALE

242 West 45th Street

Owner: The Shubert Organization
Box Office: 245-5760
Box Office.Hours: Monday–Saturday, 10 a.m.–8:30 p.m.; Sunday, 10 a.m.–6 p.m., if performance
Credit Cards: AE, DC, MC, V TELECHARGE Personal checks
Group Sales: Shubert Group Sales (944-4100)
Total Seating: 1,058 (Orchestra, 622; Mezzanine, 420; Boxes, 16; Standing room, 28)
Stage Type: Proscenium stage
AC
Handicapped: Semi-accessible

The Royale opened January 11, 1927, with *Piggy* and got its first hit the next season with Mae West in *Diamond Lil* (three years earlier, Mae had been fined $500 and 10 days in the workhouse for her risqué performance in *Sex*). In a less controversial vein, the 1930s saw Claude Rains in *They Shall Not Die;* Paul Muni in *Counsellor-at-Law,* and Sir John Gielgud in *The Importance of Being Earnest.* Producer John Golden leased the theatre and changed its name to (surprise!) the Golden before CBS took it over in 1936 and used it as a radio studio until 1940. Back in action with its original name, the Royale in the 1950s saw Gielgud return with the young Richard Burton in Christopher Fry's *The Lady's Not for Burning;* Eartha Kitt and Alice Ghostly were among the *New Faces of 1952;* Laurence Olivier appeared in both *The Entertainer* and *Becket.* In 1961, Tennessee Williams's *The Night of the Iguana* opened here to enthusiastic acclaim. The 1964 Pulitzer Prize play, Frank Gilroy's *The Subject Was Roses* enjoyed a long run, as did Lauren Bacall in *Cactus Flower.* Most, though, will remember the Royale as the home of *Grease.* The musical opened (to tepid reviews) at the Eden Theatre Off Broadway on February 14, 1972, moved to the Broadhurst for a short time, then settled in here to become the longest-running Broadway show of all time—3,388 performance when it closed on April 13, 1980. The latest Royale hit was *A Day in Hollywood/A Night in the Ukraine.*

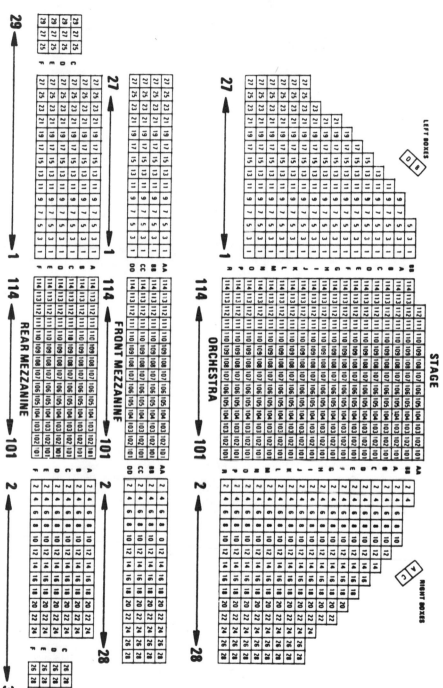

Front Mezzanine row AA overhangs Orchestra row I

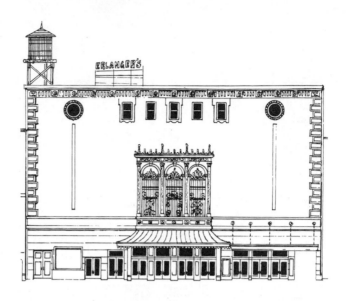

ST. JAMES

246 West 44th Street

Owner: Jujamcyn Theaters
Box Office: 398-0280
Box Office Hours: Monday–Saturday, 10 a.m.–8 p.m.; Sunday, 12 noon–5 p.m.
Credit Cards: AE, MC, V   CHARGIT   Personal checks
Group Sales: 398-8383
Total Seating: 1,601 (Orchestra, 667; Front mezzanine, 432; Rear mezzanine, 168; Balcony, 326; Boxes, 8; Standing room, 14)
Stage Type: Proscenium stage
AC
Handicapped: Semi-accessible

Originally the Erlanger, this was the top theatre of Abraham Erlanger's Theatrical Syndicate. It opened September 26, 1927, with George M. Cohan's *The Merry Malones*. In 1932, it changed hands and was renamed for the St. James Theatre in London. In its early days Mrs. Leslie Carter starred in *She Stoops to Conquer,* Tyrone Power in *Diplomacy,* and Mrs. Fiske in *Ladies of the Jury.* In the 1930s, Walter Slezak appeared in *May Wine* by Oscar Hammerstein and Sigmund Romberg; Maurice Evans triumphed in *Richard II* and *Hamlet* and, in 1941, in *Twelfth Night.* The Orson Welles production of *Native Son* starred Canada Lee. A smash hit arrived in 1943, Rodgers and Hammerstein's *Oklahoma!* and stayed five years. Other hits here included *Where's Charley?* (1948), *The King and I* (1951), *The Pajama Game* (1954), *Li'l Abner* (1956), and *Flower Drum Song* (1959). In 1960 came *Becket* with Anthony Quinn and Laurence Olivier. Nancy Walker and Phil Silvers followed with *Do Re Mi.* Another Comden and Green creation here, *Subways Are for Sleeping,* starred Carol Lawrence and Sydney Chaplin. In 1963, Albert Finney starred in John Osborne's *Luther.* On January 16, 1964, *Hello Dolly!* starring Carol Channing opened and stayed until late 1970. (For trivia buffs, the other Dollys in the production were Ginger Rogers, Pearl Bailey, Martha Raye, Betty Grable, and Ethel Merman.) Joseph Papp presented his modern version of *Two Gentlemen of Verona* in 1971. The 20th-anniversary revival of *My Fair Lady* with Ian Richardson, Christine Andreas, and George Rose was here in 1976. Betty Comden, Adolph Green, and Cy Coleman teamed up to do a musical version of *Twentieth Century,* and, since April 30, 1980, Jim Dale has been flying high in the smash musical *Barnum.*

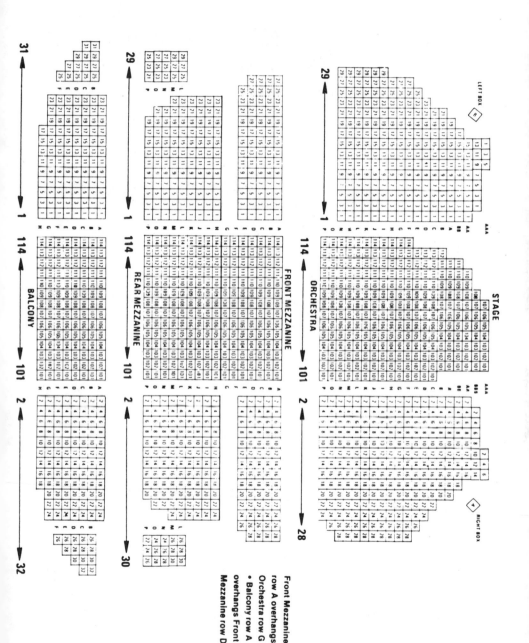

STAGE

LEFT BOX

RIGHT BOX

ORCHESTRA

FRONT MEZZANINE

REAR MEZZANINE

BALCONY

Front Mezzanine
row A overhangs
Orchestra row G
• Balcony row A
overhangs Front
Mezzanine row D

95

SHUBERT

225 West 44th Street

Owner: The Shubert Organization
Box Office: 246-5990
Box Office Hours: Monday–Saturday, 10 a.m.–8:30 p.m.; Sunday, 10 a.m.–6 p.m., if performance
Credit Cards: AE, DC, MC, V TELECHARGE Personal checks
Group Sales: 1,483 (Orchestra, 697; Mezzanine, 410; Balcony, 352; Boxes, 24; Standing room, 33)
Stage Type: Proscenium stage
AC
Handicapped: Semi-accessible

This is most people's favorite theatre and the flagship of the Shubert Organization, which has its executive offices above it in what was once Lee Shubert's apartment. (His brother, J. J., had his across the street above Sardi's.) The Shubert and the Booth comprise the western side of Shubert Alley. It opened on October 2, 1913, with *Hamlet,* starring J. Forbes Robinson, but throughout its history it has housed mostly musicals. In the 1920s, the Dolly sisters highlighted the *Greenwich Village Follies* and Texas Guinan wowed them in *Padlocks of 1927.* (Note to trivia buffs: A 1931 musical here, *Everybody's Welcome,* introduced the song "As Time Goes By.") In serious plays, Walter Huston starred in *Dodsworth,* and Alfred Lunt and Lynn Fontanne graced Robert E. Sherwood's *Idiot's Delight,* which won the 1936 Pulitzer Prize. In 1939, Katharine Hepburn, Van Heflin, Joseph Cotten, and Shirley Booth lit up the sky in *The Philadelphia Story.* Several delightful Rodgers and Hart musicals were here: *Babes in Arms; I Married an Angel; Higher and Higher;* and *By Jupiter,* starring Ray Bolger. Al Jolson and Martha Raye were in *Hold on to Your Hats* in 1940. Other hits at the Shubert: Mae West in *Catherine Was Great* (1944); *Bloomer Girl* with Celeste Holm (1944); Cole Porter's *Kiss Me, Kate* moved here from the Century (1950); Lerner and Loewe's *Paint Your Wagon* (1951); Cole Porter's *Can-Can* (1953); Judy Holliday in *Bells Are Ringing* (1956); Barbra Streisand's Broadway debut in *I Can Get It for You Wholesale* (1962); Anthony Newley's *Stop the World—I Want to Get Off* (1962); *Promises, Promises* (1969); and Stephen Sondheim's *A Little Night Music* (1973). The longest-running musical of them all? It moved from the Public Theater to here on July 25, 1975, won everything there was to win, and at this writing was still going strong—*A Chorus Line.*

STAGE

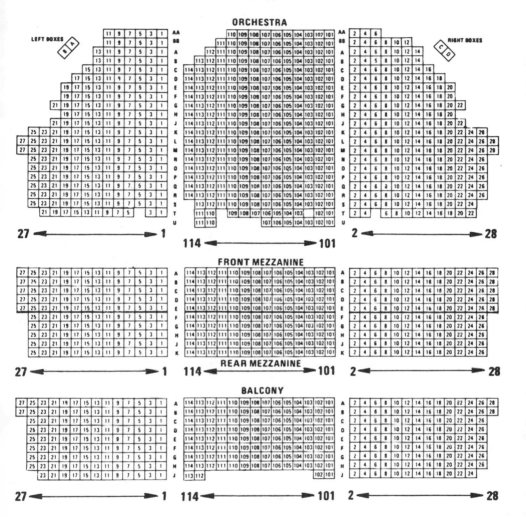

ORCHESTRA

FRONT MEZZANINE

REAR MEZZANINE

BALCONY

Front Mezzanine row A
overhangs Orchestra row L
• Balcony row A overhangs
Front Mezzanine row C

URIS

1633 Broadway (50th)

Owner: The Nederlanders
Box Office: 586-6510
Box Office Hours: Monday–Saturday, 10 a.m.–9 p.m.; Sunday, 12 noon–9 p.m.
Credit Cards: AE, DC, MC, V   CHARGIT   Personal checks
Group Sales: Through box office
Total Seating: 1,933 (Orchestra, 1,298; Loge, 46; Front mezzanine, 247; Rear mezzanine, 342)
Stage Type: Proscenium stage
AC
Handicapped: Semi-accessible

The first new Broadway theatre since 1928, the Uris opened on November 28, 1972, with a flop: *Via Galactica,* a rock musical starring Raul Julia and Virginia Vestoff. The theatre, however, has been a success. It was designed by Ralph Alswang, a set designer, who said, "The Uris represents what I think is the total philosophy of a modern musical comedy house—seating, sight lines, acoustics—the economy and aesthetics of this kind of theater." The second production here, *Seesaw,* starring Ken Howard and Michele Lee, won a Tony for Michael Bennett's choreography and for Tommy Tune's featured performance. Then came a revival of Sigmund Romberg's *The Desert Song,* followed by *Gigi,* a musical stage version of the Lerner/Loewe movie, with Alfred Drake, Daniel Massey, and Agnes Moorehead. In 1974, the Uris swung to such "evenings with . . ." as Sammy Davis, Jr.; Andy Williams; Anthony Newley and Henry Mancini; Johnny Mathis; and Nureyev and Friends. More of the same in 1975: the Dance Theatre of Harlem; Frank Sinatra in concert; Paul Anka; Margot Fonteyn and Rudolf Nureyev; the American Ballet Theatre; and the first New York production of Scott Joplin's opera, *Treemonisha.* In 1976, the season welcomed the D'Oyly Carte Opera Company; *Bing Crosby on Broadway,* and the highly acclaimed presentation of the original Gershwin full score of *Porgy and Bess.* In 1977, it was Nureyev again, then the Ballet of the Twentieth Century, before Constance Towers and the one-and-only Yul Brynner starred in the hit revival of Rodgers and Hammerstein's *The King and I.* It played until another resounding hit opened in March, 1979, Stephen Sondheim's *Sweeney Todd,* winner of eight Tony Awards. A new hit came in spring, 1981 when *Pirates of Penzance* arrived with Linda Ronstadt and Kevin Klein. Of special interest to theatregoers is the theatre Hall of Fame in the rotunda.

STAGE

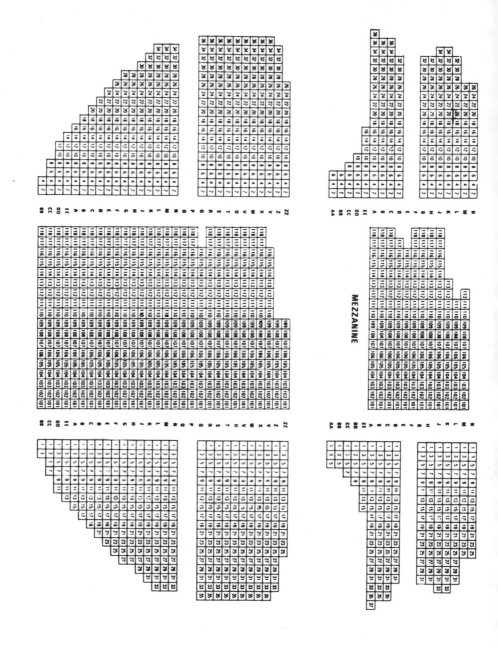

MEZZANINE

WINTER GARDEN

1634 Broadway (50th)

Owner: The Shubert Organization
Box Office: 245-4878
Box Office Hours: Monday–Saturday, 10 a.m.–8:30 p.m.; Sunday, 12 noon–6 p.m., if performance
Credit Cards: AE, DC, MC, V TELECHARGE Personal checks
Group Sales: Shubert Group Sales (944-4100)
Total Seating: 1,529 (Orchestra, 993; Mezzanine, 484; Boxes, 52; Standing room, 35)
Stage Type: Proscenium stage
AC
Handicapped: Semi-accessible

This was the first theatre to challenge 42nd Street's monopoly on musical comedy and revues. Built by the Shuberts to house their lighter offerings, it stands on the site of a horse exchange (critics in the early days claimed they could detect a lingering aroma). Al Jolson opened the Winter Garden on March 20, 1911, in a twin bill, *Bow Sing* and *La Belle Paree.* Starting the following year, the Shuberts produced 12 annual editions of their revue *The Passing Show.* Fred and Adele Astaire's first triumph, *Over the Top,* was here in 1917. Eddie Cantor was a hit here; Billie Burke's *Ziegfeld Follies* appeared in 1934; and Ray Bolger and Bert Lahr starred in *Life Begins at 8:40.* Olsen and Johnson's *Hellzapoppin* moved here from the 46th Street Theatre for a long run, followed by the comedy team's other revues, *Sons O' Fun* and *Laffin' Room Only.* Ed Wynn starred in *Hooray for What!* and a new version of the *Ziegfeld Follies* featured Fanny Brice, Josephine Baker, Bob Hope, and Eve Arden. In the 1950s, one hit musical followed another: Phil Silvers in *Top Banana;* Rosalind Russell in *Wonderful Town; Plain and Fancy;* and the biggest hit of them all, *West Side Story.* The 1960s led off with Tammy Grimes in *The Unsinkable Molly Brown,* followed with Barbra Streisand portraying her Winter Garden predecessor, Fanny Brice, in *Funny Girl,* and ended with the blockbuster *Mame* with Angela Lansbury. Here, too, was the New York Critics' Best Musical of 1971, Stephen Sondheim's *Follies,* starring Alexis Smith. In a change of pace for him and the theatre, Zero Mostel was Leopold Bloom in *Ulysses in Nighttown;* more typical for both was his 1976 revival of *Fiddler on the Roof.* The Winter Garden seemed to come full cycle recently with David Merrick's smash *42nd Street* with Tammy Grimes and Jerry Orbach, which had the dubious distinction of pushing ticket prices to a new high of $35. *42nd Street* moved to the Majestic in April 1981.

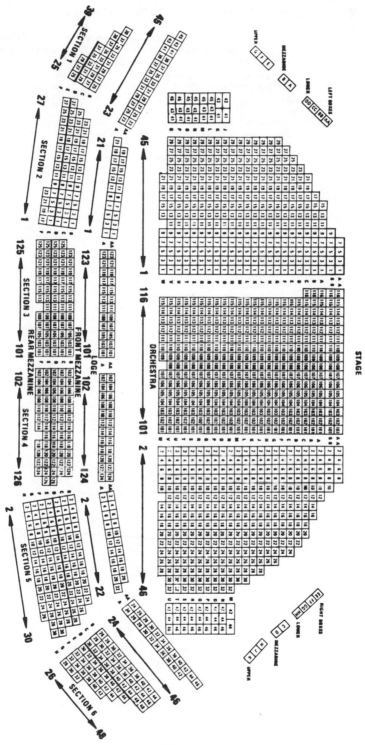

101

TWO MORE BROADWAY THEATRES—POSSIBLY.

Besides the interest in returning some of the 42nd Street theatres to legitimate use, recent attention has focused on two other theatres: the Ritz at 223 West 48th Street and the Ed Sullivan Theatre at 1697 Broadway. The Ritz opened as a Shubert house in March, 1921, and has drifted from theatre to radio studio and back over the years. In the 1960s, it was acquired by the city, renamed the RFK Center, but again fell into disuse. The city reportedly wishes to auction it off, provided it be rehabilitated as a theatre (estimated cost of rehabilitation: $1.5 million).

The Ed Sullivan was built in 1927 as Hammerstein's, renamed the Manhattan in 1931, was the Billy Rose Music Hall for a year in 1934, then the Manhattan Music Hall before CBS acquired it in 1936. As the name suggests, the Ed Sullivan television show originated from the theatre for some years. The Shubert Organization has been negotiating with CBS for the theatre, but the Nederlanders were challenging the sale on the grounds of the already extensive Shubert theatre holdings. In the spring of 1981, the matter was in the courts.

OTHER THEATRES IN THE BROADWAY AREA

ACTORS STUDIO
432 West 44th Street

Box Office: 757-0870
Box Office Hours: Monday–Saturday, 12 Noon–5 p.m.
Credit Cards: None   TDF Vouchers   Personal checks
Group Sales: Through box office
Total Seating: 125 (Orchestra, 100; Balcony, 25)
Stage Type: Thrust stage
AC
Handicapped: No access

Yes, this is *the* Actors Studio. This is where Lee Strasberg, America's leading exponent of The Method, the Stanislavski system, has trained a disproportionate number of outstanding actors and actresses—Marlon Brando, Karl Malden, Shelley Winters, Al Pacino, Ron Leibman, Ellen Burstyn, Dustin Hoffman, etc., etc., ad infinitum. If you pass the audition here (and very few do the first time), you can study free of charge with the best there are. Since the middle 1950s, the Actors Studio has played a leading, if not dominant, role in training for the stage. Its home is a former Greek Orthodox Church, and it is a rare experience to see a production here. The productions are open to the public and it's wise to reserve ahead. Phone the box office for what's happening when. Some staged readings are also open, although priority is given to studio members.

AMERICAN PLACE THEATRE
111 West 46th Street

Owner: Lawrence Wein
Box Office: 246-0393
Box Office Hours: Monday–Saturday, 10:30 a.m.–8:30 p.m.
Credit Cards: AE, DC, MC, V   CHARGIT   TDF Vouchers   Personal checks
Group Sales: Through box office
Season: September–mid-May
Total Seating: Mainstage, 299; Sub-Plot Café, 100
Stage Type: Modified thrust stage
AC
Handicapped: Semi-accessible

Wynn Handman, Michael Tolan, Sidney Lanier, and Myrna Loy founded the American Place Theatre (named after Alfred Stieglitz's American Place art gallery, where talents in many fields mingled 50 years ago) in 1964 in St. Clement's Church in Hell's Kitchen. They envisioned it as a forum for living American playwrights, and their vision has been fulfilled. More than 65 plays have been given full productions, including William Alfred's *Hogan's Goat* and Robert Lowell's *The Old Glory.* Plays by Sam Shepard, Ronald Tavel, and Maria Irene Fomes have premiered here, as have the first plays of Ronald Ribman, Steve Tesich, and Jonathan Reynold. Works by black playwrights Ed Bullins, Philip Hayes Dean, Elaine Jackson, Ron Milner, and Charles Russel; Asian-American Frank Chin; and by writers in other media—Robert Coover, Anne Sexton, Joyce Carol Oates, and Bruce Jay Friedman—also have been presented. When American Place Theatre moved here in 1971, Brooks Atkinson wrote that it was "the best new theatre in the Broadway area. The theatre building is superb." Some recent productions staged under Wynn Handman's direction include *The Grinding Machine* by Annalita Marsili Alexander; *Touching Bottom* by Steve Tesich; *Seduced* by Sam Shepard; and *Still Life* by Emily Mann. In addition, the American Humorist Series presents cabaret in the Sub-Plot Café. You might consider becoming an American Place sponsor. For $125 ($109 of which is deductible) you receive two tickets to each of the four productions in the series, plus four guest tickets. A regular series ticket is $35.

AMERICAN THEATRE OF ACTORS

314 West 54th Street

Box Office: 581-3044
Box Office Hours: Monday–Saturday, 9:30 a.m.–11 p.m.
Credit Cards: None   TDF Vouchers
Group Sales: Through box office
Total Seating: Space I; 99; Space II, 62; Space III, 41; Space IV, 50.
Stage Type: Flexible open spaces (Space IV is an outdoor theatre behind the building that operates from June to September)
AC
Handicapped: Semi-accessible

James Jennings, a director, founded this group in 1977 in a former city courthouse. It now encompasses 55 actors, 15 playwrights, and four directors, and produces 22 plays a year. A play developed here, *Heartland* by Kevin Heelan, recently moved to Broadway. The theatre concentrates on contemporary, naturalistic drama, eschewing avant-garde and conceptual productions. A new American Classic Series was opened with O'Neill's *Beyond the Horizon*. Two recent productions developed by the group were *The Greatest Play Ever Written* by Mike Sulona and *'Til Jason Comes* by Don Lauria. Lisa Lipsky is the general manager.

THE APPLE CORPS THEATRE

601 West 51st Street

Box Office: 664-0027
Box Office Hours: One hour before performance (answering machine other times)
Credit Cards: None   TDF Vouchers   Personal checks
Group Sales: Through box office
Total Seating: 86
Stage Type: Semi-thrust stage
AC
Handicapped: No access

Converted from office space in the early 1960s, this was briefly the Cuban Cultural Center before the arrival of the Apple Corps. This group has a particular fondness for the plays of Thornton Wilder and Eugene O'Neill *(Long Day's Journey into Night* was being performed when this was written). It also does two mystery trilogies each year. *Henry Apples* was given a world premiere here last season. More recent productions: Arthur Kopit's *Oh Dad, Poor Dad . . .* and Arnold Bennett's *The Honeymoon*.

CAP (CENTER FOR THE ACTING PROCESS)

276 West 43rd Street

Box Office: 840-7394
Box Office Hours: Wednesday–Thursday, 4 p.m.–11:30 p.m.; Saturday, 1 p.m.– 11:30 p.m.; Sunday, 12 noon–11 p.m.
Credit Cards: None   TDF Vouchers
Group Sales: Karen Scioli (840-7394)
Total Seating: 50
Stage Type: Proscenium stage
AC
Handicapped: No access

This West Side rehearsal studio was converted to a theatre in 1978. Since then artistic director Paul Zakrzewski has presented such plays as Philip Barry's *Hotel Universe* and Agatha Christie's *Murder Is Announced*. Most recently, Anton Chekhov's *The Seagull* was presented as "a classic soap opera laden with passion and humor."

CITY CENTER

131 West 55th Street

Owner: City of New York
Box Office: 246-8989
Box Office Hours: 12 noon–8 p.m.
Credit Cards: AE, MC, V   CHARGIT   Personal checks for advance mail sales
Group Sales: 581-7907
Season: Mid-September–June
Total Seating: 2,932 (Orchestra, 885; First balcony, 1,284; Second balcony, 763)
Stage Type: Proscenium stage
AC
Handicapped: Semi-accessible

If the facade of City Center strikes you as strange, remember that it was built in 1923 as a Masonic hall and was called Mecca Temple until 1943. Now owned by the city and run as a center for the people of the city, it offers primarily dance programs. Every now and then, however, a theatrical production comes here. The most recent was the June, 1980, revival of Meredith Wilson's *The Music Man* starring Dick Van Dyke.

THE CUBICULO

414 West 51st Street

Box Office: 265-2139
Box Office Hours: 45 minutes before performance
Credit Cards: None   TDF Vouchers   Personal checks
Group Sales: 371-9610
Season: New York, January–May
Stockbridge, Mass., June–August
Total Seating: 74
Stage Type: Black box
AC
Handicapped: No access

The Music-Theatre Performing Group/Lenox Art Center, founded in 1970 by Lyn Austin, functions as a laboratory for the development of new American music-theatre, fusing experimental theatre techniques with a wide range of musical forms—contemporary, jazz, etc.—and dance. The company trains a core of young performing artists skilled in this field and is developing into a new musical theatre repertory company. Some of its recent productions include Wallace Shawn's *The Old Man; Virgil Thomson: A Profile;* and *The Tennis Game,* book and lyrics by George W. S. Trow and music by William Schimmel. The group performs in Stockbridge, Mass., in the summer.

ENSEMBLE STUDIO THEATRE

549 West 52nd Street

Box Office: 247-4982
Box Office Hours: Tuesday–Saturday, 10 a.m.–6 p.m.; Sunday, 11 a.m.–3 p.m.
Credit Cards: None   TDF Vouchers   Personal Checks
Group Sales: 247-4982
Total Seating: 99
Stage Type: Flexible stage
No AC
Handicapped: Semi-accessible

This is a membership organization of more than 200 theater professionals—playwrights, actors, directors, designers, and technicians—located in a city-owned warehouse. The Ensemble Studio Theatre develops new works for the stage and, as important, provides a permanent home for creative artists where they can work among their peers, free of commercial pressures. Each season here there are five productions of new American plays, 10 to 15 workshop productions, and 40 to 50 play readings. Now an annual event is a spring marathon of one-act plays by American writers. The Ensemble Studio Theatre was founded in

1971 by Curt Dempster, now its artistic director. One of its most commendable works is the Theater Bank, which provides financial support to playwrights, directors, and actors. In spring 1981, the theatre presented Mary Gallagher's *Father Dreams*.

INTERART THEATRE
549 West 52nd Street

Box Office: 246-1050
Box Office Hours: One hour before performance; reservations by phone
Credit Cards: None   CHARGIT   TDF Vouchers   Personal checks
Group Sales: 246-1050
Season: October–June
Total Seating: 40 to 90, depending upon show
Stage Type: Flexible open space
AC
Handicapped: Semi-accessible

This is the performance center of the Women's Interart Center, Inc., which seeks to present the breadth and quality of work by contemporary women artists. Margot Lewitin is the artistic director, and with Marjorie De Fazio, Alice Rubinstein, and Jane Chambers founded Interart Theatre in1970. Interart does not identify itself as a "feminist" theater; artists tend to work from their own lives and their personal points of view. Among the more than 40 productions mounted here have been Michel Deutsch's *Sunday* translated by Françoise Kourilsky and Lynn Greenblatt; Shakespeare's *Antony and Cleopatra*, directed by Estelle Parsons; *The Daughters Cycle Trilogy* by the Women's Experimental Theatre; and *Request Concert* by Franz X. Kroetz.

IRISH REBEL THEATER
553 West 51st Street

Box Office: 757-3318, 757-3191
Box Office Hours: Monday–Friday, 11 a.m.–7 p.m.; Friday–Saturday, 11 a.m.–8 p.m.; Sunday, 11 a.m.–3 p.m.
Credit Cards: None   TDF Vouchers   Personal checks
Group Sales: Patrick King, (757-3318)
Total Seating: 65–99 depending upon production (Standing room, 25)
Stage Type: Flexible stage
No AC
Handicapped: No access

As the name suggests, this group produces only plays by Irish and Irish-American playwrights, the gamut being from Shaw and Wilde and O'Casey to O'Neill and Brian Friel and Hugh Leonard. Patrick King founded the group in 1974 in a building that once was a stable. Recent productions have included Leonard's *Da* and Friel's *Mundy Scheme*.

NETWORK THEATRE
754 Ninth Avenue (51st)

Box Office: 586-1260
Box Office Hours: Wednesday–Saturday, 9 a.m.–11 p.m.; Sunday, 11 a.m.–9 p.m.
Credit Cards: None
Total Seating: 74
Stage Type: Proscenium stage or modified thrust
AC
Handicapped: Semi-accessible

In a former furniture store, showcase productions are mounted by artistic director Cecil Gorey and Stanley Harrison, who is in charge of the affiliated acting school. Productions in 1981 included *The Shepherd* by Tim Wortham and Lanford Wilson's *The Gingham Dog*.

THE NEW DRAMATISTS

424 West 44th Street

Reservations: 757-6960
Free admissions to readings
Season: September–July
Total seating: Studio, 40; Theatre, 90
Stage Type: Modified Thrust Stage (Theatre), Arena (Studio)
No AC
Handicapped: No access

A distinguished theatre group (Moss Hart, John Golden, Richard Rodgers, Michaela O'Harra, Oscar Hammerstein II, Howard Lindsay, and John Wharton) founded the New Dramatists in 1949 to encourage and develop new American playwrights. An applicant submits two plays; once admitted, he is a full participating member for a three- to seven-year period. New Dramatists alumni include Robert Anderson, William Inge, Ed Bullins, Richard Foreman, and John Guare. In all, current members and past alumni have contributed more than 200 plays to the American theatre. Some recent readings: *Father Dreams* by Mary Gallagher; Jack Gilhooley's *The Ravelle's Comeback* and *Dancin' to Calliope;* Robert Lord's *Singles;* and Edward H. Mabley's *The Feathered Serpent.*

NO SMOKING PLAYHOUSE

354 West 45th Street

Box Office: 582-7861
Box Office Hours: Monday–Saturday, 11 a.m.–6 p.m.
Credit Cards: None   TDF Vouchers   Personal checks
Group Sales: Through box office
Total Seating: 79 in permanent seating, 20 in folding chairs
Stage Type: Proscenium stage
AC
Handicapped: Semi-accessible

Artistic director Norman Thomas Marshall's group Merry Enterprises Theatre started in a Chelsea storefront before moving to this former Con Ed substation in 1977. Among their recent productions were J. B. Priestley's *Dangerous Corner; Reflected Glory;* John von Hartz's *Mothers and Daughters; Hamlet,* starring Adam Redfield; and *Smaze—An Environmental Musical,* lyrics by Charlotte Lampert and music by Peter Schickele. The playhouse offers a subscription series of five major productions and several readings. The cost is $15.

PUERTO RICAN TRAVELLING THEATRE COMPANY

304 West 47th Street

Box Office: 354-1293
Box Office Hours: Thursday–Sunday, 6 p.m.–curtain
Credit Cards: MC, V   TDF Vouchers   Personal checks
Group Sales: Through box office
Season: January–September
Total Seating: 199
Stage Type: Thrust stage
AC
Handicapped: Semi-accessible

The purpose of the Puerto Rican Travelling Theatre Company is to bring contemporary, relevant, bilingual theatre free of charge to the people of the city. The permanent theatre offers bilingual presentations year-round and the company's touring unit takes productions to community centers, churches, streets, and parks. HEW sponsors the company's in-school arts programs, which holds workshops in three Upper West Side junior high schools. The company was founded in 1967 by Miriam Colon Edgar, George P. Edgar, Anibal Otero, and José Ocasio. A Broadway-area firehouse has been converted into a permanent 199-seat home for the company. A recent production here was *Death Shall Not Enter the Palace.*

QUAIGH THEATRE

Hotel Diplomat
108 West 43rd Street

Box Office: 221-9088
Box Office Hours: Monday–Saturday, 10 a.m.–5 p.m. (until 8 p.m. if evening performance)
Credit Cards: None   TDF Vouchers   Personal checks
Group Sales: Through box office
Total Seating: 99
Stage Type: Three-quarter thrust stage
AC
Handicapped: Semi-accessible

A popular year-round lunchtime theatre series has been running in the little theatre on the mezzanine of this hotel since 1976. The shows begin at 12:15 p.m. and last 45 to 50 minutes, and the audience is encouraged to bring its lunch (there's a luncheonette in the hotel and a delicatessen next door). The presentations, under the artistic direction of Will Lieberson, range from O'Neill's sea plays to René Taylor's *Benny,* and each has a two-week run. The shows are popular with senior citizens, many coming from the far reaches of the city, and with young people who work in the area. "We try to give them things they won't see on TV," explains Mr. Lieberson. Admission is free, although a $1.50 donation is suggested. The theatre is also used in the evening for showcase presentations, including *Victim,* starring Gretta Tyssen; *Mama's Little Angels* by Lou LaRusso III; *Darkness at Noon; Counsellor at Law* (very popular with lawyers in the area); and Elliot Kaplin's play about his brother, cartoonist Al Capp, *A Nickel for Picasso.*

RADIO CITY MUSIC HALL

1260 Avenue of the Americas (50th)

Box Office: 246-4600
Box Office Hours: Monday–Wednesday, 10 a.m.–8:30 p.m.; Thursday, 10 a.m.–8 p.m.; Friday–Saturday, 10 a.m.–8:30 p.m.; Sunday, 11 a.m.–8:30 p.m.
Credit Cards: AE   CHARGIT
Group Sales: 541-9436
Total Seating: 5,882 (Reserved seats: First mezzanine only)
Stage Type: Proscenium stage
AC
Handicapped: Semi-accessible

This is one of the great theatres in the world, the apogee of Art Deco as applied to theatre design and a monument to the magnitude of the dream of those who designed and built it in the early years of the Depression. Consider the size: It approaches twice the seating capacity of the Metropolitan Opera (and three times the population of the Vermont village I grew up in). It was designed for spectacular stage shows at the moment when movies were taking over. A compromise: movies (family movies, of course) and spectacular stage shows—part of growing up for so many of us was seeing the Christmas or Easter show here. When family movies ceased to draw crowds sufficient to fill the Music Hall, there was talk of demolishing it for office space. Happily, the theatre got landmark status and a new lease on life. Now movies are a rarity here, and big revues alternate with performances by such stars as Frank Sinatra. Radio City Music Hall is not legitimate theatre in the sense that the other theatres in this guide are—nor has it ever been—but if you haven't seen it, you should. As a theatre facility, it is a glory. Dreams seldom come in this size anymore.

"A novelist may lose his readers for a few pages; a playwright never dares lose his audience for a minute."

TERRANCE RATTIGAN

ROYAL COURT REPERTORY

301 West 55th Street

Box Office: 997-9582
Box Office Hours: 12 noon–8 p.m. (answering machine, if unattended)
Group Sales: Through box office
Total Seating: 60
Stage Type: Proscenium stage
AC
Handicapped: Semi-accessible

Mystery plays have been the recent strength of this repertory company. Artistic director Phyllis Craig's thriller *Bargain for Murder,* for example, now has passed its third anniversary here. Other productions include Agatha Christie's *Witness for the Prosecution* and Sir Arthur Conan Doyle and Paul W. Oakley's *The Hound of the Baskervilles.*

ST. MALACHY'S THEATRESPACE

239 West 49th Street

Box Office: 480-1340
Hours: One hour before performance (answering machine, other times)
Credit Cards: None   TDF Vouchers
Total Seating: 99
Stage Type: Flexible open space
AC
Handicapped: Semi-accessible

Productions are staged here, but that's a small part of the story. For more than 75 years, St. Malachy's Actors' Chapel had been the spiritual home of Catholic actors in the theatre district, and the church has special theatre masses (Saturday, 5 p.m., 7 p.m., and 10:45 p.m.; Sunday, 12:30 p.m. and 5 p.m.). To help meet the physical, emotional, and spiritual needs of the elderly poor in the area, most of them retired actors, Father George Moore closed the chapel and turned it into a day center. The communion rail given by George M. Cohan was sold, and Our Lady of Lourdes grotto became a rock garden. The center now serves more than 1,000 midday meals, made possible by government funding, each week. A small stage was built by Local 1 stagehands with lumber provided by the Shubert Organization. Area businessmen made donations and now there are curtained-off reading, sitting, and television-viewing areas, a library, a barber's chair, a piano, and garden tables with umbrellas. Father Moore has further plans: a Green Room, that would be a meeting ground and information center for actors, and a carillon to ring out over the area as a reminder that St. Malachy's is committed to the welfare of the theatre district.

THEATRE FOUR

424 West 55th Street

Box Office: 246-8545
Box Office Hours: Monday, 10 a.m.–6 p.m.; Tuesday–Saturday, 10 a.m.–8:30 p.m.
Credit Cards: AE, MC, V   TDF Vouchers   Personal checks
Group Sales: 575-5860
Season: September–June
Total Seating: 299 (Orchestra, 241; Mezzanine, 48)
Stage Type: Proscenium stage
No AC
Handicapped: No access

The productions of the Negro Ensemble Company have provided a major share of the body of contemporary black dramatic literature. Since it was founded in 1967 by Doublas Turner Ward (now its artistic director), Robert Hooks, and Gerald S. Krone, the company has premiered more than 80 new works. The company has made six national and four international tours. Among its recent productions were *Nevis Mountain Dew* by Steve Carter; Judi Ann Mason's *Daughters of the Mock; Zooman and the Sign* by Charles Fuller; and *Weep Not for Me* by Gus Edwards.

TOWN HALL

123 West 43rd Street

Box Office:	840-2824
Box Office Hours:	12 noon–6 p.m.
Credit Cards:	Varies with producer
Group Sales:	Through box office
Total Seating:	1,498 (Orchestra, 832; Loges, 78; Balcony, 588; Standing room, 50)
Stage Type:	Proscenium stage
	AC
	Handicapped: Semi-accessible

A superb concert hall, Town Hall has presented sufficient theatrical productions to make it of interest to the theatre. In the spring of 1981, for example, a revival of *Jacques Brel Is Alive and Well and Living in Paris* was here for three weeks. An elegant building that was designed by McKim Mead & (Stanford) White, Town Hall also boasts exceptional acoustics. This is where Margaret Sanger attempted to lecture on birth control and got carted off to the West 47th Street police station; where Lotte Lehmann and Joan Sutherland made their New York debuts; where Eddie Condon's jazz concerts were presented. Town Hall fell on hard times after the opening of Lincoln Center, and it has been fighting for its life. It is now both a city and national landmark, and a massive fundraising drive is under way to keep it in operation. Help if you can—they don't make them like Town Hall anymore.

VETERANS ENSEMBLE THEATRE

314 West 54th Street

Box Office:	977-4217
Box Office Hours:	Monday–Saturday, 10 a.m.–6 p.m. (answering machine other times)
Credit Cards:	None TDF Vouchers
Season:	October–July
Group Sales:	Through box office (to veteran and senior citizen groups only)
Total Seating:	72
Stage Type:	Proscenium stage
	No AC
	Handicapped: Semi-accessible

A group of veterans of Viet Nam was formed in 1978 by artistic director Tom Bird to present plays dealing with war and the aftermath of war. The first production, in 1979, was Rod Serling's *The Strike,* an original dramatization of the life of artist Jackson Pollock. Other productions by the group have included: *All My Sons;* Irwin Shaw's *Bury the Dead; Home of the Brave; A Place Called Heartbreak* by Robert Stokes; and Jonathan Polansky's *In Pursuit of Liberty,* a dramatization of the seizing of the Statue of Liberty.

WESTSIDE MAINSTAGE I & II

424 West 49th Street

Box Office:	664-9102
Box Office Hours:	Varies with production
Credit Cards:	Varies with production
Group Sales:	Varies with production
Total Seating:	100, Mainstage I; 100, Mainstage II
Stage Type:	End stage (Mainstage I), Semi-thrust (Mainstage II)
	AC
	Handicapped: No access

Two actors, Craig Noble and Gary Wertheim, converted a restaurant in a partially burned-out building into two theatre spaces. While they do not produce themselves, they rent the spaces to a wide range of independent producers. In March, 1980, Gryphon Theatricals opened Mainstage II with the first New York production of Norman Mailer's *Deer Park;* Mainstage I opened the following month with Robert Patrick's new play, *T-Shirts.* Other recent productions include Penumbra Production's *Last Stop Bluejay Lane* by Wendy Russell, the Glines production of *Blue Heaven,* and Shaw's *Candida.*

RESTAURANTS AND NIGHTSPOTS

There are no great restaurants in the theatre district—no Lutèce, no Palace, no Le Cygne—and perhaps it's just as well. Great dining and great theatre both deserve enough time and attention to fill an evening. Happily, there are a number of good Broadway restaurants and more than a few excellent ones—certainly enough to dine well within an easy walk of any theatre, unless you should seek a particular cuisine or wish to revisit an old favorite.

What follows is not a complete listing but all the important restaurants plus a generous sampling of others that, over the years, have proven personally rewarding or especially convenient. The restaurants are rated against these standards and given one, two, or three stars, accordingly. Particular attention has been paid to those representing bargains. In every instance, the first criterion has been, "Does this restaurant add to the pleasure of going to the theatre?" Serious gourmets should consult other, more knowledgeable sources. It is fair to say that any of these restaurants, except on the rare "off" night, should please all but the most exacting of palates.

Some cautions and suggestions are in order. Quite a few restaurants, including many that are bargains, still do not take credit cards. Some of them will take personal checks if you show them a major credit card, but it's safer to bring an adequate supply of cash.

All Broadway restaurants are at the busiest in the pre-theatre hours; reservations are a must, and you'll fare better if you phone a few days in advance. If your schedule permits, ask the maitre d' when you should come to allow sufficient time to be served properly. Also, it's a good idea to let your waiter know you're going to the theatre.

When making reservations for after the theatre, tell the maitre d' what show you're seeing. He has a list of closing times and will know to the minute when you'll be coming through the door. After-theatre dining is less crowded and more leisurely, but reservations are still suggested unless you don't mind a long wait at the bar. Most places have a special supper menu, and none seem to mind if you simply want to have dessert.

With most shows out by 10:30 p.m., many theatregoers, including me, prefer to dine after the theatre. You're not looking at your watch all through dinner, part of the pleasure of the theatre is discussing what you've just seen with your friends, and if you eat heavily before you just might nod off in act one.

I was leaving Sardi's one night when I noticed a man in a dinner jacket, standing by himself with a dumfounded look on his face. I asked what what the matter and he said, "I was at the opening of the Tennessee Williams play and I must have dozed off." I didn't see the seriousness of this until he added, "Next thing I knew someone was shaking my shoulder—it was Tennessee Williams and he asked me to leave!" *Beware the heavy meal and the one-too-many drink.* The theatre's too much fun to sleep through.

For those short of time or money, just about every version of fast food is represented on Broadway: Zum Zum and Arthur Treacher's at 50th; Burger King at 46th, Beefsteak & Brew at 45th, to mention a few. If you need a fast Chinese fix, there's even a Rickshaw Express at 49th. Nathan's at 43rd is big, busy, and fun. The franks that made the original Nathan's a Coney Island landmark are delicious.

If you're hungrier, Tad's Steaks in several Broadway locations is a bona fide bargain. A reasonable-sized sirloin (tenderized, of course) broiled over a hickory fire, baked potato, salad; and garlic bread was $3.89 when this was written. Tad's is cafeteria-style, and beer and wine are available. For those who like the now-ubiquitous salad bars, there's a Beefsteak Charlie's at 52nd just below the Broadway Theatre and a Boss practically across the street. Both fall somewhere between fast food and the more conventional restaurants.

Some restaurants have live music, some late entertainment spots serve food. If their raison d'être is entertainment, it will be so indicated (🎵 for music, 😊 for comedy).

The map at the beginning of the Broadway section will enable you to locate any listed restaurant in relation to a particular theatre and parking or public transportation.

ACROPOLIS*

767 Eighth Avenue (47th)
Reservations: 247-4120
No credit cards
Inexpensive to Moderate

You could walk by the Acropolis without giving it a second galnce, but it is an attractive place serving good, if not great, Greek food at surprisingly low prices (practically everything is under $10). Most of the entrees involve lamb, and grape leaves are much in evidence. The fish is excellent, as is the coffee.

 # ACT ONE*

One Times Square (42nd)
Reservations: 695-1880
Credit Cards: AE, DC, MC
Moderate   Closed Sunday and major holidays

Act One is on a high floor in the sheathed-over building that gave Times Square its name. Later it was the Allied Chemical Tower (*ACT* One, get it?); now it is known by its address but it's still where the ball comes down at midnight on New Year's Eve. The big attraction here is the view, and it's a beauty. You look up Times Square and Broadway, and when all the lights are on your spine will tingle. A smallish, attractive room with some interesting theatrical memorabilia on the walls, Act One offers theatre dinners and an a la carte menu. (There is a cocktail lounge on the floor below.) The prices and quality are both moderate. Light fare is served after the theatre. There's live music. Act One is worth the trip if only for a drink and a generous serving of view.

A LA FOURCHETTE***

342 West 46th Street
Reservations: 245-9744
No credit cards
Moderate   Closed Sunday and August

The city now has officially recognized what theatregoers knew all along: West 46th between Eighth and Ninth Avenues is Restaurant Row. Nearly 20 establishments crowd the block; an accurate count is nearly impossible as places come and go with alarming speed. One of the oldest and one of the best is my personal favorite, A la Fourchette. It's in an old brownstone, a few steps below street-level, and is tiny. Enter a narrow hall that serves as a coatroom, turn left to the small bar, then right to the dining room. Seating no more than 30; the room is broken up into three distinct areas which heightens the feeling of intimacy. The walls are covered with murals of fin-de-siècle Paris music-hall scenes; the atmosphere is warm and friendly. It's family-run and everyone seems delighted to see you.

A blackboard lists the specialties—usually duck, several varieties of sole, veal, and sometimes a cassoulet, usually in the $9–$12 range. There also is an extensive menu: the beef Wellington, rack of lamb, or sirloin for two ($34, $32, and $28, respectively) are at least a match of any West Side steak house. The basic cuisine is provincial French prepared with care. The wine list has a number of moderately priced selections. You can spend more money at dinner in the area, but it's hard to eat more enjoyably.

ALFIE'S*

225 West 47th Street
Reservations: 581-8290
Credit Cards: AE, CB, DC, MC, V
Moderate

What was a burned-out delicatessen a year or so ago has been transformed into a most attractive French restaurant convenient to Barrymore, Biltmore, Brooks Atkinson, and Edison theatres. The coquille au gratin is a delicious way to start your a la carte dinner. From the entrees, the lamb chops with mint sauce ($12.95), the roast Long Island duckling ($11.95), or the sea scallops broiled with shallots, garlic, butter, and tomatoes ($11.95) are recommended, as are the daily specialties. The cold soufflé du jour ($2.95) brings down the curtain nicely.

ALGONQUIN**

59 West 44th Street
Reservations: 687-4400
Credit Cards: AE, CB, DC, MC, V
Moderate to Expensive   Closed Sunday and major holidays

As Sardi's is *the* theatrical restaurant, the Algonquin is *the* theatrical hotel. Practically every big name in the theatre has stayed here at one time or another, and you usually see a few luminaries each time you visit. There are plush chairs and small tables in the lobby—veddy British—where you can have a drink before dinner, summoning your waiter by tapping a nickel-plated bell. For dinner, choose either the Oak Room or the Rose Room. The beautifully paneled Oak Room is the site of the legendary Round Table: Dorothy Parker, Robert Benchley, F. P. Adams, et al. The food is American-French, above-average hotel fare. Some suggestions: red snapper in dilled mustard sauce, ($10.50); wiener schnitzel holstein with asparagus ($10.75); frog's legs provençale ($9.75); and first-rate prime ribs with Yorkshire pudding ($14.25). The Rose Room, really an area at the end of the lobby, serves a nice after-theatre buffet as well as the a la carte menu. The Algonquin is worth a pilgrimage, particularly if you're not immune to nostalgia; it's an integral part of the Broadway scene and a lovely reminder of more gentle times. (If you're dining before the theatre, there's complimentary parking until 1 a.m.)

ARTIST AND WRITERS**

213 West 40th Street
Reservations: 840-0022
Credit CArds: AE, CB, DC, V
Moderate to Expensive   Closed Saturday, Sunday, and major holidays

To alumni of the late, great *Herald Tribune* like myself, Artist and Writers (Bleeck's—pronounced Blake's—to the cognoscenti) still is a second home; it was only 25 feet or so from the paper's back door. It survived the loss of the *Trib* as it had the closing of the old Metropolitan Opera House down the street, so it must be doing something right. Truly gumutlich, it has one of the best old-time, stand-up bars in the city. Curious mementos and ephemera abound: a suit of armor, a giant enlargement of Nat Fein's Pulitzer-Prize-winning photograph of Babe Ruth's farewell, James Thurber drawings of odd characters playing the match game—on a slow night ask the owner to teach it to you but don't play him for money; you'll lose. The food is good and Germanic and very filling. A new door links the restaurant to the lobby of the Nederlander Theater on 41st Street, convenient for an intermission drink.

BARBETTA**

321 West 46th Street
Reservations: 246-9171
Credit Cards: AE, CB, DC
Expensive   Closed Sunday

Barbetta, the grand dame of Restaurant Row, is elegant and attracts an elegant crowd. Crystal chandeliers cast their light on a beautiful room: arched windows, upholstered chairs, good linen. In the summer you can dine in the garden where there's a small pool and several pieces of statuary. (At lunch on summer Wednesday matinee days there is a fashion show in the garden.) The maitre d' is a charmer and convinces you that your arrival has made his day. A reasonably priced pre-theatre dinner is offered and to venture into the realm of a la carte is to court financial disaster, although there are some real enticements: the veal steak tartare alla piemontese that combines ground veal, lemon juice, olive oil, garlic, raw mushrooms, and fresh pepper in a sort of pancake is a true joy, as are the arugula and raw mushroom salad and the pasta. A nice touch: Barbetta welcomes diners back after the theatre to enjoy a leisurely dessert.

BERNARD'S*

218 West 48th Street
Reservations: 664-8617
Credit Cards: AE, DC, MC, V
Inexpensive

Since it opened next door to the Longacre three years ago, Bernard's has become popular for a light meal or an intermission drink. The burgers ($3.95 for a cheeseburger with steak fries, lettuce, tomato, and pickle) are popular but by no means the extent of the menu. There's a good quiche that comes with a salad ($5.95), omelettes, chicken Kiev ($6.50), and eight or so daily specials that invariably include good fish. The strawberry crepes ($2.95) are a nice finish. The bar is big, well-run, and moderately priced for the Broadway area.

BROADWAY JOE STEAK HOUSE**

315 West 46th Street
Reservations: 246-6153
Credit Cards: AE
Expensive   Closed Sunday

The name says it and if you're not in the mood for a serving of red meat that would satisfy a lumberjack, wait until you are before coming here. As you enter, there's an interesting mural filled with faces representing "Fifty Years of Broadway"—if you have a drink at the bar see how many you can name. The waiter probably will greet you with, "How do you want it?" (say "rare" or whatever and you'll be one up on him). The one-pound steaks are excellent: thick, juicy, charred, tender. A good baked potato and a salad come with your steak ($18.75), although I suggest you order something other than the house dressing. The lamb chops ($15.75) are excellent; so is the broiled half chicken ($10.50), but why come here for chicken? If you come after the theatre to this Restaurant Row standby, there's a steak sandwich platter at $12.50. In case you were wondering, this Broadway Joe, whoever he was, was not Joe Namath.

CABANA CARIOCA*

123 West 45th Street
Reservations: 581-8088
Credit Cards: AE, CB, DC, MC, V
Inexpensive

An informal, pleasant Brazilian-Portuguese restaurant, Cabana Carioca offers a number of interesting specialties: black bean soup, several spicy shrimp dishes, caldo verde (a vegetable and potato laced with garlic), plus daily specials that usually are worth exploring. One of the theatre-district bargains.

CAFÉ DE FRANCE**

330 West 46th Street
Reservations: 586-0088
Credit Cards: AE, DC, MC
Moderate   Closed Sunday

Many people treasure the Café de France and for good reason. It is a warm, friendly place with good French food at moderate prices. Move it to the East Side, give it a chic decor and it would be an instant hit. A complete dinner is offered pre-theatre, and usually the daily special is worth a try. There's an excellent quiche lorraine and an equally good coquille for appetizers. A favorite entree is the canard montmorency and the filet of sole or filet of beef in red wine are both excellent choices. Your check should average $15 to $20 per person plus drinks. Incidentally, this is one of the few restaurants in the area that offer rabbit. The wine list is extensive, and the prices are moderate. The Café de France offers a lot for the money, and it's well worth a visit.

CAFÉ DES SPORTS*

329 West 51st Street
Reservations: 974-9052
No credit cards
Moderate

A small, unpretentious bistro that seems to have a vague connection with soccer and bicycle racing, Lucien Lozach's Café des Sports has a devoted and predominantly Gallic following. Dinner is a la carte, ranging from grilled chicken or roast pork at $6.90 up to a first-class sirloin steak at $11.25. For variety: frog's legs provençale ($9.50), or tête de veau vinaigrette at $7.50 merit your attention. The cold salmon at $3.50 makes a nice overture. A good selection of moderately priced wines.

🎵 CAFÉ ZIEGFELD***

227 West 45th Street
Reservations: 840-2964
Credit Cards: AE, DC, MC, V
Moderate

Flo would have loved the place: big, multileveled, handsome in soft grays and silvers, mirrors, and flattering lights—a perfect backdrop for a bevy of Follies chorines. Nat Asch, who looks as if he should have been a White Russian cavalry officer, is the host. Try to talk him into a table up front to watch the beautiful people pass by. The menu is extensive, continental, and moderately priced: scampi à la provençale ($9.95); a tasty veal mascotta with artichoke and mushrooms ($8.95); a chicken champagne with wild rice ($8.95), plus excellent fish dishes and steaks. There are excellent salads—chef's, niçoise, shrimps with avocado—for the calorie counters. There's a special menu available after the theatre also crammed with nice things. You might like to start with a Broadway Baby, decribed as "a somewhat cynical blend of Benedictine, Creme de Cacao and cream." Salads, sandwiches (Nova Scotia salmon, cream cheese, and Bermuda onion on a bialy, $5.75), cold chicken Wellington with mustard sauce ($7.95), quiches, eggs benedict or florentine. Wind up with carrot cake, fresh berries, or if you're coming from *Annie*, ice cream and Famous Amos chocolate chip cookies. There's almost always a big-league pianist (a Hank Jones or a Jimmy Rowles) in residence. All this—plus the Café Ziegfeld is convenient to more theatres than any other restaurant. Unfortunately the Café Ziegfeld is on the Portman hit list.

🎵 CALL BACK**

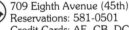

709 Eighth Avenue (45th)
Reservations: 581-0501
Credit Cards: AE, CB, DC, MC, V
Inexpensive

An interesting new addition to the theatre district's late scene, Call Back describes itself as a piano saloon, which is accurate up to a point. It's also a place where comics and singers can drop by and try out new material on a live audience. It's good fun, and the times I've been there the entertainment has been worth the trip. Burgers, quiche, barbecued chicken, and the like are available, most in the $3.50–$5 range. There's a $2.75 minimum at the tables when the entertainment is on, or you can sit at the bar and nurse a drink. There's a dart board up front if you arrive before the fun starts. A salute to Call Back for giving a 10 percent discount to anyone showing a paid-up Equity or other theatrical union card.

CAPRI*

261 West 54th Street
Reservations: 265-9654
No credit cards
Moderate   Open seven days a week

As you might guess, Capri is a Southern Italian restaurant where the accent is on pasta—excellent pasta ($5 to $6). It's a pleasant place, informal, and you certainly won't go away hungry.

¡CARAMBA!**

918 Eighth Avenue (55th)
Reservations: 245-7910
Credit Cards: Pending
Inexpensive to Moderate   Closed Monday

This is a new and welcome addition to Eighth Avenue and an excellent Mexican restaurant. Paul Seamen, originally from Miami, Arizona, and his partner Ralph Price (the designers responsible for the interiors of such restaurants as Indian Oven, Empanadas, and Etc.), have fashioned an attractive white stucco space decorated with Mexican rugs and folk art. (The back yard is being turned into a skylighted larger dining room and should be ready when you read this.) The food is authentic Mexican, which is hard to come by in New York. Combination plates (choice of two, $6.85; three $8.85) can include tacos, enchiladas, tamales, chili rellenos, tostadas, and burritos, all in their several variations. The carne asada is marinated chuck steak, charcoal broiled with salsa picante and delicious at $11.95. Several Mexican beers are available as is sangria by the glass or pitcher.

CARNEGIE DELICATESSEN***

854 Seventh Avenue (55th)
Reservations: 757-2245
No credit cards
Inexpensive

If it's deli you crave, you can't go wrong here: Many rate the Carnegie the best in New York. The decor is no-frills, honest deli, and the service is fast and friendly. The Carnegie cures its own pastrami and it's great. A regular sandwich is $4.75. Don't order the super sandwich, though, unless your appetite is gargantuan; it's huge. Beer and wine only. There's the usual take-out department, and I think you'll be tempted to take some home.

CEYLON INDIA INN*

148 West 49th Street
Reservations: 730-9293
Credit Cards: AE, DC
Moderate

A bit east of the theatre district, but if you enjoy Indian cooking it's worth the walk. In a quiet, restful atmosphere, you can choose either the complete dinner or order from the extensive a la carte menu. The curries are particularly tasty. Beer and wine only. If you're theatre-bound and have forgotten to make a dinner reservation, the Ceylon India Inn can usually accommodate you.

CHARLIES'*

263 West 45th Street
Reservations: 354-2911
Credit Cards: AE, MC, V
Inexpensive to Moderate

Charlies' was opened in 1973 by a former partner of Joe Allen, and it shows: brick walls, brick arches separating the bar area from tne dining room, theatrical posters, same black-board menu: burgers ($3.50 and up); chili ($2.95); filet of sole ($6.95); New York-cut sirloin steak ($11.95)—plus several daily specials. Charlies' is smaller and more crowded than Joe Allen's and attracts the same young, theatrical crowd though it's not as much fun. Marvel-ously convenient, however. If you can't book a table at Charlies', there are two other Joe Allen clones practically next door doing just about the same thing. Barrymore's at 247 (541-4500) and the Footlight at 259 (354-5226). All three serve food until midnight.

CHESHIRE CHEESE**

319 West 51st Street
Reservations: 765-0616
Expensive   Closed Sunday and Monday, major holidays (closed Christmas
            through New Year's Day) and July and August

This small, charming restaurant is as British as the Old Vic. The Scotch salmon is as good as you'll find anywhere; Dover sole is flown in, the steak and kidney pie is authentic, as is the Yorkshire pudding that accompanies the generous slabs of roast beef. A nice touch: If you make a reservation, everyone greets you by name.

CHEZ CARDINALE*

347 West 46th Street
Reservations: 245-9732
Credit Cards: AE, CB, DC
Moderate ` Closed Sunday

While the decor is a bit tired, this is an honest place serving up Italian and French spe-cialties at reasonable prices. Outside a sign announces a complete dinner for $9.75, but you'll probably end up spending a bit more. On a recent visit, the specials included chicken cac-ciatore with spaghetti ($10.50); veal à la parisienne ($11.95), and filet of sole belle meunière ($10.95)—prices that included antipasto, dessert, and coffee or espresso. Chez Cardinale is a nice alternative to some of its better known Restaurant Row neighbors.

CHEZ NAPOLEON*

365 West 50th Street
Reservations: 265-6980
No credit cards
Inexpensive to Moderate   Closed Sunday

Discerning theatre regulars sing the praises of Chez Napoleon's Friday special: bouilla-baisse. And they come early because it runs out, more often than not, before everyone can be served. Don't despair, the appetizers are all good, and, as entrees, the filet of sole aman-dine, the steak, and the brook trout are excellent. Chez Napoleon is small and crowded, and if you examine the prices you'll understand why.

CHEZ RAYMOND*

240 West 56th Street
Reservations: 755-1795
Credit Cards: AE, CB, DC, V
Moderate   Closed Sunday

One of the theatre district's better French restaurants—and values—although it's a little far uptown unless you're going to the Alvin or the Broadway. Everything is well-prepared; the baked oysters, striped bass, and guinea hen, when available, deserve special mention.

♫ CHILIE'S*

142 West 44th Street
Reservations: 840-1766
Credit Cards: AE, CB, DC, MC, V
Inexpensive to Moderate   Closed Sunday

You can come here for the Mexican food or the entertainment—or both. There's after-theatre entertainment every night, often country blues singers. Tuesday is audition night for Thursday's talent showcase. (The winner gets $100 and a weekend engagement.) As to food, a combination platter of any two choices of taco, burrito, enchilada, or tostada is $6.95. The burrito bandito (a burrito stuffed with beef or chicken and guacamole) is $5.75. The chili comes hot or mild (with or without garlic) or green, with shredded lettuce. There are a few Italian dishes on the menu, for some reason or other. Nice touch: Show your ticket stubs and get a 10 percent discount on your food.

CHINA BOWL*

152 West 44th Street
Reservations: 582-3358
No credit cards
Moderate

A convenient, large, rather plain, friendly restaurant serving up all the standards of Cantonese cuisine: chow mein, fried shrimp, and sweet and sour pork. The menu is extensive, everything is a la carte, and if you like the column A, column B thing, you won't be disappointed here.

CHINA SONG*

1705 Broadway (54th)
Reservations: 256-6759
No credit cards
Inexpensive to Moderate

You should recognize the China Song from other Chinese restaurants you've visited. It's attractive with most of the usual Chinese decorating clichés, no real surprises on the menu, and a choice of ordering a la carte, family dinners, or combination platters. Order carefully and your meal will be inexpensive, and the China Song rates a star for that.

CHUCK HOWARD**

355 West 46th Street
Reservations: 586-6575
Credit Cards: AE, DC, MC, V
Moderate

As a sportswear designer for Anne Klein and Bill Blass, Chuck Howard dreamed of opening his own restaurant. Unlike most dreamers, he made his come true and his elegant, ambitious place now graces Restaurant Row. In the front, a gently curving French zinc bar contrasts nicely with the linear, architectural look; baskets of dry flowers adding spots of color. Through a tiled passageway, the immaculate kitchen visible through a picture window, is the charming dining room, once the garden of the townhouse. A skylight and wall mirrors make the room seem larger than it is. The menu is serious with overtones of nouvelle cuisine; poached salmon with dijonnaise sauce, roast duck with elderberry and ginger sauce, and three or four daily specials. Burgers, chili, and omelettes are available for after-theatre snacks. Mr. Howard apparently does quite a bit of the cooking himself, particularly the sauces. The wine list has been carefully chosen and is moderate in price. Everything–napery, glassware, even the bar gin (Gordon's)–reflects a loving attention to detail. It's well worth a visit.

DELSOMMA**

266 West 47th Street
Reservations: 757-9079
Credit Cards: AE, DC, V
Moderate   Closed Sunday and Christmas

A fine Italian restaurant that shares the block with the Brooks Atkinson, Edison, Biltmore, and Ethel Barrymore theatres. If it's your first time at Delsomma, don't let the dark bar area throw you—there's a pleasant dining area in the back. The menu covers the range of standard Italian dishes, but you will do better if you disregard it and work out your selections with the waiter. Some representative daily specials: Italian pot roast with egg noodles ($7.00); tripe à la napolitana ($6.25); osso buco of veal with risotto milanaise ($7.75). Always available are three versions of calamàri (squid) for the adventurous. Most of the wines are available in half-bottles, a nice practice.

♫ DISH OF SALT**

133 West 47th Street
Reservations: 921–4242
Credit Cards: AE, DC
Moderate

For those who associate Chinese restaurants with good food and bad decor, the Dish of Salt is a pleasant surprise: This open, multileveled restaurant is as handsome as the food is scrumptious. It is owned by Kwong and Mary Ann Lum, who started Oh-Ho-So in SoHo seven years ago, and features classic Cantonese cuisine. The menu lists 48 specialties, 18 of which had never been served in the city before, including seaweed shrimp cakes ($13.25), beef with emperor mushrooms ($10.50), minced pork with clams ($11.25), baked butter lobster ($26.75), and heavenly wings ($13.50). The Dish of Salt is a good place to come for the gastronomic ritual, Peking duck. Allow sufficient time, however, as it is served in three different courses: sliced duck skin with steamed buns, stir-fried with vegetables, and as a soup with mushrooms. Manager Ronald K. Y. Chan, a 25-year-veteran of top city restaurants, gave me a look at the kitchen and if every restaurant were as impeccable, the Board of Health could shut down. The restaurant's name, by the way, comes from a Chinese saying that a bowl of rice, a jug of water, and a dish of salt are the essence of life. Neil Wolfe plays a tasty grand piano Tuesdays through Saturdays from 6 p.m. to 11:30 p.m.

DU MIDI**

311 West 48th Street
Reservations: 582–6689
No credit cards
Moderate

Here's another in that delightful category: authentic French restaurants in the theatre district providing above-average meals at reasonable prices. Not a large place, Du Midi has a pleasant atmosphere and prompt, attentive service. The cuisine tends toward French provincial; there are daily specials plus the usual dishes on the a la carte menu. The wine list is good and moderately priced.

EL TENAMPA*

304 West 46th Street
Reservations: 586-8039
Credit Cards: DC
Inexpensive   Closed Sunday

El Tenampa, Restaurant Row's Latin resident, is one of the nicest and one of the best Mexican restaurants in the city. It's spotlessly clean and simply decorated, and the owner brings a charming spontaneity to everything he does. The guacamole ($3) is prepared to order and it's delicious. The various standard Mexican combinations are in the $6–$7 price range, but you can get those anywhere. Try pipian estilo Veracruz (chunks of pork or chicken cooked in wine with a spicy peanut butter sauce) at $7.75, or bistec ranchero (steak sautéd in red chile sauce with peppers and onion slices) at $8.75. No liquor license so bring beer or wine to put out the fire (both are available around the corner on Eighth Avenue).

FARM FOOD*

142 West 49th Street
Reservations: 586-9369
No credit cards
Inexpensive

Broadway-area restaurants neglect no one, not even vegetarians. Farm Food offers an array of Jewish-style vegetarian dishes including several main courses that consist of artful eggplant concoctions: eggplant steak, eggplant schnitzel, and breaded (eggplant) scallops. For openers try good herring and Greek and egg salads. Finish up with strudel; it's a treat. Tables and counter service. A star for doing its thing well.

FRANKIE AND JOHNNIE'S**

269 West 45th Street
Reservations: 245-9717
Credit Cards: AE, DC, MC
Expensive   Closed Sunday, Thanksgiving, and Christmas

Climb a narrow, rickety flight of stairs and you seem to come out right in the small, noisy kitchen. There's a small bar—where Jason Robards, Jr., once told off Richard Nixon—and a small, crowded dining room. It looks like a former speakeasy and it is. Steak is the big attraction here, and it's delicious. The appetizers are Jewish: chopped chicken liver mixed with oil and garnished with minced onions and chopped egg, matzo-ball soup, and pickled herring. For some reason, it's de rigueur here for the waiter to slice your steak for you; he makes a little production out of it, and it is fun to watch. Everything is a la carte. The house tomato and onion salad is worth it, the potatoes are not. For dessert there is a blueberry pie that beggars description and luscious chocolate cheescake. Beware: Frankie and Johnnie's plays a bit fast and loose with reservations and despite its exceptionally convenient location you may be late for your curtain unless you insist on being treated properly.

FUJI*

238 West 56th Street
Reservations: 245-8594
Credit Cards: AE, DC, MC
Moderate

Here's a good Japanese restaurant that doesn't make you contort your Western frame to fit under those low tables. Fuji is attractive and the service is good. Special dinners and a la carte with the usual Japanese specialties: tempura, sukiyaki, teriyaki, et al. Wine and liquor are available, but if you haven't been introduced to Japanese beer, try it with your meal.

FUNDADOR*

146 West 47th Street
Reservations: 265-3690
Credit Cards: AE, CB, DC, MC
Moderate

Fundador offers up all the old favorites of both Spanish and Mexican cuisine—gazpacho, paella, the inevitable tamales, tacos, and enchiladas—in a warm, friendly setting. Nothing is outstanding but nothing is disappointing either. Service tends to be slow, so allow enough time to make your curtain.

GALLAGHER'S**

228 West 52nd Street
Reservations: 245-5336
Credit Cards: AE, CB, MC, V
Expensive

Gallagher's anchors the north end of the theatre district as Sardi's does the south. Like Sardi's, it is big, convivial, and a bit noisy—sports, though, not the theatre sets the tone here. (This was *the* sports restaurant when Madison Square Garden was nearby on Eighth Avenue.) Photographs of fighters, ballplayers, and horsemen fill the walls; inexplicably, there are lovely turn-of-the-century lithographs of Ethel Barrymore and Billie Burke flanking the coat room. There's no confusion about Gallagher's intent—a large, refrigerated glass room near the entrance is crammed with exquisite beef and strawberries. The bar is a large square and staffed by some of the city's ablest bartenders.

The food is consistently good with few, if any, surprises. Start with chopped liver ($2.95), shrimp ($5.75), or herring ($3.50). For the main course try a sirloin ($15.95), prime ribs ($14.95), or lamb chops ($15.50). (Note: A baked potato and a salad will add $5.45 to your meal.) There's also mulligan stew ($8.50), chopped beef ($8.50), and a particular favorite of mine—sliced steak on toast with a piquant mustard sauce ($11.95). The cheesecake ($2.75) is excellent. Gallagher's is one of the better steak houses around, although somewhat overpriced. It's quite crowded before and after the theatre, due in no small part to *Annie,* a few doors away at the Alvin.

HO SHIM*

120 West 44th Street
Reservations: 575-9774
Credit Cards: AE, DC, MC
Inexpensive   Open seven days a week

If you want to try something different, good, inexpensive, and convenient, Ho Shim is for you. At this Korean restaurant you sit at regular tables, not squat on the floor, and are served by waitresses in their national costume. The yakitori is an exceptional appetizer or main course: marinated bits of chicken boiled on a skewer. Or try the Korean national dish, which is marinated strips of beef and is called bolgoki. The short ribs and the deep-fried fish are also excellent. There's music after the theatre every evening except Monday.

THE IMPROVISATION***

358 West 44th Street
Reservations: 765-8268
Moderate   Closed Sunday

The Improv is the oldest and best of the city's comedy showcases and helped launch the careers of such stars as Robert Klein and the late Freddy Prinz. The atmosphere is completely informal in this barn of a place, and you never know whom you might see performing. For sure, you'll see a lot of talented young people giving it their best shot. Weekday shows are at 9 p.m., Friday and Saturday, 9 p.m. and 11:30 p.m. (First-timers appear early in the week, the more experienced talent on the late weekend shows.) Whenever you go, you'll get more than your money's worth. Moderate priced burgers and sandwiches are available. Weekend drink minimum is $5 with $4 cover charge; weekdays both are $1 less.

JACK'S EPICURE**

344 West 46th Street
Credit Cards: AE, DC, MC, V
Moderate   Open seven days but pre-theatre dining only on Sunday

A former speakeasy on Restaurant Row, Jack's Epicure is lovingly presided over by its owner, a stocky, jovial Walloon named Victor Marlier, who enjoys his many regular customers as much as they enjoy him and his excellent kitchen. A complete theatre dinner is $17.50 and includes a choice from a wide selection of appetizers—stuffed claims, little necks or blue points, pâté, or antipasto—soup, entrees like duck bigarrade, coq au vin, trout meunière, rollatine of chicken with fettuccini Alfredo, the house salad, dessert, and coffee. An a la carte is available for the less hungry. Two entrees out of many worth mentioning: the braised sweetbreads au vin blanc ($11) and the breast of chicken gismonda ($8.25). Would that all New York restaurants were this warm and friendly.

JIM DOWNEY'S*

705 Eighth Avenue (between 44th and 45th)
Reservations: 757-0186
Credit Cards: AE, CB, DC
Moderate   Closed Sunday

Downey's is an attractive Victorian restaurant with a real honest-to-goodness men's bar, frequented by a number of the theatre crowd. The food is acceptable and moderately priced. The steaks, however, are expensive and not up to the standards of a Broadway Joe or Frankie and Johnnie's. An excellent choice, however, for an after-theatre drink.

JOE ALLEN**

326 West 46th Street
Reservations: 581-6464
Credit cards: MC, V
Inexpensive to Moderate

The theatre establishment uses Sardi's to conduct business. Aspirants come to Joe Allen for informal dining, gossip, and mutual support. Not that the establishment doesn't come as well: On various recent visits I've seen Lauren Bacall, Roy Scheider, Luci Arnaz, and Tennessee Williams. But usually the crowd is young and always very involved in the theatre. Joe Allen's is a big, brick-walled room with arches dividing the main dining area from the bar. Blackboards at the ends of the dining room serve as menus. The waiters are out-of-work actors and actresses and the service can be erratic but cheerful. There are no gustatory surprises: shrimp cocktail, chopped liver, various soups and burgers, steak and roast beef, fish, chili. The spinach and mushroom and the chef's salad are generous portions, served in big wooden bowls. The prices are reasonable! Burgers and salads are under $5 and almost everything else is under $10. Notice the framed theatrical posters on the wall of the dining room. After a minute or two, you realize that they all heralded spectacular flops. A nice in-joke.

JOE'S PIER 52*

144 West 52nd Street
Reservations: 295-6652
Credit Cards: AE, CB, DC, MC, V
Expensive   Open seven days a week

The Joe of Joe's Pier 52 is Joe Kipness, one of Broadway's more active producers. The restaurant is quite a production, too. It's big, attractive, noisy, and frankly the service is not up to snuff although the clams, oysters, lobsters, and most of the other offerings are. There's a lobster tank for you to select the crustacean you fancy. Stone crab is often available but only cold, which I, for one, don't care for. You'll do better if you stick to the dishes that are simply prepared; sauces are something the kitchen has yet to master. As this was written, a new branch was opening in the Milford Plaza Hotel at 44th Street and 8th Avenue, Joe's Pier 44.

K.C. PLACE*

807 Ninth Avenue (54th)
Reservations: 246-4258
No credit cards
Inexpensive to Moderate

If you're going to, say, the ANTA or the Alvin and don't mind the short walk to Ninth Avenue, K.C. Place at 52nd Street offers delicious seafood at attractive prices. A small but succulent whole lobster is $8.95; shrimp scampi ($6.50) and red snapper ($6.95) are also good. The first is invariably fresh and there are some Oriental entrees that are worth sampling: Pla lad plik, deep-fried whole sea bass with hot sauce ($7.95), and a seafood combination with hot sauce (also $7.95). On my last visit, a veal marsala ($7.95) and two Oriental versions of chicken had been added. The restaurant is handsomely decorated in Victorian style and is popular with television people from the nearby production houses.

♫ KENNY'S STEAK PUB**

221 West 46th Street
Reservations: 719-5799
Credit Cards: AE, CB, DC, MC, V
Moderate to Expensive   Closed Sunday

Beef lovers should note this new entry, across from the Helen Hayes. An offshoot of Kenny's Steak Pub on Lexington Avenue near 50th, it serves up some of the best steaks in town. The entrees come in generous portions, the meat is excellent, and the prices reflect the value: prime ribs ($14.95), filet mignon ($16.95), and T-bone ($19.95). Italian dishes are less: fettucine Alfredo ($9.95), scampi Mediterranean with rice pilaf ($13.95), and veal marsala ($12.95). Entrees usually come with potatoes, a salad will add $2.95. The restaurant is large and handsome. Piano music from 7 p.m. until 11 p.m.

KING CRAB**

871 Eighth Avenue (52nd)
Reservations: None (765-4393)
Credit Cards: AE, DC
Inexpensive

King Crab is new, small, and attractive, and it is immensely popular. It takes no reservations and there is a line waiting to get in even on cold winter nights. The reason is simple: fresh seafood, well-prepared at bargain prices. Alaskan king crab legs as an entree ($8.95); sea bass ($5.50); red snapper ($6.95); and lobsters, priced by weight a lot less than the going rate in the theatre district. A shrimp cocktail, for example, is $2.95; for the same you'll probably pay around $5 elsewhere. The kitchen is open until midnight.

LA GRILLADE*

845 Eighth Avenue (51st)
Reservations: 265-1610
Credit Cards: AE, DC, MC, V
Moderate

This unprepossessing French steak house (formerly Le Caneton) offers up a special theatre dinner in the $13–$15 range, depending upon your entree. It includes your choice of shrimp cocktail, pâté, smoked salmon, or other appetizer; potatoes; vegetables; and salad; and such desserts as French pastries and chocolate mousse. A wide selection of entrees: roast duckling, boeuf bourguignon, paupiettes of sole, poached striped bass, paupiettes of sole chablis. Should you wish to try La Grillade's specialties, a sirloin steak au poivre is $17.25; entrecôte double grill bernaise for two, $32.75. The wine list is small, well-chosen, and priced below most of the comparable places in the area.

LE ALPI*

234 West 48th Street
Reservations: 582-7792
Credit Cards: AE, CB, DC
Moderate   Closed Sunday and Christmas

An attractive little Italian restaurant near the Longacre and the Playhouse, Le Alpi does the usual range of Italian specialties most competently. A complete theatre dinner is $16.75. Some representative a la carte entries: tortellini ($8.75); shrimps marinara ($10.50); osso buco ($10.75); and mignonettes of beef in sherry ($12.50). If you're not familiar with a rugola salad, try one here ($3), a different taste and a pleasant one. When strawberries are in season, fragole all siciliana (strawberries Sicilian-style) make a nice finish.

LE CHAMBERTIN**

348 West 46th Street
Reservations: 757-2154
Credit Cards: AE, DC
Moderate   Closed Sunday

Restaurant Row, 46th between Eighth and Ninth, is a revelation, in the number of restaurants on the block, the variety, and the surprising quality of many of them. Le Chambertin is a wise choice if you seek a French restaurant serving good food at reasonable prices. Some specialties: onion tarte, artichoke vinaigrette, and coquille St. Jacques among the appetizers; Dover sole, sea bass, and duck with cherries for entrees. A reasonably priced bottle of wine and a first-class pastry for dessert. Voila!

 ## LE VERT GALANT*

109 West 46th Street
Reservations: 582-7989
Credit Cards: AC, DC
Moderate   Closed Sunday

This is a handsome new restaurant located above street-level in an office building next door to the American Place Theater. For reasons that excape me, it has taken a pounding from the restaurant critics. My experiences here have been good if not great, and it seems to have become popular quickly. If you'd like to see for yourself before committing to dinner, stop by after the theatre for a drink. There's usually a first-rate performer at the piano.

LEO LINDY'S*

1515 Broadway (44th)
Reservations: 840-1054
Credit Cards: AE, CB, DC, MC, V
Inexpensive to Moderate   Open seven days a week

Leo Lindy's is not the Lindy's—that closed some years back and Broadway is the poorer for it. This one is part of a chain operation and although it's a big, nicely decorated place, it has traces of the coldness of a chain restaurant. Humor is the motif: Giant photographs of practically every comic in the past 50 years smile down at you; you may order an Adelaide's Lament from the bar, a blend of apricot liqueur, honey, and lemon, which, I suppose, is just the thing for a poison wid a cold. On the menu, the Comedy Hall of Fame lists 19 varieties of deli sandwiches named for—who else-?—famous comedians. (No. 13, Richard Pryor: corned beef and chopped liver triple decker with cole slaw and Russian dressing on rye, $6.95, while No. 17, the George Burns, is a more spartan grilled salami and fried egg on rye, $5.25). Gilda Radner presides over the salad platters; Robin Williams, the beverages . . . but you get the idea. All the baking, including bread, is done on the premises and the quality shows. Cheesecakes and pies may be purchased to take home; a small cheesecake is $6.50.

LES PYRENEES**

251 West 51st Street
Reservations: 246-0044
Credit Cards: AE, DC
Moderate   Closed Sunday

Another quality French provençale restaurant, most convenient to the Mark Hellinger and the Princess, charming and reasonably priced. The pre-theatre dinner, served from 5 p.m. to 9 p.m. is $12.95. Start with pâté maison, clams baked in chablis, or a tarte alsacienne. Move on to coquille St. Jacques parisienne, duck with cherries, or contre filet bordelaise (all come with a vegetable and the house salad). Close with, say, fraises au vin or a peach melba.

Considering the high quality and good service, this is true value. A la carte dining from 5 p.m. until closing with entrees from $9.50 to lamb chops or filet mignon bearnaise at $12.95. Ask host Jean Claude for the wine list; it's a good one.

MA BELL'S

218 West 45th Street
Reservations: 869-0110
Credit Cards: AE, CB, DC, MC, V
Inexpensive to Moderate   Closed Sunday

This is a large, touristy place on the east side of Shubert Alley, arguably the most convenient location in the Broadway area. The theme is a gimmick; Ma Bell is stockbroker slang for the telephone company. Big blowups of celebrities—all using the phone—are the principal decorations, and if you're seated in a booth along the wall there are Front Page-type phones where you can make free local calls. The bar is 80 feet long and adequately staffed, so it's a good place for a between-acts drink if you're at the Shubert or the Booth. There also is food service at the bar and the sandwiches are quite good. Ma Bell's is a good place for a quick meal, and an excellent choice if you're bringing children to the theatre. Besides the sandwiches, the burgers are good, as is the steak. Their English trifle for two is a treat.

MAMMA LEONE'S**

239 West 48th Street
Reservations: 586-5151
Credit Cards: AE, CB, DC, MC, V
Moderate

Mamma Leone's is huge, cheerful, noisy, touristy without being a tourist trap, and ridiculously overdecorated. The name of Mamma's game is quantity and she plays it well: for $14.95 you choose from antipasti (including shrimp cocktail or melon with prosciutto), pasta (including manicotti with meat sauce or fettuccine all' Alfredo), pesce or arrosto (filet of sole, chicken cacciatore, veal steak, broiled tenderloin of pork, roast duck, or eggplant parmigiana), dessert, and coffee. Only a handful of the offerings involve an extra charge. And if that won't hold you, there's a plate of celery, olives, tomatoes, and green peppers, a giant hunk of cheese, and good fresh bread on your table. This is an excellent place to take children; if they're under 12 $6.95 buys fruit cup, veal steak parmigiana or spaghetti with meat balls, a Coke or milk, and a bugie-tortoni. There's an a la carte menu available from 9:30 p.m., entrees in the $9–$15 range. Mamma Leone's is extra nice during the pre-Lenten Carnevale with music, dancing, and other nice surprises. My only complaint is even with reservations you can have a long wait at the bar. Many New Yorkers turn their noses up at Mamma Leone's; they're wrong.

MARTA'S OF BERGEN STREET*

249 West 49th Street
Reservations: 265-4317
Credit Cards: AE, DC, MC
Inexpensive   Closed Christmas

If the name puzzles you, it's because Marta's moved here from Bergen Street in Brooklyn some years back and, apparently, didn't want to confuse its regular patrons. Choose from 21 varieties, from spaghetti with butter sauce at $5.25 to fettucini Alfredo at $6.50. A number of fish, chicken, and veal entrees, none of which hit the $10 mark. Some treats: french-fried zucchini ($2.75); calamari (squid) in cassuola ($7.50), and zabaglione ($2.50). A glass of Chianti is $1.50. Marta's is only seconds away from the Ambassador and the Eugene O'Neill.

♫ MICKEY'S CABARET-RESTAURANT**

44 West 54th Street
Reservations: 247-2979
Credit Cards: AE, CB, MC
Shows: Friday and Saturday only, 8 p.m. and 10:30 p.m.

On weekends, Mickey's usually matches a singer and a comic in its pleasant dining room. The food is well above the usual comic showplace standard. The cover charge is $5 with a $5 minimum.

♫ MILDRED PIERCE**

345 West 46th Street
Reservations: 582-4801
Credit Cards: AE, DC, MC, V
Inexpensive to Moderate

A bright, shiny addition to Restaurant Row that pays tongue-in-cheek homage to the late Joan Crawford. (She owned a restaurant in *Mildred Pierce,* remember?) This Mildred already seems to have attracted a following from the theatre. The bar is handsome (if you overlook the bad paintings of La Crawford) and you can sit in director's chairs and order goodies from the supper menu: chili ($3.95); mussels ($4.95), and barbecued chicken wings ($4.25). The attractive dining room makes no pretense to haute cuisine but it served up quite acceptable dishes at attractive prices. Tapes of show tunes are played over an excellent sound system, and on Friday and Saturday nights there usually is a piano player in the bar.

MOLFETAS*

307 West 47th Street
Reservations: 586-9278
No credit cards
Inexpensive

Another bargain, this one Greek. Molfetas is part cafeteria, part restaurant, and has a number of interesting specialties: kasseri saganaki, a hot melted cheese dish; lemon and egg soup; moussaka; a number of lamb dishes including delicious lamb chops; and a variety of fish broiled with oil and lemon. Before you order, go to the back of the restaurant and look over the dishes on display; it will give you more ideas than the menu.

♫ MOLLY BLOOM'S**

150 West 47th Street
Reservations: 944-8815
Credit Cards: AE, MC, V
Inexpensive to Moderate   Closed Sunday

A welcome new addition to the theatre district, Molly Bloom's is as Irish as its Joycean namesake. Owner Charlie Wicklow, the bartenders, and the waitresses all have brogues that remind you what a beautiful language English can be. A comfortable, no-nonsense place decorated with etchings of Joyce's Dublin, Molly Bloom's is a hop, skip, and a jump from the Duffy Square TKTS booth and around the corner from the Palace. Man-sized drinks are $1.75, and the bartenders still practice that almost extinct custom of buying an occasional round. At the cocktail hour there's a hot buffet near the bar and it's free. The food is good and if you choose one of the chef's daily specials, it's a bargain: curried shrimp on rice ($5.95); country-style shepherd's pie ($5.05), sweet and sour chicken ($4.75). The regular menu is a la carte ranging up to a filet mignon at $12. The jukebox is a little loud but at these prices, can one complain? From 5 p.m. to 8 p.m. talented Craig Jones plays and sings at the piano bar.

NICK & GUIDO*

322 West 46th Street
Reservations: 265-9095
No credit cards
Inexpensive to Moderate   Closed Monday

The best Italian buy on Restaurant Row and one of the best in the theatre district, Nick & Guido's is small and unlovely but serves up first-rate pasta, fish dishes, and eggplant parmigiana, either a la carte or on complete dinners. The veal, though, doesn't measure up. Excellent cheese, which is a rarity in Broadway Italian restaurants. This is a hangout for Alitalia stewardesses and pilots.

PANTHEON*

689 Eighth Avenue (43rd)
Reservations: 586-9672
No credit cards
Moderate   Open seven days a week

Most convenient to a number of theatres, this small, friendly Greek restaurant has been popular for years. The avgolemono (Greek for lemon egg soup) is a good way to start; the lamb dishes are good but not great; the feta cheese salads are a joy. The Pantheon makes its own yogurt, and you owe it to yourself to taste it.

PATSY'S**

236 West 56th Street
Reservations: 247-3491
Credit Cards: AE, DC
Moderate to Expensive   Closed Monday

A little north of the theatre district, Patsy's is worth the trip, for it is one of the very best Southern Italian restaurants in the city. (Southern Italian cooking uses a generous amount of garlic and it isn't polite to go to the theatre with too lethal a breath.) Patsy's is an attractive, popular two-story restaurant that has a devoted following—Frank Sinatra usually eats here when he's in town. The homemade antipasto is delicious, as are the many forms of pasta (about $8). The menu is extensive, and they do veal in just about every way imaginable. The chicken cacciatore is first-rate; so are the steak dishes. Entrees range from $12 to $20. The homemade cheesecake shouldn't be overlooked either.

PIERRE AU TUNNEL**

250 West 47th Street
Reservations: 582-2166
Credit cards: AE
Moderate   Closed Sunday

This popular restaurant recently moved to new, attractive quarters on 47th Street between the Biltmore and the Ethel Barrymore and now, happily, accepts American Express, so its already large following should increase. A complete pre-theatre dinner is in the $12.50–$15.50 price range, more if you choose certain appetizers and desserts. Daily specials include Wednesday's special sausage crepe ($12); Friday's la bouillabaisse à la marseillaise ($15.50); and, on Saturdays, a piquant boeuf sauté bourguignonne. The pâté maison is recommended, as is la coupe du tunnel ($2 extra). While not extensive, the wine list shows careful thought and is moderately priced.

♫ RAINBOW ROOM***

30 Rockefeller Center (49th)
Reservations: 757-9090
Credit Cards: AE, CB, DC, MC, V
Moderate

On the 65th floor of the RCA Building, the Rainbow Room is as elegant and as comfortable a restaurant as there is in the city: plum-colored silk walls, mirrored columns, sparkling chandeliers, and magnificent cityscapes seen through two-story-high windows. Name musicians play for dancing here every night of the week and if you feel romantic, the dance floor is the place to be. An excellent bargain is the pre-theatre dinner (soup, entree, and dessert: $13.50) served from 5 p.m. to 7 p.m. The a la carte dinner menu offers such attractive entrees as roast Cornish hen with tarragon ($10.75), roast Long Island duckling ($12.75), and an entrecôte au poivre ($14). A special supper menu is available after 11 p.m. Gentlemen must wear jackets and ties.

RENÉ PUJOL**

321 West 51st Street
Reservations: 246-3023
Credit Cards: AE, MC, V
Expensive   Closed Sunday

This looks like a French auberge—beamed ceilings, copper pots on brick walls, a grandfather's clock, and a table where a mouth-watering smoked salmon is on view along with pastries and gateaus. An appetizer (quiche, pâté, celeri remoulade) entree, and salad will cost from $17 for the dover sole to $19 for green pepper steak or $19.50 for gratin de homard au whiskey at $19.50. There's chateaubriand for two at $38, and it's a rare treat. Crepes suzettes at $8.50, perhaps, as a curtain call. Caution: Let the captain know you're going to the theatre. Most of your fellow diners aren't and the service is leisurely.

♫ ROSELAND**

239 West 52nd Street
Reservations: 247-0200
Credit Cards: AE, MC
Moderate   Closed Mondays and Tuesdays

If you like to dance, Roseland can be marvelous fun. For more than 61 years this vast Art Deco music box has been the home of happy feet. Most nights a big band alternates with a Latin orchestra until midnight, then disco dancing until 4 a.m. On Saturday nights the average crowd is 3,500 on the dance floor, which is half a city block in size. The Rose Bar is commodious and the Terrace Restaurant seats 700 with a menu that ranges from burgers to adequate steaks. Shoe fetishers will delight in the Wall of Fame displaying the dancing shoes of such stars as Anna Held, Bill "Bojangles" Robinson, Ruby Keeler, Joel Grey, Sandy Duncan, and the like. Nearby is a plaque listing those who met at Roseland and later danced down the aisle. (Shades of Queen of the Stardust Ballroom!) To dismiss Roseland is to miss a most pleasant way to wind up an evening at the theatre. Admission ranges from $5 to $8 per person depending on the night and how late you come.

SARDI'S***

234 West 44th Street
Reservations: 221-8440
Credit Cards: AE, CB, DC, MC, V
Expensive

Sardi's succeeds in spite of itself. The decor is scruffy; only the famous caricatures of the theatre great and near-great that line the walls and the red-checked tablecloths take the edge. The service can be brusque, particularly when it's busy. While they pour a good drink, the food is barely adequate and no bargain. Why then three stars? Because no other restaurant crackles with the same kind of theatrical excitement, no other Broadway restaurant is as much *fun*. Sardi's is the quintessential theatre restaurant, as much an adornment to the Broadway scene as is the beautiful Shubert Theater across 44th Street. Out-of-towners come here with the look of Moslems on a hadj to Mecca and leave fulfilled.

You wait in the crowded foyer, a small bar to your right, for the all-important decision: Will you be led into the dining room or sent upstairs? Decor, service, food, and prices are the same. Only the magic is missing. (Phone early for reservations, request downstairs, and hope for a slow night.) Usually there are celebrities in abundance downstairs, invariably in the banquettes and at the tables near the entrance. It's a treat to be in Sardi's on an opening night when the stars enter to a standing ovation—a charming custom that started spontaneously when Shirley Booth opened in *Come Back, Little Sheba*. (Understandably, Sardi's gets more than its share of opening night parties, but most are in the third-floor Belasco Suite and private.)

Expectedly, there are many Italian dishes on the extensive menu, including a famous specialty: cannelloni au gratin. Many love it, many don't. I'm partial to the deviled roast beef bones with mustard sauce, especially after theatre. Simple dishes—steaks, chops, fish—are good choices.

Another way to enjoy Sardi's is to have a drink at the long upstairs bar, although it can be unpleasantly crowded just before curtain. It attracts a nice crowd—theatre pros and a sprinkling of *New York Times* people. A picture window overlooking Shubert Alley has recently been added; a table with a view is a delight.

SPINDLETOP**

254 West 47th Street
Reservations: 245-7326
Credit Cards: AE, DC, MC, V
Moderate to Expensive   Open seven days a week

The Spindletop, a fixture in the theatre district for 30 years, is synonymous with good beef. The decor is Godfather Italian but there's nothing sinister about the steaks, except possibly the prices: a prime sirloin is $19.75; steak calabrese with mushrooms, peppers, pimentos, and onions is $20.75. A heavy cut of prime ribs is fine at $18.75. There are several choices of seafood, veal, and chicken in the $12–$15 range. Salads and vegetables are extra. A thoughtful plus: If you have children in tow there's a half-price children's menu, or they can share with you for a $5.50 surcharge.

STAGE DELICATESSEN*

834 Seventh Avenue (54th)
Reservations: Not accepted
No credit cards
Inexpensive   Closed Rosh Hashana and Yom Kippur

The Stage used to be a rather spartan cafeteria sort of a place; now it looks like a restaurant and something got lost in the remodeling. The food still is good, however, and it's as crowded as ever. The standard deli fare—chopped liver, herring, smoked sturgeon, borscht, chicken soup with matzo balls—but a cut above average. The sandwiches are big and flavorful ($4.50–$6.50). Unlike most delis, the Stage now has a liquor license.

♫ TED HOOK'S BACKSTAGE**

319 West 45th Street
Reservations: 265-3800
Credit Cards: AE, DC, MC, V
Moderate   Open seven days a week

Ted Hook, a hoofer in many movies of the fifties and later personal secretary to Tallulah Bankhead, became a restaurateur—and a good one—when he opened Backstage five years ago next door to the Martin Beck. It's a big place: a long bar, a piano bar area where, at last report, Charles DeForest was having his way with little gems of show tunes. The decor is ultra-theatrical: The walls are the backs of scenery flats and autographed by the better-known customers; on the tables are little lamps on the base of which a tiny Romeo pleads his case to a balconied Juliet. The food is good and the prices are attractive: little necks or blue points ($3.95); veal marsala or piccata ($11.95); filet of sole ($9.95). Burgers are available after the theatre. You might like to wind it up with a café romano (made from Sambucca Romana) or Irish coffee. Incidentally, it's a pleasure to see fresh flowers in a restaurant.

♫ TED HOOK'S ONSTAGE**?

349 West 46th Street
Reservations: 265-3800
Credit Cards: AE, DC, MC, V
Moderate   Sunday, brunch show only

Apparently not content with the success of his Backstage, Ted Hook has created a jewel-box of a cabaret on Restaurant Row. The room is intimate, very handsome, and terraced so that there isn't a bad table in the place. The lighting and the sound system also are first rate. Interplay, an improvisation group, was in the room Fridays and Saturdays when this was written; Teresa Bowers from *Ain't Misbehavin'* and Dale Gonyea, a hilarious young musical comic, were regulars. When the entertainment is right, Onstage well deserves three stars. There's an 8:30 p.m. dinner and an 11:30 p.m. supper show every night except Sunday. Prix fixe dinners are available at $10.95 and $12.95, depending on entree, and light offerings are available at the late show. Add in a $5 cover, and it's still excellent value.

THAI PALACE**

261 West 54th Street
Reservations: 582-6640
Credit Cards: AE, DC
Inexpensive

Here's your chance to be both adventurous and thrifty. The Thai Palace is a little jewel. The only caveat is that Thai food is very spicy: The crabmeat with hot coconut milk, for example, may make your eyes water. The shrimp with grass noodles is milder; sweet and sour pork milder still. Definitely worth trying is mee krob , bits of pork and shrimp with crunchy noodles. The portions are smaller than usual so it's best to sample a number of dishes. Allow $10 per person for dinner.

♫ 37TH STREET HIDEAWAY**

32 West 37th Street
Reservations: 947-8940
Credit Cards: AE, CB, DC, MC, V
Moderate to Expensive   Closed Sunday, all major holdiays, Saturday in July and August, and the first two weeks of July

This charming, romantic restaurant is a bit far from the theatre district but how can we not include a place that is in John Barrymore's former townhouse. To sit by The Great Profile's fireplace on a cold winter's night has to be a special treat for any theatre-lover. There is a prix fixe pre-theatre dinner at $14.25 and it's good: clams, crepe farsie (sausage crepe), and other appetizers, pasta or soup, such entrees as grilled sole, chicken gizmonda, and Long Island duckling, dessert, and coffee. Your dinner can be expensive if you choose to order a la carte. A trio plays for dancing until the wee hours, a nice way to end an evening. Knowing the John Barrymore legend, it seems somehow fitting that the building was for a time one of the city's better-known speakeasies.

"21" CLUB***

21 West 52 Street
Reservations: 582-7221
Credit Cards: AE, CB, DC, MC, V
Expensive   Closed Sunday

This is possibly the most famous restaurant in America, and probably the best American restaurant. First-quality ingredients, cooked to perfection, albeit without the nuances of classic French cuisine, service that is a model of perfection, and, to me, the best ambiance anywhere. This is the watering hole of the power elite and you can feel it in the atmosphere. "21" is really two restaurants. Downstairs, a large room is dominated by a 50-foot bar, the best stand-up men's bar in the city. The walls are paneled, and from the ceiling hang seemingly hundreds of model planes, trucks, football helmets, and other power symbols of the regular customers. Upstairs are several elegant dining areas. It's quieter than downstairs, and more leisurely. Both have their supporters. (I like to dine downstairs if I'm with a man; upstairs, if I'm with a woman.) The menu is the same in both, and entrees range from $14.50 to about $20. The wine list is an oenophile's dream of heaven. (One of the special treats here is to be given a tour of the wine cellar, which dates back to when "21" was a speakeasy—the best speakeasy in the city, I'm told. Speak to your captain, and if it isn't too busy, he'll arrange it.) It's fashionable to knock "21" as a place where people unknown to the management are treated badly. I've been coming here for 25 years with some regularity and I've seen no evidence of it. If you make a reservation, dress appropriately (coats and ties are musts), and behave properly, you'll have a wonderful time. If you don't dress appropriately, you probably won't get in. But the rules apply to regulars, too. Messrs. Burns and Kriendler run a tight ship, and bless 'em for it.

UN DEUX TROIS**

123 West 44th Street
Reservations: Not accepted
Credit Cards: AE
Moderate

Those who know Paris swear they've been in this restaurant before. There's a déjà vu feeling about the high-ceilinged room, ceramic-tile floor, and Gallic waiters. The cuisine is provençale: a choice of pâté canard, campagne, or forestier ($4.25), an excellent salade niçoise ($6.75), brochette de poulet à l'orange ($9.25), sole meunière ($11.95), and entrecôte au poivre ($15.95). The wine list is small and moderately priced. For those who are artistically inclined, crayons are supplied at each table to doodle on the white paper table coverings. The café, which is next door to the Belasco, does not take reservations, so leave ample time if you're making a curtain; the wait at the bar can be long.

UN RINCON ARGENTINO*

1626 Broadway (50th)
Reservations: 245-2580
No credit cards
Inexpensive to Moderate

This is an Argentinian steak house and there are usually enough Argentinians dining here to guarantee its authenticity. The strange device in the window is a Argentinian charcoal broiler roasting beef on a revolving spit, and all the entrees seemed to be cooked that way. The steaks are quite good; so is the chicken, and the combination platter—sweetbreads, kidney, steak, pork, and sausage—is a real winner. Allow $10 to $15 per person for dinner. There's a dish of green sauce on your table that is explosively hot, so be careful. Beer and wine only.

VESUVIO**

163 West 48th Street
Reservations: 245-6138
Credit Cards: AE, CB, DC
Moderate to Expensive   Closed Sunday

Gourmet Magazine rates Vesuvio as the best Italian restaurant in the theatre district, and it certainly would be in the finals by any standards. The decor and ambiance are pleasant enough, and the service is friendly. Everything is a la carte and uniformly good, particularly the lobster. The pasta dishes can't be faulted (average price: $6). Caution: This is southern Italian cooking and the garlic content is dangerously high for the theatre.

VICTOR'S CAFE 52**

236 West 52nd Street
Reservations: 586-7714
Credit Cards: AE, CB, DC, MC, V
Moderate to Expensive

Be glad you weren't in this chic Cuban restaurant the night Roberto Duran walked away from Sugar Ray Leonard; it must have been like Wall Street in October, 1929. This was the Panamanian fighter's New York hangout. Outside, his footprints are enshrined a la Grauman's Chinese Theater and the menu offers "Duran Victory Cuban Style Steak with Julian Potatoes, White Rice and Black Beans" at $14.95. An offshoot of the successful Victor's on Columbus Avenue, Victor's Café 52 has earned a good reputation for interesting food in its first year of operation: suckling roast pig, a genuine Cuban delicacy, is truly delicious. If you like paella you might like paella valenciana with pork and chicken added to the usual fish. The dining room is large with canted mirrors edged with tiny lights, giving the illusion of being under the Havana stars. The special after-theatre supper menu is moderately priced.

WALLY'S***

224 West 49th Street
Reservations: 582-0460
Credit Cards: AE
Expensive   Closed Sunday

Here, arguably, are the best steaks, chops, and lobsters in the theatre district. The decor is New York-steak-house blah, but the meat makes up for it. Everything is a la carte and pricy: shrimp cocktail ($6.25); melon and prosciutto ($6.25); prime sirloin or filet mignon ($17.95); the gargantuan lobsters are priced by weight. Side orders are particularly dear: sliced tomatoes and onions ($4.25); home fries ($3.25); asparagus, when available ($4.25). Surprisingly, there are a number of good, less expensive Italian specialties, including veal in its many forms. A bar treat to sample here is a Bloody Bull, half way between a Bloody Mary and a Bullshot and, in my opinion, better than either. In sum, you pay for what you get at Wally's, but everything is strictly first-class. Most convenient, too, if you're going to the Ambassador or the Eugene O'Neill.

XOCHITL

146 West 46th Street
Reservations: 757-1325
No credit cards
Inexpensive to moderate   Closed Sunday

A small, not too attractive restaurant serving excellent tacos, enchiladas, and the like, including a fine Texas-style chili. Leave a little extra time if you're coming before the theatre because the service can be slow. And, yes, they have Mexican beer. You can eat well here for less than $10 per person. No two people I know pronounce the name of this restaurant exactly the same, but "zow-sheel" is reasonably accurate.

"Drama—what literature does at night."

GEORGE JEAN NATHAN

"The play's the thing."

HAMLET, Act V, Scene 2

"An actor is a sculptor who carves in snow."

LAWRENCE BARRETT

"Each loves the play for what he brings to it."

GOETHE

"Men go to the theater to forget; women, to remember."

GEORGE JEAN NATHAN

42nd STREET AREA

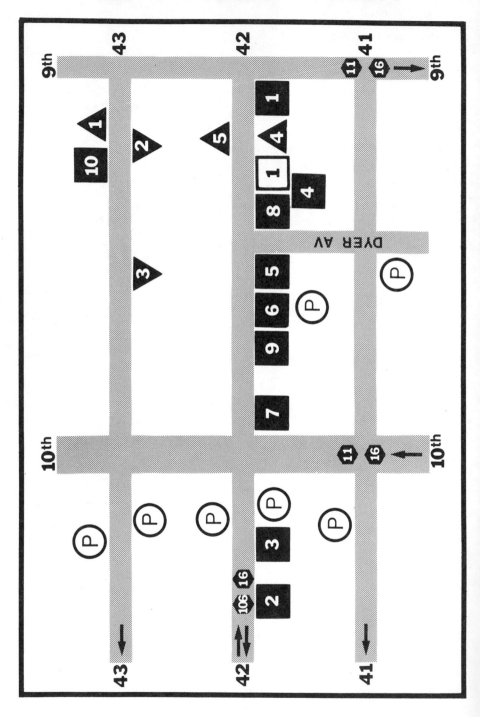

■ Theatres

1. Black Theatre Alliance / 410 West 42
2. Chicago City Limits / 534 West 42
3. Fantasy Factory / 524 West 42
4. Harold Clurman Theatre / 412 West 42
5. Intar / 420 West 42
6. Lion Theatre Company / 422 West 42
7. Nat Horne Musical Theatre / 440 West 42
8. Playwrights Horizons / 416 West 42
9. South Street Theatre / 424 West 42
10. WestSide Arts Theatre / 407 West 43

▲ Restaurants

1. Café Madeleine / 405 West 43
2. Curtain Up! / 402 West 43
3. Food Work Shop / 424 West 43
4. La Rousse / 414 West 42
5. West Bank Café / 407 West 42

□ Other Attractions

1. Ticket Central / 414 West 42

17 Bus Number

Ⓟ Parking

→ One-way Street

Some six years ago, the 42nd Street Corporation was formed for the express purpose of revitalizing 42nd Street west of Seventh Avenue. Headed by Fred Papert, a former advertising *wunderkind,* the not-for-profit corporation has already made significant progress, not only in breathing new life into the street but in creating new theatres and the beginnings of a home for the city's theatrical community.

First, five derelict tenements that once housed massage parlors, porno operations, and peep shows were converted into five 99-seat, attractive, modern theatres and 10 floors of office space. The section, on the south side of 42nd Street between Ninth and Tenth Avenues, now is known as Theatre Row.

While this was going on, Fred and the corporation were able to convince HUD to allow the twin towers under construction across the street to be used, in large part, as rental housing for professional theatre people. Today Manhattan Tower is full of the talent that powers the New York theatre scene. Interestingly, an actor or actress's rent is adjusted up or down within certain guidelines as his or her fortunes go up or down: eviction no longer looms if a performer's show closes opening night. (One of the last to get an apartment in Manhattan Tower, after a 14-month wait, was Angela Lansbury.)

Theatre Row was Phase I in the corporation's grand plan. Besides the new theatres, it also included a residential building with a new French restaurant, La Rousse, leasing the ground floor.

The tenants of Theatre Row are the Black Theatre Alliance, Actors and Directors Lab, Lion Theatre Company, Intar, Harlem Children's Theatre, Harold Clurman Theatre, and the South Street Theatre. They join two existing theatres on the block, Playwrights Horizons and the Nat Horne Theatre Company.

Theatre Row was the first development in the city under a new building code easement for Off-Off Broadway theatres. The city also extended needed tax relief for the program.

Phase II now is under way and should be nearing completion when you read this. Adjacent to Theatre Row, between Dyer and Tenth Avenues, derelict tenements, empty lots, and abandoned buildings are being converted into a series of theatres and commercial space. The most exciting part of the project is a projected 700-seat theatre to house the productions of the country's leading non-profit theatre companies: The Center Theatre Group/Mark Taper Forum of Los Angeles, the Tyrone Guthrie Theatre of Minneapolis, and the Long Wharf Theatre of New Haven; these will be the theatre's "resident" companies, while productions from other companies will be presented as artistic merit warrants.

On the western edge of the Phase II project is the former West Side Airlines Terminal. It has been converted by National Recording Studios, a major audio and television production company, to contain two sound stages, recording studios, and complete post-production facilities.

East of the former terminal, Theatre Row Market Place will be constructed. It will include two experimental theatres (of 99 and 225 seats), a 260-seat dance theatre, rehearsal facilities, retail space, a restaurant, and an urban garden. The financing for this $9.5-million venture was as convoluted and brilliant as the plot of a Pinter play and does the corporation proud.

Artist Richard Haas has executed two large wall paintings that face each other at Dyer Avenue and serve as a visual gateway to Theatre Row, and they are worth a visit all by themselves.

East of Theatre Row and around the corner south on Ninth Avenue, five existing buildings will be converted for appropriate retail use. A new restaurant on 42nd Street will share with Theatre Row a sort of "mini-Shubert Alley" with an outdoor intermission garden. This will lead to a parking lot behind the theatres.

Concurrently, the stretch of 42nd Street will be improved with new concrete and brick sidewalks, groups of trees, and street furnishings.

Phases I and II are hardly all the tricks up Fred Papert's well-tailored sleeve. The corporation purchased a building on the north side of the street, between Eleventh and Twelfth Avenues and is creating in it a new home for the Midtown Mounted Division of the New York Police Department, housing 25 horses on a round-the-clock operation. Reason: Mounted policemen trooping to and from patrols at the United Nations, midtown, and in the Broadway theatre district will create a comforting presence on West 42nd Street.

In the works is a $12-million acquisition taking on the upgrading and refurbishing of the 350-room Holland Hotel (between Eighth and Ninth Avenues on the north side of the street) into a moderately priced hotel. The hotel is under consideration as the international headquarters for the American Youth Hostel.

New housing is planned as well. The former Army Reserve training center, across and down the street from Theatre Row, is being converted into luxury loft condominiums. Next door, at the corner of 42nd and Eleventh, a $30-million, 450-unit apartment building is planned in concert with a private developer. It is hoped that this mostly private, market-level rental building will lure new private construction into the area. And why not? The building will be three blocks north of the new convention center, a block east of the new Peoples Republic of China trade delegation residence, in addition to its proximity to the amenities of Theatre Row.

Fred Papert thinks big; no one has challenged that in years. He is working to turn back the clock to when the block between Seventh and Eighth was a row of the finest theatres in the world, not double-bill movie theatres where winos sleep. One has already been converted, the New Apollo, although its entrance has been changed from 42nd to 43rd Street. A particular plum is the New Amsterdam where Florenz Ziegfeld's held sway; it is an architectural treasure and probably the finest musical theatre ever built.

The culmination of Fred Papert and the corporation's redevelopment plans is a project called "The City at 42nd Street," and it would irrevocably change the face of the city. Here's how the corporation describes it:

> The project would build on the existing assets of the area—its history, its architecture, its extraordinary accessibility, the purchasing power of the two-hundred thousand people who daily rush to get away from its present blight—with the restoration of a half dozen of the street's legendary theaters and the creation on a mezzanine level above them of a complex of exhibits and retail/restaurant atriums which, in sum, would celebrate cities. It would serve as a gateway to New York, an information center, an arts, communications and entertainment center, a launching pad for city visitors.

More than $1 million, primarily in the form of Ford Foundation grants, has gone into planning and studying the feasibility of The City at 42nd Street. The project, strongly supported by the Koch administration, was moving into the critical stage of attracting private development monies. One can only cross one's fingers and say, "Break a leg!"

Every visionary scheme needs a little tin hat. Here it is a trolley or, more precisely, a light rail transit line, running from the United Nations to Eleventh Avenue, possibly turning south to the new Convention Center, then looping around 34th Street to take in Penn Station, Madison Square Garden, and Herald Square, then back to 42nd Street. Preliminary studies show that the concept is financially feasible and would be an energy-efficient, nonpolluting, amenable public transit and, equally important would help draw new private and commercial development to the west side. So don't be too surprised if you hear a "clang-clang" and see a trolley zipping along 42nd Street; stranger things have happened.

I talked to Fred at the corporation's office on a high floor of the old green McGraw-Hill building near Theatre Row. "I can look out the window and see things I have helped make happen. Places where new things can happen. And that sure beats helping Proctor and Gamble sell soap." Smiling, he added, "Now if we can just figure out a way to put St. Patrick's on wheels and roll it down Fifth Avenue, we could have the St. Patrick's Day Parade on 42nd Street."

TICKET CENTRAL

414 West 42nd Street

Phone: 279-4200
Hours: 1 p.m.–8 p.m.
Credit Cards: AE, MC, V (50¢ service charge for phone credit card sales; none at box office) Personal checks TDF Vouchers depending on show
Group Sales: Through Theatre Row offices (279-8822)

All the theatres on Theatre Row, except the Harold Clurman and the Nat Horne, share one ticket office, Ticket Central, located near the middle of the block. (Information on shows at the Howard Clurman and the Nat Horne can be obtained by phoning Ticket Central.) Ticket prices vary from $4 to $12 depending upon the theatre and the production. Many performances are free of charge.

THEATRES

BLACK THEATRE ALLIANCE

410 West 42nd Street

Box Office: (Ticket Central)
Total Seating: 110 (89 permanent seats; 20–25 folding chairs)
Stage Type: Black box stage
AC
Handicapped: Semi-accessible

This theatre serves as a rental theatre for the 61 black theatre and dance companies (40 of which are in New York) that are members of Black Theatre Alliance. The alliance has a number of important goals: It strives to uphold a standard of excellence for black theatre and dance; works to develop new and growing audiences; seeks public and private funding for the common needs; and serves as a central source of information on all aspects of black theatre and dance. Brooke Stephens is the executive director. The season's productions depend on which companies are booking the theatre. Phone Ticket Central (279-4200) for current offerings.

CHICAGO CITY LIMITS

534 West 42nd Street

Box Office: 695-2351
Credit Cards: None
Shows: Wednesday–Thursday, 8 p.m.; Friday–Saturday, 8 p.m. and 10:30 p.m.
Stage Type: Cabaret

The attraction here is satirical reviews featuring true improvisation: the audience tosses subjects out to the actors who weave them into skits. When it works, as it does much more often than not, it is hilarious. Admission is $6.

FANTASY FACTORY

524 West 42nd Street

Box Office: 575-9654
Box Office Hours: Answering machine (will hold tickets reserved by phone until half-hour before curtain)
Credit Cards: None TDF Vouchers for some productions
Group Sales: Through box office
Season: October–May
Total Seating: 139 (Orchestra, 99; Balcony, 40; Standing room, 20)
Stage Type: Flexible stage
No AC
Handicapped: Semi-accessible

In the gymnasium of the Children's Day Care Center, the Fantasy Factory, under the artistic direction of Bill Vitale, stages its productions. The name, says Mr. Vitale, means a place "where performing dreams are created and can hopefully come true." They came through with *A Mass Murder in the Balcony of the Old Ritz-Rialto,* recipient of a National Endowment for the Arts award, which moved to an extended run Off Broadway.

HAROLD CLURMAN THEATRE

412 West 42nd Street

Box Office: 594-2370
Box Office Hours: Tuesday–Saturday, 1 p.m.–8:30 p.m.
Credit Cards: AE, MC, V TELECHARGE
Group Sales: Through box office Usually closed during summer
Total Seating: Mainstage, 100 (Orchestra, 88; Balcony, 12; Up to 25 folding chairs can be added) Workshop, 75
Stage Type: Proscenium stage (Mainstage), Black box
AC
Handicapped: Semi-accessible (Workshop)

Harold Clurman, who died in 1980, wrote in his book *The Fervent Years:* "Theatres may be socially, politically, or religiously motivated, but each of them must develop an identity, a style, a 'face,' a meaning of its own. . . . Above all, true theatre sets itself a goal and plans its work as a lifelong community, very much as the individual artist does." Jack Garfein, who made his New York directing debut in the 1950s at the age of 23, is dedicated to perpetuating the artistic vision he shares with Mr. Clurman that this theatre should not only discover new playwrights and performers but rediscover classic plays that are no longer suited to the economics of Broadway. Founded in 1978, the theatre's productions include Celeste Holm as Janet Flanner in *Paris Was Yesterday,* adapted and directed by Paul Shyre; Alix Eliam and Jill Larson in Mayo Simon's new play *These Men,* directed by Zoe Caldwell; Bill Morrison's *Flying Blind,* directed by Christopher Ward, and Arthur Miller's new play, *The American Clock.* In addition, the theatre presents a workshop series, a film program, and a season of late-night, weekend cabaret theatre.

INTAR

420 West 42nd Street

Box Office: (Ticket Central)
Total Seating: 108
Stage Type: Proscenium floor, no arch
AC
Handicapped: Semi-accessible

INTAR (International Arts Relations, Inc.) began in 1966 when a group of Hispanic artists recognized the need to establish a permanent showcase facility. Starting in a city-owned building with a shoestring budget, INTAR now is a multiarts Hispanic-American cultural organization introducing Latin artists and helping them compete successfully in the American market. INTAR has four major components: a theatrical performing company, a playwrights-in-residence laboratory, a master training program, and an art gallery. Early in 1980, INTAR presented *La Vida Es Sueno,* a free Spanish adaptation with music of Calderon de la Barca's 16th-century classic, and a free English adaptation of the same play. Under the guidance of Max Ferra, artistic director, INTAR in association with Ballet Hispanico of New York City and El Museo del Barrio presented a major spring festival celebrating the "Golden Age of Spain."

LION THEATRE COMPANY
422 West 42nd Street

Box Office:	(Ticket Central)
Total Seating:	100
Season:	September–June
Stage Type:	Black box
	AC
	Handicapped: Semi-accessible

This is a resident company of some 35 actors, eight designers, three directors, two playwrights, a composer, a choreographer, several technicians, and an administrative staff, practically all of whom have been associated with the company since its founding in 1974. Lion is a collaborative of artists believing in ensemble and continuity as the keys to fine theatre, and the company has, to an extent, a modified European idea of repertory—the feeling of home base is ever-present, with members of the company free to come and go as necessary. The Lion was a pioneer here, giving productions before Theatre Row was conceived. Under the artistic direction of Gene Nye, some of the company's productions have been the company-developed *K: Impressions of Kafka's The Trial; Music-Hall Sidelights: A Theatrical Scrapbook* (from Colette's *L'envers du music-hall*); and, more recently, *Vanities* and *Peg O' My Heart.*

NAT HORNE MUSICAL THEATRE
440 West 42nd Street

Box Office:	736-7128
Box Office Hours:	Monday–Saturday, 10 a.m.–9 p.m.; Sunday, 10 a.m.–3 p.m.
Credit Cards:	None TDF Vouchers Personal checks
Group Sales:	Through box office
Total Seating:	115
Stage Type:	Proscenium stage
	AC
	Handicapped: Semi-accessible

The Nat Horne Musical Theatre prepares the dancer for professional employment in the American musical theatre. Its graduates have worked in such shows as *Eubie, The Wiz, The Best Little Whorehouse in Texas,* and *Bubbling Brown Sugar.* The Nat Horne specialty is jazz dance but classes—35 of them a week at four levels—include modern dance, ballet, tap, voice, and acting. There is a misical theatre workshop and a professional performing company. Productions, under the supervision of Nat Horne, choreographer and artistic director, and Al Reyes, producing director, include *The Phantom of the Opera, Ham,* and *The Memory of You.* When this was written, the performing company, called Dancing Plus, was touring with the production *The Legend of Frankie and Johnnie.*

PLAYWRIGHTS HORIZONS
416 West 42nd Street

Box Office:	(Ticket Central)
Total Seating:	Theatre, 150
	Workshop space, 99
Stage Type:	Proscenium stage (Theatre), Black box (Workshop space)
	AC
	Handicapped: Semi-accessible (theatre only)

Playwrights Horizons was founded in 1971 to support and develop new American playwrights: from readings through workshops to full productions, writers are offered a professional facility in which to develop their work and refine their talents. Over the years, Playwrights Horizons has helped more than 200 playwrights, many of whom have subsequently been produced on regional theatres around the country or on Broadway. Among the successes of producing director Robert Moss, managing director Rojin J. Gold, and artistic director André Bishop are the world premieres of *Kennedy's Children, Gemini* (still going strong on Broadway at this writing), *Vanities, Table Settings, Passione,* and most recently, Ted Talley's *Coming Attractions.*

SOUTH STREET THEATRE

424 West 42nd Street

Box Office: (Ticket Central)
Total Seating: 94
Stage Type: Nonproscenium raked stage
AC
Handicapped: Semi-accessible

Artistic directors Michael Fischetti and Jean Sullivan founded the South Street Theatre in 1973 as an outdoor theatre on an empty pier at the South Street Seaport Museum. For 10 weeks they presented Edgar Lee Masters' *Spoon River Anthology.* The next year, with a grant from the New York Community Trust, a permanent environmental theatre was built on Pier 17 and, with some additional grants, Michael Fischetti's original adaptation of Melville's *Moby Dick* was presented. South Street moved here in 1978 and now its seasons are year-round. Among its productions have been several American premieres: Stephan Poliakoff's *Hitting Town;* Joe Orton's *Funeral Games; Terrible Sunlight* by Michael Brodsky, and in 1980 *Occupations,* a new play by British playwright Trevor Griffiths. South Street Theatre also provides free classes in the theatre for disadvantaged children from the Clinton community. Next season, it plans a series of free lunchtime theatre featuring the work of new directors. (Note to movie buffs: Co-artistic director Jean Sullivan played opposite Erroll Flynn in *Uncertain Glory.*)

WESTSIDE ARTS THEATRE

407 West 43rd Street

Box Office: 541-8394
Box Office Hours: Monday, 12 noon–6 p.m.; Tuesday–Saturday, 12 noon–8 p.m.; Sunday, 12 noon–3 p.m.
Credit Cards: AE, DC, MC, V TDF Vouchers (depends upon show)
CHARGIT Personal checks
Group Sales: Through box office
Total Seating: Cheryl Crawford theatre, 210; (Downstairs theatre, 190);
Stage Type: Proscenium stage (Cheryl Crawford)
Thrust (Downstairs)
AC
Handicapped: No access

These two theatres are houses in an 1860-ish building that once was an Episcopal church. In 16 seasons under the artistic guidance of producing director Robert Kalfin, the Center has produced over 100 plays including *AC/DC, The Contractor, Kaddish, The Screens, Kaspar, Polly,* and *The Crazy Locomotive.* Four Chelsea productions have moved to Broadway: *Candide, Yentl, Happy End,* and *Strider: The Story of a Horse.* Two others, *The Prince of Homburg* and *The Contractor,* were televised as part of the PBS Theater in America series. The Chelsea production of *Vanities* closed last summer after five years. Among the awards presented to Chelsea presentations are five Tonys (including a special one to the theatre for "Outstanding Contribution to the Artistic Development of Musical Theater") and 23 Obies.

"There is no more offensive act of theatrical rudeness than coming late to a performance."

MAURICE ZOLOTOW

RESTAURANTS AND NIGHTSPOTS

CAFÉ MADELEINE**

405 West 43rd Street
Reservations: 246-2993
No credit cards
Inexpensive
Tuesday–Saturday, 10:30 a.m.–9:30 p.m.; Sunday, 10:30 a.m.–8:30 p.m.;
Monday, 10:30 a.m.–9:30 p.m.

Next door to the Chelsea Theatre, former Parisian Gilles Delouette serves what he calls French snaks: charcuterie, cheese and fruit, an assortment of quiches, croque monsieur (a hot ham, cheese, and cream sandwich), salads, and pastries from La Côte Basque. Everything is good and the prices are reasonable (the most expensive item on the menu is assiette madeleine—an assortment of cheeses and pâtés—at $4). A hot croissant with jam and butter ($1) and a pot of tea (90¢)—brewed from any of nine varieties—is a delightful way to wrap up an evening. If it's summer, there's a garden in back or a sidewalk café in front and a glass of Perrier lemonade ($1.75) is refreshing. Pastries, pâtés, and cheeses can be taken home. No wine or liquor is served, but you're welcome to bring your own.

CURTAIN UP!***

402 West 43rd Street
Reservations: 564-7272
Credit Cards: AE, CB, DC, MC, V
Inexpensive

In a corner of Manhattan Plaza, Robert Nahas has created a theatre restaurant that is both a delight and a bargain. It's handsome: The powder-blue seats along the walls and two floor-to-ceiling mirrors once graced the Harkness Theatre; the bar and the sign above it that spells out "New York" came from the old Commodore Hotel; and a wall is filled with names of personalities who have appeared on Broadway. The quality of the ingredients here is excellent: All the meat is from the Ottomanelli Brothers, the fish is from the Fulton Street Market. And check the prices: One of the best and biggest (a full half-pound of meat) is $2.75; filet of sole ($6.50); a broiled half-chicken ($5.95). The most expensive item on the menu is a 10-ounce prime shell steak at $8.95. There are daily specials. Friday evenings and Sunday afternoons there is a classical guitarist; in the summer, an outdoor café.

When this was written, Mr. Nahas was about to open a "Chinese theatre restaurant" around the corner, across from Theatre Row. Pearl of the famous Pearl's on West 48th Street was helping to plan the menu, and Angela Lansbury (who lives in Manhattan Tower) is one of the investors. Sounds like a welcome addition to the area.

FOOD WORKSHOP**

424 West 43rd Street
Reservations: 695-3602
No credit cards
Inexpensive
Monday–Saturday, 9:30 a.m.–11:30 p.m.; Sunday, 12 noon–9 p.m.

If you enjoy natural food well prepared, this is your place. Nothing is canned or frozen, and they serve brown, fertile eggs and brown rice and bake with brown flour. Some interesting entrees include: tuna salad with romaine in a whole-wheat pita with salad ($3.95); stir-fried vegetables and almonds with brown rice and salad ($5.50); and to restore your energy level, a protein shake made of bananas, protein powder, brewers yeast, lecithin, and apple juice ($2.25). There is a fish special daily; the price varies with the choice. This is as much a store as it is a café, and a good place to catch up on your natural food shopping.

♫ LA ROUSSE**

414 West 42nd Street
Reservations: 736-4913
Credit Cards: AE, DC, MC, V
Moderate

La Rousse means "the redhead," in this case the charming Aline Landais, whose days begin with shopping the markets of Ninth Avenue for the freshest ingredients for her French peasant-style cuisine. The dinner menu is constantly changing as she discovers seasonal varieties on her rounds. Chicken done Basque-style, for example, with green and red peppers and zucchini. Or tonight's vegetables might be kale and mustard greens. Prices range from $5.95 for a beef and cheese torte with béchamel sauce to $14.95 for the filet mignon. Ms. Landais makes her own pâté and desserts, including a sinful cheesecake. The restaurant is nestled between the theatres on Theatre Row. There's a jazz quartet on Thursdays from 9:30 p.m. to 1:30 a.m.

WEST BANK CAFÉ**

407 West 42nd Street
Reservations: 695-6909
Credit Cards: AE, DC, MC, V
Moderate

The West Bank Café is in Manhattan Plaza across the street from Theatre Row, serving good, uncomplicated food in a friendly atmosphere. A blackboard serves as a menu, the offerings ranging from chili ($3.25) and omelettes ($3.95), through pasta ($6.75 or so) and coq au vin ($7.50) to a tasty sirloin at $11.95. Entrees come with vegetables and a potato. A new diversion is a downstairs cabaret, which opened last winter with a shortened version of *Feiffer's People*. At last report, show times were 8 p.m. and 11 p.m. There's a $7 entry charge, no minimum, and only drinks are served.

LINCOLN CENTER AREA

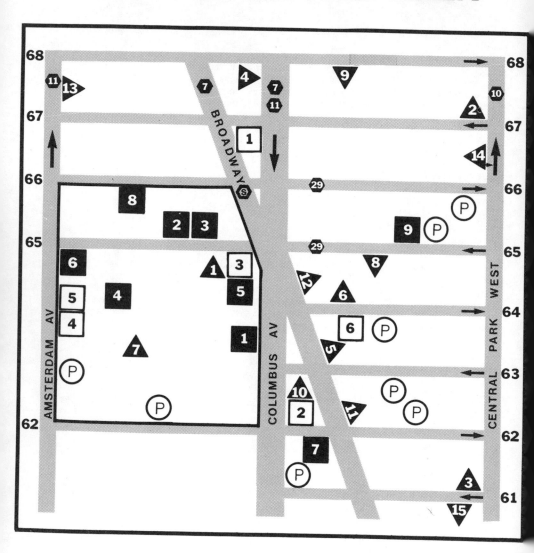

■ Lincoln Center Theatres

1. Bruno Walter Auditorium / Lincoln Center Plaza
2. Julliard Drama Workshop / 155 West 65
3. Julliard School Theatre / 155 West 65
4. Mitzie E. Newhouse / 150 West 65
5. New York State Theater / Lincoln Center Plaza
6. Vivian Beaumont / 150 West 65

■ Other Theatres

7. Chamber Theatre / 36 West 62
8. Encompass Music Theatre / 152 West 66
9. First All Children's Theatre Company / 37 West 65

▲ Restaurants

1. Allegro Café & Adagio Café / Avery Fisher Hall / Lincoln Center Plaza
2. Café des Artistes / 1 West 67
3. The Conservatory / 1 West 61
4. Dimitri / 152 Columbus
5. Fiorello's / 1900 Broadway
6. The Ginger Man / 51 West 64
7. Grand Tier / Metropolitan Opera House / Lincoln Center Plaza
8. Maestro Café / 58 West 65
9. Milestone / 70 West 68
10. O'Neals' Baloon / 48 West 63

11. Orloff's / 1900 Broadway
12. The Saloon / 1920 Broadway
13. Sweetwater's / 170 Amsterdam
14. Tavern on the Green / Central Park at West 67
15. Top of the Park / Gulf & Western Plaza (Columbus Circle)

□ Other Attractions

1. Applause / 100 West 67
2. The Ballet Shop / 1887 Broadway
3. The Center at the Center / below Avery Fisher Hall
4. Library of the Performing Arts / Lincoln Center Plaza
5. Shelby Cullom Davis Museum / Library
6. Travel & Theatre Shoppe / 1900 Broadway

🅱 Bus Numbers

Ⓢ Subway Stations

Ⓟ Parking

➡ One-way Street

⇄ Two-way Street

▢ Outlined area is Lincoln Center

The opera, the orchestra, and the ballet had no trouble settling comfortably into Lincoln Center when it was built more than 20 years ago. Not so the theatre. For many reasons, it always has been a stepchild, although often an extraordinarily gifted stepchild. It began in 1962 with a repertory company; Robert Whitehead was the producer, Elia Kazan, the director. Construction on what was to be the Vivian Beaumont Theatre was behind schedule, so a temporary theatre was built at Washington Square. It opened January 23, 1964, with the premiere of Arthur Miller's *After the Fall*. At worst, it was a failure; at best, it did not live up to the expectations of the new company. Several genuine failures followed: a revival of *Marco Millions*, *But for Whom Charlie*, *The Changeling*. The company seemed to find itself with Arthur Miller's *Incident at Vichy* and Molière's *Tartuffe*. But the damage had been done. The board tried to edge Messrs. Whitehead and Kazan out; they found out about the plot and resigned.

Herbert Blau and Jules Irving of San Francisco's Actors Workshop took over as the company moved into the Vivian Beaumont that Whitehead and Kazan had helped design along with architect Eero Saarinen and Jo Mielziner, who designed the large convertible stage and the backstage area and facility. Messrs. Bleu and Irving had trouble adjusting to the new theatre and the first several seasons reflected their uneasiness in spotty productions. In the years that followed there were many memorable presentations: Anthony Quayle in Bertolt Brecht's *Galileo;* a revival of Sean O'Casey's *The Plough and the Stars; In the Matter of J. Robert Oppenheimer;* and a revival of *A Streetcar Named Desire* among them. But the Beaumont was losing money; attendance was good, near 90 percent, but when the theatre was being built Lincoln Center management blundered into some of the most abusive union contracts ever written. After more than eight years, Mr. Irving resigned and the board again sought new direction.

It came in the person of Joseph Papp, an Off Broadway producer and founder of the New York Shakespeare Festival. Papp had two qualities that made him perfect for Lincoln Center: He was a dynamic and protean producer, and he could raise money. (He got George T. Delacorte to build a theatre in Central Park; the little theatre in the Beaumont was renamed the Mitzi E. Newhouse after she gave $1 million to help offset the deficit of the Beaumont. Under a new name, New York Shakespeare Festival Lincoln Center, Papp began. The first production was David Rabe's *Boom Boom Room* and it was a shock to those accustomed to the Beaumont's more genteel earlier efforts. Then came Hugh Leonard's *The Au Pair Man, What the Wine Seller Buys*, Strindberg's *The Dance of Death*, and the biting prison drama, *Short Eyes*. That first season set a tempo that Mr. Papp has maintained. Other success were *Streakers, Threepenny Opera, The Cherry Orchard*, and *Agamemnon*.

But the alliance of Lincoln Center and Joseph Papp was not made in heaven, and he left in the summer of 1977 as conflicting versions of a power struggle filled the newspapers. His string of innovative and successful productions continued from his Astor Place complex; the Beaumont went dark for more than three years. The next phase began when the board brought Richmond Crinkley, one of the founders of Washington's Folger Theatre Group, to be executive director of the Beaumont. Some time went by as Mr. Crinkley raised money, worked to renegotiate union contracts, co-produced *Ladyhouse Blues, Tintypes,* and the Tony Award winner *The Elephant Man* and assembled a disparate artistic directorate composed of Edward Albee, Woody Allen, Sarah Caldwell, Liviu Ciulei, Robin Phillips, and Ellis Rabb. The first season under the new management opened with a revival of Philip Barry's *The Philadelphia Story,* with Blythe Danner and Edward Herrman, which Mr. Rabb directed. It received mixed reviews. The next production was not so fortunate: Sarah Caldwell's production of *Macbeth* with Philip Ang-

146

lim (who had starred in Mr. Crinkley's *The Elephant Man*) and Maureen Audeman, who was roundly panned by the critics. The third and final play of the season, was *The Floating Light Bulb,* a new comedy by Woody Allen which drew lukewarm reviews.

In May, 1981 a grant of $4 million was received from the Fan Fox and Leslie R. Samuels Foundation to convert the Beaumont to a proscenium theatre. Other improvements will be made, but construction will rule out a 1981–82 season.

LINCOLN CENTER CALENDAR
Ms. Doreen Lown, editor
140 West 65th Street
Lincoln Center publishes a bi-monthly comprehensive calendar of events. It will be mailed to you free of charge if you write to the above address (New York, N.Y. 10023).

THEATRES

BRUNO WALTER AUDITORIUM
Library of the Performing Arts Lincoln Center
Entry from Lincoln Center Plaza and at 111 Amsterdam Avenue (65th)

This is a lovely 212-seat theatre with a proscenium stage that is used almost daily for showcase productions and music recitals. Admission is free, but you must apply in person after 3 p.m. on the day of the program (after 12 noon on Saturday) at the Amsterdam Avenue entrance. Professional theatre groups in the city can use the theatre for a three-performance showcase presentation at no cost. Arrangements are made through the Equity Library Theatre. There is roughly a one-year waiting list for such use.

CHAMBER THEATRE
Richard Allen Center For Culture & Art
36 West 62nd Street

Box Office:	496-0120
Box Office Hours:	Tuesday–Saturday, 1 p.m.–9 p.m.
Credit Cards:	None TDF Vouchers
Group Sales:	Through box office
Season:	October–May
Total Seating:	99
Stage Type:	Proscenium stage or three-quarter round, depending on production
	No AC
	Handicapped: No access

The Richard Allen Center offers training in acting, designing, and theatre management and stages its productions in this former parking garage that was converted into a theatre in 1977. Some recent productions: Langston Hughes's *Black Nativity* and *Fly Blackbird* by Jackson and Hatch. Hazel Jay Bryan is the artistic director.

ENCOMPASS MUSIC THEATRE
Church of the Good Shepherd
152 West 66th Street

Box Office:	594-7880
Box Office Hours:	Monday–Saturday, 10 a.m.–6 p.m.
Credit Cards:	MC, V TDF Vouchers Personal checks
Group Sales:	Through box office
Season:	September–June
Total Seating:	220
Stage Type:	Thrust stage
	No AC
	Handicapped: No access

With a song in their hearts, Nancy Rhodes, artistic director, and Roger Cunningham, producer, founded the Encompass Music Theatre in 1975 to develop and present American musical theatre and opera. Their presentations have included Virgil Thomson and Gertrude Stein's *Mother of Us All,* Aaron Copland's *The Tender Land,* and Marc Blitzstein's *Regina,* based on Lillian Hellman's *The Little Foxes.* Estelle Parsons starred in a new musical here, *Elizabeth and Essex,* based on Maxwell Anderson's *Elizabeth the Queen,* book by Michael Stewart and Mark Bramble, lyrics by Richard Engquist, and music by Doug Katsaros. There is a once-a-week composer-librettist workshop at the Encompass which, so far, has developed 10 new works.

FIRST ALL CHILDREN'S THEATRE COMPANY
37 West 65th Street

Box Office: 873-6400
Box Office Hours: Monday–Friday, 10 a.m.–6 p.m.; Saturday, 11 a.m.–5 p.m.
Credit Cards: None   TDF Vouchers   Personal checks
Group Sales: 875-6400
Season: October–May; touring June and July
Total Seating: 100–200, depending upon production
Stage Type: Thrust stage
No AC
Handicapped: No access

Meridee Stein founded the First All Children's Theatre (First ACT) in 1969 to produce professional theatre with and for young people. Now First ACT consists of two interracial companies: the Meri Mini Players (ages six to 13) and the Teen Company (ages 14 to 17) and has developed a unique repertory style. Five original musicals are produced each season, including one by a major playwright. For example, Elizabeth Swados's *The Incredible Feeling Show* was developed and produced here. All told, First ACT has produced more than 20 original plays and musical scores. First ACT has performed at the New York Shakespeare Festival, the Ontario Summer Festival of the Arts, the Eugene O'Neill Theater Center, the Berkshire Theatre Festival, the Paul Robeson Performing Arts Center, the John Drew Theatre, all three television networks, and a "Benefit on Broadway" at the Shubert Theatre. Its quarters have recently been renovated.

MITZI E. NEWHOUSE
Lincoln Center
150 West 65th Street

Box Office: 944-9300
Box Office Hours: Monday, 10 a.m.–6 p.m.; Tuesday–Saturday, 10 a.m.–8:15 p.m.; Sunday, 12 noon–4 p.m.
Credit Cards: AE, DC, MC, V   CHARGIT
Group Sales: 398-8383 (Special student information, 363-7600; half-price student rush and senior citizen tickets available at box office, 6 p.m. on day of performance)
Total Seating: 299
Stage Type: Thrust stage
Handicapped: No access
Cordless earphones: $1

Originally called the Forum, this jewelbox of a theatre beneath the Vivian Beaumont has presented a wide range of productions over the years, including Joseph Papp's production of David Rabe's *Streamers.* Most recently, the Newhouse has seen Robert Wilson's *Curious George,* Truman Capote reading from his own works, and a festival of one-act plays under the artistic direction of Edward Albee that included Jeffrey Sweet's *Stops Along the Way,* John Guare's *In Fireworks Lie Secret Codes,* and Percy Granger's *Vivien.*

Mitzi E. Newhouse

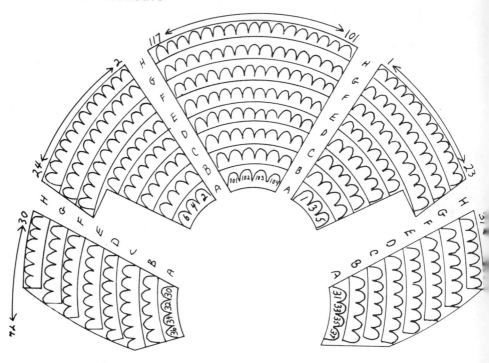

NEW YORK STATE THEATER
Lincoln Center
150 West 65th Street

Box Office: 870-5570
Box Office Hours: Monday, 10 a.m.–8 p.m.; Tuesday–Saturday, 10 a.m.–9 p.m., Sunday, 11:30 a.m.–7:30 p.m.
Credit Cards: AE, DC, MC, V CHARGIT
Group Sales: Through box office
Season: Summer only
Total Seating: 2,729 (Orchestra, 1,048; Balconies, 1,681; Standing room 40)
Stage Type: Proscenium stage
Handicapped: Fully accessible but by ramp through backstage area

This handsome theatre was the setting from 1964 to 1968 of the Music Theatre of Lincoln Centre. Under the artistic directorship of Richard Rodgers, beautifully mounted revivals were presented of such classics as *The King and I, The Merry Widow, Carousel, Oklahoma!, West Side Story, Showboat,* and *Annie Get Your Gun,* starring Ethel Merman in the role she created and featuring a new song, "An Old-Fashioned Marriage," specially written for the revival by Irving Berlin. After a decade in which the theatre presented music and dance, Sammy Davis, Jr., starred in a summer presentation of *Stop the World, I Want to Get Off,* and in the summer of 1980, Richard Burton starred in a revival of *Camelot;* in 1981, Hershel Bernardi was to star in *Fiddler on the Roof.* At press time, a grant of $4 million was announced for major renovation on the State Theater, including enlarging the orchestra pit and making accoustical improvements. Work will be done in July and August, 1982, ruling out a summer theatrical season.

VIVIAN BEAUMONT
Lincoln Center
150 West 65th Street

Box Office: 944-9300
Box Office Hours: Monday, 10 a.m.–6 p.m.; Tuesday–Saturday, 10 a.m.–8:15 p.m.;
Sunday, 12 noon–4 p.m.
Credit Cards: AE, DC, MC, V   CHARGIT
Group Sales: 398-8383 (Special student information: 362-7600; half-price
student rush and senior citizen tickets available at box office, 6 p.m.
on day of performance)
Total Seating: 1,100, varying with stage type used (Orchestra, 823; Loge, 361)
Stage Type: Variable stage
Handicapped: Full accessibility
Cordless earphones: $1

The Vivian Beaumont (named after the lady who donated half of the construction cost) is a beautiful example of what an architect and stage designer can accomplish together. Eero Saarinen's contribution is, in the opinion of many, the most elegant in the Lincoln Center complex. Jo Mielziner designed a stage that can be open, thrust, or proscenium. Both the orchestra and the loge are sharply raked and, by wrapping the orchestra around the front of the stage area, the audience feels in closer contact with the actors than it does in a conventional theatre. The stage, when thrust, works well with an intimate drama such as the revival of Lillian Hellman's *The Little Foxes,* or it can accommodate the sweep of pageantry as it did in the imaginative staging of *Agamemnon.* The backstage area has nearly as much space as a football field and is a pleasure to work in for those accustomed to the skimpy backstage of most commercial theatres. As noted in the introduction to this section, a $4 million grant has been received to convert the Beaumont to a proscenium stage, and reduce the degree to which the seating is raked. These renovations will preclude a 1981–82 season.

RESTAURANTS AND NIGHTSPOTS
ALLEGRO CAFÉ/ADAGIO CAFÉ

Avery Fisher Hall
Lincoln Center
Reservations: Not accepted (874-7000)
Credit Cards: AE, DC, MC, V
Inexpensive to Moderate
Allegro: 5:30 p.m.–8 p.m. Seven days a week
Adagio: 5:30 p.m.–8 p.m.; 9 p.m.–11:30 p.m. Performance nights.

On the right of the box office in Avery Fisher Hall is an attractive dining area known as the Allegro Café. There is a limited menu of hot and cold entrees: salads ($6.95–$7.95); a small whole salmon stuffed with pureed mushrooms ($9.50); roast ribs of beef ($11.95), with the usual appetizers and pastries. The small wine list is attractively priced.

To the right is the Adagio Café, serving a hot and cold buffet ($14.95) before Philharmonic concerts. Later it serves quiches, crepes, pastries with espresso and cappuccino. Your check should average $5 to $7 per person.

CAFÉ DES ARTISTES***

1 West 67th Street (Central Park West)
Reservations: 877-3500
Credit Cards: AE, CB, DC, MC, V
Moderate   Open seven days, Sunday until 9 p.m. Closed Christmas and New Year's Day

This is a charming, elegant restaurant that suggests London more than it does New York, and it is as much a treat for the eyes as it is for the palate. The visual stars are Howard Chandler Christie's murals of pretty girls in sylvan scenes, painted in the late 1930s when the building was a hotel and the café was the dining room. There is a prix fixe dinner at $15, the entree varying from night to night. A la carte, you might like to start with a dill marinated gravlax salmon ($5) or snails sautéed with garlic, onions, and prosciutto ($4.50). Bourride with aioli, a provençale-style fish casserole, is a delightful entree at $11.50; poularde with apples in champagne sauce ($10) and the mignon of lamb bearnaise ($13) are other excellent choices. I love the cassis sherbet here; others are partial to the pumpkin ice cream. There's a good Stilton, and your captain can find you a nice red or white wine for $10 a bottle. This is an enormously popular place for good reason, and owner-host Steve Gurgely strongly advises *early* reservations.

THE CONSERVATORY**

1 West 61st Street
Reservations: 581-1293
Credit Cards: AE, DC, MC, V
Moderate

In a corner of the Mayflower Hotel, overlooking Central Park, the Conservatory is a handsome L-shaped room, a sound choice for dinner, supper, or simply drinks in a glittery atmosphere. If you're dining before the theatre, you'll enjoy a harpist plucking away melodiously in the dining room; a pianist takes over at 9:30 p.m. Some interesting specialties brighten the menu: salmon kulibiaka, a Russian dish where the salmon is poached and put in a fluffy pastry with cucumbers, celery, onions, hard-boiled eggs, and dill for flavoring ($12.75), and Mongolian lamb chops flavored with apricot and teriyaki sauce ($16.75). A reasonably priced supper menu is available after theatre. Hint: On a cold winter's evening you might enjoy hot mulled wine—Pouilly Fuisse spiced with cloves, cinnamon, nutmeg, lemon, honey, and toasted hazel nuts ($2.75). Yum!

DIMITRI**

152 Columbus Avenue (67th)
Reservations: 787-7306
Credit Cards: AE, CB, DC, MC, V
Inexpensive to Moderate

In three years, John Venduras and chef Dimitri Phillippis have made their place a star in the Lincoln Center area. And why not? Dimitri's is handsome, the food consistently good, and the prices are a cut below comparable places on the upper West Side. Everything is a la carte (scalloped potatoes and vegetables come with the entrees), and the specialties include escargots forestière, mushroom caps stuffed with snails in garlic parsley butter ($4.50), Greek spinach pie ($2.75), whole red snapper skaras, a Greek method of open grilling ($10.50), and, for something light, an excellent spinach, bacon, and mushroom salad at $4.

FIORELLO'S**

1900 Broadway (63rd)
Reservations not accepted (595-5330)
Credit Cards: AE, MC, V
Inexpensive

Colorful, modern, and attractive, Fiorello's is a deservedly popular restaurant in the Lincoln Center area. No reservations are taken, but you are plied with free wine until a table is free, a nice touch. Good pastas, various veal and chicken dishes, and fresh fish are offered from $6.50 to $8.95. Pizza is available after the theatre. If you want something light, there's a cobb salad at $6.75 with sliced chicken, lettuce, avocado, bacon, and blue cheese that makes a delicious entree. In the late spring and summer, Fiorello's also has a sidewalk café.

 **THE GINGER MAN****

51 West 64th Street
Reservations: 399-2358
Credit Cards: AE, CB, DC, MC
Moderate to Expensive
Daily, 12 noon–1 a.m.

    The first of many restaurants created by actor Patrick O'Neal (he was starring in *The Ginger Man,* at the time) and his brother, Mike, this is one of the oldest watering holes in the Lincoln Center area. It's attractive: high-ceilings, brickwalls hung with interesting paintings and posters, and a comfortable, well-tended bar. After the theatre, burgers and omelettes are served. The salads are excellent, particuarly the salad of endive, arugula, walnuts, and oranges ($3.95). Dinner entrees fall in the $12–$16 price range. Traditional jazz groups perform throughout the week. The restaurant has lost one of its larger rooms in a landlord dispute, so make sure you have reservations if you're coming in the busy hours.

GRAND TIER RESTAURANT*

Metropolitan Opera House
Reservations: 799-3400
Credit Cards: AE, CB, DC, MC, V
Moderate to Expensive   Open two hours before curtain

    You can dine elegantly here on the grand tier level of the Met under the Chagall tapestries and the chandeliers that the Austrian government gave to the opera. The continental menu seems a bit pricy, but the ambiance makes up the difference. Note: The Grand Tier is open only when the Met has an evening performance, and reservations are a must.

MAESTRO CAFÉ*

58 West 65th Street
Reservations: 787-5990
Credit Cards: AE, DC, MC, V
Moderate

    The Maestro is a handsome new entry in the area: well-planned space, lots of trees, plants, and flowers, and, to underscore its name, enlargements of excellent candid photographs of leading maestros. The menu offers no surprises (possible exception: soft shell crabs in season at $10.25) and ranges from burgers and quiche ($4.95) up to a filet mignon au poivre ($13.50). The quality is generally excellent and the service attentive.

MILESTONE**

70 West 68th Street
Reservations: Not accepted (874-3679)
No credit cards
Inexpensive   Tuesday–Friday, 5 p.m.–10:45 p.m.; Saturday, 5 p.m.–12 midnight; closed
            Sunday and Monday

    Here's a delightful seafood restaurant an easy walk from Lincoln Center, and, wonder of wonders, it isn't decorated in standard seafood-restaurant blue, white, and fish nets. Filet of sole is $6.95, bluefish or sea trout, $5.95. Other fish entrees at comparable prices include beer batter shrimp, sea scallops, Boston scrod, and whiting with a black bean sauce. There are pork chops ($8.95) and several variations on a chicken theme, but seafood's the thing. Mushrooms à la greque make a nice appetizer, and you may want to close with homemade walnut pie. Wine and beer only. No reservations are taken so allow extra time if you're coming before the theatre.

O'NEALS' BALOON**

48 West 63rd Street
Reservations: 399-2353
Credit Cards: AE, DC, MC, V
Inexpensive

Right across Eighth Avenue from Lincoln Center, the bar and most of the tables in this informal watering hole afford an excellent view. Sit at the bar, enjoy a Guinness or a Pauli Girl and watch the center come alive; a handsome, large Hourdeau clock, thoughtfully set five minutes fast, will make sure you get to the Beaumont on time. Patrick O'Neal, the actor and successful restaurateur, originally planned to call this O'Neals' Saloon, but when it opened a decade or so ago he found it was illegal to call a New York saloon a saloon— *autres temps, autres mores!*—so he changed one letter in the sign and, *voila!*, the Baloon. The food is light and good—chili con carne with sour cream and onions ($3.95); a range of burgers from $3.95 to $4.95; quiche, fried shrimp, smoked trout, and several daily specials all usually under the $10 mark. As you enter, there is a very well-executed mural of the New York City Ballet Company. The Baloon is a very "in" place, particularly with ballet dancers.

ORLOFF'S*

1900 Broadway (63rd)
Reservations: 724-1800
Credit Cards: AE, DC, MC, V
Inexpensive

If it's deli you crave, here is a big, attractive place right across Broadway from Lincoln Center, its extensive menu offering all your favorites. A corned beef or pastrami sandwich is $4.25; combinations $1 or so more. The Nova Scotia salmon is excellent; with cream cheese on a bagel it's $6.50. For true New Yorkers, Dr. Brown's celery tonic is available at 75¢. After the theatre, homemade blintzes are an excellent choice. Counter and table service are available, and there is a large takeout department.

THE SALOON**

1920 Broadway (64th)
Reservations: 874-1500
Credit Cards: AE, DC, MC, V
Inexpensive to Moderate

Unlike the Baloon which looks like a saloon, the Saloon has a look all its own. As you come in, a small bar overlooks the high-ceilinged dining area, draped fabric overhead suggests Japanese kites, its brick walls are decorated with stunning photographs of Paris. It's a big enough place for the waiter to wear roller skates—and they do. Strangely, it's not disturbing; they glide soundlessly. A word of warning: If you pause to read the menu and the attached list of chef's specials you'll miss your curtain: if you've heard of it, they cook it here, plus a lot of things you've never heard of. Try the fresh manicotti of three cheeses, baked with a fresh plum tomato sauce with a melange of seafoods, $11.95, or the Saloon's fritti misti: bay scallops, squid, shrimp and cauliflower, zucchini, broccoli, and mushrooms, all deep-fried and served with salsa fresca, $11.95. The salads are exceptionally good—fresh, imaginative, and generous. For dessert, try either the Mississippi mudcake or the shoo-fly pie with ground hazelnuts. There's a sidewalk café in the warm months, also served by those trim people on roller skates.

 SWEETWATER'S**

170 Amsterdam Avenue (67th)
Reservations: 873-4100
Credit Cards: AE, DC, CB, MC, V
Inexpensive   Entertainment: Tuesday–Saturday, 10 p.m.–2 a.m.

You can dine here before the theatre (if you do, you get free parking at the Lincoln Towers garage at 69th and West End), but the big attraction is the entertainment: blues groups, modern jazz, calypso. (The Ink Spots played a recent engagement here.) A big, modern room with a good sound system, Sweetwater's serves a basically Italian cuisine with the usual pasta, veal, and chicken specialties. There are some light meals—burgers, salads, and the like—in the $4.95–$7.75 range. After the entertainment starts, there's a $10 minimum in the dining room. No minimum at the raised bar, however, and you can see and hear just fine.

TAVERN ON THE GREEN***

Central Park at West 67th Street
Reservations: 873-3200
Credit Cards: AE, DC, CB, MC, V
Expensive

This isn't just a restaurant, it's a production—a production that succeeds beautifully. The man responsible is Warner Le Roy. Fresh from a resounding hit with his East Side Maxwell's Plum, he took over the century-old building in 1969 and completely redid it. It's big: 60 cooks can feed more than 500 diners with no difficulty, and the various areas can be combined, which is one reason the place gets its share of opening parties, including those for Liza Minelli's *The Act, I Remember Mama, Dancin'*, and *A Chorus Line*. My choice for dining is the new Crystal Room, a glass pavilion that looks out on Sheep Meadow and the new landscaped terrace garden. There are 10 chandeliers that were originally made for Indian princes in the last century. In the winter, the bare trees decorated with some 150,000 tiny lights make you feel you're in *The Nutcracker*. In the summer, enjoy a drink on the terrace. It will make the city seem 100 miles away. The food is appropriate to the sumptuousness—basically an American menu, a la carte, carefully prepared and well-presented. Oysters, served warm with white butter ($4.50) are an interesting variation, and the basket of crudite for two ($8.50) is another good curtain-raiser. The fish is fresh, the beef excellent. Broiled red snapper with dijonnaise sauce is $13.95; a filet mignon with bearnaise sauce, $16.50. The hazelnut cheesecake with strawberries ($2.95) or any of the fresh fruits are recommended. A thoughtful touch: if you have young children in tow or are watching your budget, the dinner menu has a cheeseburger and a club sandwich, both at $5.95, and your waiter won't give you a haughty look if you order one. If you enjoy seeing celebrities—and who doesn't?—you won't be disappointed here: Many Broadway stars are regulars.

TOP OF THE PARK*

Gulf & Western Plaza (Columbus Circle)
Reservations: 333-3800
Credit Cards: AE, CB, DC, MC, V
Moderate to Expensive

From the 43rd floor of the Gulf & Western building the view is spectacular, and the surroundings appropriately luxurious. From the large cocktail lounge you look west to New Jersey and north; from the candlelit dining room the view across the park to the east is breathtaking. The complete dinners range from baked stuffed double rib pork chop with brandied prunes at $16.95, to the chef's special at $21.50: a brace of quail roasted with vine leaves and garnished with onions, carrots, and herbs. A nice selection of appetizers and desserts round out the meal. An easy 10-minute walk from Lincoln Center, the Top of the Park is well worth a visit, particularly on a clear night.

UPPER WEST SIDE

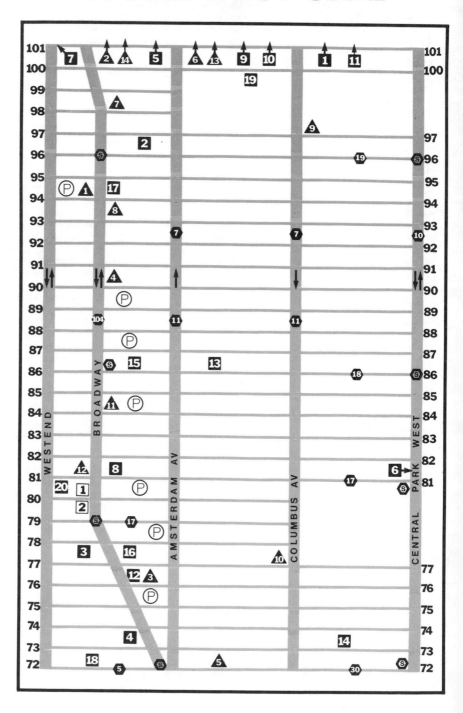

■ Theatres

1. Aaron Davis Hall at City College/134 and Convent
2. American Folk Theatre/214 West 97
3. American Lyric Theatre Workshop/236 West 78
4. American Musical Dramatic Academy Theatre/2109 Broadway
5. Cathedral of St. John the Divine/1047 Amsterdam
6. Delacorte Theatre/Central Park at 81st
7. Equity Library Theatre/310 Riverside Drive
8. The Family, Inc./251 West 80
9. Frank Silvera Writers' Workshop/317 West 125
10. Minor Latham Playhouse/606 West 120
11. Phoenix Theatre/54 Nagle
12. The Priory/2162 Broadway
13. Riverside Shakespeare Company/165 West 86
14. The Second Stage/23 West 73
15. Seventh Sign Theatre/263 West 86
16. Seventy-eighth Street Theatre Lab/236 West 78
17. Symphony Space/2537 Broadway
18. The Theatre Within/247 West 72
19. Trinity Theatre/164 West 100
20. Westside Repertory Theatre/252 West 81

▲ Restaurants

1. At Our Place/2527 Broadway
2. Au Grenier Café/2868 Broadway
3. Broadway Bay/2178 Broadway
4. Chun Cha Fu/2450 Broadway
5. Éclair/141 West 72
6. The Green Tree/1034 Amsterdam
7. Hunan Balcony/2596 Broadway
8. Hunan 94/2510 Broadway
9. Mikell's/760 Columbus
10. Museum Café/366 Columbus
11. Szechuan Taste/2332 Broadway
12. Teacher's/2249 Broadway
13. The Terrace/400 West 119
14. West End/2911 Broadway

□ Other Attractions

1. Bloomsday 2 Bookstore/ 2259 Broadway
2. Zabar's/2245 Broadway

⑰ Bus Numbers

Ⓢ Subway Stations

Ⓟ Parking

→ One-way Street

⇄ Two-way Street

This is theatre country: Actors' Equity once checked and found that more of its members live here than anywhere else. Certainly it is convenient to the theatre district, and the subway is a quick, direct access to the Village and SoHo. The lifestyle on the Upper West Side is more informal, more overtly intellectual, less business-oriented than on the East Side. (You feel a little out of things on the Upper West Side if you're not connected with the arts; on the East Side you feel that way if you are.) There is a lot of theatre activity here, as the map indicates. Even more interesting is the disproportionate number of theatre companies without permanent performance spaces that are based here. It would seem you could cast a show successfully on any block in the West Eighties. It's a shame in a way that the title has been used because the story of theatre in the city could well be entitled *West Side Story.*

THEATRES

AARON DAVIS HALL AT CITY COLLEGE

134th Street and Convent Avenue

Box Office:	690-4100
Box Office Hours:	10 a.m.–5 p.m., if performance
Credit Cards:	None Personal checks
Group Sales:	Through box office
Season:	October–May
Total Seating:	Leonard Davis Performing Arts Center (three theatres), 750; 300; 75.
Stage Type:	Proscenium stages
	AC
	Handicapped: Semi-accessible

Professor Bernard Jackson of the drama department presents student productions, including the George Wolfe musical *Summer's Sons,* Douglas Taylor's *The Agreement,* and Genet's *The Blacks,* in the various spaces here.

AMERICAN FOLK THEATER
Holy Name House

214 West 97th

Owner:	Holy Name Church
Box Office:	799-9190
Box Office Hours:	One hour before curtain
Credit Cards:	None TDF Vouchers
Group Sales:	Dick Garfield (787-1900)
Season:	Subscription series, spring; other activities year-round
Total Seating:	100–150
Stage Type:	Flexible open space
	No AC
	Handicapped: No access

In a converted gymnasium, artistic director Dick Garfield and his multiethnic company present revivals (James Baldwin's *Blues for Mister Charlie,* Langston Hughes's *Mulatto*), new plays, and, in the spring, children's theatre. Mr. Garfield describes the company's style as "direct and simply produced, story-telling theater."

AMERICAN LYRIC THEATRE WORKSHOP

236 West 78th Street

Box Office: 595-0850
Box Office Hours: Wednesday–Sunday, 6 p.m.–9 p.m.
Credit Cards: None TDF Vouchers
Group Sales: Through box office
Total Seating: 90 and 30 in second-floor theatre
Stage Type: Thrust stage, Proscenium stage (second-floor theatre)
  AC
  Handicapped: Semi-accessible

At this training and performance center, advanced actors are provided a bridge between closed laboratory workshops and public performances. In the spring of 1981, the workshop was presenting Israel Horwitz's *Primary English Class* and Meir Riblow's *Irish Coffee*. Mark Zeller is the artistic director of the five-year-old workshop.

AMERICAN MUSICAL DRAMATIC
ACADEMY THEATRE

2109 Broadway (73rd)

Box Office: 787-5300
Box Office Hours: One hour before performance (answering machine)
Credit Cards: Varies with production
Group Sales: Through box office
Total Seating: 70
Stage Type: Proscenium stage
  Handicapped: Semi-accessible

This theatre, in the landmark Ansonia apartment building, is rented out when not used by the Academy, the only institution in the city offering a two-year program in musical theatre education. Gryphon Theatricals, Inc., under the direction of William J. Lentsch and Maryellen Flynn, recently used the theatre to present *The Story of the Gadsbys,* a previously unproduced play by Rudyard Kipling.

CATHEDRAL OF ST. JOHN THE DIVINE

1047 Amsterdam Avenue

Box Office: 9 a.m.–5 p.m.
Credit Cards: Varies with performance
Group Sales: Through box office
Total Seating: Up to 3,000
Stage Type: Church interior
  No AC
  Handicapped: Semi-accessible

This is the world's largest (and latest) Gothic cathedral, and it affords a spectacular setting and excellent acoustics for certain types of productions. Work began on St. John the Divine in 1892 and the exterior isn't finished yet. Recent presentations include *Music for a Great Space, Bread and Puppet Theater,* and the *Play of Daniel.*

DELACORTE THEATER
Free Shakespeare in the Park
Central Park
Near Central Park West and 81st Street

Box Office: 535-5630
Box Office Hours: Tuesday–Sunday, 6:30 p.m.–8 p.m., if performance
Total Seating: 1,936
Season: Late June–mid-August
Stage Type: Thrust stage
Handicapped: Semi-accessible

This theatre opened in 1962 to house the New York Shakespeare Festival's productions of Free Shakespeare in the Park. The opening production was George C. Scott in *The Merchant of Venice,* and the opening night performance was telecast locally. In 1971, the John Guare and Mel Shapiro adaptation of *Two Gentlemen of Verona* moved from the Delacorte to Broadway (and a Tony Award), as did *Much Ado About Nothing* the following year. Raul Julia and Meryl Streep starred in a memorable production of *The Taming of the Shrew,* and a documentary film based on the production, *Kiss Me Petruchio,* was highly praised. Some other recent productions: *Othello, Coriolanus, All's Well That Ends Well,* and, in a departure from the traditional Shakespearean fare, Gilbert and Sullivan's *The Pirates of Penzance* with Linda Ronstadt, Kevin Kline, and George Rose was presented in 1980 and quickly moved to Broadway. I had the good fortune to see it in the park on a warm June night and as the plot unfolded a full moon slowly rose in the sky behind the stage. Unforgettable. Come early as the lines are usually long. The more crafty bring picnics to enjoy while they wait for the box office to open.

EQUITY LIBRARY THEATRE
310 Riverside Drive (103rd)

Box Office: 663-2028
Box Office Hours: 11 a.m.–9 p.m., if performance
Admission: Free, but contributions are accepted
Groups: Through box office
Season: September–May
Total Seating: 273 (Orchestra, 273; Standing room, 20)
Stage Type: Proscenium with partial thrust
No AC
Handicapped: Semi-accessible

This unique showcase theatre was founded in 1943 by Actors' Equity in association with the New York Public Library with two objectives: to create new audiences by developing a love of the theatre among those who can't afford to attend commercial productions, and to showcase artists to people in casting positions. It started out in the Lenox Hill Playhouse and moved to the Master Theatre here in 1961. Over the years, the Equity Library Theatre has become the most respected professional showcase in the nation, and more than 60 percent of the artists appearing in productions here have gotten parts as a direct result of their participation. The Equity Library Theatre has been a stepping stone for the careers of Charlton Heston, James Earle Jones, Richard Kiley, Jason Robards, Jr., Kim Stanley, Rod Steiger, Jo Van Fleet, and Freda Payne. Romance blossomed here for Anne Jackson and Eli Wallach and Ann Meara and Jerry Stiller. Extensive work is done here with community groups and area educational institutions.

"Every now and then, when you're on stage, you hear the best sound a player can hear. It's a sound you can't get in movies or in television. It is the sound of a wonderful, deep silence that means you've hit them where they live."

SHELLEY WINTERS

THE FAMILY, INC.
All Angels Church
251 West 80th Street

Box Office: 947-7193
Box Office Hours: Monday–Friday, 10 a.m.–6 p.m.; Saturday, 1 p.m.–5 p.m.
Credit Cards: None
Group Sales: Through box office
Total Seating: 130
Stage Type: Flexible stage
No AC
Handicapped: No access

Artistic director and company founder Marvin Felix Camillo was instrumental in the development of the hit *Short Eyes* and directed it at the Vivian Beaumont. His 10-year-old company moved to this church two years ago, and has presented such productions as Chekhov's *The Marriage Proposal* and *The Crucifixion,* based on a poem by James Weldon Johnson. The Family, Inc., regularly performs out-of-doors in the summer at Lincoln Center.

FRANK SILVERA WRITERS' WORKSHOP
317 West 125th Street

Box Office: 662-8463
Box Office Hours: Monday–Saturday, 10 a.m.–6 p.m.
Admission: A donation of $3.50 is suggested at showcases; readings are free
Group Sales: 662-8463
Season: September–June
Total Seating: 125
Stage Type: Flexible open space
Handicapped: No access

This workshop is a living memorial to the late Frank Silvera whose Theatre of Being in Los Angeles was active in nurturing black artists and producing black plays. Founded in 1973 by Garland Lee Thompson, the workshop now has a series of Monday-evening readings and Saturday-afternoon laboratory showcases. These are geared to the needs of each playwright and provide a session of critique following each reading. The workshop also sponsors a series of playwriting seminars conducted by such artists as Adrienne Kennedy, Richard Wesley, Owen Dodson, and Alice Childress. Recent productions include *Inacent Black and the Five Brothers* by A. Marcus Hemphill; *No Left Turn* by Buriel Clay II; and *Investments* by Ruth Ce. Jones.

MINOR LATHAM PLAYHOUSE
Barnard College
606 West 120th Street

Box Office: 280-2079
Box Office Hours: One hour before performance
Credit Cards: None
Group Sales: Through box office
Season: October–May
Total Seating: 179 (Orchestra, 127; Balcony, 52)
Stage Type: Proscenium stage
No AC
Handicapped: Semi-accessible

This theatre is used primarily by the drama department of Barnard College. Two of artistic director Kenneth Janis's 1980–81 productions were Gilbert and Sullivan's *Princess Ida* and Synge's *Playboy of the Western World.*

PHOENIX THEATRE

YM-YWHA of Washington Heights and Inwood
54 Nagel Avenue

Box Office: 569-6200
Box Office Hours: One hour before performance (also answering machine: 9 a.m.–5 p.m.)
Credit Cards: None   TDF Vouchers   Personal checks
Group Sales: Through box office
Total Seating: 300
Stage Type: Arena stage
AC
Handicapped: Semi-accessible

Built as a theatre 10 years ago, the Phoenix has been used by a number of companies: most recently, a Russian company doing classic Russian plays. In the spring of 1981, a resident company was in the process of formation.

THE PRIORY

2162 Broadway (76th)

Box Office: 362-2845
Box Office Hours: Tuesday–Saturday, 10 a.m.–8 p.m.; Sunday, 10 a.m.–3 p.m.
Credit Cards: None TDF Vouchers Personal checks
Group Sales: Through box office
Total Seating: 160
Stage Type: Proscenium stage
AC
Handicapped: Semi-accessible

This theatre is in the Hotel Opera, a tower filled with luxury apartments. The building was built about 60 years ago atop a cloister left from the 1800s. The cloister was a cabaret and nightclub when the building was the elegant Manhattan Towers. The building declined and became a welfare hotel, and the nightclub/cabaret fell into disuse. It had a brief life in the late 1960s as the Promenade, and *Godspell* performed here. Early in 1981, it was being rebuilt by Marcel Schmid's MSO Productions. When in operation, the Priory will present a variety of shows including original musicals, children's theatre, theatre for the deaf, and performances for cable TV. In other theatres, MSO Productions has done *A Taste of Honey* and a children's show, *Amazing Bone.*

RIVERSIDE SHAKESPEARE COMPANY
West Park Presbyterian Church

165 West 86th Street

Box Office: 877-6810
Box Office Hours: One hour before curtain
Credit Cards: None   TDF Vouchers   Personal checks
Group Sales: Through box office
Season: Year-round (tours city parks in July and August)
Total Seating: 85
Stage Type: Open 50-foot-wide stage
No AC
Handicapped: No access

The city's only year-round Shakespeare company moved here in November, 1980, and a happy move it was: No seat is more than 15 feet from the large, wide stage. Under artistic director W. Stuart McDowell the company's forte has been the Bard "in the spirit of how it was originally done." The company did an uncut *Hamlet* by torchlight outdoors at Columbia in 1978, a sunset *Romeo and Juliet;* indoor productions are often done in an American milieu: *Much Ado About Nothing* in a 1920s setting; *As You Like It* in 1770 Colonial America. The goal of Mr. McDowell and executive director Gloria Skurski: to build a modern Globe Theatre on the banks of the Hudson River.

THE SECOND STAGE (TOMI THEATER)

23 West 73rd Street

Owner: Theatre Opera Music Institute, Inc.
Box Office: 787-3980
Box Office Hours: Daily, 1 p.m.–6 p.m.
Credit Cards: None   TDF Vouchers
Group Sales: Jonathan Silver 787-3980; Monday–Tuesday, 10 a.m.–5 p.m.;
Wednesday, 3 p.m.–6 p.m.
Total Seating: 100–150
Stage Type: Open flexible stage
AC
Handicapped: Semi-accessible

This theatre is a 16th-floor penthouse with terraces overlooking the Dakota and Central Park. It was the ballroom when the building was a hotel in the 1930s and 1940s. Leasing it is the Second Stage, a company committed to producing plays of the last 10 years that, in its opinion, deserve another chance. Artistic directors Robyn Goodman and Carole Rothman point out that with the help of different actors, directors, and designers, a neglected play can be illuminated. "We are not a revival house," they say. "We are interested in keeping contemporary literature alive." Recent productions have included Michael Weller's *Split*, starring Brooke Adams; Amlin Gray's *How I Got That Story*, starring Bob Gunton and Daniel Stern; *In Trousers*, a musical by William Finn; and *Fishing* by Michael Weller.

SEVENTH SIGN THEATRE
Church of St. Paul and St. Andrew

263 West 86th Street

Box Office: 874-9317
Box Office Hours: Monday–Friday, 7 p.m.–10 p.m.; Saturday, 10 a.m.–5 p.m.;
Sunday, 1 p.m.–11 p.m.
Credit Cards: None   TDF Vouchers
Group Sales: Through box office
Season: September–December, February–May
Total Seating: 75 (varies with production)
Stage Type: Flexible open space
No AC
Handicapped: Semi-accessible

Artistic director Anthony Osnato has been concentrating on period American comedy here; John Patrick's *Lo and Behold* and John Van Druten's *I've Got Sixpence* were highlights of the 1980–81 season.

SEVENTY-EIGHTH STREET THEATRE LAB

236 West 78th Street

Box Office: 595-0850
Box Office Hours: Wednesday–Sunday, 6 p.m.–10:30 p.m.; no advance sale
Credit Cards: None   TDF Vouchers   Personal checks
Group Sales: Through box office with letter of agreement
Total Seating: 74
Stage Type: Center stage arena
AC
Handicapped: Semi-accessible

When the American Lyric Theatre Workshop moved into this converted loft in 1977, it changed its name but not its intent: to develop new productions with the hope of moving them to larger theatres. Some of the productions created under the artistic direction of Mark Zeller are Mary Gallagher's *Little Bird*; Meredith Miller's *Josie*; *The Sun Always Shines for the Cool* by Miguel Pinero; and *Say Goodnight, Gracie*, directed by Austin Pendleton. Spring 1981 productions included Israel Horovitz's *The Primary English Class*, William Inge's *Come Back, Little Sheba*, and *The Other Cinderella*.

SYMPHONY SPACE

2537 Broadway (95th)

Box Office: 865-2557
Box Office Hours: Varies with production
Credit Cards: None   TDF Vouchers   Personal checks
Group Sales: Each producer handles own sales
Season: September–May
Total Seating: 920 (Orchestra, 720; Balcony, 200; Standing room, 50)
Stage Type: Proscenium stage
AC
Handicapped: Semi-accessible

This theatre started out in 1910 as the Crystal Carnival Skating Rink and then was the Symphony movie house from the early 1930s until 1977. Allan Miller and Isaiah Sheffer converted the Art Deco building to a legitimate theatre in 1978. Recent productions have included the satirical musical revue *Late City Edition,* Eve Merriam's *Dialogue for Lovers,* based on the sonnets of Shakespeare and starring Estelle Parsons and Fritz Weaver, and several Gilbert and Sullivan light operas.

THE THEATRE WITHIN

247 West 72nd Street

Box Office: 799-1847
Box Office Hours: Monday–Saturday, 9 a.m.–8 p.m.
Credit Cards: None   TDF Vouchers   Personal checks
Group Sales: Through box office
Season: October–May
Total Seating: 50
Stage Type: Theatre in the round
Handicapped: Semi-accessible

Alec Rubin, who founded this group in the late 1960s, describes it as "concerned with gut-level commitment . . . theatre based on human feeling." Mr. Rubin also heads the Primal Theatre Workshop, which is associated with the Theatre Within and is "an extension of the Stanislavskian approach." The most noted recent production at the Theatre Within was *Y Is a Crooked Letter,* starring Al Pacino.

TRINITY THEATRE
Trinity Lutheran Church

164 West 100th Street

Box Office: 222-6641
Box Office Hours: 1 p.m.–5 p.m.; also 1 p.m.–10 p.m., if performance
Group Sales: Through box office
Total Seating: 96
Stage Type: Flexible stage
No AC
Handicapped: No access

Artistic director Wendy Kaufman's group has completed three seasons in the basement of this church; 1980–81 productions included Howard Richardson's *Dark of the Moon* and John Ford's *The Broken Heart.*

WESTSIDE REPERTORY THEATRE

252 West 81st Street

Box Office: 666-3521
Box Office Hours: Tuesday–Wednesday, 6 p.m.–8:30 p.m.; Friday–Sunday, 6 p.m.–8 p.m.
Credit Cards: None   TDF Vouchers   Personal checks
Group Sales: Through box office
Season: October–May (theatre in use year-round)
Total Seating: 38
Stage Type: Proscenium stage
AC
Handicapped: Semi-accessible

Under the artistic direction of Andres Castro, this group presents such classics as Shaw's *Candide*, Molière's *The Miser*, and Oscar Wilde's *An Ideal Husband*.

"Every actor in his heart believes everything bad that's printed about him."

ORSON WELLES

"Not to go to the theater is like making one's toilet without a mirror."

SCHOPENHAUER

"Many plays—certainly mine—are like blank checks. The actors and directors put their signatures on them."

THORNTON WILDER

RESTAURANTS AND NIGHTSPOTS

AT OUR PLACE*

2527 Broadway (94th)
Reservations: 864-1410
Credit Cards: AE, MC, V
Moderate

This used to be the Cleopatra, a handsome restaurant with not-so-good Middle Eastern food. It reopened (a 'u' added to the letters of the Cleopatra sign and it became, anagramically, At Our Place) with the same terracotta-colored interior and triangular booths but with much better Middle Eastern food. Now it's a hit. This is a good place for vegetarians, especially if you like eggplant. For dessert, try the apricot pudding ($1.25). A meal here should cost $5–$12 per person. A good choice if you're going to the Symphony Space Theatre or the Thalia, that 50-year-old movie house famous for its revivals of classics.

AU GRENIER CAFÉ*

2868 Broadway (111th)
Reservations: 666-3052
Credit Cards: AE, MC, V
Inexpensive to Moderate   Closed Christmas and New Year's Day

If you like wine and aren't too hungry, this may be the answer. Up a flight of stairs you find a small, attractive, triangular room with paneling and large mirrors. The bar stocks more than 50 wines, including sherry and port but no hard liquor. Daily wine specials are available by the glass ($1.75–$3) and are listed on a blackboard. Predictable French entrees vary daily and range from $6 to $10 at lunch and a bit more at dinner. A good alternative is the $5 platter with cheeses, fruits, cold cuts, or pâté. The pastries ($2–$2.75) make a nice finish.

BROADWAY BAY*

2178 Broadway (76th)
Reservations: 362-5234
Credit Cards: AE, DC, MC, V
Inexpensive to Moderate   Sunday from 3 p.m.

The great buy here is the one-pound lobster special at $6.95, which includes a cup of chowder and either potatoe or corn on the cob. Other fish entrees are fresh and good. Linguini mixed with different seafoods is $5.50. There's steak and veal, but why come here for meat? Try something unusual and moderately priced in wine here: the Pinot Grigio or the Corvo Bianco. As for dessert, the banana cream pie is worthy of special mention ($2.50).

CHINESE RESTAURANTS OF UPPER BROADWAY

SZECHUAN TASTE* (873-6655)
2332 Broadway (84th)

CHUN CHA FU** (362-2200)
2450 Broadway (90th)

HUNAN 94** (864-4077)
2510 Broadway (94th)

HUNAN BALCONY** (865-0400)
2596 Broadway (98th)

Next to Chinatown itself, upper Broadway has the largest concentration of Chinese restaurants, at least 25 in the one-mile stretch from 84th to 104th Streets. Here are four of the best: Chun Cha Fu, a favorite of Yul Brynner; Hunan Balcony, worth a special trip; Hunan 94, where the vegetables are superb; and one of the oldest, Szechuan Taste. Most don't accept reservations or credit cards, and some don't sell wine or beer, though you may bring your own. Dinners usually are in the $4–$10 range, and it's fun to come in a big group and

166

sample a number of entrees. Call ahead for the details, then line up with the actors, students, artists, and writers of the Upper West Side for some fine dining. Caution: If you're going to the theatre after dinner, allow for some extra time in case there's a long wait.

ÉCLAIR**

141 West 72nd Street
Reservations: 873-7700
Credit Cards: AE, MC, V
Inexpensive to Moderate

The Austro-Hungarian Empire is gone, but the cuisine is alive and well here—especially the cake. The Opera Cake, with almonds, filberts, and hazelnuts, is worth an aria all by itself. Places like this are called *Konditoreis* in the old country, and if you come in the late afternoon you'll be sitting next to elderly women from the neighborhood chatting away in Middle European accents, sipping coffee or mocha, and eating strudel and other delightful pastries ($1–$2.50). Throw caution to the winds and stop by the front counter on your way out and pick up something to bring home.

THE GREEN TREE**

1034 Amsterdam Avenue (111th)
Reservations: 864-9106
No credit cards
Inexpensive   Closed Sundays, Thanksgiving, Christmas, and New Year's Day

If you're seeing a production at St. John the Divine, across the street is this little treasure of a Hungarian restaurant, a godsend for years to poor but discriminating Columbia students. A complete meal with cold cherry soup, stuffed cabbage on a garnished plate, apple strudel, and coffee will cost you about $7, including tax and tip. Next door is the Hungarian Pastry Shop, a decidedly bohemian small café with some of the city's best strudel, sachertorte, and other pastries. Also a bargain.

♫) MIKELL'S**

760 Columbus Avenue (97th)
Reservations; 864-8832
Credit Cards: AE, MC, V
Moderate   Closed Sunday

Before Columbus in the 90s was fashionable, Mikell's was here and had earned a reputation for good jazz and honest, southern-style cooking. This is a hangout for jazz artists and recording industry executives. (Name performers like Sarah Vaughn or Stevie Wonder have turned up unannounced and sung here.) Some of the best new acts around are booked in here, along with old favorites such as Hugh Maskella. With success came a cover charge and the need for reservations. Still a bargain at a $3 weekday and $5 weekend cover plus a two-drink minimum. Or use the minimum against dining: Skip the appetizers and enjoy fried chicken or pork chops. Entrees range from $8 to $15.

MUSEUM CAFÉ**

366 Columbus Avenue (77th)
Reservations: 724-7509
Credit Cards: AE, MC, V
Inexpensive to Moderate   Closed Christmas

Columbus Avenue, from 66th to 97th, has become our version of the Boulevard St. Germain in Paris, lined with charming restaurants and cafés, boutiques and novelty shops, mimes and buskers. The Museum Café, across Columbus from the Museum of Natural History, is one of the best bets. A glass-enclosed sidewalk café area offers an excellent view and an array of fresh fish, quiches, salads, and burgers, as well as more substantial entrees. (Most everything is in the $4–$10 price range.) Many of the staff are out-of-work actors and actresses—if there were a theatre job for everyone who wanted one, half of the city's restaurants would be self-service—and with the kitchen open until two in the morning it's a good place for a late bite. Certainly Linda Ronstadt, Kevin Kline, and other members of the *Pirates of Penzance* cast thought so after a performance at the nearby Delacorte Theatre in Central Park.

TEACHER'S*

2249 Broadway (81st)
Reservations: 787-3500
Credit Cards: AE, DC, MC, V
Moderate

This is an agreeable, busy restaurant with a young crowd, including many—you guessed it!—teachers. No surprises on the blackboard menu: burgers up to steaks, fish, veal, and daily specials, ranging from $3.50 to $13, and all well-prepared. This is where Bernadine Dohrn, the 1960s Weatherman, worked as a waitress for 10 years while the FBI searched for her. It also is where Clive Barnes, who lives around the corner on West End, frequently eats. Stop by; who knows whom you'll see?

THE TERRACE**

Butler Hall
400 West 119th Street
Reservations: 666-9490
Credit Cards: AE, MC, V
Expensive   Closed Sunday, Monday, and two weeks in August

The view alone is worth the trip. Looking north or south on a clear night, you can see forever. The Terrace is atop a Columbia University residence hall and is the domain of Chef Dusan Bernic, an exponent of nouvelle cuisine. A popular appetizer is the puffy feuillete ($5.75). They have excellent fish, priced according to that day's market price. The filet de sole du gourmet, poached in vermouth, fish stock, mushrooms, herbs, and finished with crème fraiche and truffles, was $13.75 at a recent visit. Dessert wagon selections are $3.50 to $4.50. Plan on spending about $30 a person.

♫ THE WEST END CAFÉ**

2911 Broadway (114th)
Reservations: 666-8750
No credit cards
Inexpensive   Closed Christmas

Remember when you were in college how much fun it was to go to a real hangout, drink beer, and listen to live jazz. Like to do it again? Come on up to this big, bustling Columbia favorite and listen to some first-class old-timers play jazz of the 1930s and 1940s. You sit at long tables in the jazz room, eat (burgers and the like), drink, and be merry. Cover charge is a piddling $1.50 on weekdays, $3 on weekends. Call ahead or check the papers to see who is playing.

"I divide all productions into categories: those I like and those I don't like. I have no other criterion."

ANTON CHEKHOV

ZABAR'S***

2245 Broadway (80th)
787-2000
Credit Cards: AE
Daily until 7:30 p.m.; Saturday until 12 midnight
Bargain to Fabulously Expensive

This is food emporium as theatre, and if you're not a New Yorker, you've never seen anything like it. There are more varieties of everything in this large, crowded store than you would believe possible. Zabar's carries more than 100 types of cheese, plus biscuits, fresh baked breads, bagels, bialies, lox, caviar, chopped liver, pâté, pasta, croissants, and luncheon meats. Try the lemon or Romano chicken ($3.49 per pound), piroshki ($5.99 per pound), broccoli soufflé ($2.50 each), or any of dozens more tempters. Zabar's now has opened a bakery-café next door. Stop in for a capuccine ($1) and something sweet. This is the perfect place to stock your picnic basket before a concert in the park or theatre at the nearby Delacorte.

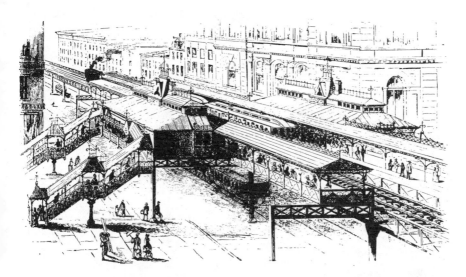

"You know, acting makes you feel like a burglar sometimes—taking all that money for all that fun."

PAT O'BRIEN

"Here [New York] the theatergoer is anxious to be surprised. He can take anything in his stride. At home, in London . . . the theater is something you do after dinner, and use it as a certain digestive pill."

KENNETH TYNAN

"A good many inconveniences attend playgoing in any large city. Certainly the greatest of them is usually the play itself."

KENNETH TYNAN

UPPER EAST SIDE

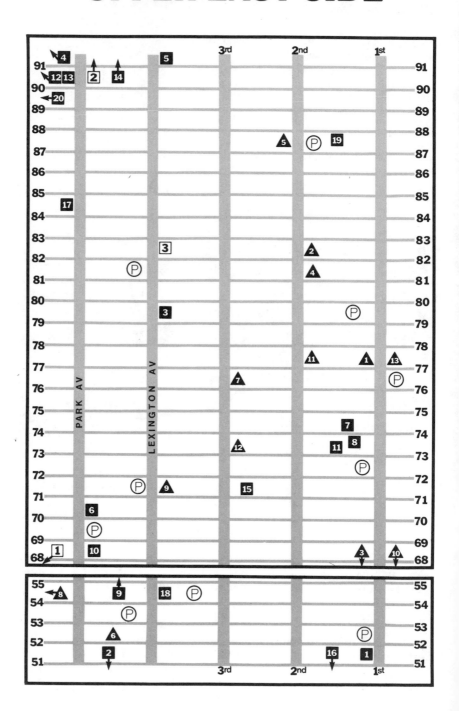

■ Theatres

1. A.A.T.C. Theatre/931 First Avenue
2. Actors Repertory Theatre/303 East 44
3. All Souls Players/1157 Lexington
4. AMAS Repertory Theatre/1 East 104
5. American Jewish Theatre/1395 Lexington
6. The Asia Society/725 Park
7. Cithaeron/351 East 74
8. Eastside Playhouse (Light Opera of Manhattan)/334 East 74
9. Folksbiene Playhouse/123 East 55
10. Hunter Playwrights/695 Park
11. Manhattan Theatre Club/321 East 73
12. National Black Theatre/9 East 125
13. New Heritage Repertory Theatre/43 East 125
14. 92nd Street YM-YWHA/1395 Lexington
15. Phoenix Theatre/221 East 71
16. St. Bart's Playhouse/109 East 50
17. Ten-Ten Players Theater/1010 Park
18. Theater of St. Peter's Church/619 Lexington
19. Theater of the Open Eye/316 East 88
20. York Players Company/2 East 90

▲ Restaurants

1. Catch a Rising Star/1487 First
2. The Comic Strip/1568 Second
3. Dangerfield's/1118 First
4. Divino Ristorante/1556 Second
5. Elaine's/1703 Second
6. Four Seasons/99 East 52
7. Jim McMullen/1341 Third
8. The King Cole/2 East 55
9. La Petite Ferme/973 Lexington
10. Maxwell's Plum/1181 First
11. Ristorante Signor Edmondo/1494 Second
12. Rusty's/1271 Third
13. Something Different/1488 First

□ Other Attractions

1. James Lowe Autographs, Ltd./667 Madison
2. Museum of the City of New York/Fifth at 103
3. Smolin Prints/1215 Lexington

⑰ Bus Numbers

Ⓢ Subway Stations

Ⓟ Parking

→ One-way Street

⇄ Two-way Street

The roots of theatre go deep in the East Side. While there isn't the intense activity of the Village or SoHo (due in part to relative real estate values), some of the oldest and most important theatres are here: the Manhattan Theatre Club, Light Opera of Manhattan, St. Bart's Playhouse, the Phoenix—all have a sense of permanency about them; they didn't arrive yesterday nor will they leave tomorrow. The theatres reflect the character of the East Side in other ways as well. They tend to deal in quality, in solid middle-class values. The untried remains untried here; one may appreciate the shock of the new, but not in one's own neighborhood. What the East Side has in abundance is intelligent theatregoers with the desire and affluence to see a lot of good theatre, wherever it may be.

THEATRES

ACADEMY ARTS THEATRE COMPANY
931 First Avenue (51st)

Owner: East Side International Center
Box Office: 4 p.m.–7 p.m., if performance
Credit Cards: None   TDF Vouchers   Personal checks
Group Sales: Through box office
Season: October–June
Total Seating: 100
Stage Type: Flexible open space
No AC
Handicapped: Semi-accessible (Shows are interpreted in sign language for deaf audience on request)

This company presenting new plays and musicals as well as the classics has produced some 80 productions in all since it was founded by artistic directors Robert and Bridget Cusack. Among the production highlights have been no less than 10 Agatha Christie revivals, and the New York premieres of Pat Staten's *Twister,* David Ives *Boarders,* David Libman's *Charlie and Belle and the Cat Box,* and David Storey's *In Celebration.* Recent productions: Rennick Steele's *Bring On the Night* and a new musical adaptation of *Snow White and the Seven Dwarfs,* adapted by Bridget Cusack. Incidentally, the East Side International Center stands on the spot where Nathan Hale expressed his regret that he had "only one life to give for his country."

ACTORS REPERTORY THEATRE
303 East 44th Street

Box Office: 687-0228
Box Office Hours: One hour before curtain
Credit Cards: None   TDF Vouchers   Personal checks
Group Sales: None
Total Seating: 89
Stage Type: Proscenium stage
AC
Handicapped: No access

In the spring of 1981, artistic director Warren Robertson moved his group to this former acting school and presented *Day's Grace* by John Fazakerley and *Toylands* by Lewis La-Rosso, both original productions.

ALL SOULS PLAYERS

1157 Lexington (81st)

Box Office: 535-5530
Box Office Hours: Two hours before performance
Credit Cards: None   TDF Vouchers   Personal checks
Group Sales: Through box office
Season: October–May
Total Seating: 99
Stage Type: Thrust or arena stage
No AC
Handicapped: No access

Since 1963, this church has housed an active theatre group doing 12 productions a year, three weekends each. In the spring of 1981, the group was presenting Pinter's *Old Times,* Shaw's *Androcles and the Lion,* the musical *Irma La Douce,* and *Carnival,* music and lyrics by Bob Merrill.

AMAS REPERTORY THEATRE

1 East 104th Street

Box Office: 369-8000
Box Office Hours: 10 a.m.–6 p.m., if performance
Credit Cards: None   TDF Vouchers   Personal checks (with ID)
Group Sales: Through box office
Season: September–June (summer street theatre tours)
Total Seating: 100 (Standing room, 100)
Stage Type: Thrust stage
No AC
Handicapped: Semi-accessible

This company, founded 10 years ago by Rosetta Le Noire, is devoted exclusively to the development of musical theatre; it also has been a pioneer in racial integration among theatre and their audiences. Here is professional showcase theatre at its best: *Bubbling Brown Sugar,* originally developed and produced here, has enjoyed successful runs on Broadway and in London. One of the objectives of AMAS (not an acroynm but Latin for "You Love") is to create a library of musical biographies. Past seasons have included new musicals based on the lives of such black artists as Bill (Bojangles) Robinson, Langston Hughes, Scott Joplin, Eubie Blake and Noble Sissle, and Ethel Waters. In 1978, AMAS was one of six national recipients of a special Kennedy Center Black Playwrights Award. The Eubie Blake Children's Theatre here is an important training center. Directors currently working at AMAS include William Mooney, Billie Allen, and Micki Grant. In the spring of 1981, AMAS was presenting the musical comedy *The Last Caravan,* by Samm-Art Williams.

AMERICAN JEWISH THEATRE

1395 Lexington Avenue (92nd)

Owner: The 92nd Street YM-YWHA
Box Office: 427-4410
Box Office Hours: 11 a.m.–8 p.m., if performance
Credit Cards: MC, V   CHARGIT   TDF Vouchers   Personal checks
Group Sales: Through box office
Season: September–June
Total Seating: 100
Stage Type: Thrust stage
AC
Handicapped: No access

The American Jewish Theatre presents five productions a subscription season ($32.50) under the supervision of managing director Michael Bavar and resident director Dan Held. The 1980–81 season started off with a special concert by Molly Picon, and included English-speaking productions of Paddy Chayefsky's *The Tenth Man; Cappella* by Israel Horovitz and David Boorstin; *The Music Keeper* by Andrea Ernotte and Elliot Tiber; Herman Wouk's *The Caine Mutiny Court-Martial,* and George Tabori's *Brecht on Brecht.* This series usually is sold out so it's wise to subscribe early.

ASIA SOCIETY
725 Park Avenue (70th)

Box Office:	371-4758
Box Office Hours:	Monday–Friday, 10 a.m.–5 p.m., plus pre-performance
Credit Cards:	None
Group Sales:	None
Total Seating:	258
Stage Type:	Proscenium stage
	AC
	Handicapped: Full access

Throughout the year, the Asia Society presents a wide variety of performers from the Far East, including theatrical troupes and puppeteers, at the Lila Acheson Wallace Auditorium in its headquarters building on Park Avenue. Admission varies with the performance, but is less expensive for members. (Annual memberships start at $35.) If you are interested in this sort of theatre, ask to be put on the society's mailing list.

CITHAERON
Jan Hus Church Theater
351 East 74th Street

Box Office:	768-3761 (24-hour answering service)
Box Office Hours:	One hour before performance
Credit Cards:	None TDF Vouchers Personal checks
Group Sales:	Through box office
Total Seating:	25–100, depending upon production
Stage Type:	Flexible open space
	Handicapped: No access

Cithaeron (named after Mount Cithaeron in Greece, the holy place where theatre began) is notable for the experimental work of director Steven Brant. A 1977 production of *Macbeth,* for example, placed the audience and the six performers in a 20-foot-wide steel and wood cage. Recently, his *Divine Comedy: The Inferno* featured puppets and masks, and the audience was taken on a walking tour of hell. The company uses a turn-of-the-century Czechoslovakian church of stone and carved wood for its productions.

EASTSIDE PLAYHOUSE
LIGHT OPERA OF MANHATTAN
334 East 74th Street

Box Office:	861-2288
Box Office Hours:	Tuesday–Sunday, 12 noon–9 p.m.; Wednesday, 11 a.m.–9 p.m.
Credit Cards:	None Personal checks for advance sale only
Group Sales:	Robert Holtman (535-6310)
Total Seating:	284 (Orchestra, 231; Balcony, 53; Standing room, 8)
Stage Type:	Proscenium stage
	AC
	Handicapped: Semi-accessible

The Broadway musicals of the first quarter of this century are alive and well and living at the Eastside Playhouse. Only they're called light opera now. But make no mistake, Victor Herbert, Rudolf Friml, and Sigmund Romberg were the Richard Rodgers, Alan Jay Lerner, and Stephen Sondheim of their day. The productions are something everyone should see: visual delights and richly melodious. The past season included *The Vagabond King, Babes in Toyland, The Merry Widow, The Desert Song, The Student Prince,* and a handful of Gilbert and Sullivan favorites: *The Gondoliers, H.M.S. Pinafore, The Mikado, Patience, The Pirates of Penzance.* A Christmas holiday special for several years has been a bang-up production of Victor Herbert's *Babes in Toyland.* The subscription series here is an excellent buy: an eight-performance ticket is $39–$60, depending upon seat and night, a five-performance ticket, $26–$40.

Eastside Playhouse/Light Opera of Manhattan

MEZZANINE
row 'A' overhangs orch. row 'H'

ORCHESTRA

-STAGE-

FOLKSBIENE PLAYHOUSE

123 East 55th Street

Box Office: 755-2231
Box Office Hours: 11 a.m.–4 p.m., and one hour before performance
Credit Cards: None   Personal checks
Group Sales: Through box office
Season: November–March
Total Seating: 445
Stage Type: Proscenium stage
AC
Handicapped: No access

When the Folksbiene was founded in 1915, Yiddish theatre flourished in the city. There were 14 such theatres, most of them on lower Second Avenue. Now the Folksbiene is the sole survivor. The troupe generally plays to full houses and has toured here and in Israel presenting works by such writers as Sholem Aleichem, Abraham Goldfadn, and I. L. Peretz. While most of the actors are young, having learned Yiddish at home or at a yeshiva, the troupe often features Leon Liebgold, Jack Rechtzeit, and other guest artists.

HUNTER PLAYWRIGHTS
LITTLE THEATRE

695 Park Avenue (69th)

Box Office: 570-5825
Box Office Hours: Two hours before performances
Credit Cards: None
Group Sales: Through box office
Season: October–May
Total Seating: 99
Stage Type: Flexible open space
No AC
Handicapped: No access

Student productions under the artistic direction of Gloria O'Donnel are presented here during the school term. Recent productions: *Night Must Fall* by Emyln Williams and Molière's *Trio*. There is a larger theatre here with a proscenium stage that seats 700. It is rented to nonprofit organizations.

MANHATTAN THEATRE CLUB

321 East 73rd Street

Box Office: 472-0600
Box Office Hours: Tuesday–Sunday, 1 p.m.–8 p.m.
Credit Cards: AE, MC, V (phone charges only)   Personal checks
Group Sales: Gary Murphy (288-2500)
Season: October–June
Total Seating: Downstage Theatre, 155; Upstage Theatre, 100; Cabaret, 75
Stage Type: Proscenium stage (Downstage); Thrust (Upstage)
AC
Handicapped: Semi-accessible

Ain't Misbehavin' started in the cabaret here, and that's how many people know the Manhattan Theatre Club. It's a shame because since its founding in 1970, it has been one of the most dynamic and creative forces on the New York theatre scene. The club's artistic policy has been the development of new theatrical works. Some highpoints: *Artichoke* by Johana Glass; *Losing Time* by John Hopkins; *The Rear Column* by Simon Gray; *Ashes* by David Rudkin; *Catsplay* by Istvan Orkeny; *The Blood Knot* by Athol Fugard; *Sea Marks* by Gardner McKay; *Life Class* by David Storey; and *The Last Street Play* by Richard Wesley. Barry Grove is the managing director, and Lynne Meadow is the artistic director. She points out that emphasis is placed on finding an "urgent voice" rather than a flawless form. Plays are sought that express compelling personal statements and can illuminate some aspect of our lives and society. Songwriter Jake Holmes recently did *Sidewalks* in the cabaret. There are two subscription series: five in the Downstage series, six in the Upstage. Both series are $75 weeknights, $80 weekends; Downstage is $40 and $45; Upstage is not available separately as a series.

Manhattan Theatre Club (Downstage Theatre)

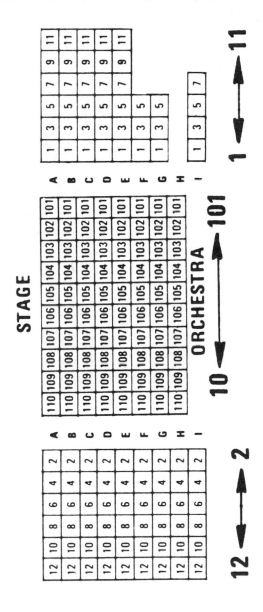

Manhattan Theatre Club (Upstage Theatre)

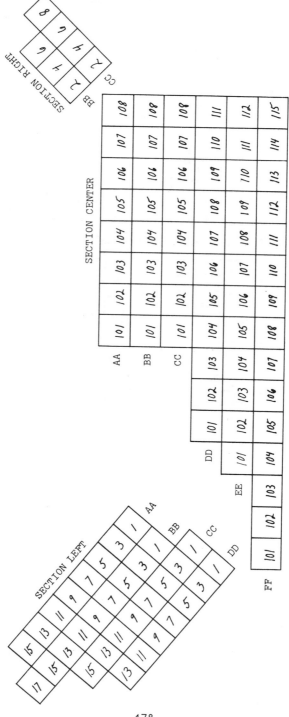

178

NATIONAL BLACK THEATRE

9 East 125th Street

Box Office: 427-5616
Box Office Hours: Monday–Thursday, 10 a.m.–5:30 p.m.; Friday–Saturday, 10 a.m.–
8:30 p.m.; Sunday, 1:30 p.m.–3 p.m.
Credit Cards: None   TDF Vouchers   Personal checks
Group Sales: 427-5616
Season: November–May
Total Seating: 99
Stage Type: Flexible stage
No AC
Handicapped: No access

Founded in 1968 by Barbara Ann Teer, the National Black Theatre's goal is "to train people to transcend the limitations of conventional theatre by developing in each person a sense of wholeness and a strong experience of self-esteem and love." NBT tries to eliminate the stereotypes of "ugly," "rich," "poor," "black," and "white" in its training program because it sees them as devices of alienation. In addition to its training facilities, NBT presents a series of workshop productions. Some recent offerings: *Softly Comes a Whirlwind Whispering in Your Ear* by Barbara Ann Teer; *The Owl and the Pussycat* by Bill Manhoff; and *Soul Fusion* by Nabii Faison, an original musical production.

NEW HERITAGE REPERTORY THEATRE

43 East 125th Street

Box Office: 876-3272
Box Office Hours: By phone two hours before performance
Credit Cards: None   TDF Vouchers   Personal checks for mail orders
Group Sales: Through box office
Season: September–June
Total Seating: 100
Stage Type: Arena stage
No AC
Handicapped: No access

This 15-year-old company, headed by Roger Furman, presents six plays a season in a former loft. Recent productions: *On Midnight Friday the 13th* by Roger Furman; *The Catwalk* by Allison West; and *Rashomon*.

NINETY-SECOND STREET YM-YWHA

1395 Lexington Avenue (92nd)

Box Office: 427-4410
Box Office Hours: Monday–Thursday, 11 a.m.–9 p.m.; Friday, 11 a.m.–3:45 p.m.;
Saturday, 6 p.m.–9 p.m.; Sunday, 12 noon–5 p.m.
Credit Cards: MC, V ($1 service charge)   Personal checks
Group Sales: Through producer
Total Seating: 75
Stage Type: Flexible open space
AC
Handicapped: Semi-accessible

Artistic director Stanley Breckner presents five plays a year here, each given for 24 performances. The 1980–81 season included Paddy Chayefsky's *The Tenth Man*, Israel Horovitz's *Cappella, From the Memoirs of Pontius Pilate* by Eric Bentley, and Martha Schlamme's *Brecht on Brecht*.

PHOENIX THEATRE
Marymount Manhattan College Theatre
221 East 71st Street

Box Office: 730-0794
Box Office Hours: Tuesday–Saturday, 1 p.m.–8 p.m.; Sunday, 1 p.m.–7:30 p.m.
Credit Cards: AE, MC, V   Personal checks
Group Sales: Audience Development Office (730-0787)
Season: October–June
Total Seating: 249
Stage Type: Proscenium stage
AC
Handicapped: No access

In 1953, T. Edward Hambleton and Norris Houghton founded the Phoenix Theatre as an alternative to Broadway when alternatives did not exist. Through the years, the Phoenix has changed as the theatrical landscape has changed, at various times embracing new plays, the classics, and a permanent ensemble performing in rotating repertory. In 1976 the focus shifted to new plays, both American and European. The theatre also collaborates with theatres outside New York to make possible the evolution of such plays as Marsha Norman's *Getting Out* and Wendy Wasserstein's *Uncommon Women and Others*. Under the artistic direction of Daniel Freudenberger several Phoenix productions, including *The Rules of the Game, Secret Service,* and *Uncommon Women and Others,* have been televised on the PBS Theatre in America series. Steven Robman became artistic director at the beginning of the 1980–81 season. Productions of the season included Wendy Wasserstein's *Isn't It Romantic?,* Romulus Linney's *The Captivity of Pixie Shedman,* Michel Tremblay's *Bonjour La, Bonjour,* and Christopher Durang's *Beyond Therapy.* A five-play subscription to the Phoenix is $60.

ST. BART'S PLAYHOUSE
109 East 50th Street

Owner: St. Bartholomew's Church
Box Office: 751-1616, Ext. 41 or 49
Box Office Hours: 12 noon–6 p.m., three weeks before performance; 12 noon–8 p.m., during run
Credit Cards: Only CHARGIT   TDF Vouchers   Personal checks
Group Sales: Through box office
Season: September–April
Total Seating: 365 (Orchestra, 260; Balcony, 105; Standing room, 12)
Stage Type: Proscenium stage
No AC
Handicapped: Semi-accessible

St. Bart's hasn't missed a season since it staged three one-act plays on February 15, 1928, and this community house is rich with history. One of the early performers here was Buddy Ebsen until Broadway, in the form of an Eddie Cantor musical, found him. A Broadway chorus boy named Jimmy Cagney often dropped by to help the players with the dance routines. In the 1940s, there was a pretty blonde angel in the Christmas pageant; she grew up to be Tuesday Weld. The playhouse does mostly musical comedy revivals with full orchestra. The 1979–80 season included: *Angel Street; Mame; Melissa, While She Sleeps; Craig's Wife; A Man for All Seasons,* and *Finian's Rainbow.* At this writing, the season's shows have been *The Importance of Being Earnest, Betjemania,* and *Anything Goes.*

Phoenix Theatre

STAGE

ORCHESTRA

Seat numbering direction: 1 → 24

Row																								
A	1	2	3	4	5	6	7	8	9	10	11	12	13	14	15	16	17	18	19	20	21	22	23	24
B		1	2	3	4	5	6	7	8	9	10	11	12	13	14	15	16	17	18	19	20			
C		1	2	3	4	5	6	7	8	9	10	11	12	13	14	15	16	17	18	19	20	21	22	
D	1	1	2	3	4	5	6	7	8	9	10	11	12	13	14	15	16	17	18	19	20	21	22	23
E	1	2	3	4	5	6	7	8	9	10	11	12	13	14	15	16	17	18	19	20	21	22		
F		1	2	3	4	5	6	7	8	9	10	11	12	13	14	15	16	17	18	19	20	21		
G		1	2	3	4	5	6	7	8	9	10	11	12	13	14	15	16	17	18	19	20			
H	1	2	3	4	5	6	7	8	9	10	11	12	13	14	15	16	17	18	19	20	21	22		
J	1	2	3	4	5	6	7	8	9	10	11	12	13	14	15	16	17	18	19	20	21	22		
K	1	2	3	4	5	6	7	8	9	10	11	12	13	14	15	16	17	18	19	20	21	22	23	24
L					1	2	3	4	5	6	7	8	9	10	11	12	13	14	15					
M					1	2	3	4	5	6	7	8	9	10	11	12	13	14	15					

TEN-TEN PLAYERS THEATER
Park Avenue Christian Church
1010 Park Avenue (85th)

Box Office: 288-3246
Box Office Hours: Monday–Saturday, 9 a.m.–10 p.m. (church takes reservations)
Credit Cards: None   TDF Vouchers
Group Sales: Through box office
Season: September–May
Total Seating: 198
Stage Type: Proscenium stage
No AC
Handicapped: No access

For 25 years the Ten-Ten Players have been presenting a range of productions, including children's musicals and original works here. Toy True handles the business side and Byron Tinsley is the artistic director. When this was written, the players were performing Robert Higgens and Byron Tinsley's *Alice the Magnificent*. During the season, the players offer a free actors' workshop and present workshop productions.

THEATER OF ST. PETER'S CHURCH
619 Lexington Avenue (54th)

Box Office: 751-4140
Box Office Hours: Monday, 1 p.m.–6 p.m.; Tuesday–Sunday, 1 p.m.–8 p.m.
Credit Cards: Determined by individual producer
Group Sales: Through box office
Total Seating: 199
Stage Type: Flexible stage
AC
Handicapped: Fully accessible

Next to the magnificent Citicorp building in the basement of St. Peter's Church is an excellent small theatre with seating on stepped platforms surrounding the performing area. In its short history it has had two plays go to Broadway: the Tony-winning *The Elephant Man* and *Tintypes*, both ANTA productions.

THEATER OF THE OPEN EYE
316 East 88th Street

Owner: Church of the Holy Trinity
Box Office: 534-6909
Box Office Hours: One hour before curtain, performance days
Credit Cards: None   TDF Vouchers   Personal checks (advance sales only)
Group Sales: Through box office
Season: September–June
Total Seating: Upstairs theatre, 150; Downstairs theatre, 100
Stage Type: Open flexible space
No AC
Handicapped: Semi-accessible

Theater of the Open Eye, founded in 1972 by Jean Erdman and Joseph Campbell, concerns itself with total theatre—a fusion of all the performing arts. Productions are inspired by the works of poets and visual artists and interweave dramatic scenes, dance, musical motifs, projected light, and pictorial effects. An outstanding work conceived here was Jean Erdman's *The Coach with Six Insides,* from the James Joyce novel *Finnegans Wake*, with music by Teiju Ito. The theatre recently held a festival of new works: a month-long staging of 17 theatre pieces in various stages of development, from readings through full production. The Children's Theater of the Open Eye presents works in this same fusion of the arts, particularly involving an exciting use of puppetry. Since 1977, Theater of the Open Eye has had a "shelter" program, which provides performing space to six homeless ensembles.

THE YORK PLAYERS COMPANY

2 East 90th Street

Owner: Church of the Heavenly Rest
Box Office: 289-3402
Box Office Hours: Three hours before curtain, performance days
Credit Cards: None TDF Vouchers Personal checks
Group Sales: Through box office
Season: October–May
Total Seating: 100
Stage Type: Proscenium stage adaptable to thrust, three-quarter, or total round
No AC
Handicapped: Semi-accessible

Since 1969 artistic director Janet Hayes Walker has been staging interesting plays and musicals in what once was the parish house of the Church of the Heavenly Rest. The theatre is a large room that adapts easily to different productions, from the classic proscenium stage to theatre-in-the-round. Productions here have included *Cyrano; A Man for All Seasons; Twelfth Night; Murder in the Cathedral; The Subject Was Roses; Rain; Golden Apple; She Loves Me; Anyone Can Whistle; Quadrille; Grass Harp; Tartuffe; John Brown's Body,* starring Celeste Holm; and *Letters of Elizabeth Barrett Browning,* starring Joan Fontaine. The company also performs Shakespeare and religious plays in the Church of the Heavenly Rest chancel.

"We read the lines so that people can hear and understand them; we move about the stage without bumping into the furniture or each other."

LYNN FONTANNE

"You need three things in the theater—the play, the actors and the audience, and each must give something."

KENNETH HAIG

". . . there is almost collusion between the stage and the audience. Everything goes. Everything carries. A magic fluid seems to be circulating. The actors have stage presence. Their characters really exist. The play has depth."

JEAN-JACQUES GAUTIER

RESTAURANTS AND NIGHTSPOTS

♫ CATCH A RISING STAR**

1487 First Avenue (78th)
Reservations:794-1906
Credit Cards: AE, MC
Shows: Friday–Saturday, 9:30 p.m. and 1 a.m.; Sunday–Thursday, 9:30 p.m.

Regulars Kelly Rogers and David Sayh maintain the pace here, alternating usually between comics and singers. The quality is uneven but that's the nature of comedy showcases. The odds swing in your favor on the weekend late shows. On weekends there is a two-drink minimum and a $5 cover; weekdays the cover is $4. Comedy workshops seem to thrive in Spartan surroundings; Catch a Rising Star is no exception.

THE COMIC STRIP**

1568 Second Avenue (78th)
Reservations: 861-9386
Credit Cards: AE, CB, DC, MC, V
Shows: Monday–Thursday, 9:30 p.m.; Sunday and Friday, 9 p.m. and
12 midnight; Saturday, 8:30 p.m. and 12 midnight

Another comic showcase, with a pleasant atmosphere, that is good or very good depending on who is there and the kind of relationship he or she establishes with the audience. Sunday through Thursday there is a $3.50 cover and a $5.50 minimum; Friday and Saturday, a $5 cover and a two-drink minimum.

DANGERFIELD'S***

1118 First Avenue (61st)
Reservations: 593-1650
Credit Cards: AE, CB, MC, V
Shows: Monday–Thursday, 9:30 p.m.; Friday–Saturday, 9 p.m. and 12 midnight;
Sunday showcase, 9:30 p.m.

Don't give Rodney any respect—it will ruin his act. Give his club some respect, though; it's the major-league comic spot in the city. If Mr. Dangerfield isn't performing, other major talents are. Sunday is new-talent night. A limited menu offers a burger ($4.95), southern fried chicken ($7.50), and filet mignon ($12.95). Monday through Saturday, there is a $7 cover and a $7 minimum; Sundays, a $4 cover and a two-drink minimum.

DIVINO RISTORANTE**

1556 Second Avenue (80th)
Reservations: 861-1096
Credit Cards: AE, DC, MC, V
Moderate   Closed Thanksgiving, Christmas, and New Year's Day

When Columbia University recently staged a festival of Italian film comedies, this is where the Italian contingent (including Giancarlo Giannini) went to eat. No wonder it's a perennial favorite with the movers and shakers in the city's Italian community. Prosciutto and melon ($3) and bresaola della valtellina ($4) are excellent openers. Delicious pastas are from $5 to $7 and half-orders are available. Veal and chicken entrees range $6.50 to $11, with a bit more for seafood dishes.

ELAINE'S*

1703 Second Avenue (88th)
Reservations: 831-9558
Credit Cards: AE
Moderate   Closed Saturday and Sunday in July and August and major holidays

Elaine's has become famous not because of its food (mostly standard Italian fare) nor its ambiance (dark) but because night after night the restaurant is chockablock with literary and show business celebrities who seem to like both the owner (Elaine) and each other's company. If you are neither a celebrity nor arrive with one, expect icy indifference; if you make the mistake of speaking to one of the celebrities unless spoken to (which won't happen), expect worse. Eschew staring and pointing, too. The squid salad and the steamed mussels are excellent; the pasta is above average. There are nightly entree specials. Dinner should cost about $15 not including wine or drinks. Yes, Elaine is the dark-haired lady by the bar.

FOUR SEASONS***

99 East 52nd Street
Reservations: 754-9494
Credit Cards: AE, CB, DC, MC, V
Moderate to Expensive   Closed Sunday

For theatregoers who want to dine in unabashed elegance, come to the Four Seasons for either the pre-theatre dinner, served in the pool area from 5:00 p.m. to 7:00 p.m., or after the show when there is a special menu with lighter selections. Both the grill and the pool area reflect the sure hand and gifted eye of Philip Johnson, who designed the restaurant to be a fitting complement to the Seagram Building, and it surely is that. The pre-theatre dinner is an exceptional value at $24.50. Start with shrimp, clams, oysters, a pate of pike and salmon, or a choice of soups. The entrees include roast baby pheasant, Boston sole with macadamia nuts, trout stuffed with crabmeat, veal, and a skillet steak with onions and peppers. A choice of desserts, the high point being a coconut soufflé (which you should order at the beginning of your meal to avoid a delay.) Notice the details here: the linens, the stemware, even the ashtrays. Everything is done to perfection. The late critic Kenneth Tynan once wrote that the height of elegance in New York was sitting at a table by the pool here and making and sailing little paper boats. Paper boats or no, dress appropriately and enjoy one of the city's handful of superlative restaurants.

JIM MCMULLEN**

1341 Third Avenue (78th)
Reservations: Not accepted (861-4700)
No Credit Cards
Moderate

Jim McMullen is one of New York's top male models, and models and other great-looking people flock to his restaurant. With no reservations accepted, unless you come early or quite late, the wait at the bar can be long, but early or late fits a theatregoer's timetable quite nicely, thank you. Seafood is a long suit here: salmon steak, red snapper, filet of sole, and swordfish are fresh, cooked to perfection, and in the $9–$10 price range. Other specialties include chicken pot pie ($8.95) and an excellent veal chop ($11.95). For dessert you would do well to order either the chocolate brownie pie ($2.25) or the hot fudge sundae ($2.95). After 11 p.m., there are burgers, other sandwiches, salads, and omelettes from $5 to $7.

♫ THE KING COLE***

St. Regis-Sheraton Hotel
2 East 55th Street
Reservations: 872-6140
Credit Cards: AE, CB, DC, MC, V
Expensive   Shows: Monday–Thursday, 9:30 p.m.; Friday–Saturday, 9:30 p.m.
and 11:30 p.m.

While I mourn the passing of one of the great standup bars in the city, I applaud the handsome, tiered supper club that replaced it. At this writing, the St. Regis has been presenting celebrations of our favorite composers: *Rhapsody in Gershwin* and, more recently, *From Rodgers and Hart with Love,* starring Mimi Hines, Larry Kert, and Mark Baker. They have all been excellent, and we sincerely hope the show policy continues. There is no minimum, but there is a $7.50 entertainment charge through the week if you're dining, $10 if drinks only; Fridays and Saturdays, $10 and $12.50, respectively.

LA PETITE FERME***

973 Lexington Avenue (71st)
Reservations: 249-3272
Credit Cards: AE, DC, MC, V
Moderate to Expensive   Monday–Saturday, 12 noon–10:30 p.m.; closed Sunday

This little farm moved up from the Village without losing its charm or the superb quality of its kitchen. Proprietor Charles Chevillot can cross spoons with any chef in town. The interior suggests a French farmhouse: fresh flowers on slab tables, a pair of doves saying silly things about the patrons. But you came for the food: a perfect petit marmite ($4) or artichaut vinaigrette ($4) to start your juices flowing, the pot-au-feu ($12), blanquette de veau ($11), or the masterly homard poché with sauce Chevillot at $17. A tarte aux framboises ($3.50) is a lovely finish. In the summer have a before-dinner drink in the small garden in back. The birds who will be there with you, incidentally, are quails.

MAXWELL'S PLUM***

1181 First Avenue (61st)
Reservations: 628-2100
Credit Cards: AE, CB, DC, MC, V
Moderate to Expensive

There are two Maxwell's Plums, both spectacular, both created by Warner Le Roy (who went on to recreate the Tavern on the Green), and both are at the same address. One is a beautiful restaurant, one of the handful of exceptional restaurants in the city. The other is the city's premier singles bar, for it is here that the pretty young East Siders come to co-mingle. Your mind being on food and the theatre, the other Maxwell's Plum is only of fleeting sociological interest. In the rear dining room is a Tiffany glass ceiling, massive chandeliers, and a Lalique fountain. (There is a glass-enclosed sidewalk café as well, but the dining room is nicer.) Some personal favorites here are the roast rib of beef with Yorkshire pudding ($14.50), the roast wild boar with gingered apples and lingonberries ($11.50), the grilled red snapper dijonnaise ($12.50), and—somehow it seems so *right* here—baked Alaska for two ($5.25). This is a must if you haven't been here before—or even if you have. Maxwell's Plum is enormously popular, so make reservations as early as you can.

RISTORANTE SIGNOR EDMONDO***

1494 Second Avenue (78th)
Reservations: 737-1337
Credit Cards: AE, MC, V
Moderate   Closed Christmas and New Year's Day

This is a fairly new restaurant and a genuine find. Two genteel brothers from Genoa, Eduardo and Raimondo, combined their names into "Edmondo" and their culinary skills to produce what is perhaps the best simple, authentic Italian cooking in the city. Pasta al pesto, panzerotti—anything "alla genovese"—is an excellent choice. Pastas cost about $7, chicken and veal dishes about $9. Desserts are first-rate, as are the espresso and cappuccino. Signor Edmondo's is a warm, attractive place, better decorated than the usual Italian restaurant.

RUSTY'S**

1271 Third Avenue (73rd)
Reservations: Not accepted (861-4508)
Credit Cards: AE, CB, MC, V
Moderate

Rusty is Rusty Staub, the home-run hitting outfielder now back with the Mets and an amateur chef of distinction. His talents are reflected in his restaurant. Personally, I love spareribs, and the city with 10,000 plus restaurants of every conceivable description is inexplicably short of places that serve good ribs. This is one of the few, and a rack of Canadian baby back ribs are $9.95. There are other delicacies as well: cold plump mussels with mustard sauce ($3.25), a "Grand Slam" salad—ham, swiss cheese, and turkey with mushrooms, cucumber, green pepper, shrimp, black olives, tomato, egg, and shredded lettuce, served with Rusty's special 16-herb vinaigrette dressing—at $6.95, or seafood New Orleans, a blend of lobster, shrimp, clams, mussels, and scallops simmered in red wine, garlic, tomatoes, and a special seafood sauce ($13.95). If your diet permits, accompany your entree with sautéed potato peels. Ribs, Rusty's barbecue sauce, and chili can be purchased to take home.

 **SOMETHING DIFFERENT**

 1488 First Avenue (78th)
Reservations: 570-6666
No credit cards
Inexpensive

Something Different certainly is something different. Billed as New York's first dessert nightclub, this is a place where the waiters and waitresses are not only aspiring actors and actresses but actually perform. And delightfully. The first show is at 8:15 p.m. and after that shows are every hour on the hour until midnight. If you have young children here's a great idea: There is a children's showcase that features tots presently working on Broadway or in movies. The children's showcases are Saturday at 7 p.m., Sunday at 3:30 p.m. and 5:30 p.m., and Monday at 7 p.m. As they say, it's desserts only, goodies like hot fudge walnut pie ($3.50), cream-me-cheese cake ($2.95), various cookies and biscotti (that's Italian for biscuits), and, if you get adequate help from your party, the Crowd Pleaser: 12 scoops of mixed flavors of ice cream with everything ($12.95)! There's a $4 minimum per person.

CHELSEA-GRAMERCY PARK-MURRAY HILL

Chelsea

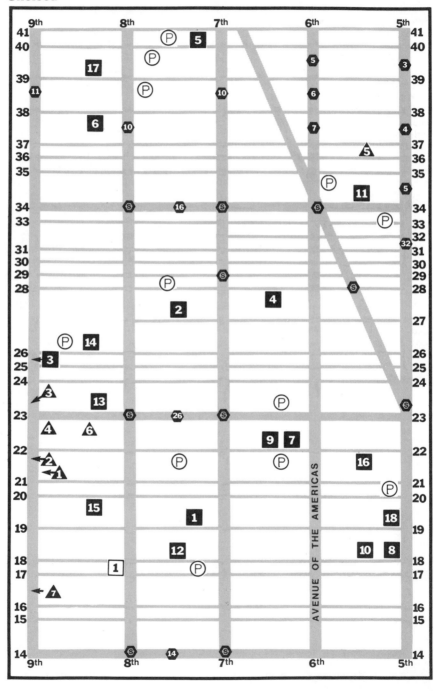

■ Theatres

1. American Theatre Laboratory/
   Bessie Schonberg Theatre/219
   West 19
2. Haft Auditorium (FIT)/227 West 27
3. Hudson Guild/441 West 26
4. Impossible Ragtime Theatre/120
   West 28
5. Manhattan Punch Line/260 West 41
6. Meat and Potatoes Company/
   Alvenia Krause Theatre/
   306 West 38
7. The Nameless Theatre/125 West 22
8. Newfoundland Theatre/1 West 18
9. New Shandol Theatre/137 West 22
10. New York Stage Works/15 West 18
11. Potter's Field Theatre/27 West 34
12. The Production Company/249
    West 18
13. Roundabout Theatre Company—
    Stage I/333 West 23
14. Roundabout Theatre Company—
    Stage II/307 West 26
15. St. Peter's Theatre/336 West 20
16. Theatre 22/54 West 22
17. The Troupe/335 West 39
18. WPA Theatre/138 Fifth

▲ Restaurants

1. Artie's Warehouse/539 West 21
2. Empire Diner/210 Tenth
3. McFeeley's/565 West 23
4. R. J. Scotty's/202 Ninth
5. Thirty-seventh Street Hideaway/32
   West 37
6. Variations/358 West 23
7. West Boondock/114 Tenth

□ Other Attractions

1. Eighth Avenue Records/153 Eighth

⑰ Bus Numbers

Ⓢ Subway Stations

Ⓟ Parking

➡ One-way Street

⬅➡ Two-way Street

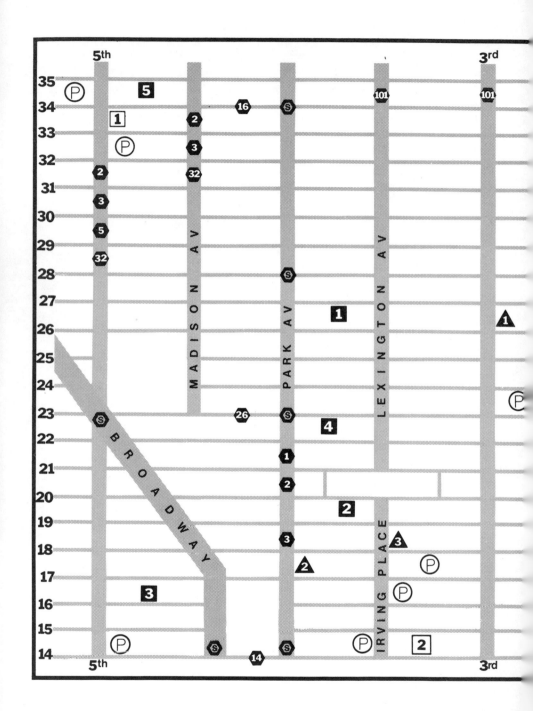

■ Theatres

1. Gramercy Art Theatre / 138 East 27
2. Heritage Theatre (National Arts Club) / 15 Gramercy Park South
3. LATE Theatre / 9 East 16
4. Nuestro Theatre / 112 East 23
5. Theatre Off Park / 28 East 35

▲ Restaurants

1. Company / 365 Third
2. Max's Kansas City / 213 Park Avenue South
3. Pete's Tavern / 129 East 18

□ Other Attractions

1. Gallery at B. Altman & Co. / Fifth and 34
2. The Silver Screen / 119 East 14

🛑 Bus Numbers

Ⓢ Subway Stations

Ⓟ Parking

→ One-way Street

⇄ Two-way Street

The three neighborhoods that lie between Greenwich Village and midtown Manhattan are rich in theatrical history. At 23rd and Sixth Avenue, Edwin Booth, the foremost actor of his day, built a theatre costing more than one million dollars. He dreamed it would be the premier classic theatre in the nation. Five years after it opened in 1869, it had bankrupted him. At Broadway and 29th was the San Francisco Music Hall, a theatre created especially for minstrel shows. The Standard Theatre, where Gilbert and Sullivan's operettas were introduced to American audiences, was torn down to make room for Gimbel's on 34th Street. The New Park Theatre, on Broadway between 21st and 22nd, burned down the day Lily Langtry was to make her American debut there. Times have changed; the old theatres are gone but a century later the spirit of theatre still flourishes here.

THEATRES

AMERICAN THEATRE LABORATORY
219 West 19th Street

Box Office:	924-0077
Box Office Hours:	One hour before performance (answering machine: Monday–Friday, 10 a.m.–10 p.m.; Saturday, 1 p.m.–10 p.m.)
Credit Cards:	None TDF Vouchers Personal checks
Group Sales:	Through box office (Mark Statman)
Season:	September–June
Total Seating:	52
Stage Type:	Proscenium stage
	No AC
	Handicapped: No access

In a loft in a former warehouse building, artistic director David White does experimental productions, such as William Burroughs's *Naked Lunch* and David Goordin's *Profile*.

"An actress's life is so transitory—suddenly you're a building."
HELEN HAYES, at the dedication of the Helen Hayes Theatre

"Playing Shakespeare is so tiring. You never get to sit down unless you're a king."

JOSEPHINE HULL

BESSIE SCHONBERG THEATRE

219 West 19th Street

Box Office: 924-0077
Box Office Hours: Answering machine, reservations taken
Credit Cards: None   TDF Vouchers   Personal checks
Group Sales: Through box office
Season: Closed July
Total Seating: 100 plus 40 cushions on floor
Stage Type: Open stage
AC
Handicapped: No access

A tire sales garage until it was converted into a theatre in 1968, this is the most active dance theatre in the country, with more than 250 performances a year. There are late-night performances by the American Theatre Laboratory and other groups.

GRAMERCY ART THEATRE
Repertorio Espanol

138 East 27th Street

Box Office: 889-2850
Box Office Hours: 10 a.m.–8 p.m., if performance
Credit Cards: None   TDF Vouchers   Personal checks
Group Sales: Through box office
Total Seating: 160 (Orchestra, 110; Balcony, 50)
Stage Type: Proscenium stage
AC
Handicapped: Semi-accessible

The building went up in 1915. First it was a Masonic temple, then an Armenian church, then the Davenport Theatre. It became the Gramercy Arts Theatre in 1952, and Repertorio Espanol has been here since 1972. What began informally in 1968 has grown into a full-time professional company trained in both the classical and modern styles. The diversity of the company with all Spanish-speaking nationalities represented is matched by its repertoire. The works the company stages extend from the classics of the Golden Age of Spain to new plays of contemporary Latin America—plays that are rarely, if ever, presented professionally in this country. A typical weekend series of Spanish-speaking performances might include a Lorca tragedy, a classic like *Celestina,* and a comedy by Mexico's Carballido, Argentina's Talesnik, or Venezuela's Chocron. Among those responsible for these worthy efforts are artistic director René Buch, designer Robert Weber Frederico, and the actors, who include Cuba's Ofelia Gonzales, Ecuador's Alfonso Manosalvas, and Puerto Rico's Raul Davilia. Gilberto Zaldivar is the producer.

HAFT AUDITORIUM
Fashion Institute of Technology (FIT)

227 West 27th Street

Box Office: 760-7710
Box Office Hours: One hour before performance (Information: Monday–Saturday, 9 a.m.–5 p.m.)
Group Sales: Tony Lamont (760-7644)
Season: September–June
Total Seating: 800 (Orchestra, 650; Balcony, 150)
Stage Type: Proscenium stage
AC
Handicapped: Semi-accessible

Basically for the use of the FIT drama department, this theatre is rented to outside groups, including the Village Light Opera Company and the Chinese Opera Company.

HERITAGE THEATRE
National Arts Club

15 Gramercy Park South

Box Office: 475-3424
Box Office Hours: 10 a.m.–10 p.m., if performance
Credit Cards: None   TDF Vouchers   Personal checks
Group Sales: Through box office
Total Seating: 65
Stage Type: Proscenium stage
AC
Handicapped: Semi-accessible

In the former library of this handsome Gramercy Park townhouse, artistic director Thomas Luce Summa revives classics that permit actors to play roles they wouldn't get the opportunity to do on the commercial stage. There are four productions a year. Included in the 1980–81 season were Ibsen's *Little Eylof; Group Portrait,* based on the novels of Henry James; and *Antigone.*

HUDSON GUILD

441 West 26th Street

Owner: Hudson Guild Theatre, Inc.
Box Office: 760-9847
Box Office Hours: Tuesday–Saturday, 11 a.m.–6 p.m.
Credit Cards: AE, MC, V (50¢ service charge)   TDF Vouchers   Personal checks
Group Sales: Through box office
Season: September–June
Total Seating: 135 (Orchestra, 135)
Stage Type: Proscenium stage
AC
Handicapped: Semi-accessible

The Hudson Guild was founded in 1922. Since 1977, it has devoted itself exclusively to the production of new plays, five in an annual subscription season. Each play has a five-week limited run. Two of the Hudson Guild's plays from the 1977–78 season moved on to Broadway: Hugh Leonard's *Da* and *My Mother Was a Fortune Teller.* The 1978–79 season's *On Golden Pond* with Frances Sternhagen and Tom Aldredge also went to Broadway. The Hudson Guild feels that, perhaps, an even more important measure of success is that it has become a place where actors love to work. The playwright is usually in residence during the four-week rehearsal period. Productions feature both new talent and such veterans as Tammy Grimes, Bernard Hughes, Shirley Knight, and Frances Sternhagen. Other recent productions included *Devour the Snow* and *Madwoman of Central Park West.* The Hudson Guild's veteran producing director, Craig Anderson, was succeeded by David Kerry Heefner at the start of the 1979–80 season. A five play subscription costs $36.

IMPOSSIBLE RAGTIME THEATRE

120 West 28th Street

Box Office: 929-8003
Box Office Hours: Monday–Saturday, 10 a.m.–6 p.m.
Credit Cards: None   TDF Vouchers   Personal checks
Group Sales: Through box office
Season: October–June
Total Seating: Stage I, 100; Stage II, 70
Stage Type: Flexible open area (Stage I); Thrust (Stage II)
AC
Handicapped: Semi-accessible

The Impossible Ragtime Theatre blooms in the city's wholesale flower district. There are many playwright theatres and performer theatres; this is a director's theatre. Since its founding in 1974 (by Ted Story, George Ferencz, Cynthia Crane, and Pam Mitchell), the Impossible Ragtime Theatre has explored a wide range of material. A season might run the gamut from Agatha Christie to Bertolt Brecht; directorial interests are major considerations in the choice of materials. Recent productions, under the artistic direction of Ted Story, include: Mel Arrighi's *The Unicorn in Captivity;* Sam Shepard's *Suicide in B Flat; Three Men on a Horse* by John Cecil Holm and George Abbot; and *Brand* by Henrik Ibsen, translation by Michael Meyer.

LATE THEATRE
9 East 16th Street

Box Office:	254-3619
Box Office Hours:	2 p.m.–5 p.m.
Credit Cards:	None TDF Vouchers
Group Sales:	Through box office
Total Seating:	99 (Varies with production)
Stage Type:	Flexible open space
	No AC
	Handicapped: No access

Artistic director Herminio Vargas formed LATE (Latin American Theatre Ensemble) in late 1980 to present Hispanic themes in productions performed both in Spanish and English. The first production here was *La Novella de las Nueve.*

MANHATTAN PUNCH LINE
260 West 41st Street

Box Office:	921-1455
Box Office Hours:	Monday–Friday, 11 a.m.–8 p.m.; Saturday, Sunday, holidays, 1 p.m.–8 p.m.
Credit Cards:	None TDF Vouchers Phone reservations accepted and held until 15 minutes before curtain
Group Sales:	Reva Cooper (921-8288)
Total Seating:	100 (Standing room, 12)
Stage Type:	Flexible stage
	No AC
	Handicapped: Semi-accessible

Since April Fool's Day, 1979, the Manhattan Punch Line has been devoted to comedy. (In response to a Theatre Guide questionnaire, the company said it handled emergencies in the theatre by "panic, yelling and screaming.") Under the direction of Steve Kaplan and Mitch McGuire, this former shoe manufacturer's loft has seen hit revivals of *Room Service* and *The Front Page.* Other productions have included: *The Male Animal, The Man Who Shot the Man Who Shot Jesse James, Will Success Spoil Rock Hunter?, The Prevalence of Mrs. Seal* with Frances Sternhagen; *A Comedy of Errors;* and W. S. Gilbert's rarely revived farce *Engaged.*

MEAT AND POTATOES COMPANY
ALVINA KRAUSE THEATRE
306 West 38th Street (4th floor)

Box Office:	584-3293
Box Office Hours:	Thursday–Friday, 4 p.m.–8 p.m.; Saturday–Sunday, 10 a.m.–8 p.m.
Credit Cards:	None TDF Vouchers Personal checks
Group Sales:	Through box office
Season:	closed August
Total Seating:	90
Stage Type:	Proscenium stage
	No AC
	Handicapped: Semi-accessible

Artistic director Neal Weaver and treasurer Jane Dwyer moved the Meat and Potatoes Company to this former manufacturing loft recently to continue the productions that began in 1976. "By the name Meat and Potatoes," Mr. Weaver explains, "we hope to suggest that we choose both classic and modern plays that are nourishing, and leave our audience with something to chew on." Recent productions have included the George Bernard Shaw comedy, *The Philanderer;* Agatha Christie's thriller *Black Coffee; The Importance of Being Earnest;* George M. Cohan's melodrama, *The Tavern;* and *Icebound,* a comedy by Owen Davis.

THE NAMELESS THEATRE
125 West 22nd Street

Box Office:	242-9768
Box Office Hours:	10 a.m. to curtain, if performance
Credit Cards:	None TDF Vouchers
Group Sales:	Through box office
Total Seating:	80
Stage Type:	Proscenium stage
	No AC
	Handicapped: No access

From 1970 to 1975 this theatre was called Stage Light Two. Patrick J. Byrne's company has been here since then, and, in 1979, major improvements were made to the space. The focus has been on classic plays, and recent productions have included *Antigone, The Master Builder, No Exit, Rattle of a Simple Man, Richard II, The Taming of the Shrew,* and *Two Gentlemen of Verona.*

NEWFOUNDLAND THEATRE
1 West 18th Street

Box Office:	255-4991
Box Office Hours:	Tuesday–Saturday, 11 a.m.–6 p.m.; Sunday, 3 p.m.–8 p.m., if performance
Credit Cards:	None TDF Vouchers Personal checks
Group Sales:	Through box office
Season:	September–June
Total Seating:	75
Stage Type:	Flexible stage
	No AC
	Handicapped: Semi-accessible

This is the home of the Medicine Show Theatre Ensemble, a company devoted to new productions of comedy, both classic and modern. Founded in 1970 by Barbara Vann and James Barbosa, the company's artistic directors, the Medicine Show has produced such diverse offerings as a contemporary production of *Frogs,* music by Yenoin Guibbory and lyrics by Carl Morse; George Bernard Shaw's *Don Juan in Hell;* and *The Tragedy of Tragedies or The Life and Death of Tom Thumb the Great* by Henry Fielding with music by Carol Henry. The Medicine Show performs with wit and imagination.

NEW SHANDOL THEATRE
137 West 22nd Street

Box Office:	243-9504
Box Office Hours:	Varies with production
Credit Cards:	Varies with production
Group Sales:	Varies with production
Total Seating:	60
Stage Type:	End stage
	AC
	Handicapped: Semi-accessible

This space was renovated in 1978 by two actors, Craig Noble and Gary Wertheim, who lease it to a variety of independent producers. Recent productions: solo mime Zwi Kanar, *The Cherry Orchard,* and Lone Wolf Productions' presentation of *The Good Doctor* and *A Late Night with John Guare.*

NEW YORK STAGE WORKS

15 West 18th Street (3rd floor)

Box Office: 242-3967
Box Office Hours: 11 a.m.–6 p.m.
Credit Cards: None TDF Vouchers Personal checks for advance sales
Total Seating: Adult theatre, 65; Children's, 75
Stage Type: Proscenium stages
AC
Handicapped: Semi-accessible

Since its founding in 1977, this group under the artistic direction of Craig La Plunt has had a busy schedule of both adult and children productions. In the adult theatre, *Matinee Idol* by Dean Corrin and *Twinenight* by Kevin Meelan were recent offerings. In the spring of 1981, there was a directors' festival of 10 one-act plays. The children's theatre features marionette shows such as *Pinocchio* and *Alice in Wonderland.*

NUESTRO TEATRO

112 East 23rd (4th Floor)

Box Office: 673-9470
Box Office Hours: Tuesday–Thursday, 2 p.m.–5 p.m.; Friday, 2 p.m.–8 p.m.;
Saturday, 6 p.m.–8 p.m.; Sunday, 1 p.m.–3 p.m.
Credit Cards: None TDF Vouchers
Group Sales: Through box office
Season: September–May
Total Seating: 75
Stage Type: Proscenium stage
AC
Handicapped: Semi-accessible

The aim of artistic director Liz Castanos is to awaken interest in Hispanic culture through the presentation of contemporary plays. Recent productions include Neil Simon and Tennessee Williams plays in Spanish. In the spring of 1981, the company presented *Anillos Para Una Dama* by Antonio Gala, a contemporary rendering of the Struggles of Jimena, the widow of El Cid, the legendary Spanish hero.

POTTER'S FIELD THEATRE COMPANY

27 West 34th Street (5th floor)

Box Office: 695-7892
Box Office Hours: Open two hours before performance
Credit Cards: None
Group Sales: Through box office
Total Seating: Up to 99, depending upon production
Stage Type: Flexible open space
AC
Handicapped: Semi-accessible

This is an acting school, affiliated with the New School for Social Research, presenting showcase productions. Recent efforts have included *Twelfth Night, Two Gentlemen of Verona,* and *Crime and Punishment* as a reading.

THE PRODUCTION COMPANY

249 West 18th Street

Box Office: 691-7359
Box Office Hours: 24-hour answering machine
Credit Cards: None   CHARGIT   TDF Vouchers   Personal checks
Group Sales: Caryl Goldsmith (691-7359)
Season: September–May
Total Seating: 75 (Standing room, 3)
Stage Type: Flexible open box
No AC
Handicapped: No access

Since 1977, the Production Company has had an enviable track record for presenting interesting and entertaining new material: *Blues in the Night; Kennedy's Children; Marry Me a Little;* Stephen Sondheim's music in cabaret; and most recently Randy Newman's music in cabaret, *Maybe I'm Doing It Wrong,* starring Treat Williams. Caren Harder is the managing director and Norman René the artistic director of this talented group.

ROUNDABOUT THEATRE COMPANY

333 West 23rd Street (Stage One)
307 West 26th Street (Stage Two)

Box Office: 242-7800
Box Office Hours: Monday–Saturday, 10 a.m.–9 p.m.; Sunday, 12 noon–3 p.m.
Credit Cards: None   CHARGIT   Personal checks
Group Sales: Through box office
Total Seating: Stage One, 350; Stage Two, 150
Stage Type: Proscenium stage (Stage One); Arena (Stage Two)
AC
Handicapped: Semi-accessible (Stage One); No access (Stage Two)

Since 1965, producing directors Gene Feist and Michael Fried have built the Roundabout into one of the major nonprofit theatrical institutions in the country with such memorable productions as *Look Back in Anger* with Malcolm McDowall and Lisa Barnes; Vincent Price as Oscar Wilde in John Gay's *Diversions and Delights;* Tammy Grimes and Amanda Plummer in Turgenev's *A Month in the Country;* Geraldine Fitzgerald in *Streetsongs;* and Ibsen's *Ghosts* with Beatrice Straight and Victor Garber. The Roundabout has a particularly attractive subscription series: six plays for the price of four (from $44 to $56 per subscription, depending upon the performances chosen). In the season just past, *Don Juan in Hell, Inadmissible Evidence, Hedda Gabler,* and *Juno and the Paycock* were at Stage One, *The Winslow Boy* and *A Taste of Honey* at Stage Two. A small, but important plus for the Roundabout is the excellence of its concession stand: quiches, pastries, cider, hot chocolate—delicious and moderately priced.

ST. PETER'S PERFORMING ARTS CENTER

336 West 20th Street

Owner: St. Peter's Episcopal Church
Box Office: 261-4616
Box Office Hours: Flexible
Credit Cards: None   TDF Vouchers   Personal checks
Group Sales: Through box office
Season: September to May
Total Seating: 99
Stage Type: Flexible open space
No AC
Handicapped: No access

Three theatres share this space. The Labor Theater, founded by Chuck Portz and Bette Craig, concentrates on dramatic material relevant to the lives of working-class people. Its productions have included Rip Torn in *Nightshift; I Just Wanted Someone to Know;* and *Con-*

Roundabout Theatre Company (Stage One)

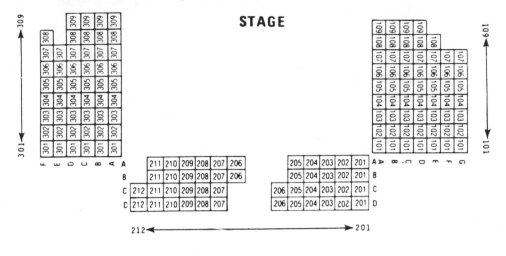

Roundabout Theatre Company (Stage Two)

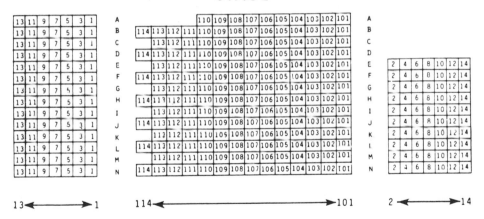

fessions of a Socialist, an Obie winner. The Modern Times Theater was founded in 1977 for the purpose of creating plays about the human realities of social change. Its productions have included Tell Me a Riddle, The Last Day, Homeland, The Eight Million, and The Bread and Roses Play. The New York Street Theater Caravan travels extensively to impoverished areas of the country, performing in migrant shacks, prisons, and Indian reservations. The company has also played extensively in Europe. One of its more recent productions was Molly Maguire, written and directed by Marketa Kimbrell.

THEATRE OFF PARK
28 East 35th Street

Owner: The Community Church of New York
Box Office: 679-6283
Box Office Hours: One hour before curtain
Credit Cards: None   TDF Vouchers   Personal checks
Group Sales: Through box office
Season: October–June
Total Seating: 73 (5 extra on stools)
Stage Type: Black box stage
AC
Handicapped: No access

Since 1975, Theatre Off Park has offered a unique range of plays and has had the satisfaction of seeing two of its productions go on to Broadway: the musical *Eubie!*, which started here as *Shuffle Along;* and *Of the Fields Lately*, by David French. Patricia Flynn Peate is the producing director, and Jay Stephens is the managing director. Other important productions here include: *Pimiento Pancakes*, an adaptation from O. Henry that was televised by WNBC to show what could be done Off-Off Broadway with a $200 budget; the premiere of Carla Conway's *The Last Days of the Wichita Kid;* the American premiere of *Emigrés* by Slawomir Mrozek; the American premiere of Thomas Kilroy's *The Death and Resurrection of Mr. Roche;* Johnny Brandon's original musical *Ain't Doin' Nothin' But Singin' My Song;* another original musical, *Give My Regards to Leicester Square;* the premiere of Paul Nathan's *Ricochet;* and *Ernest in Love*, a musical by A. Croswell and L. Pockriss based on the Wilde play, *The Importance of Being Earnest.*

THEATRE 22
54 West 22nd Street

Box Office: 243-2805
Box Office Hours: Tuesday–Sunday, 10 a.m.–8 p.m.
Credit Cards: None   TDF Vouchers   Personal checks
Group Sales: Through box office
Total Seating: 50–65, depending on production
Stage Type Flexible open space
AC
Handicapped: Semi-accessible

Owner Sidney Armus produces plays in this converted loft and rents it out to other groups. Luigi Pirandello's *The Vise* was performed here recently.

"They try to be clevah instead of watching me be clevah."
NOEL COWARD, on talkative theatregoers

"Ignorance of the Off-Off Broadway theater movement is ignorance of the American stage."
HAROLD CLURMAN

THE TROUPE

335 West 39th Street

Box Office: 244-9699
Box Office Hours: 12 noon to curtain
Credit Cards: None   TDF Vouchers
Total Seating: Upstairs, 40; Downstairs, 50
Stage Type: Variable open spaces
AC
Handicapped: Semi-accessible (Downstairs only)

In this former factory building, artistic director Andy Mulligan presents Equity showcases throughout the year. Recent productions have included *Playboy of the Western World* and John Galsworthy's *Windows;* Alexander Ostrovsky's *Diary of a Scoundrel;* and *Patsy,* a new play by Frank Addone, a New York policeman. These were performed in repertory.

WPA THEATRE

138 5th Avenue (19th)

Box Office: 691-2274
Box Office Hours: One hour before performance (reservations by phone, Monday–Friday, 11 a.m.–6 p.m.)
Group Sales: None
Season: October–June
Total Seating: 99
Stage Type: Flexible open space
OOBA
No AC
Handicapped: Semi-accessible

This company goes back to 1968 in producing a blend of new American plays and neglected American classics in a realistic idiom. A solid, professional group, its recent productions have included Larry Ketron's *The Trading Post* and *An Evening with Michael Grand.* Kyle Renick is the artistic director.

RESTAURANTS AND NIGHTSPOTS

ARTIE'S WAREHOUSE*

539 West 21st Street
Reservations: 989-9500
Credit Cards: AE, DC, MC, V
Moderate   Sunday–Thursday, open until 11 p.m.; Friday–Saturday, until 1 a.m.
Free parking

You'll think you're on the wrong street and if it weren't for the lights, you'd never know this wasn't a warehouse. Inside is something else: a big, handsome room with brick walls, natural wood, and twinkly lights. The cuisine is eclectic, some Chinese dishes, some Italian, and some standard American fare. The simpler the dish, the better. Entrees range from $8 to $15. An excellent burger ($5.75) is available after 11 p.m. on the weekends. If you enjoy lively bars, you'll like the bar here. Tip: Late at night it's best to phone for a taxi home.

♫ COMPANY**

365 Third Avenue (26th)
Reservations: 532-5222
Credit Cards: AE, CB, DC, MC, V
Inexpensive

Company is delightful and a bargain. Attractive with soft lights, fresh flowers, and high ceilings, it features live music every night from 9:30 p.m. until the 3:30 a.m. closing. The food is excellent whether you order a burger and salad ($3.75) or something more ambitious: chicken Kiev ($7.95), baked filet of lemon sole stuffed with crabmeat ($8.95), or a generous cut of prime ribs ($13.50). Give Company a try and you'll probably become a regular.

EMPIRE DINER*

210 Tenth Avenue (22nd)
Reservations: 243-2736
No credit cards
Moderate
Free parking

Glitzy is as good a word as any for this Art Deco diner. It's open 24 hours a day, and it's where many of the more flamboyant night people stop on their way home or wherever. Stick to dishes like bacon and eggs, sandwiches, or salads; the more elaborate offerings aren't worth it. Prices are about 20 percent higher here than at the usual coffee shop.

♫ MAX'S KANSAS CITY*

213 Park Avenue South (17th)
Reservations: 777-7870
No credit cards
Inexpensive

This was the "in" home of underground rock in the 1960s, and while the beautiful people have left for new diversions, the beat goes on. Max's now is a showcase for rock groups that range from a Bo Diddley sound to punk. Admission is $5 on Friday and Saturday, $3 the rest of the week (sometimes higher when there's a name performer). Music gets under way about 11 p.m. Phone during the day for a taped rundown on who's appearing. Standard saloon food. The latest in pinball machines and what is reputedly the largest jukebox in the city help keep the downstairs noisy.

♫ MC FEELY'S*

565 West 23rd Street
Reservations: 929-4432
Credit Cards: AE, MC, V
Moderate

It's a bit of a walk from the Roundabout to Eleventh Avenue, but this place is worth it. An 1890s restaurant, geared to the trade from the busy docks, McFeely's slumbered until it was restored five years ago. It's beautiful—there's no other word for it. The carved oak bar, the woodwork, the painted glass ceiling, the large, comfortable dining room—all contribute to the glow of nostalgia. The food is honest, if not inspired. Entrees are in the $7.50– $14 range. The steaks, including the steak au poivre, are excellent; so is the chicken sautéed with white wine and lemon. For an appetizer, try the smoked trout with horseradish sauce, or the black bean soup. At the other end, the chocolate mousse is delicious. And do include a leisurely drink at the bar in your visit so that you can enjoy the full beauty of the room. A piano player entertains in the dining room Tuesday through Saturday.

PETE'S TAVERN*

129 East 18th Street
Reservations: 473-7676
Credit Cards: AE, DC, MC, V
Inexpensive to Moderate   Sunday–Thursday, 11 a.m.–12 midnight; Friday–
Saturday to 1 a.m.

Drinks have been poured here since 1864; the bar is the original and so are the booths across from it. Over the first booth as you come in is O'Henry's *Gift of the Magi* (you remember: He sold his watch, she sold her hair but they had a nice Christmas anyway) as it originally appeared in the New York *World*. He wrote it in that booth. Eat in front if you can for the atmosphere—not that the rear dining room isn't nice but it isn't as old. Standard Southern Italian fare reasonably priced. A variety of pasta dishes in the $5–$6 range plus chicken tetrazzini ($6.50), veal piccata ($7.25), and shrimp scampi ($9). In the summer there's an outdoor café with a nice view up Irving Place to the statue of Edwin Booth in Gramercy Park.

R. J. SCOTTY'S**

202 Ninth Avenue (22nd)
Reservations: 741-2148
Credit Cards: MC, V
Inexpensive to Moderate

Every neighborhood needs a good Italian restaurant and R. J. Scotty's (*R. J. Scotty's???*) is Chelsea's. The walls are paneled, the bar is old, and the pasta ($6–$9) is excellent. Some special treats: steamed mussels ($5), the linguine Scotty's with a mixed seafood sauce ($9.50), and fettucine Alfredo. The cappuccino, too, is extra nice.

♫ VARIATIONS*

358 West 23rd Street
Reservations: 691-1559
Credit Cards: AE, MC, V
Moderate to Expensive

It's a surprise to find a chic French restaurant in Chelsea and a pleasant surprise at that—flowers and candles on your table and sophisticated piano music to accompany your late supper. Everything is a la carte and entrees range up to $15. The pâté de champagne is excellent, as are the duck in an apricot glaze and the steak au poivre. Don't miss the apple walnut cake that comes in a hot cranberry sauce; it alone is worth the trip.

♫ WEST BOONDOCK**

114 Tenth Avenue (17th)
Reservations: Not accepted
Credit Cards: AE, DC, MC, V
Inexpensive to Moderate

This has been the place for good soul food for more than 15 years. Good jazz, too. The atmosphere is old-timey, warm, and friendly. Fried chicken, luscious ham hocks, chitterlings, fine ribs, collard greens, and black-eyed peas. Dishes are from $5 to $9, including two vegetables. Wrap things up with an Irish coffee; it's as good as any in the city.

GREENWICH VILLAGE

West Village

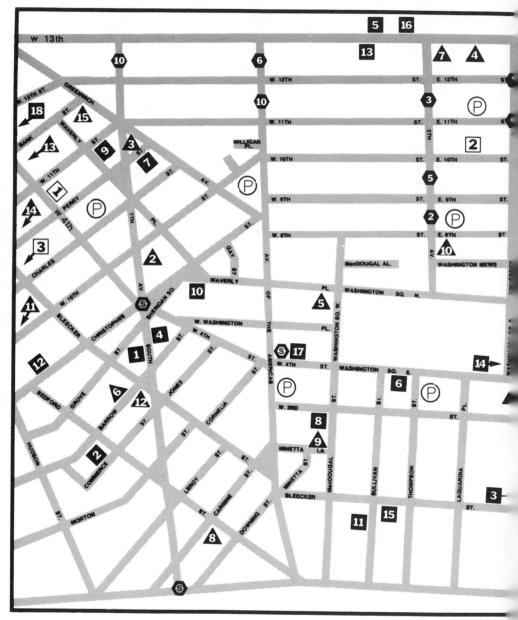

■ Theatres

1. Actor's Playhouse / 100 Seventh
2. Cherry Lane / 38 Commerce
3. Circle in the Square (Downtown) / 159 Bleecker
4. Circle Repertory Company / 99 Seventh Avenue South
5. Force 13 Theatre / 43 West 13
6. Judson Poets' Theatre / 55 Washington Square
7. Perry Street Theatre / 31 Perry
8. Players Theatre / 115 MacDougal
9. Richard Morse Mime Theatre / 224 Waverly Place
10. Ridiculous Theatre Company / 1 Sheridan Square
11. Sullivan Street Playhouse / 181 Sullivan
12. Theatre de Lys / 121 Christopher
13. Thirteenth Street Theatre Repertory Company / 50 West 13
14. University Theatre / Washington Square Players / 35 West 4
15. Village Gate / Top of the Gate / Bleecker at Thompson
16. Vital Arts Center / 78 Fifth
17. Washington Square Church / 135 West 4
18. Westbeth Theatre Center / 151 Bank

▲ Restaurants

1. Bottom Line / 15 West 4
2. Buffalo Roadhouse / 87 Seventh Avenue South
3. Caffe da Alfredo / 17 Perry
4. Café Loup / 18 East 13
5. Coach House / 110 Waverly Place
6. Le Paris Bistro / 48 Barrow
7. Lone Star Cafe / 61 Fifth
8. Mary's / 42 Bedford
9. Minetta Tavern / 113 MacDougal
10. One Fifth (⅕) / 1 Fifth
11. Sazerac House / 533 Hudson
12. Sweet Basil / 88 Seventh
13. Trattoria da Alfredo / 90 Bank
14. White Horse Tavern / 567 Hudson
15. Ye Waverly Inn / 16 Bank

□ Other Attractions

1. Chisholm Gallery / 277 West 4
2. Margo Feiden Galleries / 51 East 10
3. Quinion Books / 541 Hudson

🔴 Bus Numbers

🅢 Subway Stations

Ⓟ Parking

→ One-way Street

⇄ Two-way Street

East Village

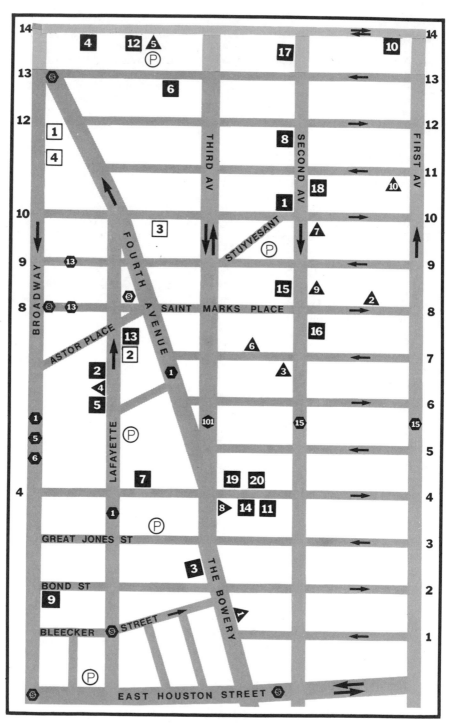

■ Theatres

1. Arts Project at St. Mark's Church/Second & 10
2. Astor Place/434 Lafayette
3. Bouwerie Lane Theatre/Jean Cocteau Repertory/330 Bowery
4. Classic Theatre/114 West 14
5. Colonnades Theatre Lab/428 Lafayette
6. CSC Repertory/136 East 13
7. Dramatis Personae/25 East 4
8. Entermedia/189 Second
9. First Amendment & Improvisation Company/2 Bond
10. Jewish Repertory Theatre/344 East 14
11. LaMama E.T.C., Inc./74A East 4
12. New York Art Theatre Institute/116 East 14
13. The New York Shakespeare Festival/Public Theatre/425 Lafayette
14. New York Theatre Ensemble/62 East 4
15. The Open Space Theatre Experiment/133 Second
16. Orpheum/126 Second
17. Shelter West Theatre Company/217 Second
18. Theatre for the New City/162 Second
19. Truck and Warehouse Theatre/79 East 4
20. Wonderhorse Theatre/83 East 4

▲ Restaurants

1. CBGB & OMFUG/315 Bowery
2. Club 57/57 St. Marks Place
3. Kiev Restaurant/117 Second
4. Lady Astor's/430 Lafayette
5. Luchow's/110 East 14
6. McSorley's Old Ale House/15 East 7
7. Second Avenue Kosher Delicatessen/156 Second
8. Phoebe's Place/361 Bowery
9. Ukranian Restaurant and Caterers/140 Second
10. Veniero's/342 East 11

□ Other Attractions

1. Dayton's/824 Broadway
2. New York Shakespeare Festival Shop/Public Theater/425 Lafayette
3. Richard Stoddard/90 East 10
4. Strand Book Store/828 Broadway

🔟 Bus Numbers

Ⓢ Subway Stations

Ⓟ Parking

→ One-way Street

⇄ Two-way Street

Off Broadway happened in the Village. Perhaps it began when Eugene O'Neill received his first New York production at the Provincetown Playhouse. Beyond question, Off Broadway became viable at the original Circle in the Square, La-Mama, and the Theatre de Lys. The seeds sown in those three theatres bore the fruit we enjoy today. Not that the Village is living on its past. It still is by far the major Off Broadway area. Surely it isn't coincidental that Joseph Papp's Shakespeare Festival found its permanent home in the Village, nor is it by chance that *The Fantasticks* threatens to play forever on Sullivan Street. The Village is the Yin to Broadway's Yang. In a strange and beautiful way they fit together to make a theatrical universe.

THEATRES

ACTOR'S PLAYHOUSE

100 Seventh Avenue South (below Sheridan Square)

Box Office:	691-6226
Box Office Hours:	Tuesday–Sunday, 10 a.m.–6 p.m.
Credit Cards:	Varies with production TDF Vouchers Personal checks
Group Sales:	Through box office
Total Seating:	150 (Standing room, 20)
Stage Type:	Proscenium stage
	AC
	Handicapped: No access

This has been one of the busier Off Broadway theatres since it was built in the 1940s. Recent productions include *Marry Me a Little* by Stephen Sondheim, *Crimes Against Nature,* and *Last Summer at Blue Fish Cove.*

ARTS PROJECT AT ST. MARK'S CHURCH

Second Avenue and 10th Street

674-0910

In this three-century-old landmark church is one of the most ambitious community multimedia art projects—and one of the best. Since the early 1960s, St. Mark's has been a powerful force in the performing arts—and the literary arts, particularly poetry. This was the home of Theatre Genesis, one of the early influences in the Off-Off Broadway movement. A bad fire here in 1978 destroyed much of the performance space, and St. Mark's still hasn't recovered its full momentum. Not to include it in this guide, however, would truly be an unpardonable oversight.

Actor's Playhouse

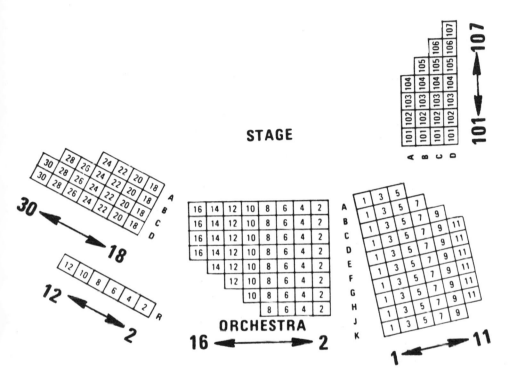

STAGE

ORCHESTRA

209

ASTOR PLACE

434 Lafayette Street

Owner: Albert Poland
Box Office: 254-4370
Box Office Hours: 11 a.m. to curtain
Credit Cards: AE, MC, V   Personal checks by mail only
Group Sales: Through theatre party agents
Total Seating: 299 (Orchestra, 216; Mezzanine, 83)
Stage Type: Proscenium stage
No AC
Handicapped: No access

The Astors lived in this landmark building, and no doubt would have approved of the quality of the productions presented here since part of it was converted into a theatre in 1969. Sixteen-year-old John Travolta made his stage debut here in *Rain*, which starred Madeleine le Roux. Al Pacino and Jill Clayburgh starred in *It's Called the Sugar Plum*, on the same bill with Israel Horovitz's *The Indian Wants the Bronx*, also starring Mr. Pacino. Other major productions have included: Sam Shepard's *The Unseen Hand;* Tom Eyen's *The Dirtiest Show in Town; Family Business; Modigliani* starring Jeffery De Munn; and Eileen Brennen and Susan Sarandan in *A Coupla' White Chicks Sitting Around Talking.*

BOUWERIE LANE THEATRE
Jean Cocteau Repertory

330 Bowery

Box Office: 677-0060
Box Office Hours: 11 a.m.–5 p.m.; phone one hour before performance at theatre
Credit Cards: None   TDF Vouchers   Personal checks
Group Sales: Through box office
Season: August–June
Total Seating: 140
Stage Type: Proscenium stage
AC
Handicapped: Semi-accessible

One of the few rotating repertory companies in America, the Jean Cocteau Repertory looks for several kinds of plays: masterpieces not recently produced in this country, such as Philip Massinger's *A New Way to Pay Old Debts;* a "closet" drama by a writer famous in another field, *i.e.,* Percy Bysshe Shelley's *The Cenci;* or a forgotten work by a well-known playwright, like *Vera* by Oscar Wilde. All plays in the repertoire are performed by members of the resident acting company, some of whom have been with the Cocteau since it was founded in 1971 by Eve Adamson. The company also presents a special matinee series of innovative productions of better-known classics for school groups. The company is involved in the promotion of the Bowery area as a revitalized arts community. There is a four-play subscription series each season; the cost per subscription is $20.

ORCHESTRA

111	109	107	105	103	101	**A**	102	104	106	108	110	112
111	109	107	105	103	101	**B**	102	104	106	108	110	112
111	109	107	105	103	101	**C**	102	104	106	108	110	112
						D	102	104	106	108	110	112
111	109	107	105	103	101	**E**	102	104	106	108	110	112
111	109	107	105	103	101	**F**	102	104	106	108	110	112
111	109	107	105	103	101	**G**	102	104	106	108	110	112
111	109	107	105	103	101	**H**	102	104	106	108	110	112
111	109	107	105	103	101	**J**	102	104	106	108	110	112
111	109	107	105	103	101	**K**	102	104	106	108	110	112
111	109	107	105	103	101	**L**	102	104	106	108	110	112
111	109	107	105	103	101	**M**	102	104	106	108	110	112
111	109	107	105	103	101	**N**	102	104	106	108	110	112
111	109	107	105	103	101	**O**	102	104	106	108	110	112
111	109	107	105	103	101	**P**	102	104	106	108	110	112
	109	107	105	103	101	**Q**	102	104	106	108	110	112
		107	105	103	101	**R**	102	104	106	108		
			105	103	101	**S**	102	104	106			

MEZZANINE

113	111	109	107	105	103	101	**AA**	102	104	106	108	110	112
113	111	109	107	105	103	101	**BB**	102	104	106	108	110	112
113	111	109	107	105	103	101	**CC**	102	104	106	108	110	112
113	111	109	107	105	103	101	**DD**	102	104	106	108	110	112
	111	109	107	105	103	101	**EE**	102	104	106	108	110	112
113	111	109	107	105	103	101	**FF**	102	104	106	108	110	112
113	111	109	107	105	103	101	**GG**	102	104	106			

Cherry Lane

-STAGE-

13	11	9	7	5	3	1
13						
	11	9				
			7			
				5	3	1

A
B
C
D
E
F
G
H
I
J
K
L
M
N
O
P

2	4	6	8	10	12

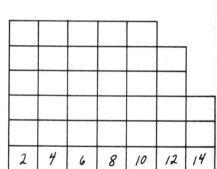

2	4	6	8	10	12	14

CHERRY LANE

38 Commerce Street

Owner: Andrea Carroad
Box Office: 989-2020
Box Office Hours: Monday, 1 p.m.–6 p.m.; Tuesday–Thursday, 1 p.m.–8 p.m.; Friday, 10 a.m.–8 p.m.; Saturday, 10 a.m.–10 p.m.; Sunday, 11 a.m.–7:30 p.m.
Credit Cards: AE, MC, V   CHARGIT   Personal checks
Group Sales: 398-8383
Total Seating: 184
Stage Type: Proscenium stage
AC
Handicapped: Semi-accessible

Since 1924, the Cherry Lane has been an important part of the Greenwich Village theatre scene. Legend has it that it was founded by Edna St. Vincent Millay, who lived in the neighborhood and was active in some of the Cherry Lane's early productions. In recent years, its presentations have included: *Godspell;* David Mammet's *Sexual Perversities in Chicago; The Passion of Dracula;* and, when this was written, David Rimmer's hit musical *Album* had moved here from Lower Fifth Avenue, starring Kevin Bacon, Jan Leslie Harding, Keith Gordon, and Jenny Wright in the WPA production.

CIRCLE IN THE SQUARE (DOWNTOWN)

159 Bleecker Street

Owner: Ted Mann
Box Office: 254-6330
Box Office Hours: 12 noon to curtain
Credit Cards: AE, MC, V ($1 service charge per order)   TDF Vouchers
Personal checks for mail orders only
Group Sales: Through New York Shakespeare Festival
Total Seating: 299 on one level
Stage Type: Three-quarter arena stage
AC
Handicapped: Semi-accessible

Circle in the Square has moved uptown now to a beautiful new theatre under the Uris. It still owns this theatre, renting it out to Off Broadway producers. Enough theatre history was made here, though, to make it worthwhile to pause a moment and reflect. Circle in the Square was founded in 1950 by Theodore Mann, José Quintero, Emile Stevens, Jason Wingreen, Aileen Cramer, and Edward Mann. The theatre opened in February, 1951, with *Dark of the Moon* and nobody took much notice. A year of struggle later, they gambled on a young actress who was supporting herself by working in a button factory and a play that had failed on Broadway. Her name was Geraldine Page and the play was Tennessee Williams's *Summer and Smoke*. Brooks Atkinson, then drama critic of *The New York Times,* came opening night and the rest is history. *Summer and Smoke* ran for a year, Ms. Page was a star, and Off Broadway was off and running. The next big break came in 1956 when Eugene O'Neill's widow gave permission to the group to produce two plays: *The Iceman Cometh,* which was to make a star of Jason Robards, Jr.; and *Long Day's Journey into Night,* which the group opened on Broadway to critical and popular acclaim. In the 1960s, Circle in the Square introduced American audiences to plays like Genet's *The Balcony* (co-produced with Lucille Lortel), revived classics like *The Trojan Women,* and worked with new playwrights like Terrance McNally, Leonard Melfi, Jules Feiffer, Israel Horovitz, and Murray Schisgal. The reputations of such actors as George C. Scott, Colleen Dewhurst, Dustin Hoffman, Peter Falk, and George Segal were, in part, established here. A theatre school was formed in the late 1960s; it is now fully accredited and has more than 250 students. The Circle in the Square moved from a one-time nightclub off Sheridan Square (which gave the inspiration for the name) to Bleecker Street to what had been the Amato Opera House. At this writing, it is the home of the long-running hit, *I'm Getting My Act Together and Taking It on the Road.*

Circle in the Square (Downtown)

CIRCLE REPERTORY COMPANY

99 Seventh Avenue South

Box Office: 924-7100
Box Office Hours: Tuesday–Saturday, 1 p.m.–8 p.m.; Sunday, 1 p.m.–7 p.m.
Credit Cards: None CHARGIT Personal checks
Group Sales: Jane Brandmeir, marketing office (691-3210)
Total Seating: 160
Season: Subscription series, October–June; summer production, July–September
Stage Type: Black box, flexible seating
AC
Handicapped: Semi-accessible

In the late 1920s, this was Billy Rose's Nut Club; in the 1960s it was the Sheridan Playhouse, and, since 1974, it has housed the only permanent company in this country of artists devoted to creating new American drama. Lanford Wilson, Marshall W. Mason, and others founded the Circle Rep in 1969 and for the first five years used a loft on the Upper West Side to house its productions. The resident ensemble of 35 actors, many of whom have worked together for the full 10 years, have turned their talents to new works by resident playwrights Lanford Wilson, Milan Stitt, John Bishop, Julie Bovasso, Albert Inaurato, and others. Original productions here have included such contemporary classics as Wilson's *The Hot l Baltimore;* Mark Medoff's *When You Coming Back, Red Rider?;* Edward J. Moore's *The Sea Horse;* Jules Feiffer's *Knock Knock;* Inaurato's *Gemini;* and Corinne Jacker's *Harry Outside.* Two more recent distinguished productions were Pat Carroll in Marty Martin's *Gertrude Stein, Gertrude Stein,* and Judd Hirsch and Trish Hawkins in Lanford Wilson's *Talley's Folly,* winner of the Pulitzer Prize.

CLASSIC THEATRE

114 West 14th Street

Box Office: 242-3900
Box Office Hours: None, telephone orders only
Credit Cards: None TDF Vouchers Personal checks for advance sales
Group Sales: Though box office
Season: Early fall–late spring
Total Seating: 60 to 70, depending upon production
Stage Type: Flexible open space
AC
Handicapped: No access

This company is currently housed in a loft and offers revivals of rarely performed classics and neglected modern masterpieces. In recent years, productions have included *Oedipus at Colonus; Danton's Death;* Hugo's *Mary Tudor;* Dostoyevsky's *Notes from the Underground;* Turgenev's *The Bachelor;* Pirandello's *Each in His Own Way; Journey's End;* and *A Moon for the Misbegotten.* Its most recent offering, when this was written, was *An Evening with Strindberg and de Maupassant*—Strindberg's *Playing with Fire* and several Guy de Maupassant short stories adapted for the stage by director Jonathan Amacker.

Circle Repertory Company

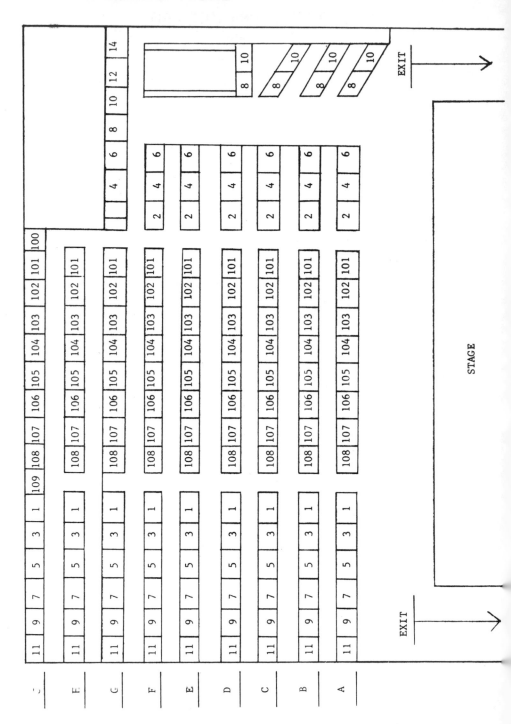

COLONNADES THEATRE LAB

428 Lafayette Street

Owner: Robert Ogden
Box Office: 673-2222
Box Office Hours: Vary with production
Credit Cards: MC, V   TDF Vouchers   Personal checks with ID   Senior citizen and student discount (with ID)
Group Sales: Through box office
Season: Usually winter–spring
Total Seating: 100
Stage Type: Flexible open space
No AC
Handicapped: No access

Artistic director Michael Lessac founded the Colonnades Theatre Lab in 1974 to provide a permanent home for a resident acting company. In a real sense, the Colonnades functions as a "regional" theatre in the heart of the city. It shares the landmark building with the Astor Place Theatre. *Molière in Spite of Himself* was developed here and moved in March, 1981, to the Hartman Theatre in Stamford, Connecticut, starring Richard Kiley. *Shakespeare's Cabaret,* developed in 1980, moved to the Bijou for a Broadway run. Another 1980 presentation, *Guests of the Nation,* was filmed by WNET for its Great Performances Series with Frank Converse and Estelle Parsons joining the original Colonnades company. More recent productions have included *Marriage by Lanternlight,* adapted by Michael Feingold, *Aryan Antics—An Evening of Caucasian Humor* by Karen Knapp and David Marsh; *Ragged Pants* conceived by Lisa Wojnovich with a new score by Eliot Sokolov; and *Two by Offenbach,* also adapted by Michael Feingold.

CSC REPERTORY

136 East 13th Street

Owner: Dennis Turner and Christopher Martin
Box Office: 677-4210
Box Office Hours: 12 noon–8 p.m.
Credit Cards: AE, MC, V   CHARGIT   Personal checks
Group Sales: Through box office
Season: October–May
Total Seating: 200
Stage Type: Semi-thrust, three-quarter round
No AC
Handicapped: Semi-accessible

"Classics in the present tense" is how Christopher Martin, CSC founder and artistic director, describes the goal of this company. The productions try to have an effect on today's audiences comparable to that of the play's original impact. The emphasis is on rarely performed classics and new plays by foreign authors. CSC also commissions new translations or adaptations. Some recent productions: *Shakespeare's Henry IV, Parts I and II;* John O'Keeffe's *Wild Oats;* Frank Wedekind's *The Marquis of Keith,* translated by Christopher Martin.

"Actors should be overheard, not listened to, and the audience is fifty per cent of the performance."

SHIRLEY BOOTH

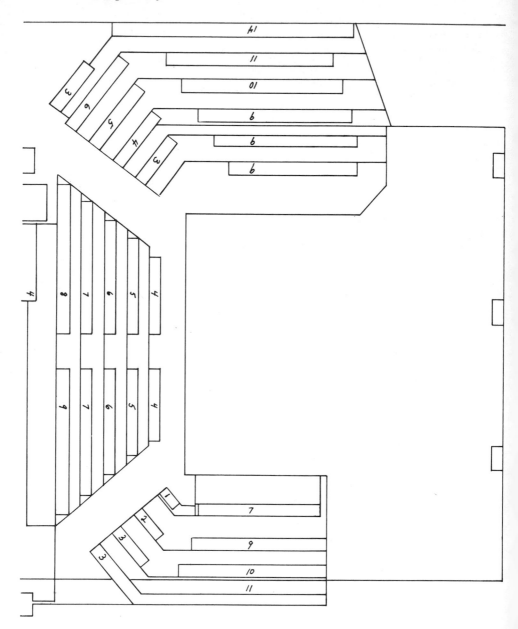

DRAMATIS PERSONAE

25 East 4th Street

Box Office: 468-8285
Box Office Hours: One hour before performance
Credit Cards: None   TDF Vouchers
Group Sales: Through box office
Total Seating: 150
Stage Type: Proscenium stage
AC
Handicapped: Semi-accessible

This company was founded in 1967 and moved to this theatre in 1979. Artistic director Steven Baker, who owns the theatre, attempts a blend of the great classics and exciting interpretations of original comedies and dramas. Recent productions have included *Evita Peron* and *Seducers,* by Guy de Maupassant as adapted by A. R. Bell.

ENTERMEDIA

189 Second Avenue (12th)

Box Office: 475-4191
Box Office Hours: 12 noon to curtain, if performance
Credit Cards: AE, MC, V
Group Sales: Through box office
Total Seating: 1,077 (Orchestra, 582; Balcony, 341; Boxes, 54; Standing room, 100)
Stage Type: Proscenium stage
AC
Handicapped: Semi-accessible

This theatre was built in 1926 as the Yiddish Art Theatre, and at different times has been known as the Phoenix and the Eden. In recent years, the Entermedia has been the Off Broadway birthplace of *Grease, Oh! Calcutta!,* and *The Best Little Whorehouse in Texas.* David Secter is the creative director of the theatre; Joseph Asaro, the executive director. There is a well-appointed lounge on the lower level.

FIRST AMENDMENT & IMPROVISATION COMPANY

2 Bond Street

Box Office: 473-1472
Box Office Hours: Reservations taken on answering machine
Credit Cards: None   TDF Vouchers   Personal checks for mail orders
Total Seating: 100
Stage Type: Cabaret seating
AC
Handicapped: Semi-accessible

This company, under the artistic direction of Barbara Contardi, does pure improvisation and presents comic sketches; *Funny Ladies* and *Strictly Improv,* both conceived by Ms. Contardi, and the company's *Crooked Teeth* are recent examples. The company, now six years old, has toured with Eddie Fisher and Donald O'Connor.

Entermedia

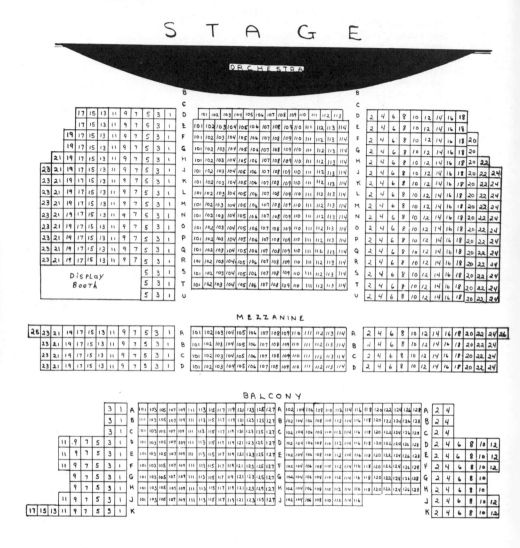

FORCE 13 THEATRE
43 West 13th Street

Owner: Margery Dignan
Box Office: 924-7277
Box Office Hours: Any time (answering machine)
Credit Cards: None   TDF Vouchers   Personal checks
Group Sales: Through box office
Season: September–June
Total Seating: 74
Stage Type: Open flexible space
No AC
Handicapped: No access

For $5 (less if you use TDF Vouchers) you sit, cabaret style, enjoy free wine and cheese and watch productions that this ensemble repertory group describe as dedicated to "the task of developing a style of drama based on the harmonious integration of conventional acting with music and acrobatic movement." Sounds heavy, but it isn't. It's a delightful hybrid of drama, acrobatics, and dancing—and it works! Recently, Force 13 (a bit above Force 12, which is the highest wind speed on the Beaufort scale) has been performing Israel Horovitz's *Acrobats,* and two versions of the Japanese Noh drama *Kiyotsune.* (*Acrobats* was in its third season here; it won a *Villager* award for outstanding ensemble.) The Noh drama was first played straight in traditional Japanese style, then in parody with the company in cowboy gear and the music, country western. At last report, performances were Wednesday at 8 p.m., Friday and Saturday at 9:30 p.m.

JEWISH REPERTORY THEATRE
344 East 14th Street

Owner: Emanuel Midtown YM-YWHA
Box Office: 674-7200
Box Office Hours: 1 p.m.–9 p.m., if performance
Credit Cards: MC   TDF Vouchers   Personal checks
Group Sales: Through box office
Season: September–June
Total Seating: 100
Stage Type: Flexible open space
AC
Handicapped: Semi-accessible

The Jewish Repertory Theatre, under the artistic direction of Ron Avoni, presents plays in English relating to the Jewish experience. Some recent productions were John Howard Lawson's *Success Story,* Harold Pinter's *The Birthday Party,* and *Marya* by Isaac Babel, adapted by Christopher Hampton. There are usually five plays in a season's series and a subscription is $24. The group is in its seventh year.

JUDSON POETS' THEATRE
Judson Memorial Church
55 Washington Square

Box Office: 777-0033
Box Office Hours: Monday–Friday, 1 p.m.–5 p.m.
Credit Cards: None   TDF Vouchers   Personal checks
Group Sales: None
Season: October–May
Total Seating: 150–200, depending on production
Stage Type: Flexible open space
No AC
Handicapped: No access

Four productions a year, running four to five weekends, of oratorios and experimental new works, are presented in this church. Some recent offerings included *Christmas Wrappings, The Agony of Paul* by Al Carmines, and *Dr. Faustus's Delights.*

LaMAMA E.T.C., INC.
74A East 4th Street

Box Office Hours: 10 a.m.–11 p.m. (sometimes answering machine)
Credit Cards: None   TDF Vouchers   Personal checks
Group Sales: Through box office
Season: October–June
Total Seating: Three spaces, one of 250, two of 60
Stage Type: Flexible open spaces
No AC
Handicapped: Semi-accessible

When Ellen Stewart used an unemployment check to put a deposit on a Greenwich Village basement in 1961, it was a small beginning for what now is now one of the city's major theatrical centers. Since the company's inception, nearly 1,000 productions have been staged, including 800 with original musical scores. Many theatrical *wunderkind* have been nurtured by LaMama: playwrights Sam Shepard, Lanford Wilson, Ed Bullins, and Tom Eyen; directors Wilford Leach (*The Pirates of Penzance*), Marshall Mason (*Fifth of July*), Tom O'Horgan (*Hair*), and Andrei Serban (*The Cherry Orchard*); composers Phillip Glass (*Einstein on the Beach*) and Elizabeth Swados (*Runaways*); and performers such as Billy Crystal, Frederic Forrest, Bette Midler, Garrett Morris, and Kevin O'Connor. LaMama was the first American theatre to present Harold Pinter (*The Room* in 1962), and plays from many countries have received their American premieres here. Recently, director Peter Brook and his Centre International de Creation Theatrales presented *L'Os, Ubu,* and *The Ik and the Conference of the Birds* and won an Obie in the process. LaMama has sent companies on European tours since 1965, the year Ms. Stewart founded the Theatre at the Center for American Students and Artists in Paris. The building, LaMama's home since 1970, was built in the 1880s as a German music hall. It was refurbished and converted into theatre spaces with the help of a Ford Foundation grant. The two smaller spaces frequently serve such troupes as the Pan-Asian Repertory Theatre and Mabou Mines.

NEW FEDERAL THEATRE
Henry Street Settlement Arts for Living Center
466 Grand Street

Box Office: 598-0400
Box Office Hours: Tuesday–Saturday, 9:15 a.m.–6 p.m.
Credit Cards: None   TDF Vouchers
Group Sales: Through box office
Season: October–June
Total Seating: 350
Stage Type: Proscenium stage
AC
Handicapped: Semi-accessible

Woodie King, Jr., founded the New Federal Theatre in 1970 in order to bring minority theatre to the audience for which it was originally intended: the people of the city's Lower East Side. The theatre has also been successful in developing minority playwrights and actors and has brought national attention to their work. Among them are J. E. Franklin (whose *Black Girl* has been filmed), Ron Milner, Ed Pomerantz, Joseph Lizardi, and Ntozake Shange. The New Federal Theatre has an arrangement with the New York Shakespeare Festival whereby plays are showcased here, then produced at one of the festival's theatres. Ms. Shange's *For Colored Girls Who Have Considered Suicide When the Rainbow Is Enuf* was done this way, and it ended up on Broadway.

NEW YORK ART THEATRE INSTITUTE

116 East 14th Street

Box Office: 228-1470
Box Office Hours: Monday–Friday, 10 a.m.–10 p.m.; Saturday, 1 p.m.–10 p.m.
Credit Cards: None   TDF Vouchers   Personal choice
Group Sales: Mark Statman (228-1470)
Season: September–December, January–June
Total Seating: 52
Stage Type: Flexible open space
No AC
Handicapped: No access

In a converted loft, artistic director Donald Sanders has been presenting an interesting series of contemporary plays since the group's founding in 1977. Representative productions: *Torrents of Spring* by Yvonne Turtenev; *Thirty-Three Scenes or the Possibility of Human Happiness* by Donald Sanders; Arnold Weinstein's *The Party;* and *Naked Lunch,* the Donald Sanders adaptation of the William Burroughs novel. Young performers are auditioned for training with the company at the Institute.

THE NEW YORK SHAKESPEARE FESTIVAL/PUBLIC THEATER

425 Lafayette Street

Box Office: 598-7150
Box Office Hours: Monday–Sunday, 1 p.m.–8 p.m.
Credit Cards: AE, DC, MC, V (Service charge of $1 per order on phone credit purchases)   TDF Vouchers (toward the purchase of Quiktix on Tuesday–Thursday nights and Saturday matinee
Group Sales: Grouptix, 598-7107 (All Public Theater productions and *A Chorus Line*)
Total Seating: Seven theatres: Newman, 299; Anspacher, 275; Martinson, 150; LuEsther Hall, 135; Other Stage, 100; Little Theater, 90; The Old Prop Shop, 100 (Except for Newman and Martinson, seating varies with production)
Stage Type: Proscenium stage (Newman), Thrust (Anspacher), Flexible open spaces (all others)
AC (except LuEster Hall)
Handicapped: Semi-accessible

"The single most important and flourishing theatrical institution in the country," said *The New York Times* about Joseph Papp's Public Theater and the New York Shakespeare Festival. There's no denying it. By any measurement this is the most dynamic and protean force in the theatre today. The huge Astor Library Building was saved from demolition and purchased by the New York Shakespeare Festival in 1966. It was converted to theatrical spaces, the headquarters of Mr. Papp and the festival, and dedicated to the production of new works by American playwrights. It opened in 1967 with the original production of *Hair.* In 1970 a financial crisis was averted, in part because of a dusk-to-dawn marathon of *The Wars of the Roses.* Also that year, the Public produced Charles Gordone's *No Place to Be Somebody,* the first play by a black writer to win the Pulitzer Prize. The city purchased the Public's landmark building in 1971, easing its financial burden. David Rabe's *The Basic Training of Pavlo Hummel* and his *Sticks and Bones* were premiered at the Public in 1971, *Sticks and Bones* moving to Broadway the following year. Then Jason Miller's *That Championship Season* premiered here and went to Broadway, a Tony Award, and a Pulitzer Prize. In 1974, Miguel Pinero's *Short Eyes* opened here, moved to the Beaumont, and won the New York Drama Critics' Award as Best American Play. *A Chorus Line* opened here in 1975 and moved to Broadway to become the hit of the decade, winning the Drama Critics' Best Musical Award, the Tony Best Musical Award, and the Pulitzer Prize. Ed Bullins's *The Taking of Miss Janie* won the Drama Critics' Best American Play Award for a clean sweep. In 1976, Ntozake Shange's *For Colored Girls Who Have Considered Suicide When the Rainbow Is Enuf* was the Public's contribution to Broadway. In 1978, the tradition continued with David Mamet's

The Water Engine and Liz Swados's *Runaways*. The following year, the Public's production of Gretchen Cryer and Nancy Ford's *I'm Getting My Act Together and Taking It on the Road* established itself as a long-run Off Broadway hit. From its various locations, the New York Shakespeare Festival has sent 11 plays and musicals to Broadway and has produced four specials for television. The Public alone does some 25 productions every year, and also runs series in New Jazz, film, and poetry. In another activity, the festival sends a touring theatre each summer, a five-trailer caravan that goes to parks and playgrounds in the five boroughs. The touring theatre makes 20 to 25 stops in a four-week season performing to audiences averaging some 1,500. The original productions (*New Lincoln Village* and *The Mighty Gents* are recent examples) focus on ghetto life.

The New York Shakespeare Festival/Public Theatre (Anspacher)

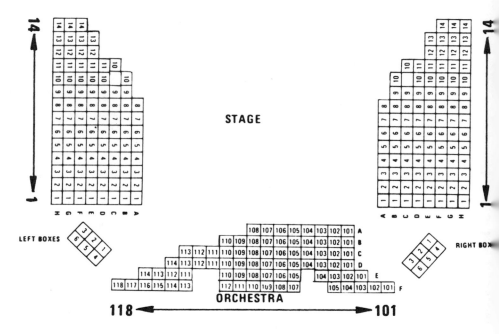

The New York Shakespeare Festival/Public Theatre (Newman)

STAGE

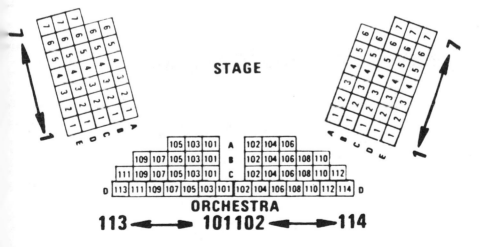

ORCHESTRA

19 ◄────────────────────► 1

The New York Shakespeare Festival/Public Theatre (The Other Stage)

STAGE

ORCHESTRA

113 ◄──► 101 102 ◄──► 114

NEW YORK THEATER ENSEMBLE

62 East 4th Street

Box Office: 477-4120
Box Office Hours: One hour before performance (answering machine other times)
Credit Cards: None TDF Vouchers
Group Sales: Through box office
Total Seating: Arena, 145; Proscenium stage, 160
Stage Type: Flexible open space, Proscenium in old music hall
AC
Handicapped: No access

In a theatre built in 1899, the New York Theater Ensemble presents a repertory of world classics, Shakespeare, musicals, and new plays. *Women Behind Bars* and *An Evening with Joan Crawford* originated here.

THE OPEN SPACE THEATRE EXPERIMENT

133 Second Avenue (8th)

Box Office: 254-8630
Box Office Hours: Tuesday–Sunday, 12 noon–8 p.m.
Credit Cards: None TDF Vouchers
Group Sales: Through box office
Total Seating: 75
Stage Type: Open stage
AC
Handicapped: Semi-accessible

In this former movie theatre, artistic director Lynne Michaels has produced a range of interesting productions, from an experimental production of Ibsen's *Peer Gynt* with an original score by Dan Erkkila to Strindberg's *A Dream Play* and Melba Thomas's *Where Have all the Dreamers Gone.*

ORPHEUM

126 Second Avenue (7th)

Owner: Eastside Theatre Corporation
Box Office: 260-8480
Box Office Hours: 1 p.m. to curtain, if performance
Credit Cards: Varies with production
Group Sales: Through box office
Total Seating: 299 (Orchestra, 249; Balcony, 50)
Stage Type: Open-end stage
AC
Handicapped: Semi-accessible (bathroom upstairs)

The Orpheum has been a legitimate theatre since it was built in 1908 and was part of the heyday of Yiddish theatre in the area. After a 1958 renovation, the Orpheum became the home of *Little Mary Sunshine, Anything Goes, Your Own Thing, The Typists and The Tiger, The Me Nobody Knows,* and *Rainbow* (from which it acquired a brass firepole). In 1978, the new owners spent two years refurbishing the Orpheum and after reopening, it has housed such productions as *The San Francisco Mime Troup, My Old Friends, Big Bad Burlesque, Fugue in a Nursery, Cocktail Party, Laurie Anderson/USA Part II,* and *Lust for Space.*

Orpheum

STAGE

MAIN FLOOR

ROW	SEATS	
1	12	12
2	12	24
3	12	36
4	12	48
5	12	60
6	12	72
7	6	78
8	13	91
9	14	105
10	14	119
11	14	133
12	14	147
13	13	160
14	13	173
15	14	187
16	14	201
17	12	213
18	12	225
19	12	237
20	10	247
21	2	249

Seating (odd-numbered seats left of letter, even-numbered right):

Left seats	Row	Right seats
11 9 7 5 3 1	A	2 4 6 8 10 12
11 9 7 5 3 1	B	2 4 6 8 10 12
11 9 7 5 3 1	C	2 4 6 8 10 12
11 9 7 5 3 1	D	2 4 6 8 10 12
11 9 7 5 3 1	E	2 4 6 8 10 12
11 9 7 5 3 1	F	2 4 6 8 10 12
	G	2 4 6 8 10 12
11 9 7 5 3 1	H	2 4 6 8 10 12 14
13 11 9 7 5 3 1	J	2 4 6 8 10 12 14
13 11 9 7 5 3 1	K	2 4 6 8 10 12 14
13 11 9 7 5 3 1	L	2 4 6 8 10 12 14
13 11 9 7 5 3 1	M	2 4 6 8 10 12 14
13 11 9 7 5 3 1	N	2 4 6 8 10 12
13 11 9 7 5 3 1	O	2 4 6 8 10 12
13 11 9 7 5 3 1	P	2 4 6 8 10 12 14
13 11 9 7 5 3 1	Q	2 4 6 8 10 12 14
11 9 7 5 3 1	R	2 4 6 8 10 12
11 9 7 5 3 1	S	2 4 6 8 10 12
11 9 7 5 3 1	T	2 4 6 8 10 12
7 5 3 1	U	2 4 6 8 10 12
3 1	V	

BALCONY

Row	Seats										Row
AA	101	102	103	104	105	106	107	108	109	110	AA
BB	101	102	103	104	105	106	107	108	109	110	BB
CC	101	102	103	104	105	106	107	108	109	110	CC
DD	101	102	103	104	105	106	107	108	109	110	DD
EE	101	102	103	104	105	106	107	108	109	110	EE

ROW	SEATS	
1	10	10
2	10	20
3	10	30
4	10	40
5	10	50

PERRY STREET THEATER

31 Perry Street

Box Office: 255 -9186
Box Office Hours: Tuesday–Sunday, 12 noon–5 p.m.
Credit Cards: None   TDF Vouchers   Personal checks
Group Sales: None
Stage Type: Flexible open stage
AC
Handicapped: Semi-accessible

Since 1975, this theatre has presented a number of Off-Off Broadway productions including *Period of Adjustment,* and Alan Bowne's *Forty-Deuce,* directed by Michael Cristofer.

PLAYERS THEATRE

115 MacDougal Street

Box Office: 254-5076
Box Office Hours: Tuesday–Friday, 1 p.m.–8 p.m. Saturday, 1 p.m.–10 p.m.
Credit Cards: AE, MC, V   CHARGIT   Personal checks for mail order sales
Group Sales: Varies by production
Total seating: 248
Stage Type: Proscenium stage
AC
Handicapped: Semi-accessible (by elevator)

This charming Greenwich Village theatre was converted from a stable-garage in 1959. Now owned by Shakespearwrights, Inc., of which Donald H. Goldman is president, it is used by individual producers for such productions as *Naomi Court, Class Enemy, An Evening with Quentin Crisp, The Secret Life of Walter Mitty,* and *The Butler Did It.*

RICHARD MORSE MIME THEATRE

224 Waverly Place (2nd floor of St. John's in the Village parish hall)

Owner: Richard Morse
Box Office: 242-0530
Box Office Hours: Monday–Friday, 10 a.m.–6 p.m.; 1 p.m.–2 p.m., 7 p.m.–8 p.m., if
performance
Credit Cards: None   TDF Vouchers   Personal checks
Group Sales: Through box office
Season: October–April
Total Seating: 103
Stage Type: Proscenium stage
No AC
Handicapped: No access

This is the only theatre in the city performing mime on a regular basis, and it is considered a major force in pioneering an original mime tradition in America. The company, under the artistic direction of Richard Morse, is in its sixth New York season here. It also has played to enthusiastic audiences across the country and has taken state department tours abroad (a tour to the Orient is being planned for this year). From its inception, the company has rejected traditional mime practices such as white face in order to give a contemporary feeling to the artform. Recent productions have included Mr. Morse's *Appeal of the Big Apple; The Play of Herod* by Noah Greenberg and William Smolden; and Rasa Lisauskas Allan's *A Chip Off the Old Munk.*

Players Theatre

STAGE

12	10	8	6	4	2		1	3	5	7	9	11
	10	8	6	4	2	**A**	1	3	5	7	9	11
12	10	8	6	4	2	**B**	1	3	5	7	9	11
12	10	8	6	4	2	**C**	1	3	5	7	9	11
12	10	8	6	4	2	**D**	1	3	5	7	9	11
12	10	8	6	4	2	**E**	1	3	5	7	9	11
12	10	8	6	4	2	**F**	1	3	5	7	9	11
12	10	8	6	4	2	**G**	1	3	5	7	9	11
12	10	8	6	4	2	**H**	1	3	5	7	9	11
12	10	8	6	4	2	**I**	1	3	5	7	9	11
12	10	8	6	4	2	**J**	1	3	5	7	9	11
12	10	8	6	4	2	**K**	1	3	5	7	9	11
12	10	8	6	4	2	**L**	1	3	5	7	9	11
12	10	8	6	4	2	**M**	1	3	5	7	9	11
12	10	8	6	4	2	**N**	1	3	5	7	9	11
12	10	8	6	4	2	**O**	1	3	5	7	9	11
12	10	8	6	4	2	**P**	1	3	5	7	9	11
12	10	8	6	4	2	**Q**	1	3	5	7	9	11
12	10	8	6	4	2	**R**	1	3	5	7	9	11
12	10	8	6	4	2	**S**	1	3	5	7	9	11
12	10	8	6	4	2	**T**	1	3	5	7	9	11
			6	4	2	**U**	1	3	5	7	9	11

THE RIDICULOUS THEATRICAL COMPANY

One Sheridan Square

Box Office: 260-7137
Box Office Hours: Wednesday–Sunday, 3 p.m. until curtain
Credit Cards: None   TDF Vouchers   Personal checks
Group Sales: Through box office
Season: September–June
Total Seating: 155 (Orchestra, 155)
Stage Type: Three-quarter round thrust stage
AC
Handicapped: No access

The Ridiculous Theatrical Company works in, as you may have guessed, the theatre of the ridiculous. This permanent ensemble of actors under the artistic direction of Charles Ludlum has produced and maintained a repertoire of 15 innovative comic dramas in the past 10 years. The company's territory is modernist works of parody, burlesque, traversity, and farce. Some of their productions are *Anti-Galaxy Nebulae, Stage Blood, Bluebeard, Utopia Incorporated,* and *Camille.* They have also created a children's theatre program, which includes *Professor Bedlam's Educational Punch and Judy Show* and *The Enchanted Pig,* a play with human actors and puppets.

SPECTRUM THEATRE

15 Vandam Street

Box Office: 475-5529
Box Office Hours: Monday–Friday, 11 a.m.–8 p.m.; Saturday–Sunday, 1 p.m.–8 p.m.
Credit Cards: AE, MC, V   TDF Vouchers   Personal checks
Group Sales: Through box office
Total Seating: 99
Stage Type: Thrust stage
AC
Handicapped: No access

Modern classics that help illuminate the human condition are presented in this former nightclub by a 150-member group, founded in 1975 by producer Ted Baird and artistic director Benno Haehnel. Some recent productions: Synge's *Playboy of the Western World;* Gorky's *The Lower Depths;* Ann Marie Barlow's *Glory Halleluiah;* Harvey Perr's *Gethsemane Springs;* and Tennessee Williams's *Orpheus Descending.* The group moved here last season from the Calvary Church on Park Avenue South.

SULLIVAN STREET PLAYHOUSE

181 Sullivan Street

Box Office: 674-3838
Box Office Hours: Tuesday–Friday, 10 a.m.–8 p.m.; Saturday, 10 a.m.–10 p.m.;
Sunday, 10 a.m.–7:30 p.m.
Credit Cards: AE, DC   CHARGIT   Personal checks two weeks in advance
Group Sales: Through box office
Total Seating: 153
Stage Type: Semi-arena
AC
Handicapped: Semi-accessible

If you go back a long way in Greenwich Village, you'll remember that this was Jimmy Kelly's nightclub before it was a theatre. If you're a theatre trivia buff you'll know that Jerry Orbach was in the original cast of *The Fantasticks.* If you're a super theatre buff you'll delight in knowing there was a production here before *The Fantasticks: Sweeney Todd,* the old English play on which the hit musical was roughly based. Practically everyone knows that Tom

Jones and Harvey Schmidt's charming musical is the longest-running production in the recent history of the America. It opened in May, 1960, and the end is nowhere in sight. If you haven't seen it, see it; if you've seen it, see it again. In all seriousness, I once asked a friend what was the hit song from this show. " 'Try to Remember,' " he said. "I am trying," I said.

Sullivan Street Playhouse

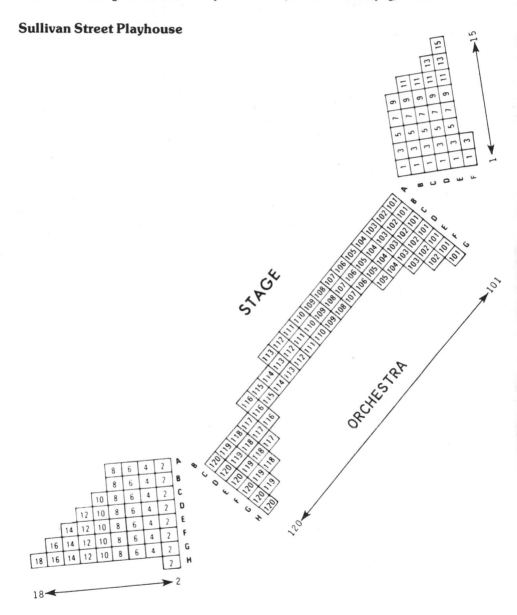

THEATER FOR THE NEW CITY

162 Second Avenue (10th)

Box Office: 254-1109
Box Office Hours: 1:30 p.m.–6 p.m., if performance
Credit Cards: None TDF Vouchers Personal checks
Group Sales: Through box office
Total Seating: 150, 96, and 50 in three theatres
Stage Type: Flexible open spaces
No AC
Handicapped: No access

In what once was a Baptist church, the Theater for the New City amalgamates song and dance, live music and poetry into diverse "total theatre" experiences: full-length dramas, musicals, operas, live music, and multimedia presentations. The company premieres 10 new plays a season by contemporary American playwrights, both established and unknown. Recent productions here include Sam Shepard's *Buried Child;* John Braden and Rosalyn Drexler's *The Writer's Opera; Clara Box Loves Garry Cooper* by Robert Dahdah and Mary Boylan; Ron Lampkin's *Liars;* Mary Karolly's *Shopping Bag Madonna;* and Crystal Field and George Bartenieff's *The Time They Turned the Water Off.* A summer street theatre with an interracial cast of 40 tours the poorer neighborhoods of the city. The Theater for the New City also presents new theatre groups from across the country.

THEATRE DE LYS

121 Christopher Street

Owner: Lucille Lortel
Box Office: 924-8782
Box Office Hours: Tuesday–Sunday, 12 noon until curtain
Credit Cards: MC, V TELECHARGE TDF Vouchers, depending on show
Group Sales: Through Ben Specher, general manager
Total Seating: 299 (Orchestra, 235; Balcony, 64)
Stage Type: Proscenium thrust stage
AC
Handicapped: Semi-accessible

The Off Broadway boom began here in 1954 with the revival of Brecht's *Threepenny Opera.* It was a hit that lasted more than six years. The producer of the hit was Lucille Lortel, who has owned the Theatre De Lys for more than a quarter of a century and has been a force in the theatre for longer than that. On Broadway, she produced Tennessee Williams's *A Streetcar Named Desire.* As artistic director of the ANTA Matinee Series, her productions included *Brecht on Brecht,* John Dos Passos's *U.S.A.,* and Paul Hunter's *Scott and Zelda.* Ms. Lortel was also the founder of the White Barn Theater in Westport, Connecticut, and there she premiered such plays as Ionesco's *The Chairs,* Schisgal's *The Typists,* and McNally's *Next.* Ms. Lortel was the recipient of the first Margo Jones Award and has received numerous other awards and tributes. Other hits seen here include *Dames at Sea, Billy Bishop Goes to War, Really Rosie,* and *Trixie True Teen Detective.*

Theatre De Lys

ORCHESTRA

7	5	3	1	A	111	110	109	108	107	106	105	104	103	102	101	A				
9				B												B	2	4	6	
				C												C			8	10
				D												D				
				E												E				
				F												F				
				G												G				
				H												H				
9				J												J				
				K												k				10
				L												L	2	4	6	8
7	5	3	1	M	111	110	109	108	107	106	105	104	103	102	101	M				

MEZZANINE

115	113	111	109	107	105	103	101	A	102	104	106	108	110	112	114	116
								B								
								C								
								D								

Mezzanine row "A" overhangs Orchestra row "F"

THIRTEENTH STREET THEATRE
REPERTORY COMPANY

50 West 13th Street

Box Office: 675-6677 or 741-9292
Box Office Hours: 10 a.m.–11 p.m.
Credit Cards: None   TDF Vouchers   Personal checks
Group Sales: Through box office
Total Seating: 75
Stage Type: Proscenium thrust stage
AC
Handicapped: Semi-accessible

In this era of public and private funding of the arts, here is a repertory company that has made it on talent, enormous energy, and grit. In 1955, an auditorium was built onto the rear of a century-old Greenwich Village townhouse and the Thirteenth Street Repertory Company was off and running. Under the direction of Edith O'Hara, the company presents two shows a night and three or four the weekend, which has to be something of a record and marvelous experience for the young performers. Israel Horovitz's *Line* was starting its sixth year here when this was written. Here's a typical Saturday schedule at this amazing theatre: *The Emperor's New Clothes,* 1 p.m., *The Taming of the Shrew,* 3 p.m., *Dog Daze,* 7 p.m., *Line,* 9 p.m., and *Brother Theodore* at 11 p.m. Phew! And it's not just quantity: The hilarious gay musical, *Boy Meets Boy,* was developed here and ran for six months in 1975. It has since played around the country and abroad.

TRUCK AND WAREHOUSE THEATRE

79 East 4th Street

Box Office: 254-5060
Box Office Hours: Tuesday–Sunday, 12 noon–8 p.m.
Credit Cards: None   TDF Vouchers   Personal checks
Group Sales: 222-7008 (Community groups free)
Total Seating: 250
Stage Type: Proscenium stage
AC
Handicapped: Semi-accessible

Artistic Director John Harry has developed a company with a reputation for its experiments in different formats. Some recent productions: *Captain Boogie and the Kids from Mars, Death Watch, Music Lives,* and *Off the Wall.*

UNIVERSITY THEATRE
WASHINGTON SQUARE PLAYERS

35 West 4th Street

Box Office: 598-3067
Box Office Hours: One hour before performance (answering machine other times)
Credit Cards: None   TDF Vouchers   Personal checks
Group Sales: Through box office
Total Seating: 347
Stage Type: Proscenium stage
AC
Handicapped: Semi-accessible

This company goes back to 1923, although it was reorganized in 1955 by William Gitelman and artistic director Dr. Lowell Schwartzell. The Players now operate in conjunction with the Program in Educational Theatre of New York University, with the goal of providing a full spectrum of productions for the university community and the stimulation of original work. In the 1980–81 season, the group presented *Cabaret; Happy Birthday, Wanda June; Our Town;* and Ibsen's *A Doll's House.*

VILLAGE GATE/TOP OF THE GATE

Bleecker at Thompson Street

Owner: Art D'Lugoff
Box Office: 475-5120/473-7270
Box Office Hours: 12 noon until 30 minutes after curtain
Credit Cards: AE, MC, V   TDF Vouchers   Personal checks
Group Sales: Through box office
Total Seating: Village Gate—450 in cabaret seating (reserved table location only)
Top of the Gate—299 in cabaret seating on terraced levels
(reserved table location only)
Stage Type: Thrust stage
AC
Handicapped: Entrance without dignity

In 1957, the Village Gate was created out of a commercial laundry, and rollicking entertainment has been the keynote here ever since. In both cabarets, you sit at tables, smoke if you like, and get a drink before the performance or at intermission. Some of the Gate's memorable productions include *MacBird, Jacques Brel Is Alive and Well and Living in Paris; 2 by 5; Oysters; Lemmings; National Lampoon Show;* and, when this was written, *One Mo' Time* had settled in for a well-deserved long run. The Top of the Gate has presented such delights as *Tuscaloosa Is Calling But I'm Not Coming; Why Hannah's Skirt Won't Stay Down; Conversations with an Irish Rascal; Night Club Cantata;* and the show business sendup *Scrambled Feet.*

VITAL ARTS CENTER

78 Fifth Avenue (14th)

Box Office: 675-1136
Box Office Hours: 90 minutes before performance
Credit Cards: None   TDF Vouchers
Group Sales: None
Total Seating: 100
Stage Type: Proscenium or thrust stage
AC
Handicapped: Semi-accessible

In the former Ray Gordon Theatre, artistic director Eleo Pomare presents performances with the accent on movement.

WASHINGTON SQUARE CHURCH

135 West 4th Street

Box Office: No telephone
Box Office Hours: 30 minutes prior to performance
Credit Cards: None   TDF Vouchers
Group Sales: No consistent policy; see program coordinator
Season: Closed August
Total Seating: 275
Stage Type: Open space with flexible seating
No AC
Handicapped: No access

Since 1968, there have been from 40 to 50 performances a season by theatre companies, dancers, and musicians in this landmark Greenwich Village Methodist Episcopal church. The setting is attractive: a 40-foot vaulted ceiling, stained-glass windows, and church pews that can be rearranged depending upon the needs of the performers. Program coordinator Alexis DiVincent has the unenviable task of keeping everything working smoothly.

WESTBETH THEATRE GROUP

151 Bank Street

Box Office: 691-2272
Box Office Hours: 12 noon until curtain
Credit Cards: None   CHARGIT   TDF Vouchers   Personal checks
Group Sales: Through box office
Total Seating: Three theatres: workshop, 60; theatre, 99; theatre II, 200
Stage Type: Proscenium stage (theatre)
Flexible open spaces (workshop and theatre II)
No AC
Handicapped: No access

Since 1976, more than 100 productions have been staged on this former commercial stage. Co-artistic directors William Hoffman and Ian McColl range from the classics to the experimental to provide varied theatrical fare for the West Village. In the spring of 1981, they were presenting *Curtains,* a new comedy.

WONDERHORSE THEATRE

83 East 4th Street

Box Office: 533-5888
Box Office Hours: One hour before performance (Answering machine other times)
Credit Cards: None   TDF Vouchers   Personal checks
Group Sales: Through box office
Season: September–May
Total Seating: 95
Stage Type: Flexible open space
No AC
Handicapped: Limited access

Since 1974, the Wonderhorse has been reviving plays of merit that have received limited exposure in New York. Recently the company has performed *You Touched Me* and Joseph Hayes's *The Desperate Hours,* directed by Marvin Kahan.

RESTAURANTS AND NIGHTSPOTS

♫ BOTTOM LINE***

15 West 4th Street
Reservations: Not accepted
No credit cards
Shows: 8:30 p.m. and 11:30 p.m., weekdays; 9 p.m. and 12 midnight, weekends
Moderate

This is where the big names in folk and rock perform. The sound system in the large room is perfection itself. It's also the scene of many record company promotion parties, so it's wise to buy tickets in advance: the box office is open from 11 a.m. to 1 p.m. and one hour before performances. Admission is $6 Sunday to Thursday, $7 on Friday and Saturday. Drinks are served from 6:30 p.m. on.

BUFFALO ROADHOUSE*

87 Seventh Avenue South (Sheridan Square)
Reservations: 243-8000
No credit cards
Inexpensive

If you're going to one of the many theatres around Sheridan Square, this is a good choice for dinner—if you can get in. The place is usually jammed. In the summer, there's a triangular terrace for alfresco dining. The small menu features fresh fish, spareribs ($6.50), chef salad ($4.50), shell steak ($9.95), the usual burgers, quiche, and the ubiquitous cheesecake ($2.50). If there's something to celebrate, you can get a bottle of New York champagne for $10. Open until 4 a.m.

CAFFE DA ALFREDO**

17 Perry Street (7th Avenue)
Reservations: 989-7028
No credit cards
Moderate   Closed Mondays

A small, crowded storefront restaurant near most of the Village theatres, Alfredo offers excellent pasta, particularly the spaghetti carbonara with little pieces of crisp bacon, and paglia e fieno alla Romana ("straw and hay" Roman-style—a green and white pasta in a cream sauce with mushrooms and sausage). Pastas are in the $6–$8 range. The veal, chicken, and fish entrees are $8 to $10, and, while good, are not as outstanding as the pasta. There are only three desserts, each exceptional: cold zabaglione with strawberries ($3), a chocolate cake with raisins ($3), and fresh fruit with cheese ($3.25). There is no liquor license, so bring your own wine. Reservations are essential here, particularly just before and after theatre.

CAFE LOUP**

18 East 13th Street
Reservations: 255-4746
Credit Cards: AE, DC, MC, V
Moderate   Closed Sunday and major holidays

This is a charming restaurant: a small bar and a dozen or so tables, beige walls hung with prints, blue napkins tucked into balloon wine glasses. A small blackboard menu circulates from table to table. Your best choices are the fowl: duck montmorency, chicken, game hens. The steak with garlic is delicious, and the most expensive dish at around $12. Both the Peter's Pan chocolate cake and the cheesecake are exceptional. There's a small, carefully chosen, and moderately priced wine list.

CBGB & OMFUG**

315 Bowery (Bleecker)
Reservations: 282-4052
Inexpensive

This is the original New Wave nightclub where the Ramones, Talking Heads, and Blondie all got their start. The atmosphere is dark and smoky, but the music and excellent sound system make up for it. Admission is $5 weekdays, $6 weekends, and the live shows are at 10 p.m. and 1 a.m. No food is served; highballs are $3, beer $2. Monday is showcase night for aspiring bands. In case you were wondering, the initials stand for Country, Bluegrass, Blues and Other Music for Uplifting Gourmandizers.

CLUB 57**

57 St. Marks Place
Reservations: Not accepted (475-9671)
Inexpensive

What's happening? Just about anything you could imagine at this hangout of young New Wavers: the Monster Movie Club, an erotic art exhibition, lady wrestling, artist performances, fashion shows, and, of course, New Wave music. Admission ranges from $2 to $5 depending upon the entertainment. No food but there's a full bar. Warning: You may be one of the few in the audience without green hair.

COACH HOUSE***

110 Waverly Place (8th)
Reservations: 777-0303
Credit Cards: AE, CB, DC, MC
Expensive   Closed Monday

Over the years, the Coach House has earned the reputation as one of the best restaurants in the city, and deservedly so. It is a warm, handsome place: high-ceilinged, brass chandeliers, flame-red banquettes, peach tablecloths. The food is distinctly American with continental overtones. Regulars here favor the black-bean soup madeira, thick and dark with bits of lemon and egg, as an appetizer, although I personally prefer the escargots for two, if I can get my guest to go along, as they are everything snails should be. For an entree, the rack of spring lamb "roasted to a crisp" is heaven. Another excellent choice and a house specialty is fresh lump crabmeat Baltimore, sautéed with julienne ham. The American chicken pie is also good. For dessert, try the fresh apple tart, or the "wonderful hot fudge ice cream cake." You won't be disappointed. Figure about $30 per person plus liquor, wine, and tips. Gentlemen will need a jacket and tie, and it's wise to reserve a day or two ahead.

KIEV RESTAURANT*

117 Second Avenue (7th)
Reservations: 674-4040
No credit cards
Inexpensive

The Kiev is a product of its environment, the East Village. Here, as outside on the streets, immigrants from Eastern Europe rub elbows with punk rockers; it's probably the only punk Russian restaurant in the world. You order kielbasa, blintzes, borscht, and boiled beef from a vast menu that also includes dishes found in most coffee shops. A full dinner shouldn't cost more than $7: a large bowl of borscht or mushroom barley soup with several pieces of buttered challah is $1.25. Open 24 hours a day, every day.

LADY ASTOR'S**

430 Lafayette Street (Astor Place)
Reservations: 228-7888
Credit Cards: None but personal checks accepted with credit card identification
Moderate to Expensive   Monday–Saturday until 12 midnight; Sunday, brunch only.
Closed Christmas and Thanksgiving

The most elegant spot convenient to the theatres of the Astor Place area is, appropriately, Lady Astor's—with stunning chandeliers, Art Deco lamps, antique mirrors. The dining room wraps around a well-tended bar where it's nice to relax and see who else is on the town. Start with coquille St. Jacques ($6.75)—they're a specialty here—as are the filet of lemon sole with mustard hollandaise ($9.75) and the steak au poivre extraordinaire, cut from the Chateaubriand ($18). Or stop by after the theatre for a burger ($3.50–$4.50).

LE PARIS BISTRO**

48 Barrow Street
Reservations: 959-5460
Credit Cards: AE, DC, MC, V
Inexpensive   Closed Thanksgiving and Christmas Day

Summer or winter, you'll like it here. In the summer there's a charming garden; in the winter, a fireplace (a WBFP, in apartment hunter's parlance). The cuisine is country French, nicely prepared from fresh ingredients: escalope de veau à la savoyarde ($8.50) is veal sautéed in butter and served with a mushroom and white wine cream sauce. Yumm! The calf's liver sautéed in red wine and shallot sauce ($7.50) is another specialty. The steak au poivre ($11.50) is a personal favorite. Ring down the curtain with a pear poached in red wine ($1.50) or fruit and cheese ($2.95).

♫ LONE STAR CAFÉ**

61 Fifth Avenue (13th)
Reservations: 242-1664
Credit Cards: AE, DC, MC, V
Inexpensive to Moderate

A little bit of whoop-it-up Texas in old New York where urban cowboys and nostalgic Texans belly up to the bar, compare their Western finery, and listen to about the best country-western music around. Dress informally, come after the theatre, and chow down on barbecued spare ribs, fried chicken, steak, and red-hot chili. Try Texas's own Lone Star beer. (Sorry to disappoint you, but the Lone Star does *not* have a mechanical bucking bronco.) Be sure to phone to reserve tickets (here one reserves tickets not tables). Tickets are $6–$10, depending on who is performing. There's a two-drink minimum which is waived if you have dinner. Occasionally blues and country jazz singers perform here, but no hard rock or punk or New Wave. Try to make it when Kinky Friedman is on—he's one whole lot of fun.

♫ LUCHOW'S**

110 East 14th Street
Reservations: 477-4860
Credit Cards: AE, CB, DC, MC, V
Moderate to Expensive

Century-old Luchow's is a reminder that 14th Street once was the heart of the city's theatre district. Recently restored to its glory, the cavernous restaurant is a joy to behold. (Most New Yorkers know Luchow's only at Christmas when a huge, decorated tree dominates the dining area.) The cuisine is German: various schnitzels in the $11–$13 range, kalbshaxer burgerlicher art (veal shanks) at $10.50 a la carte. The portions are large and filling. There always seems to be a festival of some kind here and the menu reflects it. An oompa-pa band alternates with a string ensemble playing Strauss waltzes and the like. Now a landmark building, Luchow's is well worth a visit.

MARY'S*

42 Bedford Street (7th Avenue)
Reservations: 741-3387
Credit Cards: AE, CB, DC, MC
Inexpensive to Moderate

Cozy is the word for this former private home now Giovanni Celenza's Italian Restaurant. The upstairs dining room is the nicer of the two. After you've settled in, you may wish to try the chicken cacciatore ($7.25), one of the many veal entrees (around $8), or shrimp marinara ($8.25). For a new twist on an old favorite: spaghetti with squid sauce ($6.95). The cuisine is Abruzzi-style, characterized by a passion for red peppers. You have been warned.

MINETTA TAVERN**

113 MacDougal Street (3rd)
Reservations: 475-3850
Credit Cards: AE, DC, MC, V
Inexpensive to Moderate   12 noon to 12 midnight   Closed Thanksgiving

In the 1930s and 1940s, village artists used to draw caricatures in exchange for their dinner, and their work is still on the walls here. (Note particularly the Franz Klines.) You can dine in the bar, where the drawings are, or in the quieter back room, where the walls display murals of Village life of years gone by. The cuisine is basic Italian and well turned out. The chef does nice things with fettuccine Alfredo ($5.25) and steak pizzaiolla ($10.50). The stracciatela ($2) makes a good first act. There are daily specials; watch for bay scallops or tile fish broiled with wine and lemon sauce. They're great.

McSORLEY'S OLD ALE HOUSE**

15 East 7th Street (east of Third Avenue)
Reservations: Not accepted (473-8800)
No credit cards
Inexpensive

McSorley's was established in 1854 and has changed little since. There's an old pot-bellied stove, sawdust on the floor, fading photographs and memorabilia on the walls. McSorley's is a bit dirty, but the great atmosphere more than makes up for it. (Track down a copy of late *New Yorker* writer Joseph Mitchell's *McSorley's Wonderful Saloon;* it is a pure joy to read.) McSorley's was one of the last holdouts against feminine liberation, at least as far as bellying up to *its* bar was concerned. (Curious. It was owned and run for years by a woman.) On the first day it was illegal to refuse admission to women, a tough, vocal libber was the first over the threshold. A few importune remarks were passed at the bar. "I'll serve ya!" someone said, and a pitcher of ale was poured over the lady's head. *Sic transit gloria.* Women now are most welcome and much in evidence. Beer and ale on draft, 75¢ a mug, two for $1.25. No liquor. A few entrees are listed on the blackboard (pot roast, $2.25; knockwurst, $2.25; chili, $1.50; ham, cheese, turkey, or liverwurst sandwich, $1.50). It's an easy walk from the Astor Place theatres. Weekends, McSorley's is very crowded, and it's madness to go there on St. Patrick's Day.

♫ ONE FIFTH (⅕)**

One Fifth Avenue (8th)
Reservations: 260-3434 .
Credit Cards: AE, CB, DC, MC, V
Moderate to Expensive

When the Cunard liner *Caronia* sank in the South China Sea, some of the furniture and decor from the ship's dining room were salvaged and now provide the setting for this stunning Art Deco bistro, one of the most "in" places in the city. There are some excellent dishes here: the cold pâté of bass with green sauce ($4.75), fresh Irish smoked salmon ($12.50), rack of lamb provençale ($15.50), and tasty desserts. The bar area is particularly smart, and a Dixieland band holds forth there Friday nights from about 9:30 p.m., a piano most other nights. One Fifth can get crowded and noisy, but it's fun.

PHOEBE'S PLACE*

361 Bowery (4th)
Reservations: Not accepted (473-9008)
Credit Cards: AE, DC, MC, V
Inexpensive

Phoebe's is a popular hangout for actors and other theatre people working in the area, and with the crowd from CBGB's. (It's open until 4:00 a.m.) It's big and its brick walls are decorated with Off-Off Broadway posters. There's a long, usually crowded bar. The fare ranges from burgers, salads, omelettes, and chicken-in-a-basket to steaks and chops. All is good, if unimaginatively prepared, and reasonably priced.

THE SAZERAC HOUSE*

533 Hudson Street (Charles)
Reservations: 989-0313
Credit Cards: AE, MC, V
Inexpensive to Moderate   Closed Thanksgiving and Christmas

Housed in a landmark house that was built around the time of the Revolutionary War, the Sazerac House offers the usual American fare plus some interesting New Orleans and Creole specialties: Louisiana crab chop ($8.25) is delicious, so is jambalaya with garlic bread

($6.50), shrimp creole ($8.25), and plantation chicken ($7.50). Daily specials are listed on a blackboard. The Sazerac House is an easy walk from either the Theatre De Lys or the Cherry Lane.

SECOND AVENUE KOSHER DELICATESSEN**

156 Second Avenue (10th)
Reservations: Not accepted (677-0606)
No credit cards
Inexpensive to Moderate   Closed Thanksgiving, New Year's Day, and major
                          Jewish holidays

If you crave a pastrami fix after a show at the Entremedia, you're in luck. The Second Avenue Deli is a delightful purveyor of authentic Jewish specialties. The atmosphere is strictly business, the food, strictly first-rate.

🎵 SWEET BASIL**

88 Seventh Avenue (Bleecker)
Reservations: 242-1785
Credit Cards: AE, DC, MC, V
Moderate

This top jazz club is next door to the Actor's Playhouse and near several other Sheridan Square theatres. You'll find such top talent displayed here as Benny Carter, Doc Cheatham, Chico Hamilton, and Zoot Sims. Nothing wrong with the food either. Salads range from $4.95 to $6.95; entrees from $4.50 for the hamburger platter to $12.95 for grilled shell steak. Phone to find out who is playing and to make reservations.

TRATTORIA DA ALFREDO**

90 Bank Street (Hudson)
Reservations: 929-4400
No credit cards
Moderate   Closed Tuesday

A tiny, crowded place with an exposed kitchen and walls covered with paintings, the Trattoria da Alfredo serves up some of the best pasta in the city. The baked stuffed clams oregante ($3.75) are excellent. All pastas are $5.50, and you might try either tortellini or spaghetti with pesto. Another specialty: paglia e fieno alla romano (green and white noodles with a cheese sauce). There are daily menu specials and entrees range from $7 to $10. For dessert try the hazelnut dacquoise ($2.50). No liquor is served but you may bring your own wine. Reservations in advance are a must.

UKRANIAN RESTAURANT AND CATERERS**

140 Second Avenue (8th)
Reservations: 533-6765
No credit cards
Inexpensive

This restaurant is in the Ukranian National Home, the center of the Ukranian community in the city, and has become a popular choice for Lower East Side diners. The hearty Eastern European fare comes in copious portions. For those uninitiated in this cuisine, here is a quick guide:

Bigos: Sliced kobasa mixed with sauerkraut
Bochok: smoked and marinated bacon
Borscht: beet soup
Holubsti: stuffed cabbage
Kabanose: hunter's sausage
Kasha: beef cooked and served with cracked buckwheat
Kobasa: ring sausage of pork and beef
Krakiewska: ham sausage

Krayana: coarsely ground sausage
Makivnyk: poppyseed cake roll
Pirogi: dumplings with a variety of stuffings
Siekana: finely ground sausage
Studzienna: jellied pigs' knuckles
Zayek: pork and veal loaf

Armed with this knowledge, you can eat very well for $5 to $10 a person. Try it on a Ukranian holiday when everyone is in costume. By the way, *cmacznocho* means *bon appetit.*

VENIERO'S*

342 East 11th Street
Reservations: None
No credit cards
Inexpensive

Many of the fancy pastries you find in Italian restaurants around the city are baked here. Venerable Veniero's, which has been a bakery since 1894, has a few tables where you can sample cannoli, sfogliatelle, and other delicacies while drinking espresso or cappuccino. Ideal for after-theatre in the East Village.

WHITE HORSE TAVERN**

567 Hudson Street (11th)
Reservations: Not accepted (243-9260)
No credit cards
Inexpensive

I spent one of the unforgettable nights of my life here listening to Dylan Thomas expound. (One didn't converse with Mr. Thomas, at least at a bar. One listened to him expound and loved it.) But that aside, this is THE old New York pub, 101 years old and unchanged except for the jukebox and cigarette machine. There's a back room where Norman Mailer used to hang out in his Village days. Burgers and omelettes are the extent of the menu ($2.25–$3.25), and they're good. Beck's and Heinecken are on tap. The White Horse is an easy walk from the Theatre De Lys.

YE WAVERLY INN*

16 Bank Street (Waverly)
Reservations: 929-4377
Credit Cards: AE, DC, MC, V
Moderate

You'll be reminded of a New England inn: pegged floors, beamed ceilings, lots of brass on display. The atmosphere is warm and friendly, whether you're in the main dining room or in the charming back garden. The food is straight-away American cooking, no fancy sauces or trimmings. Complete dinners—soup, entree, salad, vegetable, potato, dessert, and coffee—come from $7.95 for the meat loaf to $15.95 for the filet mignon. Recommended: fried chicken, the filet, chicken pot pie, Indian pudding, and ice cream sundaes.

243

SOHO AND BELOW

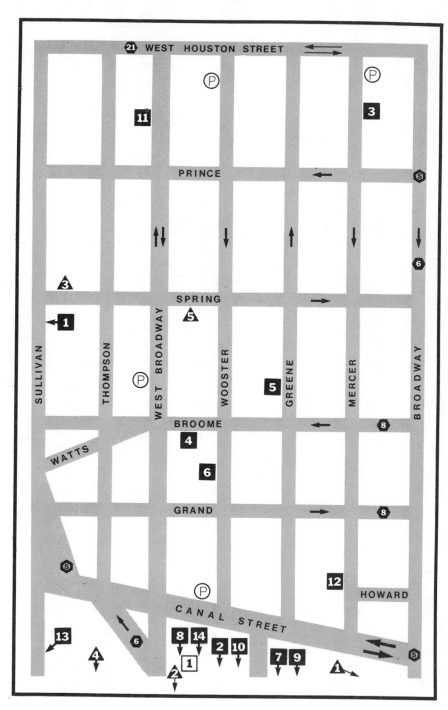

■ Theatres

1. American Renaissance
   Theatre / 112 Charlton
2. The Floating Rep / 146 Chambers
3. Inroads Multimedia Arts
   Center / 150 Mercer
4. The Kitchen / 484 Broome
5. Ohio / 59 Greene
6. Performing Garage Center / 33–35
   Wooster
7. Process Studio Theatre / 257
   Church
8. Schimmel Center for the Arts-Pace
   University / Pace Plaza
9. Shared Forms Theatre / 17 White
10. Sidewalks Theatre / 44 Beaver
11. SoHo Artists Theatre / 465 West
    Broadway
12. SoHo Repertory Theatre / 19
    Mercer
13. Spectrum Theatre / 15 Vandam
14. The Theatre Exchange / 313
    Church

▲ Restaurants

1. Mudd Club / 77 White
2. Odeon / 145 West Broadway
3. SoHo Charcuterie and
   Restaurant / 195 Spring
4. Windows on the World / One World
   Trade Center
5. WPA / 152 Spring

□ Other Attractions

1. TKTS / 100 Williams

🛈 Bus Numbers

Ⓢ Subway Stations

Ⓟ Parking

→ One-way Street

⇄ Two-way Street

This is the cutting edge of the theatre. In the lofts and performance spaces of SoHo and Tribeca, the basic principles of theatre are being challenged, rethought, and stretched to accommodate new forms and ideas. SoHo is a laboratory, and any laboratory needs a large wastebasket. The good and the bad flow freely and blend into a provocative and often frustrating mixture. This is not criticism. To paraphrase Picasso, it is hard to make something new; it is easy to make something new beautiful. Surely, future theatre historians will debate in which loft a new concept was first articulated. A spirit of adventure is basic equipment for a SoHo theatre outing. So is an open mind. Bring them and you will be rewarded.

THEATRES

AMERICAN RENAISSANCE THEATER
112 Charlton Street

Box Office: 929-4718
Box Office Hours: One hour before performance
Credit Cards: None   TD Vouchers   Personal checks
Total Seating: 70
Stage Type: Flexible open space
AC
Handicapped: Semi-accessible

This is one of the larger Off-Off Broadway companies with some 100 actors, directors, playwrights, composers, and lyricists. It mounts five productions a year, interspersed with cabaret and one-person shows that feature such company members as Martha Schlamme, Susan Reed, Ethel Smith, and Sue René Bernstein. The artistic director is Robert Elston, Elizabeth Perry is his associate, and Susan Reed is the assistant director. Formed in 1975, the company uses a former sculptor's studio to present such original productions as Joi Julian's *Act of Kindness; Do You Still Believe the Rumor?* by Jeffrey Knox; *Notes from the Underground* using material from Thoreau, Kafka, and Dostoyevski; Susan Reed's *Women of Ireland;* Elizabeth Perry's *Did You See the Elephant?;* and Stan Edelman's *Ruby, Ruby, Sam, Sam.*

THE FLOATING REP
146 Chambers Street

Owner: K & K Space and Toy Co., Inc.
Box Office: 267-5756
Box Office Hours: 9 a.m.–11 p.m.
Credit Cards: None   TDF Vouchers
Group Sales: Through box office
Season: October–May
Total Seating: 60
Stage Type: Flexible open space
No AC
Handicapped: No access

The Floating Rep seems to have found a home in this converted Wall Street area loft. Artistic directors Val Hendrickson and Gary Benson founded the company in October, 1979, and have presented mostly one-act plays: Sam Shepard's *The Unseen Hand,* Tennessee Williams's *Hello from Bertha,* Harold Pinter's *The Lover,* and Samuel Beckett's *Play.* Last season the company branched out a bit with George Abbott and John Cecil Holm's comedy *Three Men on a Horse* and Jean Giraudoux's *Tiger at the Gates.* In the summer, the company does outdoor productions and tours.

INROADS MULTIMEDIA ARTS CENTER
150 Mercer Street

Box Office: 226-6622
Box Office Hours: One hour before performance (Answering machine other times)
Credit Cards: None   TDF Vouchers
Group Sales: Through box office
Total Seating: 74
Stage Type: Flexible open space
No AC
Handicapped: Semi-accessible

Two theatrical companies are housed in this former loft: the Inroads Theatre Group and the Inroads Children's Theatre Company. The adult group, founded in October, 1980, by Gare Thompson and artistic director Fay Ran, has presented *Journey, Freeze Frames in a Jump Cut Year,* and *Self Accusation* by Peter Handke. The Children's Theatre has presented *Holiday House.* The center plans to expand its offerings to include music, film, performance, art exhibits, and poetry readings.

THE KITCHEN
484 Broome Street

Box Office: 925-3615
Box Office Hours: Tuesday–Saturday, 1 p.m.–6 p.m.
Credit Cards: None   TDF Vouchers
Group Sales: Through box office
Season: September–June
Total Seating: 199
Stage Type: Flexible open space
No AC
Handicapped: Semi-accessible

The Kitchen is right in the first rank of the avant-garde. The boundaries among the arts fade here and sometimes disappear altogether. If you are a strict constructionist, there is no theatre, *per se,* here; if you are a neo-modernist, it is *all* theatre. There is no production company connected with the Kitchen. Artists like Spalding Gray, Stuart Sherman, and Lori Anderson use the space for music, dance, performance, art exhibits, and film. The Kitchen and the Performing Garage are what SoHo is—or should be—all about.

OHIO
59 Greene Street

Box Office: 226-7341
Box Office Hours: Tuesday–Sunday, 11 a.m.–7 p.m.
Credit Cards: None   TDF Vouchers
Group Sales: Through box office
Season: October–May
Total Seating: 100 (Standing room, 50)
Stage Type: Flexible open space
No AC
Handicapped: Semi-accessible

Bill Taylor renovated one space here in the fall of 1980 and was renovating a second space in the spring of 1981. A number of companies perform here including Boston's Abrection Theatre Company, the Theatre Education Center from Taos, New Mexico, the Polish Theatre Laboratorium, the Triple Action Theatre Company of London, the Workhouse of

Munich, Actor's Lab of Toronto, and New York's Undercurrent Theatre Gang. An international theatre festival was planned for September 1981. Some recent productions: Paul Iorio's *Artificial Tears*, and the Undercurrent Theatre Gang's original production of *Heroic Acts*.

PERFORMING GARAGE CENTER

33–35 Wooster Street

Box Office: 966-3651
Box Office Hours: 30 minutes before curtain; reservations by phone
Credit Cards: None   TDF Vouchers
Group Sales: 966-9796
Total Seating: Three spaces: two of 150, the other of 75
Stage Type: Flexible open spaces
AC
Handicapped: Semi-accessible

One of the oldest experimental theatre companies in the country, the Wooster Group explores and redefines the roles of language, space, action, performer, and audience within the concept of "environmental theatre." The group was founded in 1967 by executive director Richard Schechner. He, Elizabeth LeCompte, and Spalding Gray are the driving forces behind the group. The work of the group includes company developed pieces (*Commune, Three Places in Rhode Island*), new American plays (*The Tooth of Crime, Marilyn Project, Cops*), and "reconstructions" of classics (*Dionysus in '69, Mother Courage and Her Children*). Each production generates a new space, a new way of thinking about the audience, and a renewed text. In addition to the Wooster Group, the Performing Garage Center is used by other experimental theatre companies working in New York without a permanent home.

PROCESS STUDIO THEATRE

257 Church Street

Box Office: 226-1124
Box Office Hours: 9 a.m.–8 p.m., performance days
Credit Cards: None   TDF Vouchers
Group Sales: Through box office
Total Seating: 70
Stage Type: Flexible open space
AC
Handicapped: No Access

Mickey Elias, Bonnie Laren, and John Camera share the responsibilities for the artistic direction of this four-year-old group, alternating between Shakespeare and new productions. Recent offerings: *Macbeth, Much Ado About Nothing,* and *Incorrect Is Meaning Backwards* by Richard Calabin.

SCHIMMEL CENTER FOR THE ARTS

Pace University
One Pace Plaza

Box Office: 285-3715
Box Office Hours: Two hours before performance
Group Sales: Through box office
Season: September–June
Total Seating: 668
Stage Type: Proscenium stage
AC
Handicapped: No access

This excellent theatre near City Hall is used by local theatre groups as well as the Pace University drama department. The Four Seas Players of Chinatown were here in the spring of 1981 for several performances. Pace's most recent offering was *A Funny Thing Happened on the Way to the Forum*.

SHARED FORMS THEATRE

17 White Street

Box Office: 966-6479
Box Office Hours: One hour before performance (answering machine other times)
Credit Cards: None   TDF Vouchers
Group Sales: 966-6479
Season: November–March
Total Seating: 40 (in White Street loft)
Stage Type: Flexible open space
No AC
Handicapped: No access

Shared Forms is one of the older experimental groups in the city. They develop and present original theatre works by its members, which are highly visual and often draw on works of arts from other media. Founded in 1973 by artistic director Wendy Wasdahl and Bob McBrien, the group moved to this White Street loft in 1977. Performances are held here at other spaces, including the Performing Garage on Wooster Street. Recent original presentations: *The Illustrated Journal, The Rag and Bones Café, The Epic of Gilgamesh,* and *In the Cage.*

SIDEWALKS THEATER

44 Beaver Street

Box Office: 668-9074
Box Office Hours: 11 a.m.–11 p.m.
Credit Cards: None   TDF Vouchers   Personal checks
Group Sales: Through box office
Total Seating: 100
Stage Type: Flexible open space
No AC
Handicapped: Semi-accessible

Classic comedy is the realm of this theatre company. When Sidewalks was formed six years ago, it concentrated on Italian *commedia dell'arte.* Actors rehearsed tumbling, ballet, mime, and fencing, and extensive research was done to present the attitudes, style, relationships, and spirit. Then came 17th-century French comic theatre, and in particular Molière. Artistic director Gary Beck translated four of the plays himself: *The Flying Doctor, The Doctor in Spite of Himself, The Jealous Husband,* and *Two Pretentious Maidens Ridiculed.* Now Sidewalks is exploring the stylized mannerism and wit of English Restoration comedy, presenting such plays as Aphra Behn's *The Emperor of the Moon.* Later will come Classical Greek comedy. Sidewalks performs in various places, depending on the stage of play development: Early forms go to children's psychiatric centers and hospitals, then to senior citizens' centers and outdoor events. Later forms go to schools, public parks, corporate plazas, concluding with a five-week run at Sidewalks Theater. Performances begin with a musical parade through the audience, each character introduces himself, a mime show introduces the play, and the play develops with audience interaction. The costumes are splendid, and the performances are well worth a trip downtown.

SOHO ARTISTS THEATRE

465 West Broadway

Box Office: 473-2954
Box Office Hours: One hour before performance (answering machine other times)
Credit Cards: None   TDF Vouchers   Personal checks
Group Sales: Through box office
Season: October–May
Stage Type: Flexible open space
No AC
Handicapped: Semi-accessible

In a converted manufacturing loft, artistic director Dino Narizzano presents a program

249

of original scripts. Recent productions have included *Viaduct, Bird with Silver Feathers, Brothers,* and *Out of Sight.*

SOHO REPERTORY THEATRE
19 Mercer Street

Box Office: 925-2588
Box Office Hours: Tuesday–Sunday, 1 p.m.–7 p.m.
Credit Cards: AE, MC, V (for subscription series only) TDF Vouchers   Personal checks
Group Sales: Through box office
Season: September–June
Total Seating: 100
Stage Type: Thrust stage
No AC
Handicapped: Semi-accessible

This company is in a 19th-century cast-iron building, and last season had the largest subscriber audience of any Off-Off Broadway theatre in the city. The SoHo Rep has produced more than 75 plays in its first six years, including a number of New York premieres: Picasso's *The Four Little Girls,* Rod Serling's *Requiem for a Heavyweight,* Aristophanes' *The Congresswomen,* and *October 12, 410 B.C.,* adapted by David Barrett; Michel de Ghelderode's *Miss Jairus,* Gunter Grass's *Only 10 minutes to Buffalo,* and J. P. Donleavy's *Fairy Tales of New York.* The 1980–81 season offered six plays, including four New York premieres, *Romeo and Juliet,* and Sean O'Casey's *The Silver Tassie.* Series memberships are $18.

THE THEATRE EXCHANGE
313 Church Street

Box Office: 966-3219
Box Office Hours: 9 a.m.–5 p.m. (answering machine)
Credit Cards: None   TDF Vouchers (except Friday and Saturday)
Group Sales: Through box office
Season: September–May
Total Seating: 50
Stage Type: Flexible open space
No AC
Handicapped: No access

Artistic directors Charles Clubb and Colby Willis moved their two-year-old group to this loft at the beginning of the 1980–81 season. Recent productions: Eugene O'Neill's *Beyond the Horizon* and Brecht's *Drums in the Night.*

RESTAURANTS AND NIGHTSPOTS
 **MUDD CLUB**

77 White Street
Information: 227-7777
No credit cards
Hours: 11 p.m.–4 a.m., show at 11:30 p.m.

The quintessential New Wave rock club and a sight to behold: young men with orange or green hair, girls with coifs like army sergeants, clothing somewhere between urban guerillas and characters out of *Star Wars,* along with preppy. The music is LOUD; liquor is available but no food. There's an admission charge of $5 to $8, depending upon the caliber of the talent appearing, but be prepared for an uneven door policy. Phone for a taped rundown on the night's performers. Warning: The White Street area is industrial and a bit rundown.

ODEON***

145 West Broadway (Thomas)
Reservations: 233-0507
Credit Cards: AE, MC, V
Moderate to Expensive

In less than a year, Odeon has established itself as the best restaurant between the midtown palaces of haute cuisine and the Cellar in the Sky at Windows on the World—and has a chicer crowd than either—the young, successful, beautiful people who are making it in creative arts. The ambience is art deco, but art deco with a sense of fun: chrome and leatherette chairs, banquettes around the wall, and a magnificent wood bar. Start with the oysters poached in cream ($4.50) or the mixture of duck and veal pâté ($4.50); both are scrumptious. There's a pasta special most nights (around $7.50) that's as good as you'll find anywhere. A highlight among the entrees is the breast of duck ($14), cooked rare and sliced thin. A particularly nice dessert is coffee granite: a large wine glass filled with frozen crystals of sweet coffee covered with chocolate sorbet, a treat at $4.50. Odeon serves supper from midnight until 2:30 a.m.

SOHO CHARCUTERIE AND RESTAURANT**

195 Spring Street
Reservations: 226-3545
Credit Cards: AE, MC, DC
Moderate to Expensive
Not open for dinner Sunday

Visitors to SoHo have consistently been charmed by this shop with the restaurant in back and its specialties: pâtés, quiches, homemade jams, salads, and pastries. The walls are white, the tables and chairs are birch, and there are candles and fresh flowers on the tables. Dinner is expensive here—figure $25 per person. The fish is wonderfully fresh, and the stuffed duck on wild rice garnished with fois gras, figs, and pears is an unusual variation on a great theme. Reservations are a must. The service is slow, so allow plenty of time if you go before the theatre.

WINDOWS ON THE WORLD***

One World Trade Center
Reservations: 938-1111
Credit Cards: AE, CB, DC, MC, V
Hours: *Restaurant:* Monday–Saturday, 5 p.m.–10 p.m.
      The Cellar in the Sky: Monday–Saturday, 7:30 p.m. (one seating)
      The Hors d'Oeuvrerie, Statue of Liberty Lounge, and *The City Lights Bar:* until 1 a.m.
      Sunday brunch and grand buffet, 12 noon–7:30 p.m.
Moderate to Expensive
Free parking in the World Trade Center garage

Take a living-room-sized elevator to the 107th floor of the World Trade Center to the city's most theatrical restaurant. The views are dazzling in every direction, and it may take you a minute or two before you realize just how beautiful the restaurant itself is. In the dining area, the space is terraced so that every table has a view north up the island and east to Queens and Brooklyn (on a clear night you can see the lights of both Kennedy and LaGuardia). Here you can order an excellent table d'hôte dinner for $22.95, or use the a la carte menu for such entrees as calf's liver with grilled onion ($13.95), a rainbow trout stuffed and baked in pastry ($14.95), or a roast boneless cornish stuffed with bulgar wheat and mint ($14.95). For serious gourmets, the Cellar in the Sky is a small space seating 36 that is surrounded by stacked wine bottles where a seven-course menu with five wines is offered at $55. If you come after the theatre (or for drinks before) go to the Hors d'Oeuvrerie and look out over the harbor and the Statue of Liberty. There's an excellent selection of hot and cold appetizers: sushi or sashimi ($6.50), tostados with guacamole ($3.95), lemon spareribs ($3.50), or Moroccan kefta with harisa (ground meat grilled on skewers with a spicy dip) ($3.95). Drinks are $3.25 and there is a $2.50 cover after 4 p.m. when a trio plays for dancing. High tea also is served here from 3 p.m. to 6 p.m. Except for the bar and the Hors d'Oeuvrerie, reservations are a must. Ties and jackets required, leisure suits frowned on, and jeans not allowed.

WPA**

152 Spring Street
Reservations: 266-3444
Credit Cards: AE, DC, MC
Moderate to Expensive
Closed Monday

You get 10 points if you know that WPA stands for Works Progress Administration, the Depression project that built all those post offices. (Take 50 points if you remember that its detractors said WPA stood for We Piddle Around.) Now it stands for a most handsome restaurant serving some of the best food in SoHo. Spareribs as an appetizer are an interesting change. One of the specialties is the New England kettle, a chowder of several kinds of fish and shellfish. Desserts are uniformly excellent. Most dinners will average over $20.

THE OTHER BOROUGHS

The richness of the theatre in Manhattan is mirrored in the other boroughs of the city. Myriad forms of theatre can be found in areas that were devoid of theatrical activity a few short years ago. Shakespeare at the Brooklyn Academy, Spanish theatre in Queens, theatre that goes beyond entertainment to become a positive community force, all can be found a short distance from Times Square. In assembling the material for this guide, I found the prevalent complaint that it seemed incredibly difficult to get people to come from Manhattan to see what was going on. If this is true, it is a shame. Much of what is presented outside Manhattan has merit. To ignore it is a form of reverse provincialism that speaks well of no one.

BROOKLYN

THEATRES

ALONZO PLAYERS
33 Flatbush Avenue
Brooklyn

Box Office:	522-3636
Box Office Hours:	Monday–Saturday, 11:30 a.m.–8:30 p.m.; Sunday, 11:30 a.m.–8 p.m.
Credit Cards:	None
Group Sales:	Through box office
Total Seating:	110
Stage Type:	Three-quarter round stage
	AC
	Handicapped: Semi-accessible

This is Cecil Alonzo's show: a group that was founded in 1968, in Mr. Alonzo's words, "to educate, enlighten, encourage, and entertain." Resident here since 1979, the group also tours city schools with a production by Mr. Alonzo entitled *Circus: Maxi-us.* At this theatre, the group has been performing *Behulah Johnson: The World's First Live Continuous Saga in Soap,* also by Mr. Alonzo.
7th Ave IRT to Nevins Ave; 6th Ave BMT to DeKalb.

BAM THEATER COMPANY

Brooklyn Academy of Music
30 Lafayette Avenue
Brooklyn

Box Office: 636-4100
Box Office Hours: Tuesday–Sunday, 12 noon–8 p.m.
Credit Cards: AC, MC, V (subscription series only)   CHARGIT
Group Sales: Susan Levy, 636-4126
Season: January–June
Total Seating: Opera House: 2100; Helen Owen Carey Playhouse: 1,078
Lepercq Space: 650; Attic Theatre: 199
Stage Type: Opera House, Helen Carey Playhouse, and Attic Theatre:
Proscenium stages;
Lepercq space: Flexible open space
AC (Lepercq space only)
Handicapped: Semi-accessible

The BAM Theater Company is working with David Jones, the artistic director, to explore and define a specifically American approach to the presentation of classical drama. It plans to establish a feasible rotating repertory of productions available to theatregoers at any given time. Quite simply, the company wants to establish an identity and a reputation exciting enough to make it an essential part of the New York theatre experience. Among the presentations of the company since its founding in 1976 by Frank Dunlop and Harvey Lichtenstein: *The Devil's Disciple;* Ferenc Molnar's *The Play's the Thing,* adapted by P. G. Wodehouse; *Julius Caesar,* starring Richard Dreyfuss, and, most recently, *A Midsummer Night's Dream.* The Dodger Theater, launched in 1978, serves as the company's contemporary counterpart. A subscription, which included five plays, in the 1980–81 season was $35–$45, the higher price for Friday and Saturday evenings.
7th Ave IRT to Atlantic; BMT to Pacific St.

BILLIE HOLIDAY THEATRE

1368 Fulton Street
Brooklyn

Box Office: 636-0919
Box Office Hours: Monday–Friday, 10 a.m.–7 p.m.; Saturday–Sunday, 11 a.m.–2 p.m.
Credit Cards: None   TDF Vouchers
Group Sales: Ron Macintire (636-0919)
Total Seating: 200
Stage Type: Proscenium stage
AC
Handicapped: No access

This theatre was a milk-bottling plant until 1971. Managing director Marjorie Moon and artistic director Mikell Pinkney have produced such productions as Weldon Irvine's *Young, Gifted and Broke, Tambourines to Glory* by Langston Hughes, and John Huntley's *One Monkey Don't Stop No Show,* starring Don Evans. Their production of A. Marcus Hemphill's *Inacent Black,* a musical comedy starring Melba Moore, moved to Broadway in the spring of 1981 for a short run.
8th Ave IND to Norstand Ave.

BAM Theater Company (Opera House)

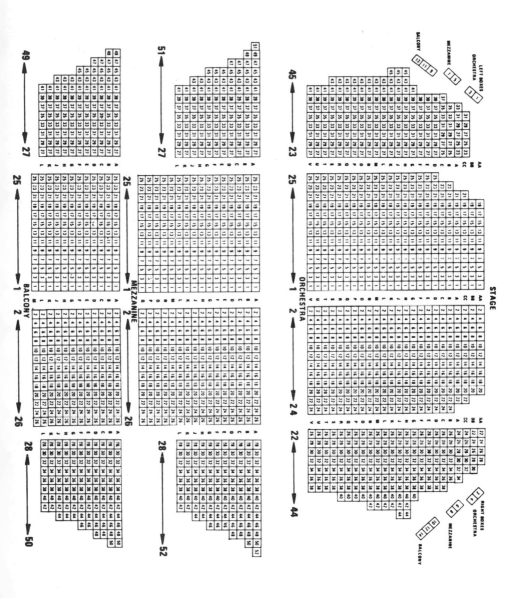

255

BAM Theater Company (Helen Owen Carey Playhouse)

STAGE

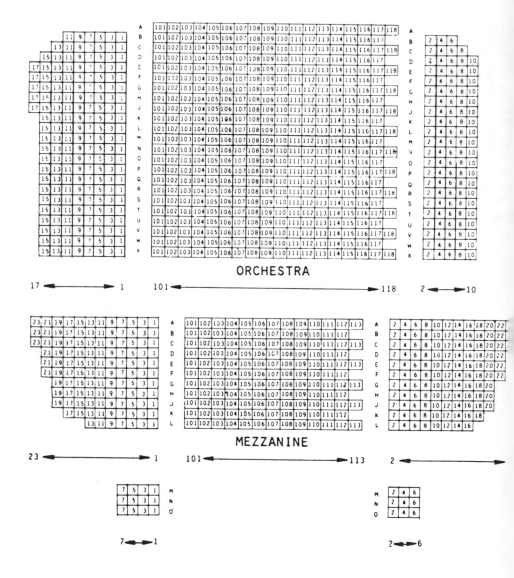

ORCHESTRA

MEZZANINE

"In New York, people don't go to the theater—they go to see hits."

LOUIS JOURDAN

"Words can be so deceitful, but pantomime necessarily is simple, clear and direct."

MARCEL MARCEAU

"She's o.k.—if you like talent."

ETHEL MERMAN, on Mary Martin

"The structure of a play is always the story of how the birds came home to roost."

ARTHUR MILLER

GALLERY PLAYERS
Old First Reform Church
Seventh Avenue and Carroll Street
Brooklyn

Box Office: 499-8239
Box Office Hours: Open 45 minutes before the 7 p.m. performances
Credit Cards: None   TDF Vouchers
Group Sales: Through box office
Season: September–June
Total Seating: 75
Stage Type: Thrust stage
No AC
Handicapped: No access

This community theatre has performed for 15 seasons in the beautiful former chapel of a Park Slope church, making it one of the senior citizens of the Off Broadway movement. Representative productions are *Annie Get Your Gun,* Tennessee Williams's *Summer and Smoke,* and *Godspell.* Siobhan Sloan is the artistic director.
7th Ave IRT to Grand Army Plaza; 6th Ave IND to 7th Ave.

HEIGHTS PLAYERS INCORPORATED
26 Willow Place
Brooklyn

Box Office: 237-2752
Box Office Hours: 9 a.m.–10 p.m. (answering machine)
Credit Cards: None   TDF Vouchers
Group Sales: John Bourne (855-5008)
Season September–May
Total Seating: 150 (varies with production)
Stage Type: Proscenium stage
AC
Handicapped: Semi-accessible

This is one of the oldest groups in the city: Founded in 1956, the players have been performing here since 1963. President John Bourne's 1980–81 offerings have included revivals of *Barefoot in the Park* and *Good News.* The sound and lighting equipment here is among the best in the city.
BMT (RR) to Court St and Borough Hall.

NEW CYCLE THEATRE
Church of St. Ann and the Holy Trinity
657 Fifth Avenue
Brooklyn

Box Office: 788-7098
Box Office Hours: Monday–Saturday, 10 a.m.–6 p.m.; Sunday, 1 p.m.–6 p.m.
Credit Cards: None   TDF Vouchers   Personal checks for mail orders
Group Sales: Through box office
Season: September–June
Total Seating: 300 (varies with production)
Stage Type: Proscenium stage
No AC
Handicapped: Semi-accessible

This three-year-old group moved to the theatre in this landmark church at the beginning of the 1980–81 season. Some of the recent productions by artistic director Berl Hash include: *A Monster Has Stolen the Sun* by Karen Malpede and Mr. Hash's *Making Peace a Fantasy.* The theatre is also used by groups associated with Brooklyn Special Projects.
BMT to Prospect Ave.

THE RYAN REPERTORY COMPANY
2445 Bath Avenue
Brooklyn

Box Office: 373-5208
Box Office Hours: One hour before performance (answering machine)
Credit Cards: None   TDF Vouchers
Group Sales: Through box office
Total Seating: 50
Stage Type: Flexible open space
AC
Handicapped: No access

This young company of eight Brooklynites, under the artistic direction of Barbara Pairi and Jonathan Rosenblum, does original musical productions. Recent offerings: *This Is It: A Matter of Life and Death* by Allan Natlick and Cindy Patish and *The Siren of Saint Milo* by Walter Smollen and Don Newey.
6th Ave BMT to 25th Ave.

WEUISI KUUMBA THEATRE
357 Summer Avenue
Brooklyn

Box Office: 289-5900, 964-9053
Box Office Hours: One hour before performance (answering machine)
Credit Cards: None   Personal checks
Seating: 150
Stage Type: Flexible open space
Handicapped: No access

Weuisi Kuumba (Swahili for "black creativity") has been performing in this former Brooklyn armory since 1979. It has presented such original productions as *What Was the Relation of the Lone Ranger to the Means of Production?*, and *Dutchman*, both by Amiri Baraka, and two plays by Ben Cordwell, *Mission Accomplished* and *Love*. The artistic director is Yusef Iman; Ami Mifu is the co-founder. *At presstime, Weuisi Kuumba was reportedly looking for another theatre.*

WHITMAN HALL
Brooklyn College
Avenue H and Campus Road
Brooklyn

Box Office: 434-1900
Box Office Hours: Tuesday–Friday, 11 a.m.–2 p.m., 5 p.m.–9 p.m.; Saturday, 10 a.m.–9 p.m.
Credit Cards: AE, MC, V   CHARGIT   TDF Vouchers
Group Sales: Ella Weiss (780-5291)
Season: September–June
Total Seating: 2,482 (Orchestra, 1,074; Balconies, 1,408)
Stage Type: Proscenium Stage
No AC
Handicapped: Semi-accessible

Named after Brooklyn's own Walt Whitman, the spacious theatre offers a broad spectrum of cultural events during its season. Among the recent productions of interest to theatre goers: Richard Henzel in *Mark Twain in Person; Theatre Without Bars;* previews of *A Midsummer Night's Dream;* and Joshua Logan's *Musical Moments.*
7th Ave IRT to Flatbush Ave.

RESTAURANTS

GAGE & TOLLNER**

372 Fulton Street
Brooklyn
Reservations: 875-5181
Credit Cards: AE, DC, MC, V
Moderate   Sunday–Friday until 9 p.m.; Saturday to 11 p.m.

If you're on your way to the Brooklyn Academy, what could be nicer than dining in this century-old seafood restaurant by gaslight. It looks the same as it did when Diamond Jim Brady used it to stop by for oysters. If you want oysters, you can choose oysters casino ($4.50), oyster bisque ($3) and, as entrees, stewed oysters ($6.50), Chicago fried oysters ($7), or oysters en brochette ($7). Some house specialties are crabmeat Dewey ($11.25), lobster a la newburg ($13.50), and English mutton chop with sausage, bacon, and kidney ($11.50). All the seafood is excellent. If you happen to like Welsh rabbit, try the Golden Buck Welsh rabbit ($4)—it's delicious.

PETER LUGER'S*

178 Broadway
Brooklyn
Reservations: 387-7400
No credit cards
Moderate to Expensive   Closed Thanksgiving, Christmas, and New Year's Day

Since 1887, Peter Luger's has been synonymous with gargantuan portions of delicious red meat. The dinner menu is as short as you'll find anywhere: steak for one to four people, a steak sandwich, double lamb chops, and roast prime rib, plus two or three specials. If you're having steak it's better to order the steak for two rather than two single steaks. (Steaks are about $15 per person; potatoes, vegetables, and salad a la carte.) The restaurant has wood walls painted black, butcher block tables, and waiters with white aprons.

THE RIVER CAFÉ**

One Water Street
Brooklyn
Reservations: 522-5200
Credit Cards: AE, DC
Expensive   Lunch, dinner to 12 midnight, supper to 2 a.m.

In New York you expect a restaurant with a view to be atop a high building. Here is a magnificent exception. It's on a barge in the East River by the Brooklyn Bridge, and wherever you sit you can see the bridge above, the Statue of Liberty, the World Trade Center, and all the rest. It's a view you'll never forget. The cuisine is American nouvelle featuring lobsters, either boiled or baked, priced by weight, feuillette of rack of lamb ($18), filet of beef in a wine sauce ($15), and daily fish specials at varying prices. You may wish to begin with a feuillete of baby snails in lime butter sauce ($6) or throw caution to the winds with poached oysters in champagne sauce and caviar ($12). Reservations and jackets for the gentlemen are recommended. The management will help you get a cab.

"I don't think the playwright has much right to expect anything from an audience, except possibly to give the play its attention for five minutes. Then he has to earn it. Certainly, I don't think he has a right to expect them to find anything subtle."

HOWARD LINDSAY

THE BRONX

LEHMAN COLLEGE CENTER FOR THE PERFORMING ARTS

Bedford Park Boulevard West
The Bronx

Box Office:	960-9933
Box Office Hours:	Monday–Friday, 10 a.m.–5 p.m.
Credit Cards:	MC, V CHARGIT Personal checks
Group Sales:	Through box office
Total Seating:	Concert hall: 2,310 (Orchestra, 1,063; Mezzanine, 960; Balcony, 287; Standing room, 25). Theatre: 500 (Standing room, 10)
Stage Type:	Proscenium Stage
	AC
	Handicapped: Semi-accessible
	Free parking

This modern theatre was built in 1980 to house performing arts presentations at Lehman College. Under the direction of Alan Light, managing director, and Valerie Simmons, assistant director, the new facility is host to a broad and ambitious program. Of interest to theatregoers were such recent productions as *A Party with Comden and Green;* Phyllis Newman in *The Madwoman of Central Park West; A Kurt Weill Cabaret* with Martha Schlamme and Alvin Epstein; and Pat Carroll in *Gertrude Stein, Gertrude Stein, Gertrude Stein.* A ticket to the theatre subscription series is $28 or $32, depending upon the seat location.
Lexington Ave IRT No. 4 train to Bedford Ave.

QUEENS

BLACK SPECTRUM THEATER

205–21 Linden Boulevard
Queens

Box Office:	527-0836, 527-1315
Box Office Hours:	Tuesday–Saturday, 11 a.m.–5 p.m.; Sunday, 1 p.m.–3 p.m.
Group Sales:	Through box office
Season:	October–July
Credit Cards:	None TDF Vouchers
Total Seating:	99
Stage Type:	Proscenium stage
	AC
	Handicapped: Semi-accessible

Since its founding in 1977, this group has been performing in a former drugstore. Representative offerings include: *Legend of the West or They Went That-A-Way* by Warren Bardine, Jr.; and *Oh, Oh Obesity* by Dr. Gerald Deas. The group also is active in filmmaking and their production of *Babies Making Babies* has been seen locally on television. Carl Clay is artistic director.
IND to 169th St, transfer to Q4 bus to 204th St, and Linden Blvd.

COLDEN CENTER FOR THE PERFORMING ARTS

Queens College

Flushing, Queens

Box Office: 793-8080
Box Office Hours: Monday–Friday, 10 a.m.–4 p.m.; also Tuesday 6 p.m.–8 p.m.
Credit Cards: None   Personal checks   (Student and senior citizen discounts available one hour before performance)
Group Sales: Through box office
Total Seating: 2,143 (Orchestra, 1,823; Balcony, 320)
Stage Type: Proscenium Stage
AC
Handicapped: Semi-accessible
Free parking

A handsome theatre, built in 1961 by Queens College, which presents a wide variety of cultural and civic events (President Carter's town meeting was held here) throughout the year. Recent events of interest to theatregoers include Marcel Marceau and the Prince Street Players. A four-event Celebrity Series subscription, which includes the theatrical presentations, was $15 to $23, depending upon seat location, for the 1980–81 season.
Flushing IRT to Main St, Q25/34 bus to Center.

QUEENSBOROUGH COMMUNITY COLLEGE THEATRE

56th Avenue and Springfield Boulevard

Bayside, Queens

Box Office: 631-6311
Box Office Hours: Monday–Friday, 10 a.m.–4 p.m.
Credit Cards: None   TDF Vouchers   Personal checks
Group Sales: Through box office
Season: October–May
Total Seating: 871 (Orchestra, 671; Balcony, 200)
Stage Type: Proscenium stage
AC
Handicapped: Semi-accessible

This attractive theatre was built in 1960 and serves the community with a subscription series of diverse cultural events. Theatrical presentations from last season included: Phyllis Newman in *The Madwoman of Central Park West;* the New Globe Theatre in Shaw's *Candida;* the National Theatre of the Deaf; Earl Wrightson and Lois Hunt in *A Salute to Noel Coward and Cole Porter;* and Gilbert and Sullivan's *The Gondoliers.* Subscriptions for the full series of eight performances range from $36 to $48, depending on seating; individual performances are $6 to $8. Of particular interest are three musicals for children. Last season's were *Beans* by the Sheffield Ensemble Theatre, *Yankee Doodle Dandy,* and the Living Theatre's *Robin Hood.* A subscription for all three is $6, individual performances, $2.50.
Flushing IRT to Main St, Q27 bus to College.

THALIA SPANISH THEATRE

41-17 Greenpoint Avenue
Sunnyside, Queens

Box Office: 729-3880
Box Office Hours: One hour before performance (answering machine)
Credit Cards: None   TDF Vouchers   Personal checks
Group Sales: Through box office
Total Seating: 99
Stage Type: Proscenium stage
AC
Handicapped: Semi-accessible

The large Hispanic community here is served by this bilingual company, which moved from Manhattan several years ago. Artistic director Zully Montero produces standard American plays (for example, *Gigi*, and *Arsenic and Old Lace*) in Spanish. The Thalia has received numerous awards for its work.
Flushing IRT to 40th St, M32 bus to Queens Blvd.

"Good plays drive bad playgoers crazy."

BROOKS ATKINSON

"If you really want to help the American theater, don't be an actress, darling. Be an audience."

TALLULAH BANKHEAD

"I never let them [the audience] cough. They wouldn't dare."

ETHEL BARRYMORE

ALSO IN THE AREA . . .

No picture of the theatre in New York would be complete any more if it did not include the major theatres in the area: the Yale Repertory and the Long Wharf in Connecticut, the McCarter and the Shakespeare Festival in New Jersey, the PAF Playhouse on Long Island. All can stand alone as important theatres; all both draw on and contribute to theatre in the city. For a suburbanite it is no longer necessary to come into the city to see good theatre. For the city dweller, an excursion to New Haven or Princeton to see a show is a welcome break in his pattern of theatregoing.

CONNECTICUT

DOWNTOWN CABARET THEATRE
263 Golden Hill Street
Bridgeport, Conn.

Box Office: (203) 576-1636
Box Office Hours: Monday–Thursday, 10 a.m.–6 p.m.; Friday–Saturday, 10 a.m.–10 p.m; Sunday, 10 a.m.–8 p.m.
Credit Cards: None   Personal checks
Group Sales: Through box office
Total Seating: 300
Stage Type: Proscenium stage
AC
Handicapped: Semi-accessible

This group is the only one in the area, if not the country, exclusively presenting original cabaret revues on a year-round basis, usually musical satires on America's past, present, and future. One show, *The Seventies—The Way We Are*, unites music, vignettes, and visual projections to demonstrate entertainingly the changes we've been through: Watergate, cults, disco fever, the influence of television, and the abuse of national resources. Decades seem a theme here; other productions have included *The Sixties*, *The Thirties*, and *The Forties— Songs of Love and War*. All the productions were conceived and written by artistic director Claude McNeal. The group, founded in 1975, also presents a year-round children's theatre company made up of advanced theatre students from the area's high schools, who are part of the theatre's free work-exchange apprentice program.

HARTFORD STAGE COMPANY
50 Church Street
Hartford, Conn.

Box Office: (203) 527-5151
Box Office Hours: Monday, 10 a.m.–5 p.m; Tuesday–Friday, 10 a.m.–8:30 p.m.; Saturday, 12 noon–9 p.m.; Sunday, 12 noon–8 p.m.
Credit Cards: AE, MC, V   Personal checks
Group Sales: Through box office
Season: September–July
Total Seating: 489 (Standing room, 20)
Stage Type: Thrust stage
AC
Handicapped: Semi-accessible. Recorded program for the blind

Since 1977, the Hartford Stage Company has been housed in a new theatre, part of a $2.5-million complex designed by noted architect Robert Venturi. The company presents a varied and balanced season with a continuing interest in black and urban themes. Under the artistic direction of Paul Weidner the company recently had a Broadway engagement of its premiere production of Ray Aranha's *My Sister, My Sister*. Its presentation of Edward Albee's *All Over* was seen nationally on the PBS series Theatre in America. In the summer, the company sponsors a youth theatre for Hartford teenagers, producing such musicals as *West Side Story* and *Two Gentlemen of Verona*. The former home of the company, active from its founding in 1964 by Jacques Cartier until 1977, is now known as the Old Place and is used occasionally for experimental and workshop productions. Some recent company presentations include Sam and Bella Spewack's *Boy Meets Girl*, Bertolt Brecht's *Galileo* as adapted by Charles Laughton, and *Passing By* written by Martin Sherman. Patti LuPone performed here in *Catchpenny Twist* before she went on to star in *Evita*.

HARTMAN THEATRE COMPANY
Box 521,
Stamford, Conn.
Landmark Square Playhouse,
1 Landmark Square
Stamford Theatre,
307 Atlantic Street

Box Office: (203) 323-2131 New York direct (212) 581-0177
Box Office Hours: Monday–Saturday, 10 a.m.–8 p.m.
Credit Cards: AE, MC, V
Group Sales: (203) 324-6781
Season: October–April
Total Seating: Stamford, 600; Landmark Square, 110
Stage Type: Proscenium stage (Stamford)
Flexible (Landmark Square)
Handicapped: Semi-accessible

Del and Margot Tenny founded the Hartman in 1974 to present a mixture of classics, new plays, and revivals. It operates in a renovated theatre that once was a vaudeville palace and in Landmark Square Playhouse, a modern space that is the site of new play readings, dark-night seminars of the theatre, and performances by visiting artists. The Hartman has presented such new works as Milan Stitt's *The Runner Stumbles*, Mark Eichman's *As to the Meaning of Words*, and A. R. Gurney, Jr.'s *The Middle Ages*. Among its revivals are Molière's *Tartuffe* and Philip Barry's *The Animal Kingdom*. The Hartman operates a professional intern program, which invites 20 qualified students to join the theatre's operation in production, administration, design, or acting. A ticket to the four-production subscription series ranges from $30 to $45 depending upon the night chosen and seat location.

LONG WHARF THEATRE
22 Sargent Drive
New Haven, Conn.

Box Office: (203) 787-4282
Box Office Hours: Monday, 10 a.m.–6 p.m.; Tuesday–Saturday, 10 a.m.–6 p.m.; Sunday, 12 noon–8 p.m.
Credit Cards: MC, V (subscription series only)   Personal checks (Telephone reservations accepted; tickets to be picked up at least two hours before performance. Main Stage is reserved seating; Stage II is not.)
Group Sales: Through box office
Season: October–June
Total Seating: Main Stage, 484; Stage II, 199
Stage Type: Three-quarter thrust (Main Stage); Thrust with flexible seating (Stage II)
Handicapped: Semi-accessible. Interpreted performances for the deaf and hearing impaired.
Free parking

The Long Wharf Theatre is in a former warehouse in the New Haven Meat and Produce

Long Wharf Theatre

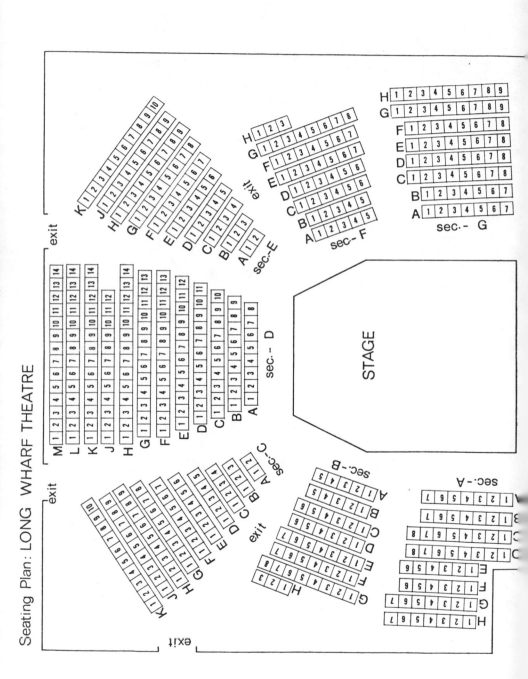

Seating Plan: LONG WHARF THEATRE

STAGE

266

Terminal. Don't let that dissuade you. It's marvellously convenient: right at Exit 46 of the Connecticut Turnpike, adjacent to the Amtrak and Conrail station, and two minutes from the bus terminal, and it's handsome with functional, unadorned cinderblock designed to focus your attention on the stage from the moment you enter. What fireworks this stage has seen! Since its founding in 1965 by Jon Jory and Harlan Lleiman, the Long Wharf has developed into a theatre of national importance. Artistic director Arvin Brown and his associate, Kenneth Frankel, have seen a number of their productions transferred intact to Broadway: D. L. Coburn's *The Gin Game,* starring Hume Cronyn and Jessica Tandy with Mike Nichols directing (winner of the Pulitzer Prize for drama); Michael Cristofer's *The Shadow Box* (a Pulitzer-Prize and Tony-Award winner); the 1979 revival of Lillian Hellman's *Watch on the Rhine;* the world premiere of David Rabe's *Streamers,* directed by Mike Nichols (New York Drama Critics' Circle Award); the American premieres of Peter Nichols's *Forget-Me-Not Lane* and *The National Health;* Stewart Parker's *Spokesong;* David Storey's *The Changing Room;* and Athol Fugard and John Kani in Winston Ntshona's *Sizwe Banzi is Dead.* Last season began with Arvin Brown's production of David Mamet's *American Buffalo,* featuring Clifton James, Al Pacino, and Thomas Waites. Three productions here have been telecast on the PBS Theatre in America series: *The Widowing of Mrs. Holroyd, Forget-Me-Not Lane,* and *Ah, Wilderness!* The Long Wharf's Stage II, now three years old, highlights works-in-progress and hosts other theatrical troupes. An eight-play subscription for the 1980–81 season ranged from $47 to $77, depending on the night and the location of the seat.

O'NEILL THEATER CENTER

305 Great Neck Road
Waterford, Conn. 06385
Box Office: (203) 443-1238; New York direct: 925-5032
Credit Cards: AE, MC, V (Reservations held until one hour before curtain)
Season: July–August
Total Seating: Theatre Barn, 200; Amphitheatre, 300; Instant Theatre, 200; Barn El, 200
Stage Type: Thrust stage (Theatre Barn and Amphitheatre)
Arena (Instant Theatre), Flexible stage (Barn El)
No AC
Handicapped: Semi-accessible

In 17 years, a number of important theatre activities have developed here under the guidance of George C. White, founder and president, and Lloyd Richards, artistic director. The first project was the National Playwrights Conference, a forum where theatre professionals can work together, free from critical pressures. In 1976, the playwrights conference in turn inaugurated the New Drama for Television Project to help playwrights conceive and develop original material specifically for TV. The conference has staged some 200 new plays by more than 150 playwrights. Another activity is the National Critics Institute, a professional workshop directed by Ernest Schier. In 1978, two more O'Neill projects began: the choreographers conference and the composer/librettist conference, both under the direction of Joseph Krakora. Another program is the National Theater Institute, a professional training program for college students directed by Lawrence J. Wilker. Joyce Schmidt directs still another program: the Creative Arts in Education Program. The center also houses the Monte Cristo Cottage Museum and Library, as well as the National Theatre of the Deaf. The productions here are always interesting, always professional, and if you are seriously interested in the American theatre, the O'Neill Theater Center is well worth a visit.

NATIONAL THEATRE OF THE DEAF

O'Neill Theater Center
305 Great Neck Road
Waterford, Conn.
Box Office: (203) 443-5378
Season: October–May

Since its founding by David Hays in 1967, this touring company has developed a unique theatrical style and visual language that is readily understood by all audiences. The second professional theatre of its kind (a Russian theatre of the deaf was founded in 1911), it has been instrumental in establishing similar troupes in Great Britain, Sweden, and Australia and has assisted the formation of community theatres of the deaf around this country. After seeing the National Theatre of the Deaf, hearing audiences (who comprise four-fifths of the attendees) invariably come away with a new understanding and appreciation of the deaf and their capabilities. The performances can be followed easily without a knowledge of sign language. The troupe has now completed more than 20 national tours totaling more than 2,000 performances, including two Broadway performances. Other tours have taken the troupe to Europe, the Middle East, and the South Pacific. More than 100,000,000 Americans have seen the group perform on commercial or public television. In 1977, it received a special Tony Award for theatrical excellence. A summer school is held at the O'Neill Theater Center to extend the company's skills, train new members, and provide training for members of deaf community troupes around the world. In September, the troupe goes into rehearsal for a new production it will tour the following season. Recent productions include Ben Jonson's *Volpone* and Dylan Thomas's *Quite Early One Morning.*

YALE REPERTORY THEATRE

Yale University
1120 Chapel Street
New Haven, Conn.

Box Office: (203) 436-1600
Box Office Hours: 11 a.m.–5:30 p.m., if no performance; 11 a.m.–8:30 p.m., performance days; closed Sunday
Credit Cards: MC, V Personal checks
Group Sales: (203) 436-1600/436-8491
Season: October–May
Total Seating: 491
Stage Type: Modified thrust
No AC
Handicapped: Semi-accessible

The Yale Repertory Theatre is a professional company affiliated with the Yale School of Drama, founded in 1966 by the school's dean, Robert Brustein. The company has devoted itself to innovative productions of the classics, and to fostering the most daring and innovative new playwriting. Under the current dean and director, Lloyd Richards, the company is also presenting classic plays from the American repertoire. Yale Rep offers a subscription series of seven plays, produced in rotating repertory over a 40-week period. Its home is in a historic former Baptist church, first occupied by the company in 1971, and completely renovated as a theatre in 1975. Among the offerings are a Sunday series of staged readings of new plays, a series of theatre-related films, a post-play discussion series, and the Yale Cabaret, a late-night weekend café featuring comic and satirical sketches. Among the productions premiered at Yale Rep are Arthur Kopit's *Wings,* Athol Fugard's *A Lesson from Aloes,* Ted Tally's *Terra Nova,* Joseph Heller's *We Bombed in New Haven,* and *The 1940s Radio Hour.*

Yale Repertory Theatre

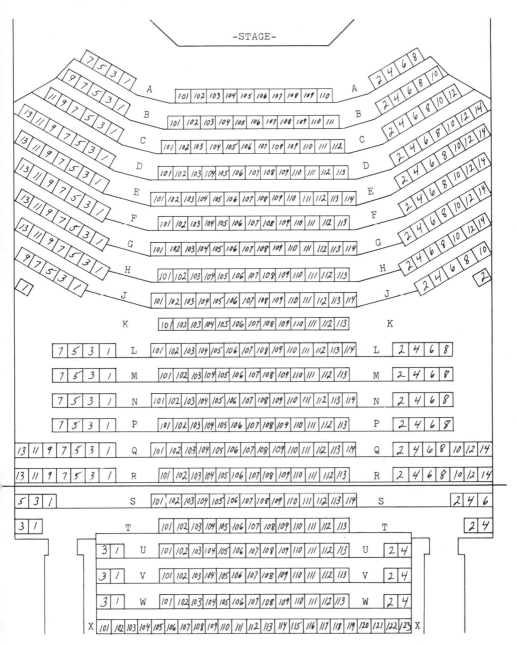

LONG ISLAND

JONES BEACH THEATRE

Jones Beach State Park
Wantagh, L.I., N.Y.

Box Office: (516) 221-1000
Box Office Hours: 10 a.m.–8 p.m., during season
Credit Cards: MC, V TELECHARGE Ticketron
Season: End of June to Sunday before Labor Day
Total Seating: 8,200
Stage Type: Unique outdoor stage
Handicapped: Fully accessible
Free parking

The spectacular outdoor theatre opened in 1952 and Mike Todd produced here the first two seasons, Guy Lombardo for the next 24 (at the theatre entrance is the Guy Lombardo Memorial Garden). The usual fare is the revival of a hit Broadway musical: *The Sound of Music, Annie Get Your Gun, Guys and Dolls,* and the like. The productions are spectacular: The stage revolves and the mainstage and the forestage are separated by a lagoon, which is integrated into the stage action. This is good family fun and a nice way to spend a summer evening. Free after-theatre dancing is provided in the Theatre Dance Tent. There is a special package trip from the city taking the Long Island Railroad from Penn Station to Freeport and a bus to the theatre.

PAF PLAYHOUSE

185 Second Street
Huntington Station, L.I., N.Y.

Box Office: (516) 271-8282
Box Office Hours: Monday–Saturday, 10 a.m.–8 p.m.; Sunday, 12 noon–3 p.m.
Credit Cards: AE, MC, V
Group Sales: Through box office.
Season: October–June
Total Seating: PAF Playhouse, 527; PAF McDonald's Theatre, 250
Stage Type: Thrust stage (PAF Playhouse)
Proscenium stage (PAF MacDonald's Theatre)
AC
Handicapped: Semi-accessible

In the spring of 1981, PAF Playhouse, the only residential professional theatre on Long Island, was fighting for its life. It had filed Chapter XI bankruptcy, closed the larger of its two theatres, and ended the season in March instead of June. It would be a tragedy if the PAF Playhouse can't reopen, for it has had a distinguished career since its founding by Clint Marantz in 1966. Normally, the playhouse stages eight productions a season. Since 1975 when Jay Broad became the producer here the accent has been on staging new plays. Some notable successes: Jack Heifner's *Vanities,* Albert Innaurato's *Gemini,* Richard Nelson's *The Killing of Yablonski,* George F. Walker's *Gossip,* and Olwen Wymark's *Loved.* This policy has been well-received and the number of subscribers has grown to nearly 14,000. In addition to the theatres, the playhouse has a touring company called Troupe, which brings full-scale productions into Long Island schools. This arts-in-education program also holds workshops in schools and has done extensive work with the handicapped.

WESTBURY MUSIC FAIR

Brush Hollow Road
Westbury, L.I., N.Y.

Box Office: (516) 333-0533
Box Office Hours: Monday–Saturday, 10 a.m.–8 p.m.; Sunday, 12 noon–8 p.m.
Credit Cards: MC, V   CHARGIT   Personal checks
Group Sales: Group Sales Department
Total Seating: 2,861 (Orchestra, 2,433; Balcony, 428)
Stage Type: Theatre in the round
AC
Handicapped: Semi-accessible
Free parking

The music fair was in a tent from 1955 to 1965, when this attractive new facility was built. It presents a mixed bag of attractions, sometimes musical comedy, sometimes celebrities such as Sergio Franchi and Abbe Lane, Fred Waring, Diana Ross, and Mitzi Gaynor.

NEW JERSEY

GEORGE STREET PLAYHOUSE

414 George Street
New Brunswick, N.J.

Box Office: (201) 846-2895
Box Office Hours: 12 noon–5 p.m.; 12 noon–8 p.m., if performance
Credit Cards: MC, V
Season: October–May
Total Seating: 260
Stage Type: Thrust stage
No AC
Handicapped: Semi-accessible. Aids for the hearing- and sight-impaired at no charge

This theatre presents a wide mixture of productions: new scripts, classics, and popular contemporary works. During the past several seasons, two world premieres have been produced including *Paris Was Yesterday*, Paul Shyre's adaptation from Janet Flanner's memoirs starring Celeste Holm, and the new musical *Pettycoat Lane* by Judd Woldin. There is no permanent company here and producer Eric Krebs and his directors cast from New York talent, for the most part. Founded in 1974 by Mr. Krebs and John Herochik, managing director, the playhouse has for the past three seasons provided support and a base of operations to a full-time children's theatre company and to Crossroads, the first Equity company in New Jersey to concentrate on black and Hispanic theatre. A subscription to the six-play series runs from $24 to $50, depending on the performance and seating.

McCARTER THEATRE COMPANY

91 University Place
Princeton, N.J. 08540

Box Office: (609) 921-8700 (telephone reservations accepted)
Box Office Hours: 12 noon until performance
Credit Cards: AE, MC, V   Personal checks
Group Sales: Through box office
Total Seating: 1,077 (Orchestra, 720; Balcony, 357)
Stage Type: Proscenium stage
AC
Handicapped: Fully accessible

This theatre was built in the late 1920s for the Triangle Club, the university group (Jim-

271

McCarter Theatre Company

STAGE

ORCHESTRA

BALCONY

my Stewart and Joshua Logan were members) that produces annual, original satirical musicals. For years it served as a popular stopover for Broadway-bound shows. The world premiere of *Our Town* was here on January 22, 1938, as well as William Inge's *Bus Stop* in 1955, Joshua Logan's *The Wisteria Trees* in 1950, Terrence Rattigan's *Separate Tables* in 1956, and *The Tooth of the Crime*, the 1972 musical by Sam Shepard. After a highly successful season by Ellis Rabb's APA Repertory Company here in 1960, the university decided to establish a permanent repertory company. The real beginning of the company, however, was the arrival in 1974 of producing director Michael Kahn. The theatre has achieved national recognition under Kahn and his successor, Nagle Jackson. The past season included: *The Taming of the Shrew*; Orson Welles's *Moby Dick Rehearsed*; Nagle Jackson's adapation of *A Christmas Carol*; Duerrenmatt's *The Visit*; Molnar's *The Play's the Thing*; and a new play by Percy Granger. A subscription membership for six plays costs up to $57 for good orchestra seats on Saturday night.

NEW JERSEY SHAKESPEARE FESTIVAL
Bowne Theatre
Drew University
Madison, N.J.

Box Office:	(201) 377-4487
Credit Cards:	MC, V Personal checks
Group Sales:	Through box office
Season:	June–November
Total Seating:	238
Stage Type:	Thrust Stage
	AC
	Handicapped: Semi-accessible

It began with a single production, *The Taming of the Shrew*, at the Cape May Playhouse in 1963. From this has grown a true repertory company, located at Drew University since 1970, that performs great English, Irish, and American plays, including at least two Shakespeare plays, each season. Some of the more innovative productions presented by founder and artistic director Paul Barry include a World War II *Coriolanus*, an 1890s Viennese *Measure for Measure*, and a Roman "black Mass" *Titus Andronicus*. This is an actor's theatre, composed of classically trained actors attracted by creative freedom, a true repertory structure, and a variety of plays presented back-to-back. The festival has a highly regarded intern program that attracts hundreds of applicants each year, of whom 80 are selected. A six-play subscription to the festival costs from $37 to $50.

THE WHOLE THEATRE COMPANY
544 Bloomfield Avenue
Montclair, N.J.

Box Office:	(201) 744-2989
Box Office Hours:	Tuesday–Saturday, 11 a.m.–9 p.m.; Sunday, 12 noon–8 p.m.
Credit Cards:	MC, V
Season:	October–June
Total Seating:	200
Stage Type:	Flexible stage
	No AC
	Handicapped: Semi-accessible

This company started in the vestibule of the First Baptist Church in 1973 and in 1978 moved into the vestibule of a renovated bank. A more important measure of its progress is that it started with 50 subscribers and now has some 3,500 from more than 160 communities. In the past season, the company presented two U.S. premieres: *The Death and Resurrection of Mr. Roche* by Ireland's Thomas Kilroy; and John Morgan Evans's *Daughters*. Other productions included the musical revue *Cole, A Thousand Clowns*, and an adaptation of Molière's *Tartuffe* in 1950 in Little Italy. The theatre is directly across the street from the Bloomfield Avenue stop of the Montclair bus from Port Authority. The theatre recently opened the Upstage Café on the second floor. Here you can supper on various quiches, crepes, and salads. No liquor license but you are welcome to bring your own.

COMPANIES WITHOUT PERMANENT THEATRES

To be accurate and complete, a theatre guide needs to discuss both theatres and what happens in theatres. The majority of Off-Off Broadway theatres are associated with particular theatre companies. Some, however, are simply performance spaces used by a number of companies. This section contains information on active theatre companies in the city that are not associated with a particular theatre but which either use whatever theatre is free and convenient when they have a production or are companies that perform somewhere other than in conventional theatres.

THE ACTING COMPANY

420 West 42nd Street
564-3510

The Acting Company got its start because John Houseman thought his first graduating class from the Theater Center of the Julliard School was too talented to be simply disbanded. He and executive producer Margot Harley formed the Class of 1972 into a professional company that was introduced as the dramatic arm of the Saratoga (New York) Performing Arts Festival. Later it was called the City Center Acting Company. When this association ceased in 1975, the company adopted its present name. The Acting Company tours a repertoire of classical and modern plays across the country; it has performed 34 plays in 165 cities in 39 states. It also provides teaching demonstrations and workshops, the only company to do so. Michael Kahn and Alan Schneider are the company's artistic directors. The company recently took a six-week tour of Australia presenting productions staged by Michael Kahn, Liviu Ciulei, and Gerald Gutierrez. Some recent offerings include: Lewis Galantière's adaptation of Jean Anouilh's *Antigone; Romeo and Juliet;* and George Abbott and Philip Dunning's *Broadway.* The company's season is from July to May.

ACTOR'S ALLIANCE

10 East 18th Street
567-9376

This group was founded in 1976 on the principle that actors can make their own artistic and business decisions. William Newman, founder and member of the board of directors, and Donald Pace, managing director, have produced such plays as Kathy Hurley's *In Beauty like the Night* about the relationship between Byron and Shelley, *The Fading of Miss Dru,* also by Ms. Hurley, and *Yes, But What Do You Really Do for a Living?,* a comedy about the lives of actors developed by the group in workshop. The last two were presented at the Samuel French Short Play Festival. Jack Poggi, a group member, did a new translation of Chekhov's *Uncle Vanya,* which the group presented. The latest effort is the workshop development of *Marriage and Other Matters,* scenes and sketches about marriage by Jeanne Schlegal. When this was written the group was looking for a new theatre (it had been using the Town House on West 64th Street) and arranging a touring schedule with the city's department of cultural affairs.

AMERICAN ENSEMBLE COMPANY

P.O. Box 5478
Grand Central Station
571-7594

Robert Petito founded this company in 1970 to present productions of both literary and social significance. Among the recent productions were Friedrich Schiller's *Mary Stuart,* Tennessee Williams's *The Glass Menagerie,* and André Gide's *The Immoralist,* most of them at the Theatre Off Park. Mr. Petito hopes to have a theatre to house his productions by the time you read this, and says the emphasis in forthcoming seasons will be on new plays.

AMERICAN STANISLAVSKI THEATRE

485 Park Avenue
755-5120
   Sonia Moore, a true disciple of the Stanislavski school of Method acting, teaches 80 or 90 students in the parish house of the Trinity Presbyterian Church on West 57th Street. The group presents two productions a year, in January and June, in such theatres as the SoHo Rep and the Nameless Theatre, as well as touring the United States and Canada. The productions are carefully chosen to stretch and display the techniques of Method acting. Recent presentations have included Tennessee Williams's *This Property Is Condemned* and *A Streetcar Named Desire,* Strindberg's *The Stronger, My Poor Murat* by Arbuzov, and several Chekhov plays.

BLUES FREEZE THEATRICAL ENSEMBLE

394 Morningside Terrace
Teaneck, N.J.
(201) 836-6058, direct New York (212) 281-8463
   Byron A. Gaspard, founder, producer, and artistic director of this group, presents both classics and original plays at correctional institutions in the area, Actors Playhouse, the Harlem Performance Center, and the Lincoln Center summer festival of one-act plays. Last season, the group presented two of Mr. Gaspard's original works: *What Is Real . . . Is What's Really Real* and *Anything and Everything.*

BOND STREET THEATRE COALITION

2 Bond Street
254-4614
   Founded in 1975 by Patrick Sciarratta and Joanne Sherman, the company originally was known as Bond Street Mime. Now it is a working ensemble of actors, mimes, acrobats, jugglers, magicians, musicians, and puppeteers. It's a touring company, performing in the streets and in theatres. Classic structures—*commedia dell'arte,* myth, cabaret, and folklore—are used by the company, as well as a theatre form that is immediately accessible to the public, spontaneous and highly improvisatory. Its goal: to bring the "theatre of dexterity and perception" to a broad spectrum of the public. In the late 1970s, the company was in residence at LaMama and produced original productions there, including *What a Mess, Power Play,* and *Capidome.* In the summer the company has a two-week intensive workshop for a small group on Shelter Island. This is a fine group; watch for their fall appearances in city theatres.

BYRD HOFFMAN FOUNDATION

147 Spring Street
966-1365
   Artistic director Robert Wilson is known for his visual approach to the performing arts, and the company presents mostly his original works. An operatic adaptation of *Medea* was seen at the Music Theatre Library at Washington's Kennedy Center. *Dialog/Curious George,* after playing at the Mitzi Newhouse Theatre at Lincoln Center, toured to Rotterdam and Warsaw. An original musical, *Golden Window,* was in rehearsal early in 1981. Lois Bianchi is executive director of the company.

CHAMELEON THEATRIX

220 West 98th Street
Amy Sophia Marashinsky (964-4482)

This group develops and produces highly theatrical presentations, choosing an appropriate performance space for the individual production. In 1979, it premiered Jean Cocteau's *The Infernal Machine* in the gymnasium of the Universalist Church at 76th Street and Central Park West. In 1980, it mounted a new swashbuckling production of *The Three Musketeers* on Columbia's Low Library steps. The group planned new productions of *Arabian Nights,* and an untitled pirate production to be performed on the sailing vessel *Peking* at the South Street Seaport.

CHAMOMILE PRODUCTIONS, INC.

Box 5 S
4 Park Avenue
679-1858

Performers and other beginning theatre people can find help from this two-year old group, now conducting seminars on various aspects of the theatre, from auditions to marketing to developing one-man showcases. Founder Dorothy Johnston and her associates—Laura Lockhart, Ken Leak, Janine Quick, and Jean Scott—are working on ways to help young performers hone their skills and polish their craft.

CREATION PRODUCTION COMPANY

127 Greene Street
674-5593

Creation is a post-modern theatre company exploring the cross between video, music, sculpture, dance, poetry, and technology. Through the use of collage and other intermedia techniques, it develops new performance concepts and integrates the visual and performing arts in original and innovative works. Matthew Maguire and Susan Mosakowski are the artistic directors. Some recent works include: *Seventy Scenes of Halloween* by Jeffrey M. Jones; *Eye Figure Fiction* by Matthew Maguire; *Eclipse* by Susan Mosakowski; and *The Ride Across Lake Constance* by Peter Handke. Creation rehearses in a SoHo loft and appears at such theatres as the Open Space, Perry Street Theatre, LaMama, and the Performing Garage.

DOUBLE IMAGE

444 West 56th Street
245-2489

Helen Waren Mayer, artistic director, and Grace L. Jones, administrative director, founded this group in 1974 to produce new plays, to encourage new playwrights, and to create work for actors looking for a place to perform. Recent productions have included: *Nothing Immediate* by Shirley Lauro; *Me Too Then* by Steven Smith and Tom Dudzick; *The Deserter* by Norman Beim; and *Forty-Deuce!* created in the group's workshop by 12 cast members. Double Image appeared in the spring of 1981 at the American Theatre for Actors.

ECCENTRIC CIRCLES THEATRE

c/o R. Hopkins, Apt. 4N
400 West 43rd Street

Original plays, written and directed by women, are the province of this group, founded in 1980 by director-producer Rosemary Hopkins, Paula Kay Pierce, Barbara Bunch, and Janet Bruders. Its productions at the Eighteenth Street Playhouse and St. Malachy's have included *Running Numbers* by Gloria Allen, *I Thought It Was a Lie* by Leslie Ava Shaw, *96A* by Nancy Henderson, *MaPa* by Janet Bruders, *The Snow Room* by Kate Ryan, and *Many Faces of Eve,* a montage of New York women.

ENCORE THEATRE COMPANY

125 Christopher Street
243-0458

In its first season, 1980–81, this repertory group used the Westside Mainstage to present Maxim Gorky's *The Lower Depths, Out of the Frying Pan* by George Swann, and comedies of the 1940s. Artistic director George Zagoren is seeking a permanent theatre for his group.

THE GLINES

28 Willow Street
Brooklyn
522-5567

The Glines founded New York's Gay Arts Festival in 1980 in which theatre companies from San Francisco and Minneapolis and a mime company participated. More recently the group presented Arch Brown's *News Boy* and Doric Wilson's *A Perfect Relationship* in repertory at the Twenty-eighth Street Playhouse in Manhattan. John Gline founded the group that bears his name in 1976 with Barry Laine. Lawrence Lane is the general manager.

HAND OVER MOUTH HIDDEN THEATRE

158 East 7th Street
473-6012

The first question has to be about the name of this group. "So many of our emotions—fear, astonishment, surprise—are expressed with a hand over the mouth," explained artistic director Craig Lowy. "And we express only a small portion of the emotions we feel inside. The expression of hidden emotions is what we're after in our group." The group, founded in 1977, has performed Gertrude Stein's *Dr. Faustus Lights the Lights*, Strindberg's *Storm*, and, more recently, Mr. Lowy's *Mercury Descending* at the JayCee Studio.

HARLEM CHILDREN'S THEATRE

420 West 42nd Street
594-0524

The Harlem Children's Theatre has permanent rehearsal space in Theatre Row but performs all over the city—and the world. The company was founded in 1971 by Aduke Aremu and Omodele Folayan, and its beginnings were in the basement of a school at 116th and First Avenue with a program trying to offer productions to delinquent children. As the group began performing, its popularity rose rapidly, and it moved to the Billie Holiday Theatre in Brooklyn before coming to Theatre Row. Now the company has a cast of 60, ranging in age from four to 18. Its repertoire includes four original musicals; *Land of the Egyptians, The Liberation of Mother Goose, Ju Ju Man,* and *Babylon II.* The company has performed at Lincoln Center, Brooklyn Academy, Town Hall, the Gene Frankel Theatre, National Black Theatre, Mr. Morris Park, Pratt Institute, Hunter College, and the Apollo Theatre. Its production of *The Liberation of Mother Goose* was telecast on PBS and produced by Joseph Papp at the New York Shakespeare Festival. The company performed at the Second International Black Arts Festival in Lagos, Nigeria, in January, 1977. The next year it toured England, Spain, France, and Germany in celebration of the International Year of the Child. Last year it performed in Barbados.

MABOU MINES

463 West Street
989-4953

Another ex-LaMama resident company, Mabou Mines (the name of a town in Nova Scotia) is one of the city's best avant-garde performance companies. It was founded and led by Lee Bruer in the 1960s, and through the years has developed techniques that have many sources: *commedia dell'arte*, mime, even kabuki. Most of their work is original, although they have done some well-received adaptations of works by Samuel Beckett. There is no set schedule of performances at this time, but Mabou Mines is worth watching for.

NATIONAL SHAKESPEARE COMPANY

414 West 51st Street
265-1340

The National Shakespeare Company tours colleges, universities, and communities nationwide presenting classical productions of Shakespeare. NSC productions are directed by such notable directors as Mario Siletti, John Houseman, Neil Flanagan, and Sue Lawless. A company of 12 tours with full scenery, lighting, and costumes. Since 1963, under the artistic direction of co-founder (with Elaine Sulka) Philip Meister, NSC has performed its repertoire in 125 cities in 35 states to a total audience of more than 250,000. NSC has developed a program of performances geared to secondary schools that not only enhance the study of Shakespeare's plays, but also serve as an aid to teachers of English, history, and drama. Last season, this matinee series was presented to more than 25,000 students in New York, Pennsylvania, Illinois, and Iowa. The company offers actors a two-year program in the city and an intensive eight-week summer program at its base in the Catskills.

NEW CONSERVATORY THEATRE

334 Bowery
777-1855

Since 1974, artistic director Joan Langue has arduously built a historical repertory company of actors and musicians who present works dating from the 12th to the 16th centuries. The oldest piece is *The Play of Anti-Christ,* an anonymous work that originated in Bavaria. Others include such secular farces as *The One Who Had Doubt and the Two Who Can't Hear* and *The New Farce of the Meatloaf and the Pie.* In *commedia dell'arte* the company works off the scenario of *The Three Cuckolds.* Another work is *Shakespeare's Sonnets: An Exploration in Imagery.* The group (usually 10 actors and six musicians playing replica instruments) tours extensively to colleges and universities in the tri-state area. In the city, Ms. Langue's group has appeared at the Cathedral of St. John the Divine and at Symphony Space. Discussion periods follow performances focusing on how the plays pertain to social conditions then and now. An extensive training program is conducted for groups of 12 to 15 in the theatre's Bowery space.

NEW YORK COLLABORATION THEATRE

102 West 80th Street
873-4991

Artistic director Gene Pelfrey frankly admits that his group is elitist, seeking to challenge intellectual audiences with provocative productions. Since its founding in 1977, the group has presented *Blood Lust,* an original study, created in the rehearsal process, of the public reaction to a Son-of-Sam-type killer and, in a co-production with Shelter West, Synge's *In the Shade of the Glen.* In spring 1981, the group was working on an original women's play.

NEW YORK THEATRE STUDIO

130 West 80th Street
595-6656

This group was founded in 1977 by artistic director Richard Romagnoli and managing director Cheryl Fardone to present new American plays and the American premieres of European plays, including several works by British playwright Snoo Wilson. The group had been using the Chelsea Theatre Club for its productions and was moving in the spring of 1981 to AMDA Studio One in the Ansonia Hotel where it is to present *Redback* by Denis Spedaliere and *As to the Meaning of Words* by Mark Eichman.

ONTOLOGICAL-HYSTERIC THEATER

463 West Street
989-4953

Presently without a production home here, this company travels to universities and museums around the country presenting the work of its founder and artistic director Richard Foreman. Founded in 1968, the theatre's early work was based upon a sort of phenomenological analysis of act, gesture, speech, and object. Now the pieces document with great rapidity in performance the ever-shifting relations among many complex production and textural elements. A book on the theatre's work, *Richard Foreman: Plays and Manifestos,* was published in 1976 by New York University Press. Recent Foreman productions include *Boulevard de Paris: I've Got the Shakes* and *Madness and Tranquility (My Head Was a Sledgehammer).*

PAPER BAG PLAYERS

50 Riverside Drive
362-0431

The Paper Bag Players have an international reputation as innovators in children's theatre. They perform in Lincoln Center, Harlem, and in rural schools in Appalachia, and tour to Israel, Egypt, and England. Director Judith Martin founded the players in 1958 with Remy Charlip, Shirley Kaplan, Sudie Bond, and Daniel Jahn. Ms. Martin writes, designs, and directs all the shows for the players, and Donald Ashwander composes the music. Irving Burton, the leading actor, joins in the collaboration in developing pieces integrating story, music, and dance with the dramatic use of paper props. Most stories are modern-day allegories: A bar of soap tries to persuade a small boy to take a bath; a girl milks a cardboard cow and out comes a carton of milk. Paper, cardboard, paints, and crayons are basic elements. Costumes and props are drawn and sometimes constructed on stage as part of the action. Some recent productions include *Dandelion, Hot Feet,* and *Everybody, Everybody.* This is children's theatre at its best so be sure to see the players when they come to your area.

PERFORMING ARTS REPERTORY THEATRE (PART)

131 West 86th Street
595-7500

PART is the largest theatre company for young audiences in the country. It was founded in 1967 by Robert K. Adams, Jay Harnick, and Charles Hull. Since then, PART has played to more than five million people in the course of more than seven thousand performances. The company seeks to produce meaningful new works for young people and many of its best-known and most widely produced works have been based on historical characters and events—*Jim Thorpe, All-American, John F. Kennedy. The Road to Camelot, Young Ben Franklin,* and *Daniel Boone,* among others. In all, PART has developed nearly 30 new productions from the collaborations of more than 40 authors, lyricists, and composers, among them Saul Levitt, Ossie Davis, Mary Rodgers, Joe Raposo, Alice Childress, Albert Hague, John Morris, and John Allen. Besides its tours, PART has a resident series at Town Hall.

PERIWINKLE PRODUCTIONS

262 Broadway
Monticello, N.Y.
(914) 794-1666

The Catskills, famous for producing comedians, now has another claim to show-business fame: Periwinkle Productions, one of the oldest and best children's theatres and a pioneer in educational theatre. Founded in 1963 by Sunna Rasch, it began by developing programs that were entertaining cultural experiences while at the same time, they challenged young people intellectually. Later the company moved to include original scripts with themes inspired by its young audiences. *Hooray for Me!,* for example, is a musical based on a teenager's search for identity. *The Mad Poet Strikes—Again!* is about an 1890s teenager who lies to make himself seem more important. In 1978, the company received the Jennie Heiden Award, the highest honor in the country for such work. Artistic director Scott Laughead has created many of the company's productions, including *Hooray for Me!* and *The Dream Show*. The company tours most of the year. Among its stops are Washington's Kennedy Center and the Lincoln Center Library.

PING CHONG AND THE FIJI COMPANY

21 Bleecker Street
228-0653

The work of this innovative company is called "bricolage—a new world created out of any and all available materials from an old world, resulting in luminosity." Another definition of the word is "a billiard shot that results in an indirect action or unexpected stroke." Both are somewhat obscure and therefore fit the symbolic image of this company. This is avantist theatre in the extreme and Ping Chong has his own original outlook and frame of reference. The company's recent productions include *Nuit Blanche, Humboldt's Current, Fear and Loathing in Gotham,* and, in collaboration with Meredith Monk, *Paris* and *Venice/Milan.* Mr. Chong and the Fiji Company have performed at LaMama, the Lee Nagrin Studio Theatre, American Theatre Lab, and Kennedy Center, in addition to touring here and abroad.

THE PROPOSITION WORKSHOP

P.O. Box 745
Radio City Station

This company started in Cambridge, Massachusetts, in 1968 and had an immediate hit with its improvisational revue *The Proposition.* It quickly became one of the principal touring companies in the country. In the past six years, the workshop has turned to creating non-fiction productions that fuse documentary materials, oral histories, and both authentic and original music. The subjects might be whaling (*The Whale Show*), trucking (*Night Riders*), or cowboys (*Corral*). Many of the shows produced in Cambridge have moved here and toured nationally. Since the company's long Off Broadway run in the early 1970s, it has maintained a base here and completed the move here in the fall of 1977. The Proposition Workshop has changed its working habits somewhat: two new works, developed in a work-shop format, are planned each season. Currently in the works are pieces on the Kerouac Fifties and Coney Island.

RAFT THEATRE LTD.

432 West 42nd Street
575-9088

If construction schedules were met, the Raft Theatre Ltd. will now be ensconced in the Phase II area of Theatre Row and the Theatre Row Ticket Central will be its box office. Its first five years, in which more than 40 full productions of new American plays were presented, were spent at the Title Theatre at Westbeth on Bank Street. To keep active while waiting for its new theatre to be finished, the Raft presented *Adult Fiction* at the Pyramid Theatre, 48th Street and Broadway, a one-time burlesque house. Artistic director Martin Zurla reports that the new Theatre Row space will be flexible, seating 40 to 70 persons, depending upon the production.

SHELTER WEST THEATRE COMPANY

217 Second Avenue
673-6341

This group, founded in 1973 by Judith Joseph, is looking for a new home, preferably in Tribeca. It first performed at St. Stephen's Church on West 69th Street, then for three years at the Vandam Theatre on Vandam Street. Much of the 1980–81 season was at the New Vic at 219 Second Avenue. Some recent productions include *Dreams,* Thomas Shanday's new play; *The Carpenters,* Sean Sutton's adaptation of *A Christmas Carol; Rooming House;* and the first revival, since the 1924 production, of John Dos Passos's *Garbage Man.*

In addition, the Shelter West Company recently has initiated a directors' workshop, and is developing a repertory group to present one-act plays.

THE SILENT PERFORMER WORKSHOP

The Hudson Street Studio

One Hudson Street
349-4251

Jim Moore, an accomplished mime, and Mark Stolzenberg, a Ringling Brothers clown, have been using this loft for advanced instruction in mime, clowning, and puppetry. Occasional public performances are given here and at other spaces and theatres around the city. Telephone for details.

STAGE LEFT

Box 12-U
235 West 102nd Street

Stage Left is a new, bright, busy production company without a permanent theatrical home. It was founded early in 1977 by a group of 15 actors, directors, and theatrical technicians as a company devoted to the development of new theatrical talent. It produced two full-length plays that summer for a one-week run in repertory at the Off Center Theatre in Chelsea: *The Haunting of Hill House* by Shirley Jackson and *The Play's the Thing* by Ferenc Molner, as adapted by P. G. Wodehouse. The next summer saw a revival of Rachael Crothers' *He and She* at the Drama Ensemble in SoHo. In 1979, the company presented an originally conceived British music-hall revue, *A Little of What You Fancy*, in several locations. Then came two one-act plays: Tom Stoppard's *The Real Inspector Hound* and Julie Bovasso's *Schubert's Last Serenade*, again at the Off Center. In April, 1980, the company had a two-week run of *The Servant of Two Masters* by Carlo Goldoni at the IRT Theatre's Stage Two. Most recently was a two-week run of Leonard Melfi's one-act plays, *Birdbath* and *Halloween* at the Open Eye. Pat Vanderbeck is Stage Left's artistic director, Mary Ellen Bernard, the executive director.

THE STREET THEATER

White Plains Armory
35 South Broadway
White Plains, N.Y. 10601
(914) 949-8558

It was a most unusual and exemplary group that Gray Smith founded in 1970. The initial purpose was to serve the black communities and prisons of Westchester County. Out of the theater's Bedford Hills workshop, a company was developed called "The Family." It was the Family that developed Miguel Pinero's *Short Eyes*. First produced by the Street Theater in 1972 at Sing Sing Prison at Ossining while Pinero was still an inmate there, it was playing to packed houses at Lincoln Center later that same year. From 1974 to 1976, the prison workshop programs were expanded to include 10 New York state correctional facilities, involving 600 inmates and 30 productions, about half of which were original pieces developed in workshops. A number of inmates have joined the staff upon release. There now are two touring companies: a professional company and a youth company. Many Westchester communities see the productions, which include *Related Voices, A Play About Us?*, and *This One's for You*.

STRUT AND FRET

303 West 87th Street
724-7776

Strut and Fret's mission is to present musicals using rock and roll and country music. Since its founding in 1978 by David Watson, the group has presented Thomas Babe's *Kid Champion* and David Hare's *Teeth and Smiles*. These were performed at West Side Stage II, but the group currently has no particular theatre affiliation.

THE THRESHOLD THEATRE COMPANY

251 West 87th Street
724-9129

This group, founded in 1978, does productions in translation from the French, Italian, and Hungarian languages. At the Community Church of New York, artistic directors Pamela Billing and Eugene Broganyi have presented *Star at the Stake* and *Cain and Abel*, both by Andress Suto.

THE WRITERS THEATRE

(American Writers Theatre Foundation, Inc.)
P.O. Box 810
Times Square Station
581-5295

As its name suggests, the Writers Theatre is attuned to the specific needs of the playwright, developing and presenting new works and adaptations of literary masterpieces. At this writing, the group had just launched a fundraising campaign to buy and renovate theatre space in SoHo, which it hopes will be ready for the 1981–82 season. It was also developing an Off Broadway production of a new work, *Anne Sexton: My Own Stranger,* based on the work of the Pulitzer-Prize poet. An earlier production, the premiere of Robin Swicord's *Last Days at the Dixie Girl Café,* also was seen Off Broadway. The group's first production, *The Gospel According to Mark Twain,* played in New York and at Scotland's Edinburgh Festival. Linda Laundra, administrative and artistic director, is the moving force behind the Writers Theatre; Marilyn Espet, special projects director, has scripted 15 productions for the group; and Thomas M. Fontana is playwright-in-residence.

YUEH LUNG SHADOW THEATRE

34-41 74th Street
Jackson Heights, Queens
Jo Humphrey, Director (478-6246)

This group was organized in 1975 to preserve and perpetuate the 2,000-year-old Chinese shadow theatre tradition which has all but disappeared today in Asia and is virtually unknown here. The classic legends of the East were first transmitted from generation to generation by itinerant shadow masters. Traditional dramas such as *Journey to the West, The White Snake Legend,* and *The Fisherman's Revenge* use colored animated figures to convey philosophical and ethical concepts drawn from religion, folk tales, and epic Chinese literature. The Yueh Lung Shadow Theatre follows ancient practice and performs with colorful calfskin figures, which are exact replicas of the Peking East-City figures in the permanent collection at the American Museum of Natural History and are constructed by the company. Animated behind a translucent screen, images appear as demons and benefactors. An endless cast of exotic characters illustrate basic moral values shared by all civilizations. Under the direction of Jo Humphrey, the company has presented programs at city schools, senior citizen centers, nursing homes, psychiatric centers, institutions for the handicapped, and, for general audiences at the United Nations, World Trade Center, Alice Tully Hall, libraries, and community centers. The company also tours extensively here and abroad.

APPENDIXES

THEATRE SHOPPING

APPLAUSE

100 West 67th Street
496-7511
Credit Cards: MC, V
Hours: 11 a.m.–12 midnight, open seven days a week

Glenn Young, a playwright and drama professor, recently opened this drama bookstore to serve the Juilliard drama students and the large upper West Side theatrical community. A big bulletin board in the store will quickly bring you up to date on the state of the art and the artists in the area. The store stocks some 5,000 titles in both hardcover and paperback. Play readings are held here on a regular basis. Stop by or phone the store for the schedule.

THE BALLET SHOP

1887 Broadway (63rd)
581-7990
Credit Cards: AE, MC, V
Hours: Monday–Saturday, 11 a.m.–8 p.m.

Although this small shop specializes in dance and opera, owner Norman Crider has a reasonable selection of out-of-print theatre books, 19th-century prints and posters, rare photographs, and autographs of interest to the serious collector. The items are one-of-a-kind and priced accordingly: a *Ben Hur* playbill, $25; an autographed photograph of Sarah Bernhardt, $175. It's fun to browse here, and the stock is constantly changing.

BLOOMSDAY 2 BOOKSHOP

2259 Broadway (80th)
724-0210
Credit Cards: AE, MC, V
Closed Christmas and New Year's Day

This two story bookshop near Zabar's is most comprehensive and has a fine theatre section. Two long tables in the rear feature stacks of intriguing books at significantly reduced prices. Upstairs is now a café where poetry readings are held most Sundays. Recently, it was the scene of a marathon reading of James Joyce's *Ulysses*, and many of the theatre's top performers, including Geraldine Fitzgerald, stopped in to read.

BROADWAY POSTERS

252 West 45th Street
997-1715
Credit Cards: MC, V
Hours: Monday–Saturday, 5 p.m.–8 p.m.; Sunday, 12 noon–3 p.m.

Tucked between the theatres of 45th Street is this small poster shop, offering a good selection of current show posters at reasonable prices. The 14″ x 22″ showcards are $6, the larger graphics range up to $20. Framing can be done here, if you wish. This is an offshoot of the Triton Gallery (further west on 45th at 323), which has a much broader selection.

THE CENTER AT THE CENTER

Lincoln Center
Credit Cards: AE, MC, V
Hours: Monday–Saturday, 10 a.m.–10 p.m.; Sunday, 10 a.m.–6 p.m.

This is a stylishly modern performing-arts gift shop on the concourse level below Avery Fisher Hall. (A smaller gift shop is located on the main level of Avery Fisher.) The theatre section has a good selection of current original cast albums and a few theatre picture books. There is an excellent gallery of Lincoln Center posters and signed prints that is well worth a visit. (As yet there are no theatre posters on display.) The shop could use more one-of-a-kind items and more bargains.

CHISHOLM GALLERY

277 West 4th Street
243-8834
Credit Cards: MC, V
Hours: Tuesday–Saturday, 12:30 p.m.–7:30 p.m.; Sunday, 2 p.m.–6 p.m.

This is one of the best sources in the city for vintage theatre posters: 1880–1945 American posters; French posters, particularly cabaret; and English vaudeville, musical hall, and D'Oyly Carte. Most are in the $50–$500 range; a few French beauties get up to $2,000. If you're looking for something for an enormous wall, owner Gail Chisholm has a few 12-sheet posters that measure 6½ feet by 13 feet at $1,500. One, she says, is framed in plexiglass and suspended from the ceiling of a bedroom in a SoHo loft.

COLONY RECORD CENTER

1619 Broadway (49th)
265-1260
Credit Cards: AE, DC, CB, MC, V
Hours: 9:30 a.m.–2:30 a.m., seven days a week

For more than 30 years, Sidney and Richard Turk's Colony Record Center has been among the best places to find out-of-print original cast albums. They stock everything available on current Broadway and Off Broadway shows, including sheet music and musical comedy song books. Out-of-print albums range in price from $20 to $100 or more for the very, very rare. They mail anywhere. A telephone call or letter will determine if they have what you want.

DAYTON'S

824 Broadway (12th)
254-5084
No credit cards
Hours: Monday–Friday, 10 a.m.–6 p.m.; Saturday, 10 a.m.–5 p.m.

If you are a true collector of original cast albums, this is Mecca. There are more than 1,000 cutouts* in this shop that bulges at the seams with stacks of records. Depending on the rarity and condition of the album, you'll pay from $20 to $100 or more. Even if those prices are too steep for you, Dayton's is worth a visit. There is a good selection of cutouts from the shop's overstock all the time. Write or phone if you are searching for particular albums and you'll be quoted a price.

---

*Books are out-of-print when publishers no longer stock them; similar record orphans are *cutouts*.

THE DRAMA BOOKSHOP

150 West 52nd Street
582-1037
Credit Cards: MC, V
Hours: Monday–Friday, 9 a.m.–6 p.m.; Saturday, 1 p.m.–5 p.m.

What Sylvia Beach's Shakespeare and Co. bookshop was to American writers in Paris in the 1920s, the Drama Bookshop has been for generations of actors. Allen Collins and Arthur Seelen have owned the bookstore for 25 years and have built it to being *the* authoritative source. Their aim is "to be so well informed that any request should elicit some response as to the whereabouts of a book." They both give credit to the labors of Margaret Seligmen during her many years in the store. There are files on every book the shop has handled. This means that if a book is out of print, reprinted, excerpted, or whatever, the staff of 15 can run it down in a jiffy. The shop is a meeting place for actors and other theatre people. A large bulletin board displays casting announcements and other items of interest to the profession. Acting students come to ask help in picking a scene to perform, authors for research material, directors for cast copies for upcoming productions. And the owners enjoy the opportunity of introducing talented people to one another. Mr. Seelen sums up the somewhat quixotic philosophy of the Drama Bookshop by saying, "We are too much of a service to be a business, yet too much of a business to be a service." Note: The Drama Bookshop does an extensive mail-order business across the country and abroad. It also periodically publishes a comprehensive bibliography of all new books relating in any way to the theatre.

EIGHTH AVENUE RECORDS

153 Eighth Avenue (17th)
675-1311
Hours: Monday–Saturday, 10 a.m.–6 p.m.

Serious record collectors consider Max Draisner's shop one of the seven wonders of the city. It is hard to find, there is little rhyme or reason to the collection, but it is packed with absolute treasures. Mr. Draisner will be glad to help you find what you're looking for. Be sure to allow enough time to browse.

GALLERY AT B. ALTMAN & CO.

Fifth Avenue and 34th Street
561-7070
Credit Cards: AE
Hours: Monday–Saturday, 10 a.m.–6 p.m.; also Thursday until 8 p.m.

One of the prime sources for quality theatre autographs, letters, posters, and other memorabilia is the eighth-floor gallery of this venerable department store. Buyer Robert Tollett was an actor (M.A. in theatre arts from Northwestern University and seven years on the stage) and a collector when a Christmas job here in 1965 led to a new career. The big three for theatrical collectors, I was told, are Sarah Bernhardt, Eleonora Duse, and Ellen Terry. Their autographs, signed photographs, and letters will range in price from $200 to $700 and more. The only actor who comes close to these prices is Edmund Kean. Some rare and unusual items pass through the gallery: the original deed to London's Convent-Garden Theatre, a contract signed by Rodgers and Hart to do the movie *Babes in Arms,* and letters signed by both Laurence Olivier and Vivien Leigh. Understandably, movie stars like Garbo, Chaplin, and Valentino command higher prices—with one notable exception: There are only seven known authentic signatures of William Shakespeare, and each is valued in excess of $1.5 million (the only rarer signature is that of Julius Caesar). The gallery also has a fine selection of old theatre posters, and sketches of costume and set designs.

HOTALINGS NEWS AGENCY

One Times Square
840-1868
Hours: 7:30 a.m.–9:30 p.m.

If you want to see what the Philadelphia critics said about a show that opened there, or if you just want a copy of your hometown newspaper, this newsstand carries the city's largest selection of out-of-town newspapers and publications, some 500 of them.

JAMES LOWE AUTOGRAPHS, LTD.

Suite 709
667 Madison Avenue (65th)
889-8204
Hours: Monday–Friday, 11 a.m.–6 p.m.; Saturday, 1 p.m.–5 p.m.

If you are just getting started as a theatrical autograph collector, or if you're looking for a gift for a theatre-lover, this is a good place to shop, for it abounds with bargains. Some samples: a small signed photograph of Judith Anderson ($17.50, unframed); a photograph and separate autograph of Ethel Barrymore ($30); autographed photographs of Jimmy Durante ($45) and Sir John Gielgud ($15); a cancelled check of Rex Harrison to a New York limousine service ($25); excellent signed and framed photographs of Edwin Booth ($175), Will Rogers ($225), and Sarah Bernhardt ($225). Serious collectors should write or phone to receive Mr. Lowe's catalogues.

MARGO FEIDEN GALLERIES

51 East 10th Street
677-5330
Credit Cards: AE, MC, V
Hours: Monday–Friday, 10 a.m.–5:30 p.m.; Saturday, 11 a.m.–5 p.m.

One of the theatrical institutions in the city is a bearded, aristocratic gentleman of 78 named Al Hirschfeld whose caricatures have graced *The New York Times* for more than 50 years. For so many of us his pen-and-ink drawings with the hidden "Ninas" is part of Sunday morning. (Nina is the name of his daughter and he first hid her name to herald her birth in 1945. Every drawing since has had at least one "Nina" in it, and once you get in the habit of looking for them, you become an addict. I speak as an addict of many years standing.) Mr. Hirschfeld is exclusively represented by this Greenwich Village gallery, and there is a permanent exhibit of his work here. Originals range from $1,000 to $2,500, depending upon the number of figures in them; his graphics are $150–400. Lithographs of Broadway doings in the 1930s and 1940s by the late Don Freeman also are here ($200–$1,000), as are colored-ink drawings by Kurt Vonnegut ($450–$500). Write or phone if you would like to be notified about upcoming exhibitions.

MUSIC MASTERS

25 West 43rd Street
840-1958
Credit Cards: MC, V
Hours: Monday–Friday, 10 a.m.–6 p.m.; Saturday, 10 a.m.–3:30 p.m.

Owner Will Lerner has tapes of live performances of thousands of Broadway, Off Broadway, and Off-Off Broadway shows from 1958 on. For $45 he will dupe one for you on either casette or reel-to-reel tape. Mr. Lerner also produces a number of records on the Music Master label that are musts for collectors: Cole Porter: 1924–44; Irving Berlin: *Louisiana Purchases*; Bert Lahr; British musicals with scores by American composers; and a number of two-record sets featuring the best songs from Broadway for a particular year in the 1920s and 1930s. These are $12.50 per record. Catalogues and bulletins are issued nine times a year. A phone call or a note will add your name to the mailing list.

NEW YORK SHAKESPEARE FESTIVAL SHOP

Public Theater
425 Lafayette Street
598-7100
No credit cards
Hours: Two hours before and through performances

In a corner of the Public Theater lobby is a small shop with a variety of merchandise relating to Shakespeare Festival productions. For example, you can buy an original cast album ($7), a T-shirt, and a song book ($6.50) for *I'm Getting My Act Together And Taking It on the Road.* There's a nice Public Theater sweatshirt with the Shakespeare logo ($16). Or perhaps you'd like the poster for the show *Joe Papp Sings,* autographed by the star himself ($10). An excellent buy: eight posters designed by Paul Davis for festival productions ($6). Playscripts for many productions here are available in book form.

ONE SHUBERT ALLEY

One Shubert Alley (between 44th and 45th)
586-7610   Toll-free: (800) 223-1290
Credit Cards: AE, MC, V
Hours: Monday–Saturday, 10:30 a.m.–11:30 p.m.; Sunday, 12 noon–7 p.m.

Across Shubert Alley from Ma Bell is a sparkling little gift shop filled with things to delight a theatrelover: T-shirts from such hits as *Barnum* and *Annie* ($7.50–$13.95); similarly emblazoned tote bags ($12.95–$18.25); satin show jackets ($55–$68.95), an assortment of 14- and 18-carat gold jewelry ($30 to $500), a Sweeney Todd apron (how droll!) at $14.95, to name a few, plus theatre books, current original cast albums, and souvenir programs. Telephone and they'll send you a catalogue so you can order by mail.

PARK SOUTH GALLERY

885 Seventh Avenue (56th)
757-5469
No credit cards
Hours: Monday–Saturday, 11:30 a.m.–6:30 p.m.

Around the corner from Carnegie Hall, Laura Gold has an exceptional selection of Art Nouveau and Art Deco original French posters, including theatre and music-hall motifs. There are also British theatre posters from time to time. These are for the serious collector, ranging in price from several hundred to several thousand dollars. If you're looking for a special poster, let Ms. Gold know. She'll keep her eyes open and give you a call if she finds it.

PROPS AND PRACTICALS

Drama Book Shop
150 West 52nd Street (5th floor)
765-4487
Credit Cards: AE, DC, MC, V
Hours: Monday–Friday, 11 a.m.–6 p.m.; Saturday, 1 p.m.–5 p.m.

You'll find an interesting selection of gifts for theatregoers here—if you don't decide to keep them for yourself. How about Theatre Notes in red leather ($12), designed for capsule reviews of shows; a deck of cards with Shakespearean characters on the back ($15); a children's toy theatre from London ($15); a most handsome man's necktie with the names of classic playwrights printed in red or yellow on a blue background ($12.50); lucite clipboards with your choice of Producer, Director, Composer, Lyricist, or Playwright printed on it ($10.50). Particularly attractive are a selection of theatrical masks; a papier-mâché Pierrot ($40) to a leather Pantalone mask ($250), with a number of choices in between. Props and Practicals is the best shop of its kind in the city.

QUINION BOOKS

541 Hudson Street
Credit Cards: AE, CB, DC, MC, V
Hours: 12 noon–8 p.m.

   This small, attractive shop is evenly divided between theatre books and cookbooks. This may strike you as strange, but not owner Jesse Feiler—the theatre and cooking are his two passions. Most current theatre books and a good selection of scripts are available here.

RICHARD STODDARD

90 East 10th Street
No credit cards
Hours: Wednesday–Saturday, 11 a.m.–6 p.m.; Sunday, 1 p.m.–6 p.m.

   This bookstore specializes in rare and out-of-print performing arts books and the theatre section is excellent. Mr. Stoddard also carries current theatre posters and, from time to time, has vintage posters at attractive prices.

SAM GOODY

235 West 49th Street (246-1708)
51 West 51st Street (246-8730)
666 Third Avenue (43rd) (986-8480)
Credit Cards: AE, MC, V
Hours: Monday–Friday, 9:30 a.m.–7 p.m.; Saturday, 9:30 a.m.–6 p.m.; Sunday,
   12 noon–5 p.m.

   Your best bet to save some money on current original cast albums is at one of the Sam Goody outlets. The stock is complete and the discounts are as good as you'll find ($4.99 for a $7.98 list album).

SAMUEL FRENCH, INC.

25 West 45th Street
582-4700
Hours: Monday–Friday, 9 a.m.–5 p.m.

   For more than 150 years, this company has been selling scripts for plays and musicals and the rights to produce them to schools and colleges and small theatre groups. There are nearly 4,000 plays and several hundred musicals in their catalogue. (Write or phone and one will be sent to you.) A well-stocked bookstore is in their second-floor headquarters. In case you were wondering: the most popular plays are *Our Town, The Mousetrap, Blythe Spirit, Spoon River Anthology,* and the comedies of Neil Simon.

THE SILVER SCREEN

119 East 14th Street
677-4485
No credit cards
Hours: Monday–Saturday, 11 a.m.–7 p.m.

   As the name says, the accent here is on the movies but there's quite a bit of interesting theatre memorabilia as well. Posters, photographs, and autographs are available and the prices vary widely depending on the rarity and condition of the item.

SMOLIN PRINTS

1215 Lexington Avenue (82nd)
876-1464
No credit cards
Hours: Monday–Saturday, 1 p.m.–6 p.m.; closed Wednesday

This shop is filled with posters, photographs, and other paper memorabilia dating from the turn-of-the-century. It's a good place to find old-time theatre posters and pictures of your favorite stars.

STRAND BOOK STORE

828 Broadway (12th)
473-1452
No credit cards
Hours: Monday–Saturday, 9:30 a.m.–6:30 p.m.; Sunday, 11 a.m.–5 p.m.

This is the largest used bookstore in the country—32,000 square feet on three floors—and a bibliophile's dream come true. In its vast stock are some 20,000 books on the theatre. Owner Fred Bass sends out a list of new acquisitions four to six times a year and a note or a phone call will add your name to his list. At the front of the store is one of the great book bargains anywhere: reviewer copies at half-price, including those stunning coffee table books. Book reviewers would need a warehouse if they kept all the books sent to them. They sell to the Strand, the Strand sells the books to us at half-price, and everyone wins.

THEATREBOOKS

1576 Broadway (47th)
757-2834
Credit Cards: MC, V
Hours: Monday–Friday, 10:30 a.m.–6 p.m.; Saturday, 12 noon–5 p.m.

Actor Robert Emerson and his wife Jane have an amazing number of used and out-of-print books on the theatre in two crowded rooms in a Broadway office building. They issue a catalogue four times a year—to get on their mailing list write to the above address—and this is an excellent place to check if you're looking for something rare.

TRAVEL & THEATRE SHOPPE

1900 Broadway (63rd)
724-9500, 800-223-1326
Credit Cards: AE, DC, MC, V
Hours: Monday–Friday, 9:30 a.m.–6 p.m.; Saturday, 10:30 a.m.–4 p.m.

An odd but somehow logical combination of a ticket agency, travel agency, and shop for current original cast albums, Broadway posters, and historical posters (e.g., a large, handsome Mistinguett in mint condition: $700). They specialize here in travel for the theatre-oriented and can get you tickets for shows and festivals anywhere in the world.

TRITON GALLERY

323 West 45th Street
765-2472
Credit Cards: MC, V
Hours: Monday–Saturday, 10 a.m.–6 p.m.

If you love theatre posters, prepare to be seduced by the beauties on display here, as fine a selection of current and past shows as you'll find anywhere. The 14″ x 22″ showcards are usually $6 and framing adds another $15 to $35 depending on your choice of style and material. The theatre graphics range in size from 23″ x 46″ to a smashing 42″ x 84″. The Triton will mount your choice on a box frame and spray it with acrylic to keep it clean for $40–$135, depending on the size. There are bins of posters from shows of the 1950s and

1960s, from $10 to $300 depending on the rarity of the poster. The Masterpiece Theatre posters are stocked, as are the classic Paul Davis posters. There are works by a cute young lady named Gacci (pronounced Jacky), who interprets musicals through clever shoe caricatures. These are $10 each or $60 for a set of seven. If you have a friend about to open in a show, how about having the Triton do a one-of-a-kind "break-a-leg" small poster, complete with your friend's name, the name of the show, and the date of opening night—$20 unframed. A color catalogue is available for 50¢ for ordering by mail. Owner Roger Puckett has been here for 15 years and is the man to talk to if you are trying to track down something special.

THEATRE MUSEUMS AND LIBRARIES

LINCOLN CENTER LIBRARY OF THE PERFORMING ARTS

Entry from Lincoln Center and at 111 Amsterdam Avenue (65th)
930-0800
Hours: *General Library:* Monday and Thursday, 10 a.m.–8 p.m.; Tuesday, 10 a.m.–6 p.m.; Friday–Saturday, 12 noon–6 p.m.; closed Wednesday and Sunday. *Research Department:* Tuesday, Wednesday, Friday, Saturday, 12 noon–6 p.m.; Monday and Thursday, 12 noon–8 p.m.; closed Sunday.

This is the largest performing arts library in the world, housed in its own handsome building designed by Eero Saarinen with interiors by Gordon Bunshaft. It is part of the New York City Public Library System, so your library card will enable you to use the general library section of books and phonograph records; the research center, which contains a unique collection of documents and programs, is available only to scholars. Robert Henderson has headed the general collection, and Thor Wood the research center since the library opened in 1966. Free readings and lectures are held almost daily in the library's Bruno Walter Auditorium on the Amsterdam Avenue level. These are listed in the bulletin *Events* available at any branch of the public library, in the Lincoln Center Calendar, and, frequently, in *The New York Times* Weekend section. An annual event worth noting is the library's Bazaar at which duplicates from the collection are sold. Often there is an auction for the rarer material. At a recent Bazaar, I bought an original playbill for the Friday, June 19, 1818, performance at the Theatre Royal in London's Covent Garden for $7. It's now framed and hangs in a place of honor in my apartment.

MUSEUM OF THE CITY OF NEW YORK

Fifth Avenue and 103rd Street
534-1672
Hours: Tuesday–Saturday, 10 a.m.–5 p.m.; Sunday, 1 p.m.–5 p.m.
Suggested donation $1

The theatre collection here is spectacular, and the exhibitions that are mounted several times a year are ample testimony to its breadth and scope; "Biography of a Hit"; "The 40th anniversary of *Life with Father*"; "Child Stars of the New York Stage"; "Katherine Cornell Remembered"; and, recently, "Lucille Lortel: Queen of Off Broadway." Unfortunately, these exhibitions are the only time anyone except scholars and researchers can see the collection, which fills more than 15,000 large, expandable envelopes, each devoted to a separate production that has appeared in the city. Files also have been kept on more than 10,000 stage personalities. The first curator of this department was May Davenport Seymour, a descendant of two great American theatrical families. Although material began flowing into the department from its founding in 1923, the first coup was 11 original scripts in Eugene O'Neill's handwriting, which he gave in 1932. A unique facet of the collection is the array of stage costumes. The earliest probably is Edwin Forrest's tunic from *The Gladiator;* one of the later, Zero Mostel's Tevye. Private papers from the estates of Daniel and Charles Frohman, William Seymour, Harry B. Smith are in the collection, as are scrapbooks and miscellaneous documents from Ethel Merman, Mary Martin, and the Barrymores. George M. Cohan's files were presented to the collection by his music publisher, E. B. Marks. Here, too, are original promptbooks dating from 1803. Hundreds of thousands of photographs, theatre programs, sheet music, posters and window cards, original theatrical portraits, sculpture, theatrical curios, models of stage sets—all are here. A special Yiddish Theatre Collection is kept in the museum's Dazian Library, and it generated a touring exhibition that has been seen throughout the world. Dr. Mary Henderson, author of the definitive *The City and the Theatre*, has been the curator since 1975 and her accomplishments have been notable. The small gift shop at the museum has a few items of interest to theatregoers, including prints of former New York theatres.

NEW YORK PUBLIC LIBRARY THEATRE INFORMATION

Library of the Performing Arts
Lincoln Center
870-1639

The above telephone number is a direct line to the theatre collection at the New York Public Library, and if you are desperate for a bit of theatre information, it is unequaled. The person who answers is an expert researcher trained by the library. Most questions can be answered after a minute or two wait; more complex ones may mean you will have to call back for the information or stop by and look at their files. This service has been invaluable in preparing this guide, and the staff of the collection have our deepest gratitude.

SHELBY CULLOM DAVIS MUSEUM

Library of the Performing Arts
Lincoln Center
Entry from Lincoln Center Plaza and at 111 Amsterdam Avenue (65th)
930-0800
Hours: Monday and Thursday, 10 a.m.–8 p.m.; Tuesday, 10 a.m.–6 p.m.; Friday, 10 a.m.–
6 p.m.; Friday–Saturday, 12 noon–6 p.m.; closed Wednesday and Sunday

The museum has two exhibit spaces in the library, the Main Gallery and the Vincent Astor Gallery, and excellent theatrical exhibits are presented periodically. Some recent examples: *commedia dell'arte* masks, stage designs of Boris Aronson, and stage designs of Beni Montesor. Admission is free.

SONGWRITERS HALL OF FAME

One Times Square (8th floor)
221-1252
Hours: Monday–Saturday, 11 a.m.–3 p.m.

This is a celebration of American popular music and the fact that for decades the Times Square area has been the heart of the music publishing business. There are fascinating things to see: Fats Waller's own piano, the piano on which Duke Ellington, Hoagy Carmichael, and Mitchell Parish auditioned their compositions for the Mills Publishing Company, the Grammy Stephen Sondheim won for "Send in the Clowns." The Hall of Fame is sponsored by the National Academy of Popular Music. Oscar Brand is the curator, and Frankie MacCormick manages the archives. The Academy was founded in 1968 by Johnny Mercer, Abe Olman, and Howard Richmond. Sammy Cahn is the current president. There are regular exhibitions featuring particular composers or eras in popular music. Well worth a visit. (When we went to press, the Songwriters Hall of Fame was looking for a new home as One Times Square had been sold.)

THEATRE MUSEUM IN THE THEATRE DISTRICT

Minskoff Theatre Arcade (1515 Broadway, between 44th and 45th Streets)
Admission: $1 donation; 50¢ for children and senior citizens

In the fall of 1981, the Museum of the City of New York was to open a branch across the arcade from the Minskoff box office for exhibits from its Theatre Collection. The first exhibition planned was "An Actor's Life" with photographs, costumes, and other memorabilia, including all the awards ever presented to Helen Hayes. The 1,500-square-foot hall exhibits audiovisual and sound-and-light presentations. Given the high quality of the theatre exhibitions at the uptown museum, this promises to be a welcome addition to the Broadway area.

THEATRICAL SCULPTURE AND LANDMARKS IN THE CITY

At the south end of the mall in Central Park stands a statue of William Shakespeare, executed in 1870 by John Quincy Adams Ward. In doublet, hose, and short cloak, the Bard stands with book in hand looking pensive. Near him on the mall is a 1927 bust by Edmond T. Quinn of Victor Herbert, the Irish immigrant who became the first important composer on the American musical stage. In Gramercy Park, a stone's throw from the townhouse in which he lived and died and which now is The Players, the actor's club he founded, stands a handsome full-length statue of Edwin Booth, America's greatest Shakespearean actor. Booth is costumed as Hamlet in the 1918 work by Edmond T. Quinn. At the northern tip of Times Square, where lines for the TKTS booth form, there is a 1959 sculpture by Georg Lober of George M. Cohan, hat and cane in hand, looking south, giving his perpetual regards to Broadway. On the west side of Broadway near 46th Street, above the entrance to an older office building, are four busts of four lovely ladies set in individual niches. The building once was the headquarters of I. Miller, then a leading manufacturer of ladies' theatrical shoes. The company chose to adorn its building with the likenesses of the four most popular women in the performing arts: Mary Pickford, Ethel Barrymore, Marilyn Miller, and Rosa Ponselle.

The only theatre to achieve landmark status is the Lyceum on West 45th Street. Three others are housed in landmark buildings: the Public Theater in the Astor Library, the Astor Place, and the Colonnades Theatre Lab in Colonnade Row, four superb joined townhouses, once occupied by the likes of John Jacob Astor and Washington Irving. (During construction, it was the scene of one of the worst riots of the period, which broke out when the Irish laborers learned that the stone for the building had been quarried by convicts from Sing Sing.) The Players at 16 Gramercy Park, former townhouse of Edwin Booth, is a landmark, as is the National Arts Club next door, once Samuel Tilden's residence. A few blocks south on 14th is the German restaurant Luchow's, built in 1880 and a beautiful reminder of the 1890s when 14th was the hub of theatre and gracious dining. (Down the street, supposedly, was the Harmonie Gardens where Dolly Levi made her triumphful return.) Luchow's is where Victor Herbert and eight of his friends formed ASCAP, the association that guarantees composers will be paid royalties for the use of their music. At 120 Madison Avenue, the American Academy of Dramatic Arts has occupied an exquisite Stanford White Building since 1963.

THEATRE TOURS

BACKSTAGE ON BROADWAY TOURS

228 West 47th Street
Reservations: 575-8065

If you have longed to get behind the scenes of a hit musical to see just how it's put together, this may be the answer. Backstage on Broadway tours are offered daily except Sunday, Christmas, and New Year's Day. The cost is $4 for adults, $3 for students, $2.50 for senior citizens; group discounts are available. Groups of about 25 are guided by a theatre professional—a stage manager or actor—to a Broadway theatre where a musical is playing. First comes a half-hour lecture on how a Broadway show is put together, from the first note written by the composer, through the agonies of casting and rehearsals, right up to opening night. Then the group goes backstage and sees just what has to heppen for the show to go on. Lloyd Meeker who operates Backstage on Broadway emphasizes that you will see "what really goes on, not what you read in the gossip columns." The tour is loaded with theatre vernacular, so you'll get a real idea of how Broadway sounds as well as looks. Note: These tours are popular so you must reserve in advance to make sure you're not disappointed.

BACKSTAGE TOUR

Metropolitan Opera House
Lincoln Center
Reservations: 582-3512
Hours: Monday–Friday, 3:30 p.m.; Saturday, 10:30 a.m.
Adults, $5; children, $2; Opera Guild members, $3

For nearly two hours you tour the cavernous backstage area of the Met, where more than 300 artisans design and produce the sets, props, costumes, and wigs that will be seen on the stage. You'll visit the rehearsal facilities, dressing rooms, and main stage set for the next performance. If you're interested in stagecraft, this tour is a must. Reservations are also a must. To order tickets send a check or money order payable to Metropolitan Opera Guild. List at least three alternate dates, enclose a stamped self-addressed envelope, and allow at least two weeks for the tickets to arrive. Mail to Backstage Tours, Metropolitan Opera Guild, 1865 Broadway, New York, N.Y. 10023.

BACKSTAGE TOUR

Radio City Music Hall
1260 Avenue of the Americas (51st)
246-4600

An interesting tour of one of the world's great theatres is given seven days a week. It leaves from the lobby and in 90 minutes you are shown the fascinating backstage areas, the recording studios, rehearsal hall, costume rooms, and technical equipment. The tour costs $3.95 (no special children's or senior citizen rate although there is a discount for groups of 15 or more). Note: Phone in advance the day of your tour, as departure times vary.

LINCOLN CENTER GUIDED TOUR

Desk: Below Metropolitan Opera on concourse level
Reservations: 877-1800, Ext. 512
Tours: Daily, 10:30 a.m.–5 p.m. Closed Christmas and New Year's Day
Adults, $3.75; students and senior citizens, $3.25; ages 6–14, $2.50
Groups: 877-1800, Ext. 512 or 551 for reservations and rates
Handicapped: Can accommodate by reservation.

This is an introduction to Lincoln Center, an overview of the buildings, the sculpture and the art, the facts and figures. You can be lucky and see part of a rehearsal; you can be unlucky and find a building not on the tour because of a performance. The tour takes approximately one hour.

MEET THE ARTIST PROGRAM

Lincoln Center
140 West 65th Street
Reservations: 877-1800, Ext. 514

Programs are arranged for groups of 20 or more with special attention paid to the special interest of the group and the age level. The artist may be a performer, stage manager, make-up expert, or director from one of Lincoln Center's resident companies, or someone from outside the center in the arts. Several programs for schoolchildren are available.

THE ART OF THEATRE TICKET-BUYING

There are many ways to buy theatre tickets and each way has advantages and disadvantages. It depends on what you want, when you want it, and what you're willing to spend in money and time to get it. And ticket-buying, like investing, rewards those who know what they are doing and can act quickly. The traditional way to buy tickets is to go to the theatre box office, wait in line, see what's available, discuss alternatives, and take what looks best. Until ticket-buying becomes completely computerized, this is still the only way to get exact seat locations before you buy. But it is a time-consuming nuisance.

Some suggestions: Lunchtime is the *worst* time to go to the box office, particularly on matinee days. Why not go by early on an evening when you're seeing another show nearby and save yourself an extra trip. Or plan ahead and go to several box offices on one trip to the theatre district. Now here's a tip that's worth the price of this guide several times over: Decide *exactly* what you want before you get to the window, and ask for it firmly and politely. The person behind the window is a human being doing an essentially boring job for long hours in a cramped space. "I want some good seats for my wife's birthday" tells him nothing. "I want two in the center no farther back than DD, Friday or Saturday, November 6th or 7th or the 13th or 14th" tells him exactly what he needs to know, and if he's got them you'll have them. And if you think cashiers don't punish unpreparedness and rudeness, keep your eyes and ears open the next time you go to the box office. That's why theatres post seating plans, and that's why there are seating plans in this book: so you'll know what to ask for. And remember to take a second and check the number of tickets, the seats, and the date. Mistakes can happen, and this is the time to correct them.

Another good way to get the seats you want on the date you want is to order them by mail from the theatre when the show is first advertised. Use the seating plan and be as specific as you would be if you went to the box office in person. List two alternate dates and enclose a stamped self-addressed envelope. You can pay by check when you order by mail.

Ticketron is an innovation in ticket-buying, an extension of the theatre's box office, through a sophisticated computer setup. Ticketron now has some 700 locations around the country in department and chain stores where you can actually purchase tickets to Broadway shows right then and there. (A list of numbers to phone to find the Ticketron outlet nearest you is on page 298.) Ticketron is given an allotment of tickets by the theatre which are programmed into its Hackensack, New Jersey, computer. If you go into a Ticketron outlet anywhere in the country and say what show you want to see when, the operator punches that information into his computer outlet and on a screen you will see the available seats for that performance. You make your selection and your tickets are printed electronically in a second or two. Most Ticketron sales are for cash, although some outlets permit you to charge them to your account at the store in which they are located.

If you have a credit card, CHARGIT offers an easy way to buy tickets by phone. (The Shubert Organization has a phone credit card system for its theatres called TELECHARGE, which operates in the same way, except that CHARGIT adds a service charge of, usually, $1.75 and TELECHARGE does not.) Tell the operator the show you want, the performance you want, and you'll be told what's available. Make your selection, give your name, type of card, card number, and expiration date. That's all there is to it. Your tickets will be waiting at the box office. It's easy to see why CHARGIT handles some 2,000,000 ticket transactions a year. (CHARGIT numbers for various areas of the country are listed on page 296.)

There's no substitute for dealing directly with the box office, though, if you're finnicky. My publisher, John Sammis, is a theatrelover who isn't happy unless he's sitting in the front row. Consequently, he's an early arrival at the box office when a show he wants to see comes to town. (My problem is somewhat different. At the tender age of 13, I went with some friends to see my first burlesque show and the box office lady talked us into buying box seats. As soon as the show started, we were spotted by a comedian and our sexual naïveté immediately became part of his routine, hilarious, apparently, to everyone but us. To this day, I don't like boxes.) I do prefer the front of the mezzanine to the back of the orchestra, and I'd rather take seats in the center farther back than sit way to the side.

Another way to buy tickets is through ticket brokers, who also serve as an extension of the box office. Ticket brokers are a convenience, particularly if you're staying in a hotel and there's a broker in the lobby. It enables you to shop around and see what's available that night, a privilege you pay for in the form of a $2–$4 markup on the tickets. You pay the broker and the tickets are held for you at the box office. A lot of companies and some individuals have accounts with brokers.

All of which brings up a taboo subject: scalpers. It's against the law in New York to scalp tickets, i.e., sell tickets for more than the legal markup. But every day, important clients arrive from out of town and announce they would like to see a certain hit show that night and, *voila!,* that night they're in the eighth row center. Now it happens you were told at the box office three weeks before that on that night the 17th row was the best they could do for you. What happened? Did the box office lie to you? (No.) Was there a scalper involved? (Yes.) Did the box office knowingly sell the tickets to a scalper? (Probably not, and couldn't make a charge stick if they did.) When someone goes to the box office and buys a lot of tickets, the box office can't demand he prove that he isn't going to scalp them. One large loophole in all this is that New Jersey doesn't have a scalping law. Look in the yellow pages under "ticket brokers," see how many have New Jersey phones and addresses, and draw your own conclusions. Scalping is part of supply and demand. (Ever notice that the good seats at the World Series are filled with people who probably haven't seen a ball game all season?) Before the curtain at a hit show you'll see people outside trying to sell a few tickets at substantial prices, but that's small potatoes compared with what really goes on. If people are willing to pay the price (two or three times the actual box-office price), they can get pretty much what they want. The responsible people in the theatre don't like it, but can't do much about it.

One of the major purchasers of theatre tickets are groups. (Ever see those buses parked in the theatre district on matinee days?) Producers and theatre owners love them, they're good, steady customers. People like them, too. They sign up for a certain number of shows and someone else worries about the tickets, transportation, and meals. Group discounts are available from practically every theatre listed in this guide (see individual listings for details), although many groups prefer to work with a theatre party specialist (see page 297.). A specialist will usually reserve blocks of seats for a group at no charge for a sufficient time to allow the group leader to collect from the members before paying the specialist. What's more fun than going to the theatre with friends?

Previews have become the rule these days, and they deserve discussion. It's much easier to get good seats to a show when it's on previews than after it has opened to rave reviews, and understandably so. You run the risk of seeing a flop in the making, or seeing a hit before it's got its acts all together. But that's not all that bad. Flops can be fun. Seeing a show before and after it opens can be an edifying experience. And there are some lovely bargains. *Billy Bishop Goes to War* was one of several shows to open recently on a progressive price structure: all seats for the first preview, $1; all seats for the second preview, $2, and so on. As this was written, an advertisement in the Sunday *Times,* announcing the coming of *A Reel American Hero* to the Rialto, states that for one day all preview tickets "will be sold at 1939 movie prices: 60¢ for adults, 30¢ for children." Both techniques have the same purpose: to build preview audiences to a show that doesn't have name stars and hope that good word-of-mouth will build momentum. I saw *Billy Bishop* for $2, loved it, and talked it up, and I'll try to be one of the bargain audiences at *A Reel American Hero.* I like previews and the uncertainty of not knowing exactly what to expect.

If you consider the TKTS booth in Duffy Square a daring innovation in the theatre, a short history lesson is in order. It all started with a man named Joseph Lebang, a young immigrant from Budapest who had a tobacco shop on Sixth Avenue and 30th Street. In the early 1920s, theatre owners would give a shop owner free tickets for displaying a show poster in his window. Joe got the idea of selling the tickets, and soon he was buying tickets from other merchants for resale. He moved his operation to Times Square and eventually 20 or 30 theatres were sending their unsold tickets to Lebang's. In 1931, according to *Broadway* by Brooks Atkinson, Joe grossed between $7 and $8 million on the sale of some 5,000,000 tickets. For a long time, half-price theatre tickets were known as Lebangs. After the Lebang era, theatre owners with lagging shows would print up "twofers" that looked like tickets but were to be taken to the box office and used to purchase two tickets for the price of one. As in the old days, twofers were distributed through drug and tobacco stores.

Now the TKTS operations at Duffy Square and Williams Street have replaced twofers, although you occasionally see someone giving them out for a show to people on line. (Note to out-of-towners: In New York one stands on line, not in line.) TKTS has been in operation since 1972 and it's still a subject of debate in the theatre world. Some say that it is building a new theatre audience and helping shows that aren't big hits stay alive; others, that people who would pay full price for tickets are buying them at Duffy Square and that, in effect, the full price buyers are subsidizing the half-price buyers. There is some validity to both sides, but the fact remains that Broadway has been growing, both in grosses and actual attendance, every year since TKTS opened. TKTS may not be solely responsible, of course, but it does vitiate the case against it. (And, as we know, the Pandora's box of half-price tickets had been opened some 50 years before.)

I personally like TKTS because it has expanded my theatregoing. I live 10 blocks away so I can stroll down, see what's on the board that evening that I want to see, and go at a reasonable price. A lot of us now say, "Let's go to the theatre tonight," as we said, "Let's go to the movies tonight," leaving the choice of show until later. I now see more shows and spend more, probably, on theatre tickets because I still see a lot of shows at full price. It's been good for me, and I don't see why it hasn't been good for the theatre, too.

The details of the TKTS operation are on page 298. You'll find that more shows are up and the seats are better the earlier in the week. (Tuesday is the best night to go to the theatre, for my money. Outside of the relative ease of getting tickets, Tuesday audiences are usually especially knowledgeable and appreciative and they spark good performances from the cast.) An insider's tip: For the very best selection, get down to Williams Street when the TKTS booth there opens at 11:30 a.m. You'll wait on line for a shorter time, too.

BONDED THEATRE TICKET BROKERS IN MANHATTAN

Some of these brokers have several locations. Most major city hotels, for example, have brokers in their lobby.

ABC Theatre Ticket Agency, 255 West 43rd Street, 840-2230
Ace Theatre Ticket Service, 1560 Broadway, 575-1422
Americana Theatre Service, Americana Hotel, 201 West 52nd Street, 581-6660
Brown's Theatre Ticket Agency, 151 West 51st Street, 581-3795
Capri Ticket Serivce, Inc., 1560 Broadway, 221-3030
Downtown Theatre Ticket Agency, 71 Broadway, 425-6410
Embassy Theatre Ticket Service, 234 West 50th Street, 757-2204
Golden Penn Theatre Ticket Service, 125 East 50th Street, 753-6644
Green's Theatre Ticket Service, 234 West 50th Street, 753-6644
Hickey's Ticket Agency, 251 West 45th Street, 586-2980
Jacobs Theatre Ticket Service, 201 West 45th Street, 247-2728
Lebang's, 207 West 45th, 757-2300
Lexington Theatre Ticket Agency, Summit Hotel, Lexington Avenue and 51st Street, 751-3260
Liberty Theatre Tickets, 210 West 45th Street, 757-6677
Luxury Theatre, 10 West 66th Street, 873-6187
Mackey's, 234 West 44th Street, 840-2800
Manhattan Theatre Ticket Service, 1501 Broadway, 582-3600
Metro Theatre Ticket Agency, 1691 Broadway, 582-5270
Keith Prouse International, 810 Seventh Avenue, 397-3200
Original R. Tyson & Co., 266 West 44th Street, 247-7600
Jack Rubin Theatre Service, 1560 Broadway, 354-3000
Saul Subber Theatre Ticket Service, 1560 Broadway, 354-3000
Gerald Schor, Hotel Royalton, 44 West 44th Street, 764-0914
Supreme Ticket Service, 301 West 45th Street, 246-5454
Travel & Theatre Tickets, 1900 Broadway, 724-9500
Turf Ticket Agency, 1650 Broadway, 246-2011
West Side Theatre Tickets, 251 West 45th Street, 247-5200

CHARGIT

To order theatre tickets from CHARGIT, use the following numbers:
New York City: (212) 944-9300
Long Island: (516) 944-9300
Westchester: (914) 423-2030

New Jersey: (201) 332-6360
Other Areas:
500-mile radius of New York: 800-223-0120
Rest of US: 800-223-1814

QUIKTIX AT THE PUBLIC THEATER

Here's a bargain. Quiktix are reduced price tickets sold at $5 (Tuesday–Thursday and Sunday evenings and Saturday matinees) or $6 (Friday and Saturday evenings and Sunday matinees) for all regular Public Theater attractions. At least 25 percent of the tickets at each theater (sometimes more) are sold as Quiktix, even for shows already sold out at full price. Here's how it works: Quiktix go on sale at 6 p.m. (matinees, 1 p.m.) on the day of performance only. The best time to arrive depends on the popularity of a given show. You can phone and the box office will estimate, but not guarantee, a suggested time for arrival. You are given a numbered slip when you arrive; this gets you a place in line when the Quiktix go on sale. No more than two tickets are sold per number; if you need more, additional people must be on line. After all those waiting in line have had a chance to buy available tickets, sales cease. If you come after that, you can either buy seats at full price or get a number and return for an additional Quiktix distribution at 7:30 p.m. (matinees, 2:30 p.m.). Unsold seats and/or unclaimed reservations are placed on sale at Quiktix prices at those times.

THEATRE DEVELOPMENT FUND (TDF)

1501 Broadway (43rd) 10036
221-0013

TDF offers two services of great value to theatregoers. *TDF Vouchers,* if you qualify, can be purchased in sets of five for $7.50. A TDF Voucher may be used for one admission to theatre and other performing-arts events at more than 200 participating theatres. Eligible to purchase TDF Vouchers are students, teachers, union members, members of youth, community, and church groups, performing-arts professionals, and retired people. If you qualify, send a stamped, self-addressed envelope to the Theatre Development Fund at the above address and you will be sent an application.

New York on Stage, published 11 times a year by TDF, contains detailed listings of performances on Broadway, Off Broadway, and Off-Off Broadway, plus dance and music. Send $10 to TDF for a year's subscription.

THEATRE PARTY SPECIALISTS

Theatre parties, in most cases, require a minimum of 20 people. In addition to the companies listed below, groups of 20 or more can usually arrange for discounted tickets directly from the individual theatres or producers.

Accent on Theatre Parties, 246 West 44th Street, 354-2062
Vic Cantor Theatre Party Services, 1650 Broadway, 581-9690
Tuddie Danter, 165 West 46th Street, 575-5060
Frances A. Drill, 165 West 46th Street, 395-6660
Leonard Fischer, 165 West 46th Street, 575-5050
Gertrude Fox, 165 West 46th Street, 575-5050
Group Sales Box Office, Inc., 234 West 44th Street, 398-8383
Larric Theatre Party Bureau, 2 West 45th Street, 575-5185
Fredye Lazarus, 246 West 44th Street, 354-2062
Lexington Theatre Ticket Service, Summit Hotel, Lexington Avenue and 51st Street, 751-3260

Liberty Theatre Ticket Corporation, 210 West 45th Street, 767-6677
Mackey's, Inc., 210 West 44th Street, 840-2800
National Theatre Club of New York, Inc., 303 West 42nd Street, 586-1644
Play of the Month Guild, Inc., 2 West 45th Street, 575-5185
Prestige Theatre Parties, Inc., 165 West 46th Street, 575-5050
Supreme Ticket Office, 301 West 45th Street, 246-5454
Theatre Party Associates, 234 West 44th Street, 398-8370

TICKETRON

For the Ticketron locations in your area, telephone:
New York City (212) 977-9020
Long Island (516) 882-7337
Northern New Jersey (201) 343-9310
Maine (207) 772-7402
Boston (617) 542-5491
Western Massachusetts (413) 584-7184
Buffalo (716) 847-8964
Rochester (716) 224-0449
Syracuse (315) 423-1300
Philadelphia (215) 885-2515
Washington, D.C. (202) 659-2601
Virginia Beach (804) 449-0597
Cincinnati (513) 421-6500
Cleveland (216) 447-0109
Chicago (312) 454-6777
Milwaukee (414) 273-6400
Houston (713) 526-7220
San Francisco (415) 393-6914
San Diego (714) 565-9949
Los Angeles (213) 642-5700

TKTS

Duffy Square North End of Times Square
Hours: 3 p.m.–8 p.m.; also from 12 noon on matinee days
Lower Manhattan Theatre Centre
100 Williams Street
Hours: Monday–Friday, 11:30 a.m.–5:30 p.m.

Tickets are sold only on the day of performance. Plaques listing the shows available for that day are posted near the ticket windows, and removed when sold out. Broadway, Off Broadway, and Lincoln Center productions use TKTS. All tickets with a face value of up to $10 are sold at half-price plus a 50¢ service charge; over $10, the service charge is $1 per ticket. All sales are for cash: no credit cards or personal checks. It is not possible to check seat locations before purchase; locations often are in the back of the orchestra and the mezzanine and to the sides. If tickets are available for hit shows, check to see if they are obstructed-view tickets. The selection of shows and seats to shows is considerably better earlier in the week. It is wise to have a second choice in mind when you reach the ticket window if there's a problem with your first choice; dawdling isn't encouraged.

IN THE WINGS: COMPUTER TICKETS

The Shubert Organization is installing a computerized ticket-selling operation that will go into limited operation late in 1981. When the system is fully operational, anyone, without going to the box office, will be able to buy the best available seat in any part of the theatre, on the preferred date for any advance performance, by telephone and credit card or at a computer terminal, anywhere in the country. When this happens, the distant ticket-buyer will be on the same footing as the New Yorker who goes to the box office—first come, first served will be the rule everywhere. Instead of the familiar racks of tickets behind the window, there will be a computer terminal. At the touch of a button, a screen will show the floor plan of the theatre and indicate the seats still unsold for a given performance; another touch of the button and the computer will print tickets and remove the sold seats from its inventory. Elapsed time: 1½ seconds. The first phase of the computerization will connect up the Shubert's 17 Broadway theatres. Other theatres will be invited into the system on a cost basis. Eventually, the plan calls for such refinements as the overnight discounting of tickets on a supply-and-demand basis, a centralized telephone service, and a ticket office in Times Square that would handle all shows. The program started with a feasibility study conducted by the League of New York Theatres and Producers. The Shubert Organization agreed to invest some $4 million when the study indicated the program would work. The hardware is being developed by Ticketron and its parent, Control Data Corporation, whose terminals in cities across the country will eventually be interconnected to give the system transcontinental capability. The system will be able to carry 25 million tickets in inventory, about twice the present volume of Broadway business.

THE HANDICAPPED AT THE THEATRE

The Theatre Development Fund (TDF) surveyed the Broadway theatres last year to determine the extent of facilities offered to people confined to wheelchairs. It is sad to report that only two theatres, the Minskoff and the Vivian Beaumont, have what TDF defines as *total accessibility*, that is, the theatre can accommodate patrons in wheelchairs via direct access, there are proper toilet facilities that the handicapped can use unassisted, and there are public telephones of a usable height. In preparing this guidebook, we have followed the TDF guidelines and terminology in our own investigations: *Semi-accessibility* means direct access seating only, no special toilet or telephone facilities; *access without dignity* means that theatre personnel are available to carry the person and the wheelchair up and down stairs or there is access via a freight elevator or other entrance; *no access* means that if you're handicapped, you're out of luck. For an art medium distinguished by its concern for the human condition, this is a sorry, sorry state of affairs.

IMPORTANT: *The theatre must know in advance when a wheelchair patron is attending. Wheelchair locations are limited in every instance, and the fire department must be given prior notice.*

For those theatregoers with a hearing impairment, help has come in the form of cordless earphones which can be adjusted to the desired level of sound magnification. Only a handful of Broadway theatres now offer them (this is noted in the individual theatre listings), but many more have them on order. The usual procedure is a dollar charge for the use of the earphones and surrendering two pieces of identification until the earphones are returned.

SOME WAYS TO ENJOY THE THEATRE MORE

As with so many other good things in life, the more you know about the theatre the more enjoyable it is. Not that it takes any special knowledge to love *Barnum* or *42nd Street;* indeed, it is now a common sight to see tourists who speak no English having the time of their lives at Broadway musicals.

But learning to love Broadway musicals is about as difficult as learning to love ice cream. This is not to demean musical comedy. It is the great American contribution to the theatre, and productions like *Sweeney Todd* and *Evita* have shown what a serious and versatile medium musical comedy can be. But it is only one part of the theatre. It is not unfair to say that Broadway itself is only one part of the theatre, though the most visible part, to be sure.

One reason for this guide is the breadth and depth and diversity of theatre in New York. There is no other place in the world where so many talented people are doing so many different things in the theatre. Consider that there are more premieres of new plays given each year in Manhattan than in the rest of the English-speaking world put together.

And what a shame not to take advantage of this phenomenon, not because of intellectual pretension but because it is enjoyable in a way unique to live entertainment. In a world of television, movies, and discos, the special power of direct human communication the theatre offers is worth seeking out.

The practical information in this guide should remove many of the stumbling blocks to extending your theatregoing experience. Here are some suggestions that may make your theatregoing experience more rewarding.

See more plays. Make theatregoing a habit. Your knowledge and critical understanding of theatre will grow in direct proportion to the number of productions you see. You become a skilled writer by writing, a good tennis player by playing tennis, an intelligent theatregoer by going to the theatre.

"But look at those Broadway prices," you say. The TKTS booths take most of the sting out of that. (Not that there aren't times you should plan ahead and get great seats to a great production. That is worth every penny.) More than half of the theatres listed in this guide cost less to attend than a movie, and many offer free theatre from time to time. So don't let your financial resources be an excuse.

Vary your playgoing. Change itself can heighten enjoyment. Seeing a Restoration comedy in the Village is the intellectual equivalent of going to a Chinese restaurant. See some avant-garde theatre. You may not like it at first, but chances are it will get you thinking. See some Shakespeare, not *Hamlet* or *Macbeth* but *The Winter's Tale* or *As You Like It.* Follow *Evita* with *The Red Mill* or *The Vagabond King* to see how far the musical has come. If you've just seen an elaborately staged production, try a reading on a bare stage. Counter Pinter with Neil Simon and both with Sam Shepard.

Do your homework. Get in the habit of clipping reviews of productions you are going to see. Find out something about the playwright, the company, the actors involved. Get the script and read it. Some years ago an actor friend suggested that before I go to see Tom Stoppard's *Rosencrantz and Guildenstern Are Dead* I should reread *Hamlet,* particularly the scenes involving Rosencrantz and Guildenstern. I did and the effect was amazing. To truly appreciate a switcheroo, you must know the original.

Be a comparison theatregoer. One of the fascinating things about the theatre is that no two performances are ever exactly alike. In a very real sense, you haven't seen *A Chorus Line,* you have seen a *performance* of *A Chorus Line.* A Broadway show can vary as much as 10 minutes in length from night to night depending upon pacing and audience reaction. A change in cast, even of one actor, can make a profound difference. To have seen Anthony Hopkins and Anthony Perkins and Richard Burton all do *Equus* was not only three great evenings in the theatre but an illumination of what the theatre is all about. When Yul Brynner took a vacation from *The King and I,* Angela Lansbury replaced Constance Towers as Anna and the whole focus changed: The king was her foil, not vice versa. Don't be afraid to go back to a production, and seize the opportunity to see new productions of great plays. A talented director, an exceptional cast can bring to *The Cherry Orchard,* say, a personal interpretation that not only is worthy in itself but will bring new insights to the production you saw before.

Use intermissions constructively. Think about what has gone before, what conflicts have developed, where the play is going. Is the play's structure sound? Are the actors building believable characters? Try to anticipate what is coming. If you make a habit of doing this, your critical judgment will improve rapidly, just as a muscle you exercise regularly will strengthen.

Keep a theatre diary. I once ran into Clive Barnes as he was coming from a theatre in the Village and asked him what he thought of the play. "I don't know," he said. "I haven't written my review yet." He may have been telling me that one simply doesn't ask a critic that question. I prefer to believe that he was reminding me what all writers learn: Writing forces you to think, sift through impressions, make judgments. That's one good reason for keeping a theatre diary; another is that we all forget so fast. Putting your impressions on paper is more than a substitute for an exceptional memory. The act of writing in some mysterious way can indelibly burn things into your memory. Don't worry about style. Jot down what you did and didn't like about the play, the cast, the staging. Then think about it, and try to put down why. Don't spend more than 15 minutes on it, and try to do it as soon as possible after the play. It may seem like hard work but try it four or five times with an open mind. My guess is you'll stick with it.

Read plays. Pick up a "best plays" collection and read a few. Reading a play usually only takes 30 or 40 minutes at most, and it's an entertaining literary form. See how various playwrights handle dialogue. Sense what accomplished actors could do with that dialogue. Visualize how the play might be staged; think what you would have the actors do if you were the director. After awhile try reading a play before you see it performed, then read it again after you've seen it, letting it replay again in your memory. See if this doesn't make the whole experience more rewarding.

Another aspect of play reading can be a lot of fun. Get several duplicate playscripts from a drama bookstore, invite some friends over, assign parts, and do a reading. It's a nice way to spend an evening, and you'll be surprised how rapidly your dramatic skills will improve.

Look for opportunities to learn. Many theatres have readings or workshop productions followed by discussion periods. Go to a few, listen, and don't be afraid to ask questions. The New School for Social Research and other educational institutions offer excellent evening courses in aspects of the theatre for the layman. Many times these involve discussion periods with major theatre talent. Shop around, find one that sounds interesting, and give it a try. Chances are you'll get the added dividend of making some new friends who share your fascination with the theatre.

Read about the theatre and its personalities. Read John Houseman's excellent memoirs, Brooks Atkinson's *Broadway,* Alan Jay Lerner's *On the Street Where I Live,* Stanislovsky's *An Actor Prepares.* Start collecting original cast and spoken arts albums and listen to them with a critical ear. See how songs advance the plot or describe character or plot development. Listen to Olivier or Gielgud doing Shakespeare with the script in front of you; feel their rhythm, what they can do with their voices. See some of the excellent theatre exhibits at the Museum of the City of New York and the Lincoln Center library. Take a backstage tour. Make it a habit to read Walter Kerr's thoughtful and provocative essays in the Sunday *New York Times.*

And, above all, enjoy. This is theatre. It can make you laugh or cry, it can bring you new understanding of the human condition, of yourself. All you have to do is meet it halfway.

THEATRE ETIQUETTE

The quality of a theatre performance depends in large measure on the quality of the audience at the performance. Something symbiotic happens in the theatre: The audience gives and the cast repays. Conversely, the best of shows can give a flat performance to a bad audience. There are a handful of things that can just about guarantee a flat performance—deadly sins, if you will.

Coming late. A good show grabs the audience's attention as soon as the curtain goes up. It can't do this if late arrivals are squeezing into their seats, obstructing the view of others, and filling the theatre with little cries of "Oops," "Pardon me," and "Sorry." Coming back late from intermission is a sin, too.

Talking. People get so accustomed to talking back to television or talking while it is on that it carries over into the theatre. It kills the show for the people around you if you talk. (If I made our nation's laws, strangling someone who talked in the theatre would be justifiable homicide.) Save "Doesn't she look lovely!" for the intermission. Only once did I find talking in the theatre excusable. When I first saw *Gemini* I found myself seated next to a blind man and throughout the play his companion quietly explained to him what was happening on the stage.

Coughing. I cough, you cough, we all cough. But drugstores sell preparations that stop the urge to cough for enough time to enjoy the theatre.

Eating. I love popcorn in the movies. In fact, I'm like Pavlov's dog: I enter a movie lobby and I invariably want popcorn. But I don't eat at the theatre. If you must eat, or take cough drops or whatever, remember this: Take the cellophane off before the curtain goes up. Shelley Berman once said, "It's not buttermilk I dislike so much; it's how the glass looks after

I drink it." It's not eating as much as it is the noise of the cellophane or cardboard.

Sleeping. How someone can pay $25 or whatever for a ticket and then drop off in Act I, Scene I, is more than I can fathom. But they do, in practically every performance. Why overindulge in food or liquor before a show. Everybody loses when you do. If you do, though, ask your companion to nudge you if you start to doze.

Sitting on your hands. It's not only polite to applaud at appropriate times; it helps ensure a better performance. A star deserves applause when he or she first appears on stage. So does a particularly well-played scene. Ray Bolger always sought what he called a "10 o'clock number" in a show he was considering doing, a number like "Once in Love with Amy" in *Where's Charley?* That number could run from five to 20 minutes depending on the audience response to Mr. Bolger. Think about who was shortchanged when the applause wasn't there and the number ran only five minutes.

The frantic departure. It always happens. The final curtain comes down, the audience is applauding, and suddenly a few people leap up and head for the exit like Little Eva chased by the bloodhounds. It's an insult to the cast, an annoyance to the audience, and where are they going anyway? Can a minute or two more be all that important?

Wandering gloves. I have spent a considerable part of my adult life looking under theatre seats for missing gloves. There must be something about the theatre that brings out the nomad in gloves. They stay quietly in place in restaurants only to roam later in the theatre. Might it not be wise to put them in one's handbag at the beginning and close it securely? You might even get a standing ovation.

On the matter of checkrooms. When you go to a hit show, it is reasonable to expect that there won't be an empty seat next to you. In the winter this means you'll have to hold your coat, hat, and whatever in your lap unless you have the foresight to check them. Holding them is an annoyance—to you and the people on either side of you. Putting them under your seat is a pretty messy business. The worst of all are shopping bags. Shopping bags are noisy by nature, and a shopping bag in the theatre can be heard 20 rows away. Almost every theatre has a checkroom. Use it.

THE CRITICS

"We don't make or break shows," say the drama critics. "The hell you don't!" say the actors and producers. The truth of the matter lies somewhere between these extremes. Shows, particularly musicals, can survive luke-warm or even bad reviews. *Grease* did and went on to be the longest-running show ever on Broadway. So did *Pippin* and a half-dozen others. Serious play, though, contract pneumonia and die when exposed to any chilliness from the critics. Comedy and mystery plays are hardier sorts. Richard Eder of *The New York Times* lambasted *Deathtrap* but it was still going strong two years later, outlasting Mr. Eder's run as drama critic, as a matter of fact. More recently, *Lunch Hour* received tepid reviews but showed box-office strength.

This is not to say that the critics aren't powerful. They certainly are, though less so than when there were seven New York daily papers instead of only three. And less powerful than they were before producers learned to sell their shows with skilfully made television commercials. But perhaps it is just as well, for that life-or-death quality tended to overshadow the true purpose of criticism.

A good critic helps us to see. His training, background, and skills bring an important element to our thinking, our response to the play. (You can sense the absence of criticism when you attend previews. There's a certain restive quality in the audience, a feeling, often, of "Yes, but . . ." If you ever have seen a play before and after opening, the contrast is remarkable.) Most of us look at reviews to determine if we want to go to the trouble and expense to see the play. After all, no one can see everything. This is fine, although it's wise to look at several reviews before making up your mind. No critic is infallible. The problem is very few of us look at reviews *after* we've seen the play. And that is when it is most important. The play is fresh in your mind, you sort out your thoughts and impressions by comparing them with the critic's thoughts and impressions. Did you see what he saw? Did you react in the same way? Did your reactions lead you to the same conclusions? If not, why not? Get in the habit of clipping reviews of plays you're going to see and re-read them when you come home. It's enjoyable, and it will sharpen your own critical facilities.

No one has a keener theatrical eye than Walter Kerr of the *Times*. A former daily critic, at the *Herald Tribune* from 1951 to 1966, and at the *Times*, he now writes thoughtful essays for the Sunday *"Arts and Leisure"* section. They sparkle with insight and well-turned phrases. Mr. Kerr was a professor of drama at Catholic University in Washington before he became a critic, and he brings the lucidity of a good professor to his writing. He is a must for anyone with a serious interest in the theatre.

The chief critic of the *Times* is Frank Rich, a 32-year-old former film critic at *New Times*, the *New York Post*, and *Time* magazine. He joined the *Times* in March, 1980, and became chief critic that September. This Harvard graduate has the most important critic's position in the city because if he likes it, the *Times* likes it, and any producer will tell you that you're just about home free if the *Times* likes it.

Another important and excellent critic at the *Times* is Mel Gussow, winner in 1978 of the George Jean Nathan Award for critical excellence. Since 1969 he has covered Off and Off-Off Broadway for the paper, written a number of magazine articles and a biography of Darryl F. Zanuck. A native New Yorker, Mr. Gussow is a graduate of Middlebury College and the Columbia School of Journalism.

Once chief critic of the *Times* (1967–77), Clive Barnes now is the chief critic of the *Post* and continues to be the best-known critic on Broadway. He has an unerring eye and a facility for the well-turned phrase. Born in London and educated at Oxford, Mr. Barnes was a critic for the *London Daily Express* before beginning his association with the *Times*. He has the singular distinction of covering dance and theatre at both papers—and with equal dexterity.

The oldest of the daily critics is Douglas Watt of the *Daily News*, its chief critic since 1971. Mr. Watt, 67, is a thoughtful, lucid writer who avoids the equivocation that sometimes plagues his fellow critics: You always know what Mr. Watt thinks of a show. A former president of the New York Drama Critics Circle, he also is a composer with a number of popular songs published and recorded.

Once the opening night party ritual was waiting for someone to run in with early editions hot off the press (openings usually are at 6:30 p.m. to permit reviewers to make the early editions). Now this is augmented by waiting for the television reviews.

Katie Kelly, from Albion, Nebraska (population: 1,982), is the theatre critic for WNBC-TV. She was a commentator on television on the "Today" show until she replaced Chauncy Howell as critic early in 1981. She was a researcher and show-business writer at *Time* before entering TV journalism.

At WABC-TV, Joel Siegel is the entertainment critic. The ebullient Mr. Siegel, a *cum laude* graduate of the University of California, was an advertising copywriter before joining KMET-TV in Los Angeles in 1972. He has won two Emmy Awards for special reporting.

Dennis Cunningham has been an able critic at WCBS-TV since June of 1978. He had been critic at WCAU-TV, the CBS outlet in Philadelphia.

Weekly magazines are important critical voices in the theatre and perhaps the most recognizable of these voices belongs to Brendon Gill of *The New Yorker*. Mr. Gill is both an astute critic and an elegant writer, and his reviews are a joy to read. He has been at the magazine since 1936 and its drama critic since 1967. Mr. Gill has written many books, including *Cole* and *Tallulah*, and co-authored with Maxwell Anderson a play based on his novel, *The Day the Money Stopped*. He also wrote the book for the musical *La Belle*. Off and Off-Off Broadway for *The New Yorker* have been the concern of Edith Oliver since 1961. Ms. Oliver, a graduate of Smith College, studied acting at the Berkshire Playhouse, and was a radio actress on "Gangbusters." Before joining the magazine in 1948, she wrote and produced the quiz programs "$64 Question" and "Take It or Leave It."

At *Newsweek*, Jack Kroll, winner of the George Jean Nathan Award in 1980, writes the drama reviews and is senior editor in charge of the arts section. His counterpart at *Time* magazine is Theodore Kalem, who succeeded Louis Kronenberger as drama critic in 1961. A Harvard graduate, he worked at *The Christian Science Monitor* as a book reviewer before joining *Time*.

The most controversial critic on the scene is erudite, often vituperative John Simon of *New York* magazine. If Mr. Simon doesn't care for you or your production, watch out. His scathing comments on Tammy Grimes, Sylvia Miles, and Liza Minnelli, to name only a few, are legendary. It's a shame for two reasons: He oversteps the limits of good taste and fair play and hurts people, and when he does, it tends to obscure the fact that he is a gifted critic and splendid writer, often a needed voice of intelligent dissent to the daily critics. Born Jovan Ivan Dimon in Subotica, Yugoslavia, he was educated in England before attending Harvard, where he received his A.B., M.A. and Ph.D. in comparative literature. He has written a number of books of criticism and has received several fellowships and awards. Before *New York,* he was a critic for *The Hudson Review, The New Leader, Commonweal,* and *Esquire.*

The Village Voice has done an outstanding job for years of covering and reviewing Off and Off-Off Broadway. It's understandable, for the *Voice* and Off and Off-Off Broadway theatre grew up together. (It is the *Voice* that created and annually awards the Obies.) Erika Munk is a senior editor and critic. Her articles deal with subjects ranging from guerrilla and environmental theatre to all aspects of political theatre to the current avant-garde and its relationship to mainstream theatrical performances. Her column, "Cross Left," explores the link between theatre and society, here and abroad. Ms. Munk is the author of *Brecht, Buchner's Woyzeck,* and *Stanislavski and America.* Terry Curtis Fox is the critic of Off Broadway. A University of Chicago graduate, Mr. Fox is the author of the play *Cops,* which has been produced at the Performing Garage and other theatres around the country.

SoHo News does an excellent and comprehensive job of covering the many aspects of noncommerial theatre in the city. Don Shewey is the paper's theatre editor. Formerly a theatre critic for the *Boston Phoenix,* he has written on the theatre for a number of publications. His staff includes: James Leverett, a veteran actor and prolific writer on theatre who is also director of the literary services department at Theatre Communications Group; Jeremy Gerard, a graduate of SUNY at Purchase, former theatre editor of *Our Town,* and currently editor of the *American Theatre Critics Association Newsletter;* Elinor Fuchs, dramaturge, scholar, and playwright (*Year One of the Empire*), who also serves as radio theatre critic for the Canadian Broadcasting Corporation; Bethany Haye, who trained as an actress in London and toured here for three years with the Third Eye Theatre Company and is the U.S. arts liaison for *Tageszeitung* in Berlin; and Joseph Hurley, who has written extensively for documentary television and other newspapers and magazines.

THEATRE PUBLICATIONS

No one publication covers the full range of theatre activity in the city, let alone the country or the world, but several cover various aspects of the theatre in depth and with regularity. *Variety,* the "bible of show business," is a weekly tabloid that celebrated its 75th anniversary early in 1981. Although it started out as a theatre paper, "legit," as the theatre is referred to by *Variety,* trails behind movies, television, music, records, and nightclub acts in both position and amount of coverage. But *Variety* is the place to look if you're interested in such things as Broadway grosses, who's casting what, the shows now playing in London, regional and road company grosses, and the like. One thing *Variety* does particularly well is review Broadway-bound shows in tryout cities, the reviews usually presage the New York reviews. *Variety* has made a reputation over the years for the hipness of its headlines (*Wall Street Lays An Egg; Stix Nix Hix Pix*—referring to the 1929 stock market crash and to a report that small towns were not overly enamored of movies that protrayed people in small towns as amusing oafs), a practice that continues to this day. As this was written, a *Variety* headline informed me that *Babes On B'way Blitz Looms On Legit Schedules.* I read on to learn that the impending arrival of shows starring Elizabeth Taylor, Lauren Bacall, Glenda Jackson, Beatrice Arthur, Lena Horne, Claudette Colbert, and Rita Moreno proves that the old star system is alive and well on Broadway. In sum, *Variety* is fun to read and the best barometer around of the financial, if not the artistic, health of Broadway. (*Variety,* weekly, $1 per copy; subscription, $50 a year. 154 West 46th Street, New York, N.Y. 10036.)

Producers read *Variety;* aspiring actors read Leo Shull's *Show Business* for the excellent reason that the weekly tabloid is chock full of casting news. Mr. Shull, who has strong opinions on anything and everything, writes a diary in most issues that's fun to read. Besides *Show Business,* he also publishes annuals and guide books: *How to Break into Show Business* ($7), *Summer Theatre Directory* ($8), and *Theatre Angels* ($60), a listing of investors names, addresses, and amounts invested in productions during the previous year. (*Show Business,* weekly, 75¢ per copy; subscription, $30 per year. 134 West 44th Street, New York, N.Y. 10036.)

On the far other end of the scale are two scholarly journals: *Theatre,* published by the Yale School of Drama, and *The Drama Review,* published by the New York University School of the Arts. Both are recondite and tend to be intimidating to anyone who doesn't have a doctorate in dramaturgy. Both stress the avant-garde in the noncommercial theatre with lengthy monographs on performance and the interaction between abstract dance and the theatre. (*Theater,* published three times a year, $3.50 per copy; subscription, $9 per year. Box 2046, Yale Station, New Haven, Conn. 06520. *The Drama Review,* published quarterly, $4 per copy; subscription, $14.50 per year. Room 600, 721 Broadway, New York, N.Y. 10013.)

For those with a professional interest in Broadway and Off Broadway, by far the most important and informative publication is *Theatrical Index,* produced by Price Berkley and published every Monday. It contains every bit of pertinent information on every show, even those in the formative stages. *Theatrical Index* is accurate, well organized, and indispensable. There are various subscription options depending upon frequency and method of delivery, which affect the cost. For additional information: Price Berkley, 888 Eighth Avenue (586-6343).

The best publication for the theatregoer is *The New York Times.* Daily and Sunday, in the regular paper and often in the magazine, there is an abundance of news, criticism, and feature stories on the theatre in and around the city. Frankly, it is hard to conceive of anyone with a genuine interest in the theatre doing without it.

IMPORTANT THEATRE ORGANIZATIONS

ACTORS' EQUITY

165 West 46th Street
869-8530

Actors' Equity Association is the labor union encompassing all professional performers in the legitimate theatre in the United States, some 30,000. The problem with Equity is the problem every actor faces: unemployment. At almost any given time, four out of five Equity members have no jobs in legitimate theatre. In a typical year, less than 5 percent of its members earned more than $10,000 in the theatre. To become a member, an actor must be offered a part in a show with an Equity contract (which means the producer has agreed to cast only Equity members). The actor pays a one-time initiation fee of $500. He also can become a member by first being a membership candidate, something like being an apprentice in other unions. After a certain length of time, usually 50 weeks, in a stock company or similar acting situation, he is eligible for full Equity membership. Incidentally, part of what makes Off-Off Broadway possible is an easement of Equity rules permitting Equity actors to appear with non-Equity actors in theatres below a certain size for a limited number of engagements. It is the definitions contained in the 85-to-100 page contract that spell out what is Broadway, Off Broadway, and Off-Off Broadway. Nothing else. As to wages, the current Broadway minimum is $475 a week plus an 8.5 percent pension and welfare payment. National company actors receive the same plus a per-diem expense allowance. Off Broadway the minimum is about $160 per week, somewhat less than the average secretary makes. If this sounds grim, however, it is infinitely better than in the days when Equity was founded by 112 actors in New York on May 26, 1913. The exploitation of actors was the rule then: Each manager drew his own agreement, there was no minimum wage, rehearsal time was unlimited and unpaid for, there was no guarantee of playing time, holiday matinees were numerous and actors weren't paid for doing them, actors could be laid off during lean weeks, actors furnished their own costumes, and they could be laid off without notice. To join a traveling company was to run the real risk of being stranded out there somewhere without money. All that's changed now, but it didn't come easy. A strike in 1919 lasted 30 bitter days and closed 37 plays in eight cities, prevented the opening of 16 others, and cost those concerned the then-large sum of $3 million. George M. Cohan sided with management against Equity; Marie Dressler, who had begun her career as a chorus girl at $8 a week, helped bring the chorus performers to Equity's side. She later became the first president of the Chorus Equity Association, which later merged with Actors' Equity. Through the years, Equity has been in the forefront of the civil rights movement and has labored in Washington to promote the passage of legislation favorable to the arts and the theatrical profession. Equity has been a remarkably stable union with only 10 presidents in its more than 60-year history. Theodore Bikel has been its president since 1974.

THE DRAMA LEAGUE

One of the most durable of the city's theatre organizations is the Drama League of New York, now in its 65th year. Its members attend more than a dozen Broadway and several Off Broadway shows each season. The League doesn't stop there. Julia Hansen, League president, recently noted, "We're not merely a theatregoing group. Our members form an educative, supportive audience for the New York theatre, attend luncheons to hear theatre professionals speak and extend financial support to theatrical projects." Ms. Hansen is particularly proud of the League's expanded interest in Off Broadway theatre projects. It recently awarded an annual $1,000 grant to the Circle Repertory Company to assist playwrights. League members make a special effort to follow the careers of particular performers. Currently they are watching the activities of John Lithgow, an actor who has appeared in *The Changing Room, My Fat Friend,* and *Division Street.* Mr. Lithgow recently was made a member of the League's advisory board. The League also grants scholarships to such institutions as Juilliard and the American Academy of Dramatic Arts. A recent recipient was Christine Ebersole, who played Ado Annie in the revival of *Oklahoma!,* and opposite Richard Burton in *Camelot* at Lincoln Center. Since 1935, the League has awarded the Delia Austrian Medal for "the most distinguished performance of the season." Information on membership may be obtained by writing the Drama League of New York, P.O. Box 5179, New York, N.Y. 10163.

THE LEAGUE OF NEW YORK THEATRES AND PRODUCERS

226 West 47th Street
582-4455

The League was founded in 1930 to combat ticket speculation, an evil it still wrestles with. Its mandate was broadened shortly after to include the conservation and promotion of the general welfare of the theatre and the interests of its members. In 1938, it added a key function as it became the bargaining unit for management in negotiations with theatrical unions. Now its 215 members are an important force. Their concern includes the condition of the theatre district and nearby neighborhoods. Many of the good things that have happened in the area in recent years can be traced to efforts of the League. Through a system of financial grants and other technical assistance, the League serves a number of city arts organizations: the Theatre Development Fund, the International Theatre Institute, the Off-Off Broadway Alliance, the Actors Fund, Theatre Row, In-Touch Networks, St. Malachy's Green Room, the Board of Education's Drama Enrichment Curriculum, and the Theatre Collection of the Museum of the City of New York. Currently, the League is supervising a theatre marketing study in conjunction with the Theatre Development Fund, the Cultural Assistance Center, and the American Express Company. It encompasses both the commercial theatre and not-for-profit theatre. A more immediately noticeable effort came out of the League's Special Projects Department, headed by Harvey Sabinson: the successful "I Love New York" commercials, featuring current Broadway shows to stimulate tourism. The League has the responsibility for coordination and administration of the annual Tony Awards.

OFF-OFF BROADWAY ALLIANCE

162 West 56th Street
757-4433

The Off-Off Broadway Alliance (OOBA, which rhymes with tuba) is a not-for-profit organization that, since its founding in 1972, has sought "to nurture the conditions and processes which encourage the theatre artist to survive." If OOBA can be judged by the proliferation of Off-Off Broadway theatre since the early 1970s, it has been successful indeed. Some 90 member theatres and theatre groups now look to OOBA for a variety of services that include being a spokesman and information center for the Off-Off Broadway movement and an advocate in dealings with government, businesses, and unions, and for training in such areas as fundraising, record-keeping, and box-office management. Executive director Nancy Heller says, "If OOBA went out of business, it would have to be reinvented." OOBA is supported by the following foundations and corporations: Celanese Corporation; The Chase Manhattan Bank, N.A.; The Dramatist Guild Fund, Inc.; Robert Sterling Clark Foundation, Inc.; The Ford Foundation; The League of New York Theatres and Producers, Inc.;

Metropolitan Life Foundation; Morgan Guaranty Trust Company; and the Shubert Foundation, Inc.

OOBA Membership
Academy Arts Theatre Company
AMAS Repertory Theatre
American Ensemble Company
American Jewish Theatre at the Y
American Renaissance Theatre
American Stanislavski Theatre
Bond Street Theatre Coalition
Cherubs Guild
Circle Repertory Company
Cithaeron Theatre
Classic Theatre
Colonnades Theatre Lab
Counterpoint Theater Company
CSC Repertory
Direct Theatre
Frederick Douglass Creative Arts Center
DORT at the Martinique
Encompass Theatre Company
Ensemble Studio Theatre
Fantasy Factory
First All Children's Theatre
Force 13 Theatre Company
Gene Frankel Theatre Workshop
The Glines
Golden Fleece Ltd.
Hudson Guild Theatre
Impossible Ragtime Theatre
INTAR
Interart Theatre
Irish Rebel Theatre
Jean Cocteau Repertory
Jewish Repertory Theatre
LaMama E.T.C.
Latin American Theatre Ensemble
Lion Theatre Company
Manhattan Punch Line
Manhattan Theatre Club
Medicine Show Theatre Ensemble
Medusa's Revenge
Nat Horne Musical Theatre
New Federal Theatre at Henry Street
  Settlement
New World Theatre
New York Collaboration Theatre
New York Shakespeare Festival

New York Stageworks
New York Street Theatre Caravan
New York Theatre Strategy
New York Theatre Studio
Nuestro Teatro
Off Center Theatre
The Open Space
Pan Asian Repertory Theatre
Playwrights Horizons
The Production Company
The Proposition Workshop
Puerto Rican Travelling Theatre
Quaigh Theatre
Raft Theatre
Repertorio Espanol
Richard Allen Center for Culture and Art
Richard Morse Mime Theatre
Riverside Shakespeare Company
The Second Stage
Seven Ages Performance Ltd. at Perry
  Street Theatre
78th Street Theatre Lab
Shelter West
Shirtsleeve Theatre
Sidewalks of New York Productions
SoHo Rep
South Street Theatre Company
Spectrum Theatre
Spiderwoman Theatre Workshop
Stage Left
Ten-Ten Players
Thalia Spanish Theatre
Theatre Matrix
Theatre for the New City
Theatre Off Park
Theatre of the Open Eye
Theatre of the Riverside Church
Theatre at St. Clement's
Theatre XII
TRG Repertory Company
Veterans Ensemble Theatre Company
Westside Community Repertory Theatre
The Wooster Group
WPA Theatre
The York Players Company
Yueh Lung Shadow Theatre

THE THEATRE GUILD

226 West 47th Street
265-6170

The Theatre Guild is the oldest continuing theatrical producing organization in the country. Since its founding in 1919, it has produced more than 200 Broadway plays and introduced to American audiences the plays of 60 of Europe's major dramatists. It produced 18 of George Bernard Shaw's plays here, five of which were world premieres. Eugene O'Neill's relationship with the Theatre Guild lasted until his death. Other important American playwrights who were first produced by the Guild include: Robert Sherwood, Maxwell Anderson, Sidney Howard, S. N. Behrman, William Saroyan, and Philip Barry. George Gershwin's *Porgy and Bess* was originally produced by the Guild, as were Rodgers and Hammerstein's *Oklahoma!* and *Carousel*. Other memorable Guild productions: *Bells Are Ringing, Come Back, Little Sheba, The Iceman Cometh, The Lady's Not for Burning, Liliom, The Matchmaker, The Philadelphia Story, Picnic, Saint Joan, Sunrise at Campobello, They Knew What They Wanted, Royal Hunt of the Sun, The Homecoming,* and *Golda*. Since 1960, the Guild also has been active in producing motion pictures through Theatre Guild Films. Among its productions or co-productions: *The Pawnbroker, Judgment at Nuremberg,* and *A Child Is Waiting*. Besides its role as producer, the Guild maintains a system of organized theatre audiences in six U.S. cities with an enrollment of some 75,000 members. Almost every play that tours the country is seen by these audiences and supported by them. This division of the Guild has organized the theatrical subscription audiences of the John F. Kennedy Center in Washington. The Guild also operates Theatre Guild Abroad, in which participants travel on cultural exchange programs to sample the theatre and exchange views with theatrical personalities in other countries, and Theatre at Sea, a series of theatre cruises to the Caribbean and Mediterranean. Philip Langner, co-director of the Guild, has been with the Guild for more than 25 years. One of the most recent productions was *Absurd Person Singular,* the second-longest-running English comedy in Broadway history. He also owns the Westport Country Playhouse in Connecticut, one of the country's most famous summer theatres. His wife, Marilyn, is in charge of the Theatre at Sea activities. A former actress, Mrs. Langner (stage name: Marilyn Clark) was in several John Cassavetes's movies including *Faces* and *Husbands*. The other co-director of the Guild is Armina Marshall, formerly an actress who appeared in many Guild productions. With her late husband, Lawrence Langner, one of the Guild's original founders, she co-authored several plays, including *Pursuit of Happiness, Suzanna and the Elders,* and *On to Fortune*. Ms. Marshall is chairman of the Theatre Guild–American Theatre Society. Information on the activities of the Guild may be obtained by writing to its New York headquarters.

LONGEST RUNNING PRODUCTIONS

BROADWAY

(as of June 1, 1981. An asterisk indicates a show still running)

Performances

Grease	3,388	Barefoot in the Park	1,532
Fiddler on the Roof	3,242	Mame	1,503
Life with Father	3,224	Arsenic and Old Lace	1,444
Tobacco Road	3,182	Same Time, Next Year	1,444
Hello, Dolly!	2,844	The Sound of Music	1,443
My Fair Lady	2,717	How to Succeed in Business	
A Chorus Line*	2,409	Without Really Trying	1,417
Man of La Mancha	2,329	Hellzapoppin'	1,404
Abie's Irish Rose	2,327	The Music Man	1,375
Oklahoma!	2,212	Deathtrap*	1,361
Oh! Calcutta!*	1,967	Funny Girl	1,348
Pippin	1,944	The Best Little Whorehouse in	
South Pacific	1,925	Texas*	1,317
The Magic Show	1,920	Mummenschanz	1,316
Harvey	1,775	Dancin'*	1,311
Hair	1,742	Ain't Misbehavin'*	1,300
Annie*	1,717	Angel Street	1,295
Gemini*	1,702	Lightnin'	1,291
The Wiz	1,661	Promises, Promises	1,281
Born Yesterday	1,642	The King and I	1,246
Mary, Mary	1,572	Cactus Flower	1,234
The Voice of the Turtle	1,557	Sleuth	1,222

1776	1,217		Kiss and Tell	962
Equus	1,209		Anna Lucasta	957
Guys and Dolls	1,200		The Moon Is Blue	924
Cabaret	1,166		Bells Are Ringing	924
Mister Roberts	1,157		Beatlemania	914
Annie Get Your Gun	1,147		Luv	902
The Seven Year Itch	1,141		Can-Can	895
Butterflies Are Free	1,128		Carousel	890
Pins and Needles	1,108		Hats Off to Ice	890
Plaza Suite	1,097		Fanny	888
Kiss Me Kate	1,071		Follow the Girls	882
Don't Bother Me, I Can't			The Bat	878
Cope	1,065		Camelot	873
The Pajama Game	1,063		My Sister Eileen	866
The Teahouse of the August			White Cargo	864
Moon	1,027		No, No Nanette	861
Damn Yankees	1,019		Song of Norway	860
Never Too Late	1,007		A Streetcar Named Desire	855
Any Wednesday	984		Comedy in Music	849
A Funny Thing Happened on			You Can't Take It with You	837
the Way to the Forum	964		La Plume de Ma Tante	835
The Odd Couple	964		Three Men on a Horse	835

OFF-BROADWAY

	Performances			
The Fantasticks*	8,769		Oh! Calcutta!	704
Threepenny Opera	2,611		The Knack	685
Godspell	2,124		The Club	680
Jacques Brel Is Alive and Well			One Mo' Time*	672
and Living in Paris	1,847		The Balcony	672
You're a Good Man, Charlie			The Passion of Dracula	660
Brown	1,547		America Hurrah	634
The Blacks	1,408		Hogan's Goat	607
Let My People Come	1,327		The Trojan Women (r)	600
Vanities	1,313		Krapp's Last Tape and The	
The Hot l Baltimore	1,166		Zoo Story	582
Little Mary Sunshine	1,143		The Dumbwaiter and The	
El Grande de Coca Cola	1,114		Collection	578
One Flew over the Cuckoo's			Dames at Sea	575
Nest (r)	1,025		The Crucible (r)	571
Boys in the Band	1,000		The Iceman Cometh (r)	565
Your Own Thing	933		The Hostage (r)	545
Curley McDimple	931		Six Characters in Search of an	
Leave It to Jane (r)	928		Author (r)	529
I'm Getting My Act Together			The Dirtiest Show in Town	509
& Taking It on the Road**	900		Happy Ending and Day of	
The Mad Show	871		Absence	504
Scrambled Feet*	823		The Boys from Syracuse	500
The Effect of Gamma Rays on				
Man-in-the-Moon Marigolds	819		* As of June 1, 1981 (still running)	
A View from the Bridge (r)	780		** Number of performances at the Circle in	
The Boy Friend (r)	763		the Square Downtown. Prior to this engage-	
The Pocket Watch	725		ment, the show was done for six months at	
The Connection	722		the Public Theatre	
Adaptation and Next	707		(r) revival	

ACTORS AND ACTRESSES
(Birthplace, birthdate, and New York debut)

George ABBOTT. Forestville, N.Y., June 25, 1887. Babe Merrill in *The Misleading Lady* at the Fulton Theater, Nov. 25, 1913

Edie ADAMS. (née Edith Adams Enke) Kingston, Pa., April 16, 1928. Eileen in *Wonderful Town* at the Winter Garden, Feb. 25, 1953

Luther ADLER. New York City, Feb. 10, 1902. *Schmendrick* at Thalia Theater on the Bowery, 1908

Stella ADLER. New York City, Feb. 10, 1902. With her father at his theatre, the Grand, in *Broken Hearts,* 1906

Eddie ALBERT. (né Edward Albert Heimberger) Rock Island, Ill., April 22, 1908. *O Evening Star* at the Empire, Dec. 25, 1935

Jack ALBERTSON. Revere, Mass. *Meet the People* at the Mansfield

Robert ALDA. (né Alphonso Giovanni Giuseppe Roberto D'Abruzzo) New York City, Feb. 26, 1914. Vaudeville at the RKO in 1933

Tom ALDREDGE. Dayton, Ohio, Feb. 28, 1928. The messenger in *Electra* at the Jan Hus House, May 9, 1958

Jane ALEXANDER. (née Quigley) Boston, Oct. 28, 1939. *The Great White Hope* at the Alvin, Oct. 3, 1968

Woody ALLEN. (né Allen Konigsburg) Brooklyn, N.Y., Dec. 1, 1935. Allan Felix in *Play It Again, Sam* (which he also wrote) at the Broadhurst, Feb. 12, 1969

Dame Judith ANDERSON. (née Frances Margaret Anderson-Anderson) Adelaide, Austrailia, Feb. 10, 1898. Small parts in a stock company at the Fourteenth Street Theater

Dana ANDREWS. Collins, Miss., Jan. 1, 1912. Jerry Ryan in *Two for the Seesaw* at the Booth, June 30, 1958

Julie ANDREWS. Walton, England, Oct. 1, 1935. *The Boy Friend*

Eve ARDEN. Mill Valley, Cal., April 30, 1912. *Ziegfeld Follies* at the Winter Garden, Jan. 4, 1934

Alan ARKIN. New York City, March 26, 1934. *From the Second City* at the Royale, Sept. 26, 1961

Beatrice ARTHUR. (née Bernice Frankel) New York City, May 13, 1926. *Lysistrata* at the New School Dramatic Stage, 1947

Dame Peggy ASHCROFT. Croydon, England, Dec. 22, 1907. Lise in *High Tor* at the Martin Beck, Jan. 8, 1937

Elizabeth ASHLEY. (née Cole) Ocala, Fla., Aug. 30, 1939. Jessica in *Dirty Hands* at Actors Playhouse, July, 1959

René AUBERJONOIS. New York City, June 1, 1940. Fool in *King Lear* at the Vivian Beaumont on Nov. 7, 1968

Jean-Pierre AUMONT. Paris, France, Jan. 5, 1909. Pierre Renault in *My Name Is Aquilon* at the Lyceum, Feb. 9, 1949

Lauren BACALL. (née Betty Joan Perske) New York City, Sept. 16, 1924. Walk-on in *Johnny 2 X 4* at the Longacre, March 16, 1942

Pearl BAILEY. Newport News, Va., March 29, 1918. Butterfly in *St. Louis Woman* at the Martin Beck, March 30, 1946

Josephine BAKER. St. Louis, Mo., June 3, 1906. That Comedy Chorus Girl in *The Chocolate Dandies* at the Plantation Club, 1924

Kaye BALLARD. (née Catherine Gloria Balotta) Cleveland, Nov. 20, 1926. *Three to Make Money* at the Adelphi, 1946

Martin BALSAM. New York City, Nov. 4, 1919. The Villian in *Pot Boiler* at the NYC Playground

Anne BANCROFT (née Anna Maria Italiano) Sept. 17, 1931. Gittel Mosca in *Seesaw,* January, 1958

Barbara BARRIE. Chicago, May 23, 1931. Jane Stewart in *The Wooden Dish* at the Booth, Oct. 6, 1955

Richard BASEHART. Zanesville, Ohio, Aug. 31, 1914. Weiler in *Counterattack* at the Windsor, Feb. 3, 1943

Alan BATES. Derbyshire, England, Feb. 17, 1934. Cliff Lewis in *Look Back in Anger* at the Lyceum, October, 1958

Barbara BAXLEY. Stockton, Cal., Jan. 1, 1927. Sibyl Chase in *Private Lives* at the Plymouth, October, 1948

Anne BAXTER. Michigan City, Ind., May 7, 1923. Elizabeth Winthrop in *Seen But Not Heard* at the Windsor, March, 1938

Orson BEAN. (né Dallas Frederick Burroughs) Burlington, Vt., July 22, 1928. Edgar Grassthal in *Men of Distinction* at the 46th Street Theatre, April, 1953

Brian BEDFORD. Morley, Yorks, England, Feb. 13, 1935. *Five Finger Exercise* at the Music Box, December, 1959

Barbara BEL GEDDES. New York City, Oct. 31, 1922. Dottie Coburn in *Out of the Frying Pan* at the Windsor, Feb. 10, 1941

Joan BENNETT. Palisades, N.J., Feb. 27, 1910. As Daisy in *Jarnegan* with her father at the Longacre, September, 1928

Ingrid BERGMAN. Stockholm, Sweden, Aug. 29, 1915. Julie in *Liliom* at the 44th Street Theatre, March 25, 1940

Milton BERLE. (né Berlinger) New York City, July 12, 1908. Bit part in *Floradora* at the Century, April 5, 1920

Theodore BIKEL. Vienna, Austria, May 2, 1924. Inspector Massoubre in *Tonight in Samarkand* at the Longacre, November, 1955

Vivian BLAINE. (née Stapleton) Newark, N.J., Nov. 21, 1921. Miss Adelaide in *Guys and Dolls* at the 46th Street Theatre, Nov. 24, 1950

Claire BLOOM. London, Feb. 15, 1931. Juliet in *Romeo and Juliet* at the Winter Garden, October, 1956.

Ray BOLGER. Dorchester, Mass., Jan. 10, 1904. *The Merry World* at the Imperial, June 8, 1926

Shirley BOOTH. (née Thelma Booth Ford) New York City, Aug. 30, 1907. Nan Winchester in *Hell's Bells* at Wallack's, Jan. 26, 1925

Tom BOSLEY. Chicago, Oct. 1, 1927. Dupont Dufour in *Thieves' Carnival* at the Cherry Lane, June, 1947

Joseph BOVA. Cleveland, May 25, 1924. Chip in *On The Town* at the Carnegie Hall Playhouse, Jan. 15, 1959

Eddie BRACKEN. Astoria, N.Y., Feb. 7, 1920. Western Union Boy in *The Man on Stilts* at the Plymouth, Sept. 9, 1931

Carol BURNETT. San Antonio, Texas, April 26, 1933. Princess Winnifred in *Once upon a Mattress* at the Phoenix, May, 1959

Richard BURTON. Pontrhydfen, South Wales, Nov. 10, 1925. Richard in *The Lady's Not for Burning* at the Royale, Nov. 8, 1950

Sid CAESAR. Yonkers, N.Y., Sept. 8, 1922. *Tars and Spars* at the Strand, 1944

Zoe CALDWELL. Australia, 1934. Prioress in *The Devils* at the Longacre, Febraury, 1966

Kitty CARLISLE. New Orleans, Sept. 3, 1914. Title role in *Rio Rita* at the Capitol, 1932

Ian CARMICHAEL. Hull, England, June 18, 1920. Robert in *Boeing-Boeing* at the Cort, February, 1965

Art CARNEY. Mount Vernon, N.Y., Nov. 4, 1918. James Hyland in *The Rope Dancers* at the Cort, Nov. 20, 1957

Carleton CARPENTER. Bennington, Vt., July 10, 1926. Tittman in *Bright Boy* at the National, May 23, 1944

John CARRADINE. (né Richmond Reed) New York City, Feb. 5, 1906. Johnathan Brewster in *Arsenic and Old Lace* at Town Hall, August, 1946

Peggy CASS. Boston, May 21, 1924. Maisie in *Burlesque* at the Broadhurst, October, 1949

Richard CHAMBERLAIN. (né George Richard) Beverly Hills, Cal., March 31, 1935. Jeff Claypool in *Breakfast at Tiffany's* at the Majestic, December, 1966

Carol CHANNING. Seattle, Jan. 31, 1921. *No for an Answer* at the Center, January, 1941

Imogene COCA. Philadelphia, Nov. 18, 1908. Chorus girl in *When You Smile* at the National, Oct. 5, 1925

James COCO. New York City, March 21, 1929. Tavu in *Hotel Paradiso* at the Henry Miller, April 11, 1957

Claudette COLBERT. (née Lily Chauchoin) Paris, Sept. 13, 1905. Sybil Blake in *The Wild Wescotts* at the Frazee, December, 1923.

Betty COMDEN. (née Cohen) Brooklyn, May 3, 1919. Cabaret act (with Adolph Green and Judy Holliday) at the Adelphi, December, 1944

Barbara COOK. Atlanta, Oct. 25, 1927. Sandy in *Flahooley* at the Broadhurst, May, 1951

Peter COOK. Torquay, England, Nov. 17, 1937. *Beyond the Fringe* at the Golden, October, 1962.

Robert COOTE. London, Feb. 4, 1909. Col. Rinder Sparrow in *The Love of Four Colonels* at the Shubert, January, 1953

Joseph COTTEN. Petersburg, Va., May 15, 1905. Understudy and assistant stage manager for David Belasco's last two productions at the Belasco Theater, 1929

Paddy CROFT. Worthing, Sussex, England. Miss McKay in *The Prime of Miss Jean Brodie* at the Helen Hayes, 1968

Hume CRONYN. London, Ontario, July 18, 1911. The Janitor in *Hipper's Holiday* at the Maxine Elliott, 1934

John CULLUM. Knoxville, Tenn., March 2, 1930. A Citizen, a Cobbler, and a Servant in *Julius Caesar* at the Shakespearewrights, Oct. 23, 1957

Constance CUMMINGS. Seattle, May 15, 1910. In the chorus of *Treasure Girl* at the Music Box, April, 1928.

Jim DALE. (né Smith) Rothwell, England, Aug. 15, 1935. Petruchio in *Taming of the Shrew* and *Scapino* (for which he wrote the music and co-directed) at the Brooklyn Academy, March, 1974

Blythe DANNER. Philadelphia, The Girl in *The Infantry* at the 81st Street Theater, Nov. 14, 1966

Bette DAVIS. (née Ruth Elizabeth) Lowell, Mass., April 5, 1908. Floy Jennings in *The Earth Between* at the Provincetown Playhouse, March 5, 1929

Ossie DAVIS. Cogdell, Ga., 1917. In *Joy Exceeding Glory* with the Rose McClendon Players in Harlem, 1941

Sammy DAVIS, Jr. New York City, Dec. 8, 1925. Charley Welch in *Mr. Wonderful* at the Broadway, March, 1964

Ruby DEE. (née Ruby Ann Wallace) Cleveland, Oct. 27, 1923. A Native in the drama *South Pacific* at the Cort, Dec. 29, 1943

Gabe DELL. (né del Vecchio) Barbados, B.W.I., Oct. 7, 1923. Ring Foy (a child part) in *The Good Earth* at the Guild, Oct. 17, 1923

Sandy DENNIS. Hastings, Neb., April 27, 1937. Millicent Bishop in *Face of a Hero* at the Ethel Barrymore, November, 1961

Colleen DEWHURST. Montreal, June 3, 1926. One of the neighbors in *Desire Under the Elms* at the ANTA, January, 1952.

Bob DISHY. In the review *Chic* at the Orpheum.

Roy DOTRICE. Buernsey, Channel Islands, May 26, 1925. *Brief Lives* at the Golden, December, 1967.

Melvyn DOUGLAS. Macon, Georgia, April 5, 1901. Ace Wilfong in *A Free Soul* at the Playhouse, Jan. 12, 1928

Stephen DOUGLASS. (né Fitch) Mount Vernon, Ohio, Sept. 27, 1921. Billy Bigelow in *Carousel* at the Majestic, May, 1947

Alfred DRAKE. (né Capurro) New York City, Oct. 7, 1914. In chorus of *The Mikado* at the Adelphi, July 15, 1935

Keir DULLEA. Cleveland, N.J., May 30, 1936. Timmie Redwine in *Season of Choice* at the Barbazon-Plaza, April 13, 1959

Faye DUNAWAY. Tallahassee, Fla., Jan. 14, 1941. Margaret More in *A Man for all Seasons* at the ANTA (Washington Square), September, 1962

Sandy DUNCAN. Henderson, Texas, Feb. 20, 1946. Zaneeta Shinn in *The Music Man* at City Center, June 16, 1965

Mildred DUNNOCK. Baltimore, Jan. 25, 1900. Miss Pinty in *Life Begins* at the Selwyn, March 28, 1932

Nancy DUSSAULT. Pensacola, Fla., June 30, 1936. In the revue *Diversions* at the Downtown, Nov. 7, 1958

Patricia ELLIOTT. Gunnison, Col., July 21, 1942. Regan in *King Lear* at the Vivian Beaumont, Nov. 7, 1968

Tom EWELL. Queensboro, Ky., April 29, 1909. Red in *They Shall Not Die* at the Royale, Feb. 21, 1934

Nanette FABRAY. (née Ruby Nanette Fabares) San Diego, Cal., Oct. 27, 1920. In the revue *Meet the People* at the Mansfield, Dec. 25, 1940

Mia FARROW. California, Feb. 9, 1946. Cecily Cardew in *The Importance of Being Earnest* at the Madison Avenue Playhouse, 1963

José FERRER. Santurce, Puerto Rico, Jan. 8, 1912. Second Policeman in *A Slight Case of Murder* at the 48th Street Theatre, Sept. 11, 1935

Betty FIELD. Boston, Feb. 8, 1918. A reporter in *Page Miss Glory* at the Mansfield, Nov. 27, 1935

Frank FINLAY. Franworth, England, Aug. 6, 1926. Percy Elliott in *Epitaph for George Dillon* at the Golden, November, 1958

Albert FINNEY. Salford, Lancaster, England, May 9, 1936. Martin Luther in *Luther* at the St. James, September, 1963

Geraldine FITZGERALD. Dublin, Ireland, Nov. 24, 1914. Ellie Dunn in *Heartbreak House* at the Mercury, April 29, 1938

Nina FOCH. Leyden, Holland, April 20, 1924. Mary McKinley in *John Loves Mary* at the Booth, Feb. 4, 1947

Henry FONDA. Grand Island, Neb., May 16, 1905. Walk-on in *The Game of Life and Death* at the Guild, Nov. 25, 1929.

Jane FONDA. New York City, Dec. 21, 1937. Toni Newton in *There Was a Little Girl* at the Music Box, February, 1960

Lynn FONTANNE. Woodford, England, Dec. 6, 1892. Harriet Budgeon in *Mr. Preedy and the Countess* at Nazimova's 39th Street Theatre, Nov. 7, 1910

Henderson FORSYTHE. Macon, Miss., Sept. 11, 1917. Mr. Hubble in *The Cellar and the Well* (which he also directed) at the ANTA, Dec. 10, 1950

John FORSYTHE. (né John Lincoln Freund) Carney's Point, N.J., Jan. 29, 1918. Private Cootes in *Vickie* at the Plymouth, Sept. 22, 1942

Arlene FRANCIS. (née Arlene Kazanajian) Boston, Oct. 20, 1908. Anne in *One Good Year* at the Fulton, February, 1936

Martin GABEL. Philadelphia, June 19, 1912. Emmett in *Man Bites Dog* at the Fulton, December, 1934

Vincent GARDENIA. (né Scognamiglio) Naples, June 7, 1922. At the age of five he appeared as the Shoe Shine Boy in *Shoe Shine* at the Fifth Avenue Theatre, Brooklyn

Betty GARRETT. St. Joseph, Mo., May 23, 1919. *Danton's Death* at the Mercury, November, 1938

Ben GAZZARA. New York City, Aug. 28, 1930. Jocko De Paris in *End as a Man* at the Theatre De Lys, Sept. 15, 1953

Alice GHOSTLEY. Eve, Mo., Aug. 14, 1926. *New Faces of 1952* at the Royale, May, 1952

Sir John GIELGUD. London, April 14, 1904. Grand Duke Alexander in *The Patriot* at the Majestic, Jan. 19, 1928

Jack GILFORD. (né Jacob Gellman) New York City. Revue with Elsie Janis at the Music Box, January, 1939

Anita GILLETTE. (née Luebben) Baltimore, Aug. 16, 1936. Thelma in *Gypsy* at the Broadway, 1959

Hermione GINGOLD. London, Dec. 9, 1897. In the revue *John Murray Anderson's Almanac*, December, 1953

Lillian GISH. Springfield, Ohio, October, 1893. Danced in one of Sarah Bernhardt's productions at the Republic, Jan. 8, 1913

Ruth GORDON. Wollaston, Mass. Oct. 30, 1896. Nibs in *Peter Pan* at the Empire, Dec. 21, 1915

Cliff GORMAN. New York City. Peter Boyle in *Hogan's Goat* at the American Place, Nov. 11, 1965

Elliott GOULD. (né Goldstein) Brooklyn, Aug. 29, 1938. In the chorus of *Rumple* at the Alvin, November, 1957

Rubert GOULET. Lawrence, Mass. Nov. 26, 1933. Lancelot in *Camelot*, Dec. 3, 1960

Ronny GRAHAM. Philadelphia, Aug. 26, 1919. In the revue *New Faces of 1952* at the Royale, May 16, 1952

Dolores GRAY. Chicago, June 7, 1924. In *Seven Lively Arts* at the Ziegfeld, Dec. 7, 1944

Joel GREY. (né Katz) Cleveland, April 11, 1932. In *The Littlest Revue* at the Phoenix, May 22, 1956

Hugh GRIFFITH. Marian Glas, Anglesey, North Wales, May 30, 1912. In *Legend of Lovers* at the Plymouth, Dec. 26, 1951

Tammy GRIMES. Lynn, Mass., Jan. 30, 1932. Replaced Kim Stanley in *Bus Stop* at the Music Box, 1955

George GRIZZARD. Roanoke Rapids, N.C. April 1, 1928. Hank Griffin in *The Desperate*

Hours at the Ethel Barrymore, February, 1955

Charles GRODIN. Pittsburgh, April 21, 1935. Robert Pickett in *Tchin-Tchin* at the Ambassador, September, 1964

Sir Alec GUINNESS. London, April 2, 1914. On leave from the Royal Navy, as Flight-Lieut. Graham in *Flare Path* at the Henry Miller, December, 1942

Fred GWYNNE. New York City, July 10, 1926. Stinker in *Mrs. McThing* at New York City Center, Feb. 20, 1952

Uta HAGEN. Gottingen, Germany, June 12, 1919. Nina in *The Seagull* at the Shubert, March 28, 1938

Margaret HAMILTON. Cleveland, Sept. 12, 1902. Helen Hallam in *Another Language* at the Booth, April, 1932

Barbara HARRIS. (née Markowitz) Evanston, Ill., 1937. In *From the Second City* at the Royale, Sept. 16, 1971

Julie HARRIS. Grosse Pointe Park, Mich., Dec. 2, 1925. Atlanta in *It's a Gift* at the Playhouse, March, 1945

Rosemary HARRIS. Ashby, England, Sept. 19, 1930. Mabel in *The Climate of Eden* at the Martin Beck, November, 1952

Rex HARRISON. Luyton, England, March 5, 1908. Tubbs Barrow in *Sweet Aloes* at the Booth, March 2, 1936

Helen HAYES. Washington, D.C., Oct. 10, 1900. Little Mimi in *Old Dutch* at the Herald Square, Nov. 22, 1909

Eileen HECKART. Columbus, Ohio, March 29, 1919. In *Tinker's Dam* at the Blackfriars Guild, 1943

Florence HENDERSON. Dale, Ind., Feb. 14, 1914. New Girl in *Wish You Were Here* at the Imperial, June, 1952

Katharine HEPBURN. Hartford, Conn., Nov. 9, 1909. A hostess in *Night Hostess* (under the name Katharine Burns) at the Martin Beck, Sept. 12, 1928

Eileen HERLIE. Glasgow, Scotland, March 8, 1920. Mrs. Molloy in *The Matchmaker* at the Royale, December, 1955

Charlton HESTON. Evanston, Ill., Oct. 6, 1922. Proculeius in *Antony and Cleopatra* (with Katharine Cornell) at the Cort, January, 1949

Arthur HILL. Melfort, Saskachewan, Canada, Aug. 1, 1922. Cornelius Hackl in *The Matchmaker* at the Royale, December, 1955

Dame Wendy HILLER. Bramhall, Cheshire, England, Aug. 15, 1912. Sally in *Love on the Dole* at the Shubert, February, 1936

Pat HINGLE. Denver, Col, July 19, 1923. Herbert Kolbe in *End as a Man* at the Theatre De Lys, September, 1953

Dustin HOFFMAN. Los Angeles, Aug. 8, 1937. The Young Man in *Yes Is for a Very Young Man* at Sarah Lawrence College, 1960

Hal HOLBROOK. Cleveland, Feb. 17, 1925. In his one-man show, *Mark Twain Tonight!*, at the Purple Onion, February, 1955

Geoffrey HOLDER. Port-of-Spain, Trinidad, Aug. 1, 1930. The Champion and Baron Samedi in *House of Flowers* at the Alvin, Dec. 30, 1954

Celeste HOLM. New York City, April 29, 1919. Lady Mary in *Gloriana* at the Little Theatre, Nov. 25, 1938

Robert HOOKS. Washington, D.C., April 18, 1937. Dewey Chipley in *Tiger Tiger Burning Bright* at the Booth, Dec. 22, 1962

Anthony HOPKINS. Port Talbot, South Wales, Dec. 31, 1937. Petruchio in *The Taming of the Shrew* at the Plymouth, July, 1972

Ken HOWARD. El Centro, Cal., March 28, 1944. Karl Kubelik in *Promises, Promises* at the Shubert, December, 1968

Sally Ann HOWES. St. John's Wood, London, Eliza in *My Fair Lady* at the Mark Hellinger, February, 1958

Bernard HUGHES. Bedford Hills, N.Y., July 16, 1915. The Son in *Please, Mrs. Garibaldi* at the Belmont, March 16, 1936

Kim HUNTER (née Janet Cole) Detroit, Nov. 12, 1922. Stella Kowalski in *A Streetcar Named Desire* at the Ethel Barrymore, Dec. 3, 1947

Wilfred HYDE-WHITE, Bourton-on-the-Water, Glos, England, May 12, 1903. Sir Alec Dunne in *Under the Counter* at the Shubert, Oct. 3, 1947

Earle HYMAN. Rocky Mount, N.C., Oct. 11, 1926. The Diaperman in *Three's a Family* at the American Negro Theatre, 1943

Anne JACKSON. Allegheney, Pa., Sept. 3, 1926. A guest in *The Cherry Orchard* at the City Center, Jan. 1, 1945

Glenda JACKSON. Birkenhead, England, May 9, 1936. Charlotte Corday in *Marat/Sade* at the Martin Beck, December, 1965

Derek JACOBI. London, Oct. 33, 1938. The lead in *The Suicide* at the ANTA, October 1980

Lou JACOBI. Toronto, Dec. 28, 1913. Mr. Van Daan in *The Diary of Ann Frank* at the Cort, Oct. 5, 1955

Salome JENS. Milwaukee, Wis., May 8, 1935. Miss Ferguson in *Sixth Finger in a Five Finger Glove* at the Longacre, Oct. 8, 1956

Van JOHNSON. Newport, R.I., Aug. 25, 1916. A chorus boy in *New Faces of 1936* at the Vanderbilt, May 19, 1936

Glynis JOHNS. Pretoria, South Africa, Oct. 5, 1923. Title role in *Gertie* at the Plymouth, Jan. 30, 1952

James Earl JONES. Arkabutla, Miss., Jan. 17, 1931. Sgt. Blunt in *Wedding in Japan* at the Graystone Hotel, 1957

Raul JULIA. San Juan, Puerto Rico, March 9, 1940. Astolfo in *La Vida Es Sueno* at the Astor Place Playhouse, March 17, 1964

Kurt KASZNAR. (né Serwischer) Vienna, Austria, Aug. 13, 1913. Seven parts in *The Eternal House* at the 44th St. Theatre, 1931

Stacy KEACH. Savannah, Ga., June 2, 1941. Marcellus and the First Player in *Hamlet* at the Delacorte, June, 1964

Howard KEEL. Gillespie, Ill., April 13, 1919. Succeeded John Raitt as Billy Bigelow in *Carousel* at the St. James, 1946

Ruby KEELER, Halifax, Nova Scotia, Canada, Aug. 25, 1909. A chorus girl in *The Rise of Rosie O'Reilly* at the Liberty Theatre, Dec. 23, 1923

Arthur KENNEDY. Worcester, Mass., Feb. 17, 1914. In *Merrily We Roll Along* at the Music Box, September, 1934

Deborah KERR. Helensburgh, Scotland, Sept. 30, 1921. Laura Reynolds in *Tea and Sympathy* at the Ethel Barrymore, Sept. 30, 1953

Larry KERT. (né Frederick Lawrence) Los Angeles, Dec. 5, 1930. In cabaret group, Bill Norvas and the Upstarts, at the Roxy, 1950

Richard KILEY, Chicago, March 31, 1922. Poseidon in *The Trojan Women* at the Equity Library Theatre, 1947

Lisa KIRK. Brownsville, Pa., Sept. 18, 1925. Vickie in *Good Night, Ladies* at the Royale, Jan. 17, 1945

Sally KIRKLAND. New York City, Oct. 31, 1944. An understudy in *Step on a Crack* at the Ethel Barrymore, 1962

Eartha KITT. North, S.C. Jan. 26, 1930. A member of Katherine Dunham's dance troup in *Blue Holiday* at the Belasco, 1945

Jack KLUGMAN. Philadelphia, April 27, 1922. In the Equity Library Theatre production of *Stevedore,* Feb. 18, 1949

Frank LANGELLA. New Jersey, 1940. Michel in *The Immoralist* at the Bouwerie Lane, Nov. 7, 1963

Angela LANSBURY. London, England, Oct. 16, 1925. Marcelle in *Hotel Paradiso* at the Henry Miller, April 11, 1957

Linda LAVIN. Portland, Maine, Oct. 15, 1937. Izzy in the revival of *Oh Kay!* at the East 74th Street Theatre, April 16, 1960

Carol LAWRENCE. Melrose Park, Ill., Sept. 5, 1935. In *New Faces of 1952* at the Royale, May 16, 1952

Eva LE GALLIENNE. London, Jan. 11, 1899. Rose in *Mrs. Boltay's Daughters* at the Comedy Theatre, Oct. 26, 1915

Ron LEIBMAN. New York City, Oct. 11, 1937. Orpheus in *Legend of Lovers* at the 41st Street Theatre, Oct. 27, 1959

Margaret LEIGHTON. Barnt Green, Worcestershire, England, Feb. 26, 1922. Lady Percy in *Henry IV, Part I,* May 6, 1946

Rosetta LENOIRE. (née Burton) New York City, Aug. 9, 1911. Inez Cabral in *I've Got Sixpence* at the Ethel Barrymore, Dec. 2, 1952

Hal LINDEN. (née Harold Lipshitz) New York City, March 20, 1931. Replaced Sydney Chaplin in *Bells Are Ringing,* July 1958

Cleavon LITTLE. Chickasha, Okla., June 1, 1939. In *Macbeth* at the Mobile Theater, June 28, 1966

Dorothy LOUDON. Boston, Sept. 17, 1933. Wilma Risqué in *Nowhere to Go But Up* at the Winter Garden, Nov. 10, 1962

Laurence LUCKINBILL. Fort Smith, Ark., Nov. 21, 1934. The Old Shepherd in *Oedipus Rex* at the Carnegie Playhouse, April 29, 1959

Kevin McCARTHY. Seattle, Feb. 15, 1914. Jasp in *Abe Lincoln in Illinois* at the Plymouth, Oct. 15, 1938

Alec McCOWEN. Tunbridge Wells, England, May 26, 1925. The Messenger in *Antony and Cleopatra* at the Ziegfeld, Dec. 20, 1951

Roddy McDOWALL (née Roderick Andrew) London, Sept. 17, 1928. Bentley Summerhayes in *Misalliance* at the City Center, March, 1953

Dorothy McGUIRE. Omaha, Neb., June 14, 1918. Understudy in *Stop-Over* at the Lyceum, January, 1938

Aline MacHAHON. McKeesport, Pa., May 3, 1899. Laura Huxtable in *The Madrass House* at the Neighborhood Playhouse, Oct. 29, 1921

Donna, McKECHNIE. Detroit, November, 1940. A dancer in *How to Succeed in Business Without Really Trying* at the 46th Street Theatre, Oct. 14, 1961

Ian McKELLEN. Burnley, England, Leonidik in *The Promise* at the Henry Miller, November, 1967

Siobhan McKENNA. Belfast, Northern Ireland, May 24, 1923. Miss Madrigal in *The Chalk Garden* at the Ethel Barrymore, Oct. 26, 1955

Patrick MAGEE. Armagh, Northern Ireland. De Sade in *Marat/Sade* at the Martin Beck, December, 1965

Nancy MARCHAND. Buffalo, N.Y., June 18, 1928. Hostess of the Tavern in *The Taming of the Shrew* at the City Center, April, 1951

Hugh MARLOWE. (né Hugh Herbert Hipple) Philadelphia, Jan. 20, 1911. Wayne Kincaid in *The Land Is Bright* at the Music Box, October, 1941

E. G. MARSHALL. Owatonna, Minn., June 18, 1910. Henry Onstott in *Prologue to Glory* at the Ritz, Sept. 19, 1938

Mary MARTIN. Weatherford, Texas, Dec. 1, 1913. Dolly Winslow in *Leave It to Me* at the Imperial. Nov. 9, 1938

Walter MATTHAU. (né Matthow) New York City, Oct. 1, 1920. Sadovsky in *The Aristocrats* at the President, 1946

Elaine MAY. (née Elaine Berlin) Philadelphia, April 21, 1932. *An Evening with Mike Nichols and Elaine May* at the Golden, Oct. 8, 1960

Kay MEDFORD. (née Regan) New York City, Sept. 14, 1920. Cherry in *Paint Your Wagon* at the Shubert, November, 1951

Ralph MEEKER. (né Rathgeber) Minneapolis, Nov. 21, 1920. Chuck in *Strange Fruit* at the Royale, Nov. 29, 1945

Burgess MEREDITH. Cleveland, Nov. 16, 1908. Walk-ons in Civic Repertory Theatre Company productions, December, 1929

Ethel MERMAN. (née Zimmerman) Astoria, N.Y. Jan. 16, 1909. With Clayton, Jackson, and Durante at the Palace, 1928

Ann MILLER. (née Lucy Ann Collier) Houston, Texas, April 12, 1919. A dancer in *George White's Scandals* at the Alvin, August, 1939

Jason MILLER. Long Island City, N.Y., April 22, 1939. Pip in *Pequod* at the Mercury Theatre, June 29, 1969

Jonathan MILLER. London, England, July 21, 1934. *Beyond the Fringe* at the Golden, October, 1962

Jan MINER. Boston, Oct. 15, 1917. In *Obbligato* at the Theatre Marquee, Feb. 18, 1958

Liza MINNELLI. Los Angeles, March 12, 1946. Ethel Hofflinger in *Best Foot Forward* at Stage 73, April 2, 1963

Dudley MOORE. London, April 18, 1935. *Beyond the Fringe* at the Golden, October, 1962

Rita MORENO (née Rosita Dolores Alverio) Humancao, Puerto Rico, Dec. 11, 1931. Angela in *Skydrift* at the Belasco, Nov. 13, 1945

Michael MORIARTY. Detroit, April 5, 1941. Octavius Caesar in *Antony and Cleopatra* at the Delacorte, June 13, 1963

Robert MORLEY. Semley, Wilts, England, May 26, 1908. In the title role in *Oscar Wilde* at the Fulton, Oct. 10, 1938

Robert MORSE. Newton, Mass., May 18, 1931. Barnaby Tucker in *The Matchmaker* at the Royale, Dec. 5, 1955

Anthony NEWLEY. Hackney, London, Sept. 24, 1931. In the revue *Cranks* at the Bijou, November, 1956

Phyllis NEWMAN. Jersey City. N.J., March 19, 1935. Sarah in *Wish You Were Here* at the Imperial, June 25, 1953

Mike NICHOLS. Berlin, Germany, Nov. 6, 1951. *An Evening with Mike Nichols and Elaine May* at the Golden, October, 1960

Carrie NYE. Inez in *A Second String* at the Eugene O'Neill, April 13, 1960

Russell NYPE. Zion, Ill., April 26, 1924. Leo Hubbard in *Regina* at the 46th Street Theatre, Oct. 31, 1949

Kevin O'CONNOR. Honolulu, May 7, 1938. Harry in *Up to Thursday* at the Cherry Lane, Feb. 10, 1965

Sir Laurence OLIVIER. Dorking, England, May 22, 1907. Hugh Bromilow in *Murder on the Second Floor* at the Eltinge Theatre

Patrick O'NEAL. Ocala, Fla., Sept. 26, 1927. Took over the role of Arthur Turner in *Oh, Men! Oh, Women!* at the Henry Miller, 1954

Jerry ORBACH. Bronx, New York, Oct. 20, 1935. The Streetsinger and Mack the Knife in *Threepenny Opera* at the Theatre De Lys, Sept. 20, 1955

Maureen O'SULLIVAN. Roscommon, Ireland, March 17, 1917. Edith Lambert in *Never Too Late* at the Playhouse, November, 1962

Al PACINO. New York City, April 25, 1940. Murps in *The Indian Wants the Bronx* at Astor Place, January, 1968

Geraldine PAGE. Kirksville, Mo., Nov. 22, 1924. The Sophomore in *Seven Mirrors* at the Blackfriars Guild, Oct. 25, 1945

Estelle PARSONS. Lynn, Mass., Nov. 20, 1927. The Girl Reporter in *Happy Hunting* at the Majestic on Dec. 6, 1956

Anthony PERKINS. New York City, April 4, 1932. Took over as Tom Lee in *Tea and Sympathy* at the Ethel Barrymore, June 1954

Bernadette PETERS. Ozone Park, L.I., N.Y., Feb. 28, 1948. Tessie in *The Most Happy Fella* at the City Center, Feb. 10, 1959

Molly PICON. New York City, June 1, 1898. In *Yankele* at Kessler's Theatre, 1923

Alice PLAYTEN (née Plotkin) New York City, Aug. 28, 1947. Baby Louise in *Gypsy* at the Broadway, May, 1959

Joan PLOWRIGHT. Bigg, England, Oct. 28, 1929. The Old Woman in *The Chairs* and the pupil in *The Lesson* (double bill) at the Phoenix, January, 1958

Christopher PLUMMER. Toronto, Dec. 13, 1927. George Phillips in *The Starcross Story* at the Royale, January, 1954

Sidney POITIER. Miami, Feb. 20, 1924. In *Days of Our Youth* with the American Negro Theatre, 1945

Tom POSTEN. Columbus, Ohio, Oct. 17, 1921. Took over a part in *Cyrano de Bergerac* at the Alvin, 1947

Robert PRESTON. (né Meservey) Newton Highlands, Mass., June 8, 1918. Oscar Jaffe in *20th Century* at the Fulton, 1951

Vincent PRICE. St. Louis, Mo., May 27, 1911. Prince Albert in *Victoria Regina,* October, 1955

William PRINCE. Nichols, N.Y., Jan. 26, 1913. Walk-on in *The Eternal Road* at the Manhattan Opera House, 1937

Anthony QUAYLE. Ainsdale, Lancashire, England, Sept. 7, 1913. Mr. Harcourt in *The Country Wife,* December, 1936

Anthony QUINN. Chihuahua, Mexico, April 21, 1915. Stephen S. Christopher in *The Gentleman from Athens* at the Manfield on Dec. 9, 1947

Ellis RABB. Memphis, Tenn., June 20, 1930. Starveling in *A Midsummer Night's Dream* at the Jan Hus House on Jan. 13, 1956

Charlotte RAE. (née Lubotsky) Milwaukee, April 22, 1926. Tirsa Shanahan in *Three Wishes for Jamie* at the Mark Hellinger, March 21, 1952

John RAITT. Santa Ana, Cal., Jan. 19, 1917. Billy Bigelow in *Carousel* at the Majestic, April 19, 1945

Tony RANDALL. Tulsa, Okla., Feb. 26, 1920. The Brother in *The Circle of Chalk* at the New School, 1941

Lester RAWLINS. (né Rosenberg) Sharon, Pa., Sept. 24, 1924. Lodovico in *Othello* at the City Center, Sept. 8, 1955

Lynn REDGRAVE. London, March 8, 1943. Carol Melkett in *Black Comedy* at the Ethel Barrymore, February, 1967

Michael REDGRAVE. Bristol, England, March 20, 1908. Title role in *Macbeth* at the National Theatre, March 31, 1948

Venessa REDGRAVE. London, Jan. 30, 1937. Ellida in *The Lady from the Sea* at Circle in the Square, March, 1976

Kate REID. London, Nov. 4, 1930. Martha (matinees only) in *Who's Afraid of Virginia Wolf?* at the Billy Rose, 1965

Charles Nelson REILLY. New York City, Jan. 13, 1931. In the Equity Library production of *Best Foot Forward* at Lenox Hill Playhouse, Feb. 22, 1956

Clive REVILL. Wellington, New Zealand, April 18, 1930. Bob Le Hotu in *Irma La Douce* at the Plymouth, September, 1960

Sir Ralph RICHARDSON. Cheltenham, Gloucestershire, England, Dec. 19, 1902. As Chorus and Mercutio in *Romeo and Juliet* at the Martin Beck on Dec. 23, 1935

Diana RIGG. Doncaster, Yorks, England, July 20, 1938. Cordelia in *King Lear* at the New York State Theatre, May, 1964

Chita RIVERA. (née Concita del Rivero) Washington, D.C., Jan. 23, 1933. Dancer in *Call Me Madam* at the Imperial, 1952

Jason ROBARDS, Jr. Chicago, July 22, 1922. The rear end of the Cow in *Jack and the Beanstalk* at the Children's World Theatre, October, 1947

Tony ROBERTS. New York City, Oct. 22, 1939. Air Cadet in *Something About a Soldier* at the Ambassador, January, 1962

Ginger ROGERS. (née Virginia Katherine McNath) Independence, Mo., July 16, 1911. Babs Green in *Top Speed* at the Alvin, October, 1930

George ROSE. Bicester, England, Feb. 19, 1920. Peto in *Henry IV, Part I,* at the Century, May 6, 1946

Patricia ROUTLEDGE. Birkenhead, Cheshire, England, Feb. 17, 1929. Violet, Nell, and Rover in *How's the World Treating You?* at the Music Box, October, 1966

Paul SCOFIELD. Hurstpierpoint, England, Jan. 21, 1922. Thomas More in *A Man for All Seasons* at the ANTA Theatre, November, 1961

George C. SCOTT. Wise, Va., Oct. 18, 1927. Richard, Duke of Gloucester, in *Richard III* at the Heckscher, November, 1957

Martha SCOTT. Jamesport, Mo., Sept. 22, 1914. Emily Webb in *Our Town* at the Henry Miller, Feb. 4, 1938

Marian SELDES. New York City, Aug. 23, 1928. Attendant in *Medea* at the National, Ocotber, 1947

William SHATNER. Montreal, Canada, March 22, 1931. Robert Lomax in *The World of Suzie Wong* at the Broadhurst, October, 1956

Martin SHEEN. (né Ramon Estevez) Dayton, Ohio, Aug. 3, 1940. Took over role of Ernie in *The Connection* at the Living Theatre, 1959

Carole SHELLEY. London, Aug. 16, 1939. Gwendolyn Pigeon in *The Odd Couple* at the Plymouth, March 6, 1955

Alexis SMITH. (née Gladys Smith) Penticton, Canada, June 8, 1921. Phyllis Stone in *Follies* at the Winter Garden, April 4, 1971

Maggie SMITH. Ilford, England. In revue *New Faces of 1956* at the Ethel Barrymore, June, 1956

Paul SORVINO. New York City, 1939. Patrolman in *Bajour* at the Shubert, Nov. 23, 1965

Kim STANLEY. (née Patricia Reid) Tularosa, N.M. Iris in *The Dog Beneath the Skin* at the Carnegie Recital Hall, December, 1948

Jean STAPLETON. (née Jeanne Murray) New York City, Jan. 19. 1923. Mrs. Watty in *The Corn Is Green* at the Equity Library Theatre, Feb. 4, 1948

Maureen STAPLETON. Troy, N.Y., June 21, 1925. Sarah Tansey in *The Playboy of the Western World* at the Booth, October, 1946

Frances STERNHAGEN. Washington, D.C., January 13, 1930. Miss T. Muse in *The Skin of Our Teeth* at the ANTA, August, 1955

James STEWART. Vinegar Hill, Pa., May 20, 1908. Constable Gano in *Carrie Nation* at the Biltmore, Oct. 20, 1932

Beatrice STRAIGHT. Old Westbury, L.I., N.Y., Aug. 2, 1918. One of the Spinning Girls in

Bitter Oleander at the Lyceum, Feb. 11, 1935

Barbra STREISAND. Brooklyn, April 24, 1942. Miss Marmelstein in *I Can Get It for You Wholesale* at the Shubert, March, 1962

Elaine STRITCH. Detroit, Feb. 2, 1926. A Tiger and a Cow in the New School children's show *Bambino,* April, 1944

Shepperd STRUDWICK. Hillsboro, N.C., Sept. 22, 1907. In a revival of *The Yellow Jacket* at the Charles Coburn Theatre, October, 1928

Jessica TANDY. London, June 7, 1909. Toni Rakonitz in *The Matriarch* at the Longacre, March, 1930

Joan TETZEL. New York City, June 21, 1921. Renie in *Lorelei* at the Longacre, Nov. 29, 1938

Rip TORN. (né Elmore Raul Torn) Telmpe, Texas, Feb. 6, 1931. Took over role of Brick in *Cat on a Hot Tin Roof* at the Morosco, June, 1956

Constance TOWERS. Whitefish, Mont., May 20, 1933. The title role in *Anya* at the Ziegfeld, Nov. 29, 1965

Dorothy TUTIN. London, April 8, 1930. In *The Hollow Crown* at the Henry Miller, January, 1963

Cicely TYSON. New York City. Understudied Eartha Kitt in *Jolly's Progress* at the Longacre, December, 1959

Peter USTINOV. London, April 16, 1921. The General in *Romanoff and Juliet* (which he wrote) at the Plymouth, October, 1957.

Brenda VACCARO. Brooklyn, Nov. 18, 1939. Gloria Gulock in *Everybody Loves Opal* at the Longacre, Oct. 11, 1961

Dick VAN PATTEN. Kew Gardens, L.I., N.Y., Dec. 9, 1928. The Child in *Tapestry in Grey* at the Shubert, December, 1935

Joyce VAN PATTEN. New York City, March 9, 1934. Took over a Mae Yearlin in *Love's Old Sweet Song* at the Plymouth, 1940

Gwen VERDON. Culver City, Calif., Jan. 13, 1925. Dancer in a revue, *Alive and Kicking,* at the Winter Garden, January, 1950

Ben VEREEN. Miami, Oct. 10, 1946. Took over a role in *The Prodigal Son* at the Greenwich Mews, October, 1965

Christopher WALKEN. Astoria, L.I., N.Y. Took over the role of David in *J.B.* at the ANTA, 1959

Nancy WALKER. (née Anna Myrtle Swoyer) Philadelphia, May 10, 1921. The Blind Date in *Best Foot Forward* at the Ethel Barrymore, October, 1941

Eli WALLACH. Brooklyn, Dec. 7, 1951. The Crew Chief in *Skydrift* at the Belasco, Nov. 8, 1945

Ray WALSTON. New Orleans, Nov. 2, 1917. An attendant in the Maurice Evans production of *Hamlet* at the Columbus Circle, December, 1945

Ruth WARRICK. St. Joseph, Mo., June 29, 1915. In *The Thorntons* at the Provincetown Playhouse, February, 1956

Sam WATERSTON. Cambridge, Mass., Nov. 15, 1940. Replacement for Jonathan in *Oh Dad, Poor Dad, Mama's Hung You in the Closet and I'm Feeling So Sad* at the Phoenix, 1962

David WAYNE. (né Wayne James McMeekan) Traverse City, Mich. Jan. 30, 1914. Walk-on in *Escape This Night* at the 44th Street Theatre, April, 1938

Fritz WEAVER. Pittsburgh, Jan. 19, 1926. Fainall in *The Way of the World* at the Pheonix, January, 1955

Jack WESTON. (né Morris Weinstein) Cleveland, Aug. 24, 1915. Michael Lindsey in *Season in the Sun* at the Cort, Sept. 28, 1950

James WHITMORE. White Plains, N.Y., Oct. 1, 1921. Sgt. Harold Evans in *Command Decision* at the Fulton, Oct. 1, 1947

Billy Dee WILLIAMS. New York City, April 6, 1937. The Page in *The Firebrand of Florence* at the Alvin, March 22, 1945

Emlyn WILLIAMS. Flintshire, Wales, Nov. 26, 1905. In *Pepys' Boy* at the Shubert, Nov. 9, 1927

John WILLIAMS. Chalfon St. Giles, Bucks, England, April 15, 1903. Clifford Hope in *The Fake* at the Hudson, Oct. 6, 1924

Nicol WILLIAMSON. Hamilton, Scotland, September, 1938. Bill Maitland In *Inadmissible Evidence* at the Belasco, December, 1965

Shelley WINTERS. (née Shirley Schrift) St. Louis, Mo., Aug. 18, 1922. Flora in *Night Before Christmas* at the Morosco, April, 1941

Norman WISDOM. London, Feb. 4, 1920. Will Mossop in *Walking Happy* at the Lunt-Fontanne, November, 1966

Joseph WISEMAN. Montreal, May 15, 1918. A Soldier in *Abe Lincoln in Illinois* at the Plymouth, Oct. 15, 1938

John WOOD. Derbyshire, England. Guildenstern in *Rosencrantz and Guildenstern Are Dead* at the Alvin, Oct. 18, 1967

Irene WORTH. Nebraska, June 23, 1916. Cecily Harden in *The Two Mrs. Carrolls* at the Booth, Aug. 3, 1943

Teresa WRIGHT. New York City, Oct. 27, 1918. Joined the cast of *Our Town* in small part and understudy to Dorothy McGuire as Emily, at the Henry Miller, October, 1938

AWARDS

ANTOINETTE PERRY AWARD

The Tony Award is the major award of the Broadway theatre. It was established in 1946 in honor of the late Antoinette Perry, head of the American Theater Wing during the war. The Tonys are presented by the League of New York Theaters and Producers under the authorization from the American Theater Wing. A decade ago, producer Alexander Cohen decided that the Broadway theatre would benefit from a national broadcast of the Tony Awards, which now takes place every June.

Best Play
1980–81 *Amadeus*, Peter Shaffer
1979–80 *Children of a Lesser God*, Mark Medoff
1978–79 *The Elephant Man*, Bernard Pomerance
1977–78 *Da*, Hugh Leonard
1976–77 *The Shadow Box*, Michael Cristofer
1975–76 *Travesties*, Tom Stoppard
1974–75 *Equus*, Peter Shaffer
1973–74 *The River Niger*, Joseph A. Walker
1972–73 *That Championship Season*, Jason Miller
1971–72 *Sticks and Bones*, David Rabe
1970–71 *Sleuth*, Anthony Shaffer
1969–70 *Borstal Boy*, Frank McMahon
1968–69 *The Great White Hope*, Howard Sackler
1967–68 *Rosencrantz and Guildenstern Are Dead*, Tom Stoppard
1966–67 *The Homecoming*, Harold Pinter
1965–66 *Marat/Sade*, Peter Weiss
1964–65 *The Subject Was Roses*, Frank Gilroy
1963–64 *Luther*, John Osborne
1962–63 *Who's Afraid of Virginia Woolf?* Edward Albee
1961–62 *A Man for All Seasons*, Robert Bolt
1960–61 *Becket*, Jean Anouilh
1959–60 *The Miracle Worker*, William Gibson
1958–59 *J.B.*, Archibald MacLeish
1957–58 *Sunrise at Campobello*, Dore Schary
1956–57 *Long Day's Journey into Night*, Eugene O'Neill
1955–56 *The Diary of Anne Frank*, Frances Goodrich and Albert Hackett
1954–55 *The Desperate Hours*, Joseph Hayes
1953–54 *The Teahouse of the August Moon*, John Patrick
1952–53 *The Crucible*, Arthur Miller
1951–52 *The Fourposter*, Jan de Hartog
1950–51 *The Rose Tattoo*, Tennessee Williams
1949–50 *The Cocktail Party*, T. S. Eliot

1948–49 *Death of a Salesman,* Arthur Miller
1947–48 *Mister Roberts,* Thomas Heggen and Joshua Logan
1946–47 No award

Best Musical
1980–81 *42nd Street*
1979–80 *Evita*
1978–79 *Sweeney Todd*
1977–78 *Ain't Misbehavin'*
1976–77 *Annie*
1975–76 *A Chorus Line*
1974–75 *The Wiz*
1973–74 *Raisin*
1972–73 *A Little Night Music*
1971–72 *Two Gentlemen of Verona*
1970–71 *Company*
1969–70 *Applause*
1968–69 *1776*
1967–68 *Hallelujah, Baby!*
1966–67 *Cabaret*
1965–66 *Man of La Mancha*
1964–65 *Fiddler on the Roof*
1963–64 *Hello, Dolly!*
1962–63 *A Funny Thing Happened on the Way to the Forum*
1961–62 *How to Succeed in Business Without Really Trying*
1960–61 *Bye, Bye Birdie*
1959–60 *Fiorello!*
1958–59 *Redhead*
1957–58 *The Music Man*
1956–57 *My Fair Lady*
1955–56 *Damn Yankees*
1954–55 *The Pajama Game*
1953–54 *Kismet*
1952–53 *Wonderful Town*
1951–52 *The King and I*
1950–51 *Guys and Dolls*
1949–50 *South Pacific*
1948–49 *Kiss Me Kate*
1947–48 No award
1946–47 No award

Best Actor—Play
1980–81 Ian McKellen, *Amadeus*
1979–80 John Rubenstein, *Children of a Lesser God*
1978–79 Tom Conti, *Whose Life Is It Anyway?*
1977–78 Barnard Hughes, *Da*
1976–77 Al Pacino, *The Basic Training of Pavlo Hummel*
1975–76 John Wood, *Travesties*
1974–75 John Kani and Winston Ntshona, *Sizwe Banzi Is Dead* and *The Island*
1973–74 Michael Moriarty, *Find Your Way Home*
1972–73 Alan Bates, *Butley*
1971–72 Cliff Gorman, *Lenny*
1970–71 Brian Bedford, *The School for Wives*
1969–70 Fritz Weaver, *Child's Play*
1968–69 James Earl Jones, *The Great White Hope*
1967–68 Martin Balsam, *You Know I Can't Hear You When the Water's Running*
1966–67 Paul Rogers, *The Homecoming*
1965–66 Hal Holbrook, *Mark Twain Tonight!*
1964–65 Walter Matthau, *The Odd Couple*
1963–64 Alec Guinness, *Dylan*

1962–63 Arthur Hill, *Who's Afraid of Virginia Woolf?*
1961–62 Paul Scofield, *A Man for All Seasons*
1960–61 Zero Mostel, *Rhinoceros*
1959–60 Melvyn Douglas, *The Best Man*
1958–59 Jason Robards, Jr., *The Disenchanted*
1957–58 Ralph Bellamy, *Sunrise at Campobello*
1956–58 Fredric March, *Long Day's Journey into Night*
1955–56 Paul Muni, *Inherit the Wind*
1954–55 Alfred Lunt, *Quadrille*
1953–54 David Wayne, *The Teahouse of the August Moon*
1952–53 Tom Ewell, *The Seven Year Itch*
1951–52 José Ferrer, *The Shrike*
1950–51 Claude Rains, *Darkness at Noon*
1949–50 Sidney Blackmer, *Come Back, Little Sheba*
1948–49 Rex Harrison, *Anne of the Thousand Days*
1947–48 (tie) Henry Fonda, *Mister Roberts*
              Paul Kelly, *Command Decision*
              Basil Rathbone, *The Heiress*
1946–47 (tie) *José Ferrer, Cyrano de Bergerac*
              Fredric March, *Years Ago*

Best Actress–Play
1980–81 Jane LaPotaire, *Piaf*
1979–80 Phyllis Frehlich, *Children of a Lesser God*
1978–79 (tie) Constance Cummings, *Wings*
              Carole Shelley, *The Elephant Man*
1977–78 Jessica Tandy, *The Gin Game*
1976–77 Julie Harris, *The Belle of Amherst*
1975–76 Irene Worth, *Sweet Bird of Youth*
1974–75 Ellen Burstyn, *Same Time, Next Year*
1973–74 Colleen Dewhurst, *A Moon for the Misbegotten*
1972–73 Julie Harris, *The Last of Mrs. Lincoln*
1971–72 Sada Thompson, *Twigs*
1970–71 Maureen Stapleton, *Gingerbread Lady*
1969–70 Tammy Grimes, *Private Lives*
1968–69 Julie Harris, *Forty Carats*
1967–68 Zoe Caldwell, *The Prime of Miss Jean Brodie*
1966–67 Beryl Reid, *The Killing of Sister George*
1965–66 Rosemary Harris, *The Lion in Winter*
1964–65 Irene Worth, *Tiny Alice*
1963–64 Sandy Dennis, *Any Wednesday*
1962–63 Uta Hagen, *Who's Afraid of Virginia Woolf?*
1961–62 Margaret Leighton, *The Night of the Iguana*
1960–61 Joan Plowright, *A Taste of Honey*
1959–60 Anne Bancroft, *The Miracle Worker*
1958–59 Gertrude Berg, *A Majority of One*
1957–58 Helen Hayes, *Time Remembered*
1956–57 Margaret Leighton, *Separate Tables*
1955–56 Julie Harris, *The Lark*
1954–55 Nancy Kelly, *The Bad Seed*
1953–54 Audrey Hepburn, *Ondine*
1952–53 Shirley Booth, *Time of the Cuckoo*
1951–52 Julie Harris, *I Am a Camera*
1950–51 Uta Hagen, *The Country Girl*
1949–50 Shirley Booth, *Come Back, Little Sheba*
1948–49 Martita Hunt, *The Madwoman of Chaillot*
1947–48 (tie) Judith Anderson, *Medea*
              Katharine Cornell, *Antony and Cleopatra*
              Jessica Tandy, *A Streetcar Named Desire*
1946–47 (tie) Ingrid Bergman, *Joan of Lorraine*
              Helen Hayes, *Happy Birthday*

Best Actor—Musical
1980–81 Kevin Kline, *The Pirates of Penzance*
1979–80 Jim Dale, *Barnum*
1978–79 Len Cariou, *Sweeney Todd*
1977–78 John Cullum, *On the Twentieth Century*
1976–77 Barry Bostwick, *The Robber Bridegroom*
1975–76 George Rose, *My Fair Lady*
1974–75 John Cullum, *Shenandoah*
1973–74 Christopher Plummer, *Cyrano*
1972–73 Ben Vereen, *Pippin*
1971–72 Phil Silvers, *A Funny Thing Happened on the Way to the Forum*
1970–71 Hal Linden, *The Rothschilds*
1969–70 Cleavon Little, *Purlie*
1968–69 Jerry Orbach, *Promises, Promises*
1967–68 Robert Goulet, *The Happy Time*
1966–67 Robert Preston, *I Do!, I Do!*
1965–66 Richard Kiley, *Man of La Mancha*
1964–65 Zero Mostel, *Fiddler on the Roof*
1963–64 Bert Lahr, *Foxy*
1962–63 Zero Mostel, *A Funny Thing Happened on the Way to the Forum*
1961–62 Robert Morse, *How to Succeed in Business Without Really Trying*
1960–61 Richard Burton, *Camelot*
1959–60 Jackie Gleason, *Take Me Along*
1958–59 Richard Kiley, *Redhead*
1957–58 Robert Preston, *The Music Man*
1956–57 Rex Harrison, *My Fair Lady*
1955–56 Ray Walston, *Damn Yankees*
1954–55 Walter Slezak, *Fanny*
1953–54 Alfred Drake, *Kismet*
1952–53 Thomas Mitchell, *Hazel Flagg*
1951–52 Phil Silvers, *Top Banana*
1950–51 Robert Alda, *Guys and Dolls*
1949–50 Ezio Pinza, *South Pacific*
1948–49 Ray Bolger, *Where's Charley?*
1947–48 Paul Hartman, *Angel in the Wings*
1946–47 No award

Best Actress—Musical
1980–81 Lauren Bacall, *Woman of the Year*
1979–80 Patti LuPone, *Evita*
1978–79 Angela Lansbury, *Sweeney Todd*
1977–78 Liza Minnelli, *The Act*
1976–77 Dorothy Loudon, *Annie*
1975–76 Donna McKechnie, *A Chorus Line*
1974–75 Angela Lansbury, *Gypsy*
1973–74 Virginia Capers, *Raisin*
1972–73 Glynis Johns, *A Little Night Music*
1971–72 Alexis Smith, *Follies*
1970–71 Helen Gallagher, *No, No Nanette*
1969–70 Lauren Bacall, *Applause*
1968–69 Angela Lansbury, *Dear World*
1967–68 (tie) Patricia Routledge, *Darling of the Day*
            Leslie Uggams, *Hallelujah, Baby!*
1966–67 Barbara Harris, *The Apple Tree*
1965–66 Angela Lansbury, *Mame*
1964–65 Liza Minnelli, *Flora, the Red Menace*
1963–64 Carol Channing, *Hello Dolly!*
1962–63 Vivien Leigh, *Tovarich*
1961–62 (tie) Anna Maria Alberghetti, *Carnival*
            Diahann Carroll, *No Strings*

1960–61 Elizabeth Seal, *Irma La Douce*
1959–60 Mary Martin, *The Sound of Music*
1958–59 Gwen Verdon, *Redhead*
1957–58 (tie) Thelma Ritter, *New Girl in Town*
            Gwen Verdon, *New Girl in Town*
1956–57 Judy Holliday, *Bells Are Ringing*
1955–56 Gwen Verdon, *Damn Yankees*
1954–55 Mary Martin, *Peter Pan*
1953–54 Dolores Gray, *Carnival in Flanders*
1952–53 Rosalind Russell, *Wonderful Town*
1951–52 Gertrude Lawrence, *The King and I*
1950–51 Ethel Merman, *Call Me Madam*
1949–50 Mary Martin, *South Pacific*
1948–49 Nanette Fabray, *Love Life*
1947–48 Grace Hartman, *Angel in the Wings*
1946–47 No award

Best Supporting Actor—Play
1980–81 Brian Backer, *The Floating Light Bulb*
1979–80 David Rounds, *Morning's at Seven*
1978–79 Michael Grough, *Bedroom Farce*
1977–78 Lester Rawlins, *Da*
1976–77 Jonathan Pryce, *Comedians*
1975–76 Edward Herrman, *Mrs. Warren's Profession*
1974–75 Frank Langella, *Seascape*
1973–74 Ed Flanders, *A Moon for the Misbegotten*
1972–73 John Lithgow, *The Changing Room*
1971–72 Vincent Gardenia, *The Prisoner of Second Avenue*
1970–71 Paul Sand, *Story Theatre*
1969–70 Ken Howard, *Child's Play*
1968–69 Al Pacino, *Does a Tiger Wear a Necktie?*
1967–68 James Patterson, *The Brithday Party*
1966–67 Ian Holm, *The Homecoming*
1965–66 Patrick Magee, *Marat/Sade*
1964–65 Jack Albertson, *The Subject Was Roses*
1963–64 Hume Cronyn, *Hamlet*
1962–63 Alan Arkin, *Enter Laughing*
1961–62 Walter Matthau, *A Shot in the Dark*
1960–61 Martin Gabel, *Big Fish, Little Fish*
1959–60 Roddy McDowall, *The Fighting Cock*
1958–59 Charlie Ruggles, *The Pleasure of His Company*
1957–58 Henry Jones, *Sunrise at Campobello*
1956–57 Frank Conroy, *The Potting Shed*
1955–56 Ed Begley, *Inherit the Wind*
1954–55 Francis L. Sullivan, *Witness for the Prosecution*
1953–54 John Kerr, *Tea and Sympathy*
1952–53 John Williams, *Dial M for Murder*
1951–52 John Cromwell, *Point of No Return*
1950–51 Eli Wallach, *The Rose Tattoo*
1949–50 No award
1948–49 Arthur Kennedy, *Death of a Salesman*
1947–48 No award
1946–47 No award

Best Supporting Actress—Play
1980–81 Swoosie Kurtz, *Fifth of July*
1979–80 Dinah Manoff, *I Ought to Be in Pictures*
1978–79 Joan Hickson, *Bedroom Farce*
1977–78 Ann Wedgeworth, *Chapter Two*
1976–77 Tarzana Beverly, *For Colored Girls Who Have Considered Suicide/*
                     When the Rainbow is Enuf

1975–76 Shirley Knight, *Kennedy's Children*
1974–75 Rita Moreno, *The Ritz*
1973–74 Frances Sternhagen, *The Good Doctor*
1972–73 Leora Dana, *The Last of Mrs. Lincoln*
1971–72 Elizabeth Wilson, *Sticks and Bones*
1970–71 Rae Allen, *And Miss Reardon Drinks a Little*
1969–70 Blythe Danner, *Butterflies Are Free*
1968–69 Jane Alexander, *The Great White Hope*
1967–68 Zena Walker, *Joe Egg*
1966–67 Marian Seldes, *A Delicate Balance*
1965–66 Zoe Caldwell, *Slapstick Tragedy*
1964–65 Alice Ghostely, *The Sign in Sidney Brustein's Window*
1963–64 Barbara Loden, *After the Fall*
1962–63 Sandy Dennis, *A Thousand Clowns*
1961–62 Elizabeth Ashley, *Take Her, She's Mine*
1960–61 Colleen Dewhurst, *All the Way Home*
1959–60 Anne Revere, *Toys in the Attic*
1958–59 Julie Newmar, *The Marriage-Go-Round*
1957–58 Anne Bancroft, *Two for the Seesaw*
1956–57 Peggy Cass, *Auntie Mame*
1955–56 Una Merkel. *The Ponder Heart*
1954–55 Patricia Jessell, *Witness for the Prosecution*
1953–54 Jo Van Fleet, *The Trip to Bountiful*
1952–53 Beatrice Straight, *The Crucible*
1951–52 Marian Winters, *I Am a Camera*
1950–51 Maureen Stapleton, *The Rose Tattoo*
1949–50 No award
1948–49 Shirley Booth, *Goodbye, My Fancy*
1947–48 No award
1946–47 No award

Best Supporting Actor—Musical
1980–81 Hinton Battle, *Sophisticated Ladies*
1979–80 Mandy Patinkin, *Evita*
1978–79 Henderson Forsythe, *The Best Little Whorehouse in Texas*
1977–78 Kevin Kline, *On the Twentieth Century*
1976–77 Lenny Baker, *I Love My Wife*
1975–76 Sammy Williams, *A Chorus Line*
1974–75 Ted Ross, *The Wiz*
1973–74 Tommy Tune, *Seesaw*
1972–73 George S. Irving, *Irene*
1971–72 Larry Blyden, *A Funny Thing Happened on the Way to the Forum*
1970–71 Keene Curtis, *The Rothschilds*
1969–70 René Auberjonois, *Coco*
1968–69 Ronald Holgate, *1776*
1967–68 Hiram Sherman, *How Now, Dow Jones*
1966–67 Joel Grey, *Cabaret*
1965–66 Frankie Michaels, *Mame*
1964–65 Victor Spinetti, *Oh, What a Lovely War*
1963–64 Jack Cassidy, *She Loves Me*
1962–63 David Burns, *A Funny Thing Happened on the Way to the Forum*
1961–62 Charles Nelson Reilly, *How to Succeed in Business Without Really Trying*
1960–61 Dick Van Dyke, *Bye, Bye Birdie*
1959–60 Tom Bosley, *Fiorello!*
1958–59 (tie) Russell Nype, *Goldilocks*
           Cast, *La Plume de Ma Tante*
1957–58 David Burns, *The Music Man*
1956–57 Sydney Chaplin, *Bells Are Ringing*
1955–56 Russ Brown, *Damn Yankees*

1954–55 Cyril Ritchard, *Peter Pan*
1953–54 Harry Belafonte, *John Murray Anderson's Almanac*
1952–53 Hiram Sherman, *Two's Company*
1951–52 Yul Brynner, *The King and I*
1950–51 Russell Nype, *Call Me Madam*
1949–50 Myron McCormick, *South Pacific*
1948–49 No award
1947–48 No award
1946–47 No award

Best Supporting Actress—Musical
1980–81 Marilyn Cooper, *Woman of the Year*
1979–80 Priscilla Lopez, *A Day in Hollywood/A Night in the Ukraine*
1978–79 Carlin Glynn, *The Best Little Whorehouse in Texas*
1977–78 Nell Carter, *Ain't Misbehavin'*
1976–77 Dolores Hall, *Your Arms Too Short to Box with God*
1975–76 Kelly Bishop, *A Chorus Line*
1974–75 Dee Dee Bridgewater, *The Wiz*
1973–74 Janie Sell, *Over Here!*
1972–73 Patricia Elliott, *A Little Night Music*
1971–72 Linda Hopkins, *Inner City*
1970–71 Patsy Kelly, *No, No Nanette*
1969–70 Melba Moore, *Purlie*
1968–69 Marian Mercer, *Promises, Promises*
1967–68 Lillian Hayman, *Hallelujah, Baby!*
1966–67 Peg Murray, *Cabaret*
1965–66 Beatrice Arthur, *Mame*
1964–65 Maria Karnilova, *Fiddler on the Roof*
1963–64 Tessie O'Shea, *The Girl Who Came to Supper*
1962–63 Anna Quayle, *Stop the World—I Want to Get Off*
1961–62 Phyllis Newman, *Subways Are for Sleeping*
1960–61 Tammy Grimes, *The Unsinkable Molly Brown*
1959–60 Patricia Neway, *The Sound of Music*
1958–59 (tie) Pat Stanley, *Goldilocks*
                Cast, *La Plume de Ma Tante*
1957–58 Barbara Cook, *The Music Man*
1956–57 Edith Adams, *Li'l Abner*
1955–56 Lotte Lenya, *The Threepenny Opera*
1954–55 Carol Haney, *The Pajama Game*
1953–54 Gwen Verdon, *Can-Can*
1952–53 Sheila Bond, *Wish You Were Here*
1951–52 Helen Gallagher, *Pal Joey*
1950–51 Isabel Bigley, *Guys and Dolls*
1949–50 Juanita Hall, *South Pacific*
1948–49 No award
1947–48 No award
1946–47 No award

CLARENCE DERWENT AWARDS

The Clarence Derwent Awards, of which there are two, are given annually by Actors' Equity Association to the actor and actress considered the most promising newcomers on the New York theatre scene. Supporting performers from both Broadway and non-Broadway shows are eligible. The Derwent winners are selected by a committee of drama critics. Each recipient is given a $1,000 cash prize and an engraved crystal egg.

1981 Mia Dillon, *Crimes of the Heart*
      Robert Gunton, *How I Got That Story*
1980 Dianne Wiest, *The Art of Dining*
      Eric Peterson, *Billy Bishop Goes to War*

1979 Laurie Kennedy, *Man and Superman*
     Richard Cox, *Platinum*
1978 Margaret Hilton, *Molly*
     Morgan Freeman, *The Mighty Gents*
1977 Rose Gregorio, *The Shadow Box*
     Barry Preston, *Bubbling Brown Sugar*
1976 Nancy Snyder, *Knock, Knock*
     Peter Evans, *Streamers*
1975 Marybeth Hurt, *Love for Love*
     Reyno, *The First Breeze of Summer*
1974 Ann Reinking, *Over Here!*
     Thom Christopher, *Noel Coward in 2 Keys*
1973 Mari Gorman, *The Hot l Baltimore*
     Christopher Murney, *Tricks*
1972 Pamela Bellwood, *Butterflies Are Free*
     Richard Backus, *Promenade All*
1971 Katherine Helmond, *The House of Blue Leaves*
     James Woods, *Saved*
1970 Pamela Payton-Wright, *The Effect of Gamma Rays on Man-in-the-Moon Marigolds*
     Jeremiah Sullivan, *A Scent of Flower*
1969 Marlene Warfield, *The Great White Hope*
     Ron O'Neal, *No Place to Be Somebody*
1968 Catherine Burns, *The Prime of Miss Jean Brodie*
     David Birney, *Summertree*
1967 Reva Rose, *You're a Good Man, Charlie Brown*
     Austin Pendleton, *The Alchemist*
     Special Citation, Philip Bosco, *Hail Scrawdyke*
1966 Jean Hepple, *Sgt. Musgrave's Dance*
     Christopher Walken, *The Lion in Winter*
     Special Citation, Tom Ahearne, *Hogan's Goat*
1965 Elizabeth Hubbard, *The Physicist*
     Jaime Sanchez, *Conerico Was Here to Stay*
1964 Joyce Ebert, *The Trojan Women*
     Richard McMurray, *A Case of Libel*
1963 Jessica Walter, *Photo Finish*
     Gene Hackman, *Children from Their Games*
1962 Rebecca Darke, *Who'll Save the Plowboy?*
     Gene Wilder, *Complaisant Lover*
1961 Rosemary Murphy, *Period of Adjustment*
     Eric Christmas, *Little Moon of Alban*
1960 Rochelle Oliver, *Toys in the Attic*
     William Daniels, *The Zoo Story*
1959 David Hurst, *Look After Lulu*
     Lois Nettleton, *God & Kate Murphy*
1958 George C. Scott, *Richard III*
     Colin Wilcox, *The Day the Money Stopped*
1957 Ellis Rabb, *The Misanthrope*
     Joan Croydon, *The Potting Shed*
1956 Gerald Hiken, *Uncle Vanya*
     Frances Sternhagen, *The Admiral Bashville*
1955 Fritz Weaver, *The White Devil*
     Vivian Nathan, *Anastasia*
1954 David Lewis, *King of Hearts*
     Vilma Murer, *The Winner*
1953 David J. Stewart, *Camino Real*
     Jenny Egan, *The Crucible*
1952 Iggie Wolfington, *Mrs. McThing*
     Anne Meacham, *The Long Watch*
1951 Logan Ramsey, *High Ground*
     Frederic Warriner, *Getting Married*

Phyllis Love, *The Rose Tattoo*
1950 Douglas Watson, *Wisteria Trees*
Gloria Lane, *The Consul*
1949 Ray Watson, *Summer and Smoke*
Leonra Dana, *Madwoman of Chaillot*
1948 Lou Gilbert, *Hope Is a Thing with Feathers*
Catherine Ayers, *Moon of the Caribbean* and *Long Way from Home*
1947 Tom Ewell, *John Loves Mary*
Margaret Phillips, *Another Part of the Forest*
1946 Paul Douglas, *Born Yesterday*
Barbara Bel Geddes, *Deep Are the Roots*
1945 Frederick O'Neal, *Anna Lucasta*
Judy Holliday, *Kiss Them for Me*

DELIA AUSTRIAN MEDAL

The Drama League of New York awards this bronze medal annually to the outstanding actor or actress of the Broadway season. (Performers in one-man shows are not eligible.)

1981 Ian McKellen, *Amadeus*
1980 Roy Scheider, *Betrayal*
1979 Frank Langella, *Dracula*
1978 Frances Sternhagen, *On Golden Pond*
1977 Tom Courteney, *Otherwise Engaged*
1976 Eva Le Gallienne, *The Royal Family*
1975 John Wood, *Sherlock Holmes*
1974 Christopher Plummer, *The Good Doctor*
1973 Alan Bates, *Butley*
1972 Eileen Atkins, Claire Bloom, *Vivat! Vivat! Regina*
1971 Anthony Quayle, *Sleuth*
1970 James Stewart, *Harvey*
1969 Alec McCowen, *Hadrian the Seventh*
1968 Zoe Caldwell, *The Prime of Miss Jean Brodie*
1967 Rosemary Harris, *The Wild Duck*
1966 Richard Kiley, *Man of La Mancha*
1965 John Gielgud, *Tiny Alice*
1964 Alec Guinness, *Dylan*
1963 Charles Boyer, *Lord Pengo*
1962 Paul Scofield, *A Man for All Seasons*
1961 Hume Cronyn, *Big Fish, Little Fish*
1960 Jessica Tandy, *Five Finger Exercise*
1959 Cyril Ritchard, *The Pleasure of His Company*
1958 Ralph Bellamy, *Sunrise at Campobello*
1957 Eli Wallach, *Major Barbara*
1956 David Wayne, *The Ponder Heart*
1955 Viveca Lindfors, *Anastasia*
1954 Josephine Hull, *The Solid Gold Cadillac*
1953 Shirley Booth, *Time of the Cuckoo*
1952 Julie Harris, *I Am a Camera*
1951 Claude Rains, *Darkness at Noon*
1950 Grace George, *The Velvet Glove*
1949 Robert Morley, *Edward, My Son*
1948 Judith Anderson, *Medea*
1947 Ingrid Bergman, *Joan of Lorraine*
1946 Louis Calhern, *The Magnificent Yankee*
1945 Mady Christians, *I Remember Mama*
1944 Elisabeth Bergner, *The Two Mrs. Carrolls*
1943 Alfred Lunt and Lynn Fontanne, *The Pirate*
1942 Judith Evelyn, *Angel Street*
1941 Paul Lukas, *Watch on the Rhine*
1940 Paul Muni, *Key Largo*

1939 Raymond Massey, *Abe Lincoln in Illinois*
1938 Cedric Hardwicke, *Shadow and Substance*
1937 Maurice Evans, *Richard III*
1936 Helen Hayes, *Victoria Regina*
1935 Katharine Cornell, *Romeo and Juliet*

GEORGE JEAN NATHAN AWARD FOR DRAMATIC CRITICISM

The heads of the English departments of Cornell, Princeton, and Yale Universities choose one American who has written outstanding criticism in the past theatrical year. The award carries a $5,000 prize.

1979–80 Sean Mitchell, staff writer and drama critic, *Dallas Times-Herald*
1978–79 Jack Kroll, senior editor, drama and film critic, *Newsweek*
1977–78 Mel Gussow, drama critic, *The New York Times*
1976–77 Bernard Knox, Center for Hellenic Studies, Washington, D.C., for a review of *Agamemnon* published in *The New York Review of Books*
1975–76 Michael Goldman, professor of English, Princeton University, for *The Actor's Freedom: Toward a Theory of Drama*
1974–75 No award
1973–74 Albert Bermel, theatre critic, *The New Leader*
1972–73 Stanley Kauffmann, film and theatre critic, *The New Republic*
1971–72 Jay Carr, theatre and music critic, *The Detroit News*
1970–71 Richard Gilman, professor of playwriting and criticism, Yale University Drama School, for *Common and Uncommon Masks: Writings on Theatre 1961–1970*
1969–70 John Simon, drama critic, *Hudson Review* and *New York Magazine*
1968–69 John Lahr, drama critic, *Evergreen News* and *The Village Voice*
1967–68 Martin Gottfried, drama critic, *Women's Wear Daily,* for *A Theater Divided: The Postwar American Stage*
1966–67 Elizabeth Hardwick, advisory editor, *The New York Review of Books*
1965–66 Eric Bentley, professor of dramatic literature, Columbia University
1964–65 Gerald Weales, associate professor of English, University of Pennsylvania
1963–64 Elliot Norton, drama critic, *Boston Record American and Sunday Advertiser*
1962–63 Walter Kerr, drama critic, *The New York Herald Tribune,* for *The Theater in Spite of Itself*
1961–62 Robert Brustein, theatre critic, *The New Republic*
1960–61 Jerry Tallmer, drama critic, *The Village Voice*
1959–60 C. L. Barber, professor of English, Amherst College, for *Shakespeare's Festive Comedy*
1958–59 Harold Clurman, drama critic, *The Nation,* for *Lies like Truth*

NEW YORK DRAMA CRITICS CIRCLE AWARDS

In a season that presented Lillian Hellman's *The Children's Hour,* Robert E. Sherwood's *The Petrified Forest,* Maxwell Anderson's *Valley Forge,* and Clifford Odets's *Awake and Sing,* the 1935 Pulitzer Prize for Drama went to Zoe Akins's dramatization of Edith Wharton's *The Old Maid.* In reaction, the New York critics started an award of their own to honor the best productions of a play and musical during the past season. Most years, two plays are honored: If the best play is American, the second play is foreign, and vice versa.

1980–81
Play, *A Lesson From Aloes,* Athol Fugard
American play, *Crimes of the Heart,* Beth Henley
Special citations, *Lena Horne: The Lady and Her Music,* and the New York Shakespeare Festival production of *The Pirates of Penzance*
1979–80

Play, *Talley's Folly*
Foreign play, *Betrayal*
Musical, *Evita*
Special citation, *Peter Brook's Centre International de Creations Theatrales*
1978–79
Play, *The Elephant Man*
Musical, *Sweeney Todd*
1977–78
Play, *Da*

Musical, *Ain't Misbehavin'*
1976–77
Play, *Otherwise Engaged*
American play, *American Buffalo*
Musical, *Annie*
1975–76
Play, *Travesties*
American play, *Streamers*
Musical, *Pacific Overtures*
1974–75
Play, *Equus*
American play, *The Taking of Miss Janie*
Musical, *A Chorus Line*
1973–74
Play, *The Contractor*
American play, *Short Eyes*
Musical, *Candide*
1972–73
Play, *The Changing Room*
American play, *The Hot l Baltimore*
Musical, *A Little Night Music*
1971–72
Play, *That Championship Season*
Foreign play, *The Screens*
Musical, *Two Gentlemen of Verona*
Special citations, *Sticks and Bones* and *Old Times*
1970–71
Play, *Home*
American play, *The House of Blue Leaves*
Musical, *Follies*
1969–70
Play, *Borstal Boy*
American play, *The Effect of Gamma Rays on Man-in-the-Moon Marigolds*
1968–69 Play, *The Great White Hope*
Musical, *1776*
1967–68
Play, *Rosencrantz and Guildenstern Are Dead*
Musical, *Your Own Thing*
1966–67
Play, *The Homecoming*
Musical, *Cabaret*
1965–66
Play, *The Persecution and Assassination of Marat as Performed by the Inmates of the Asylum of Charenton Under the Direction of the Marquis de Sade*
Musical, *Man of La Mancha*
1964–65
Play, *The Subject Was Roses*
Musical, *Fiddler on the Roof*
1963–64
Play, *Luther*
Musical, *Hello, Dolly!*
Special citation, *The Trojan Women*
1962–63
Play, *Who's Afraid of Virginia Woolf?*
Special citation, *Beyond the Fringe*

1961–62
American play, *The Night of the Iguana*
Foreign play, *A Man for All Seasons*
Musical, *How to Succeed in Business Without Really Trying*
1960–61
American play, *All the Way Home*
Foreign play, *A Taste of Honey*
Musical, *Carnival*
1959–60
American play, *Toys in the Attic*
Foreign play, *Five Finger Exercise*
Musical, *Fiorello!*
1958–59
American play, *A Raisin in the Sun*
Foreign play, *The Visit*
Musical, *La Plume de Ma Tante*
1957–58
American play, *Look Homeward, Angel*
Foreign play, *Look Back in Anger*
Musical, *The Music Man*
1956–57
American play, *Long Day's Journey into Night*
Foreign play, *The Waltz of the Toreadors*
Musical, *The Most Happy Fella*
1955–56
American play, *The Diary of Anne Frank*
Foreign play, *Tiger at the Gates*
Musical, *My Fair Lady*
1954–55
American play, *Cat on a Hot Tin Roof*
Foreign play, *Witness for the Prosecution*
Musical, *The Saint of Bleecker Street*
1953–54
American play, *Teahouse of the August Moon*
Foreign play, *Ondine*
Musical, *The Golden Apple*
1952–53
American play, *Picnic*
Foreign play, *The Love of Four Colonels*
Musical, *Wonderful Town*
1951–52
American play, *I Am a Camera*
Foreign play, *Venus Observed*
Musical, *Pal Joey*
Special citation, *Don Juan in Hell*
1950–51
American play, *Darkness at Noon*
Foreign play, *The Lady's Not for Burning*
Musical, *Guys and Dolls*
1949–50
American play, *The Member of the Wedding*
Foreign play, *The Cocktail Party*
Musical, *The Consul*
1948–49
American play, *Death of a Salesman*
Foreign play, *The Madwoman of Chaillot*
Musical, *South Pacific*

1947–48
American play, *A Streetcar Named Desire*
Foreign play, *The Winslow Boy*
1946–47
American play, *All My Sons*
Foreign play, *No Exit*
Musical, *Brigadoon*
1945–46
Musical, *Carousel*
1944–45
American play, *The Glass Menagerie*
1943–44
American play, no award
Foreign play, *Jacobowsky and the Colonel*
1942–43
American play, *The Patriots*
1941–42

American play, no award
Foreign play, *Blithe Spirit*
1940–41
American play, *Watch on the Rhine*
Foreign play, *The Corn Is Green*
1939–40
American play, *The Time of Your Life*
1938–39
American play, no award
Foreign play, *The White Steed*
1937–38
American play, *Of Mice and Men*
Foreign play, *Shadow and Substance*
1936–37
American play, *High Tor*
1935–36
American play, *Winterset*

NOBEL PRIZE

Many dramatists have been recipients of the Nobel Prize for literature, though some were honored for their work in poetry or fiction. Henrik Ibsen, often called the father of modern drama, is said to have been bitter that he never received a Nobel. Ironically, the first dramatist to receive a Nobel was Ibsen's contemporary and sometime rival, Bjornstjerne Bjornson, who was honored for his poetry. Eugene O'Neill was the only American dramatist ever to receive a Nobel Prize.

1974 Edmund Martinson, Sweden
1969 Samuel Beckett, Ireland
1964 Jean Paul Sartre, France (declined)
1951 Par F. Lagerkvist, Sweden
1948 T. S. Eliot, Great Britain (for poetry)
1936 Eugene O'Neill, United States
1934 Luigi Pirandello, Italy
1932 John Galsworthy, Great Britain (for his novels)
1925 George Bernard Shaw, Great Britain
1913 Rabindranath Tagore, India
1912 Gerhart Hauptmann, Germany
1911 Maurice Maeterlinck, Belgium
1910 Paul J. L. Heyse, Germany
1904 José Echegaray, Spain
1903 Bjornstjerne Bjornson, Norway (for poetry)

OBIE AWARDS

The Off-Broadway (OBIE) Awards were established by *The Village Voice* to recognize major achievements in the non-Broadway New York theatre. Though the categories have changed from year to year (note 1969), the Obies serve to bring attention to up-and-coming performers and playwrights, many of whose works could never be realized on the larger and more costly Broadway stage.

Distinguished Performances
1981 Giancarlo Esposito, *Zooman and the Sign*
     Bob Gunton, *How I Got That Story*
     Mary Beth Hurt, *Crimes of the Heart*
     Kevin Kline, *The Pirates of Penzance*
     John Lone, *FOB* and *The Dance and the Railroad*
     Mary McDonnel, *Still Life*
     Timothy Near, *Still Life*
     William Sadler, *Limbo Tales*
     Michele Shay, *Meetings*

Meryl Streep, *Alice in Concert*
John Spencer, *Still Life*
Christopher Walken, *The Sea Gull*
1980 Michael Burrell, *Hess*
Michael Cristofer, *Chinchilla*
Lindsay Crouse, *Reunion*
Elizabeth Franz, *Sister Mary Ignatius Explains It All for You*
Morgan Freeman, *Mother Courage* and *Coriolanus*
John Heard, *Othello* and *Split*
Michael Higgins, *Reunion*
Madeleine Le Roux, *La Justice*
John Polito, for performances with the Dodger Theatre Company and the BAM
    Theatre Company
Bill Raymond, *A Prelude to Death in Venice*
Dianne Wiest, *The Art of Dining*
Hattie Winston, *Mother Courage* and *The Michigan*
1979 Fred Gwynne, *Grand Magic*
Mary Alice, *Julius Caesar* and *Nongogo*
Philip Anglim, *The Elephant Man*
Elizabeth Wilson, *Taken in Marriage*
Meryl Streep, *Taken in Marriage*
Marcell Rosenblatt, *Vienna Notes*
Joseph Buloff, *The Price*
Constance Cummings, *Wings*
Judd Hirsch, *Talley's Folly*
1978 Richard Bauer, *Landscape of the Body* and *The Dybbuk*
Nell Carter, *Ain't Misbehavin'*
Alma Cuervo, *Uncommon Women*
Swoosie Kurtz, *Uncommon Women*
Kaiulani Lee, *Safe House*
Bruce Myers, *The Dybbuk*
Lee S. Wilkof, *The Present Tense*
1977 Danny Aiello, *Gemini*
Martin Balsam, *Cold Storage*
Lucinda Childs, *Einstein on the Beach*
James Coco, *The Transfiguration of Benno Blimpie*
Anne DeSalvo, *Gemini*
John Heard, *G. R. Point*
Jo Henderson, *Ladyhouse Blues*
William Hurt, *My Life*
Joseph Maher, *Savages*
Roberta Maxwell, *Ashes*
Brian Murray, *Ashes*
Lola Pashalinski, *Der Ring Gott Farblonjet*
Marian Seldes, *Isadora Duncan Sleeps with the Russian Navy*
Margaret Wright, *A Manoir*
1976 Robert Christian, *Blood Knot*
Pamela Payton-Wright, *Jesse and the Bandit Queen*
Priscilla Smith, *The Good Woman of Setzuan*
David Warrilow, *The Lost Ones*
June Gable, *Comedy of Errors*
Sammy Williams, *A Chorus Line*
Priscilla Lopez, *A Chorus Line*
Joyce Aaron, *Acrobatics*
Mike Kellin, *American Buffalo*
Roberts Blossom, *Ice Age*
Crystal Field, *Day Old Bread*
Tony LoBianco, *Yankees 3, Detroit 0*
T. Miratti, *The Shortchanged Revue*
Kate Manheim, *Rhoda in Potatoland*

1975 Reyno, *The First Breeze of Summer*
     Moses Gunn, *The First Breeze of Summer*
     Dick Latessa, *Philemon*
     Kevin McCarthy, *Harry Outside*
     Stephen D. Newman, *Polly*
     Christopher Walken, *Kid Champion*
     Ian Trigger, *The True History of Squire Jonathan*
     Cara Duff-McCormick, *Craig's Wife*
     Priscilla Smith, *Trilogy*
     Tanya Berezin, *The Mound Builders*
     Tovah Feldshuh, *Yentl the Yeshiva Boy*
1974 Barbara Barrie, *The Killdeer*
     Conchata Ferrell, *The Sea Horse*
     Loretta Greene, *The Sirens*
     Barbara Montgomery, *My Sister, My Sister*
     Zipora Spaizman, *Stepnyu*
     Elizabeth Sturges, *When You Comin' Back, Red Ryder?*
     Joseph Buloff, *Hard to Be a Jew*
     Kevin Conway, *When You Comin' Back, Red Ryder?*
1973 Maria Gorman
     Lola Pashalinski
     Alice Playten — Ron Liebman
     Roxie Roker — Austin Pendleton
     Jessican Tandy — 1969 (See separate listing.)
     Hume Cronyn — 1968 Jean David
     James Hilbrant — Mari Gorman
     Stacy Keach — Peggy Pope
     Christopher Lloyd — John Cazale
     Charles Ludlam — James Coco
     Douglas Turner Ward — Cliff Gorman
     Sam Waterston — Moses Gunn
1972 Salome Bey — Roy R. Scheider
     Jeanne Hepple — 1967 Bette Henritze
     Marilyn Chris — Tom Aldredge
     Marilyn Sokol — Robert Bonnard
     Kathleen Widdoes — Alvin Epstein
     Maurice Blanc — Neil Flanagan
     Alex Bradford — Stacy Keach
     Ron Faber — Terry Kiser
     Danny Sewall — Eddie McCarty
     Ed Zang — Robert Salvio
1971 Susan Batson — Rip Torn
     Margaret Braidwood — 1966 Clarice Blackburn
     Joan Macintosh — Marie-Claire Charba
     Hector Elizondo — Gloria Foster
     Donald Ewer — Sharon Gains
     Sonny Jimm — Florence Tarlow
     Stacy Keach — Frank Langella
     Harris Laskawy — Michael Lipton
     William Schallert — Kevin O'Connor
     James Woods — Jess Osuna
1970 Rue McClanahan — Douglas Turner
     Roberta Maxwell — 1965 Margaret De Priest
     Fredericka Weber — Rosemary Harris
     Pamela Payton-Wright — Frances Sternhagen
     Beeson Carroll — Sada Thompson
     Vincent Gardenia — Brian Bedford
     Harold Gould — Roberts Bolssom
     Anthony Holland — Robert Duvall
     Lee Kissman — James Earl Jones

1964 Joyce Ebert
Lee Grant
Estelle Parsons
Diana Sands
Marian Seldes
Philip Bruns
David Hurst
Taylor Mead
Hack Warden
Ronald Weyand
Gloria Foster
1963 Jacqueline Brooks
Olympia Dukakis
Anne Jackson
Madeleine Sherwood
Joseph Chalkin
Michael O'Sullivan
James Patterson
Eli Wallach
1962 Sudie Bond
Vinnette Carroll
Rosemary Harris
Ruth White
Clayton Corzatte
Geoff Garland
Gerald O'Laughlin
Paul Roebling
1961 Joan Hackett
Gerry Jedd
Surya Kumari
Godfrey M. Cambridge
James Coco
Lester Rawlins
1960 Patricia Falkenhain

Alissa Loti
Nancy Marchand
William Daniels
Donald Davis
Vincent Gardenia
John Heffernan
Jack Livingston
1959 Rosina Fernhoff
Anne Fielding
Nancy Wickwire
Zero Mostel
Lester Rawlins
Harold Scott
1958 Tammy Grimes
Grania O'Malley
Nydia Westman
Leonardo Cimino
Jack Cannon
Robert Geiringer
Michael Higgins
1957 Marguerite Lenert
Betty Miller
Julia Wolf
Thayer David
Michael Kane
Arthur Maiet
1956 Peggy McKay
Shirlee Emmons
Frances Sternhagen
Nancy Wickwire
Gerald Hiken
Alan Ansara
Roberts Blossom
Addison Powell

Best Play
1981 *FOB*, David Henry Hwang
Still Life, Emily Mann
1980 *A Prelude to Death in Venice*, Lee Breuer
Sister Mary Ignatius Explains It All for You, Christopher Durang
Tennessee, Romulus Linney
Full Confessions of a Socialist, Roland Muldoon
That's How the Rent Gets Paid (Part Three), Jeff Weiss
1979 *Josephine*, Michael McClure
1978 *Shaggy Dog Animations*, Lee Breuer
1977 *Curse of the Starving Class*, Sam Shepard
1976 No award
1975 *The First Breeze of Summer*, Leslie Lee
1974 *Short Eyes*, Miguel Pinero
1973 *The Hot l Baltimore*, Lanford Wilson
The River Niger, Joseph A. Walker
1972 No award
1971 *House of Blue Leaves*, John Guare
1970 *The Effect of Gamma Rays on Man-in-the-Moon Marigolds*, Paul Zindel
Approaching Simone, Megan Terry
1969 See separate listing

1968 No award
1967 No award
1966 *The Journey of the Fifth Horse*, Ronald Ribman
1965 *The Old Glory*, Robert Lowell
1964 *Play*, Samuel Beckett
   Dutchman, LeRoi Jones
1963 No award
1962 *Who'll Save the Plowboy?*, Frank D. Gilroy
1961 *The Blacks*, Jean Genet
1960 *The Connection*, Jack Gelber
1959 *The Quare Fellow*, Brendan Behan
1958 *Endgame*, Samuel Beckett
1957 *A House Remembered*, Louis A. Lippa
1956 *Absalom*, Lionel Abel

Best Actress
1968 Billie Dixon, *The Beard*
1967 No award
1966 Jane White, *Coriolanus* and *Love's Labour's Lost*
1965 No award
1964 No award
1963 Colleen Dewhurst, *Desire Under the Elms*
1962 Barbara Harris, *Oh Dad, Poor Dad, Momma's Hung You in the Closet and I'm Feelin' So Sad*
1961 Anne Meacham, *Hedda Gabler*
1960 Eileen Brennan, *Little Mary Sunshine*
1959 Kathleen Maguire, *The Time of the Cuckoo*
1958 Anne Meacham, *Suddenly Last Summer*
1957 Colleen Dewhurst, *The Taming of the Shrew, The Eagle Has Two Heads,* and *Camille*
1956 Julie Bovasso, *The Maids*

Best Actor
1971 Jack MacGowran, *Beckett*
1970 No award
1969 No award
1968 Al Pacino, *The Indian Wants the Bronx*
1967 Seth Allen, *Futz*
1966 Dustin Hoffman, *The Journey of the Fifth Horse*
1965 Roscoe Lee Browne, *The Old Glory*
   Frank Langella, *The Old Glory*
   Lester Rawlins, *The Old Glory*
1964 No award
1963 George C. Scott, *Desire Under the Elms*
1962 James Earl Jones, *Clandestine on the Morning Line, The Apple,* and *Moon on a Rainbow Shawl*
1961 Khigh Dhiegh, *In the Jungle of Cities*
1960 Warren Finnerty, *The Connection*
1959 Alfredo Ryder, *I Rise in Flame, Cried the Phoenix*
1958 George C. Scott, *Richard III, As You Like It,* and *Children of Darkness*
1957 No award
1956 Jason Robards, Jr., *The Iceman Cometh*
   George Voskovec, *Uncle Vanya*

1969 Awards
The Living Theatre, *Frankenstein*
Jeff Weiss, *The International Wrestling Match*
Julie Bovasso, *Gloria and Esperanza*
Judith Malina and Julian Beck, *Antigone*
Israel Horvitz, *The Honest-to-Goodness Schnozzola*
Jules Feiffer, *Little Murders*
Ronald Tavel, *The Boy on the Straight Back Chair*
Nathan George and Ron O'Neal, *No Place to Be Somebody*
Arlene Rothlein, *The Poor Little Match Girl*
Theatre Genesis
The Open Theatre, *The Serpent*
Om Theatre, *Riol*
The Peformance Group, *Dionysus in '69*

OUTER CIRCLE AWARDS

The Outer Circle Awards have been presented annually since 1951 by the Outer Circle, an organization of writers who review New York theatre productions for out-of-town newspapers and national publications.

1980 Ian McKellen (*Amadeus)*
       Swoosie Kurtz (*Fifth of July*)
       The Pirates of Penzance (best revival of a musical)
       William Finn (*March of the Falsettos*)
       Robert Phillips (set design, body of work)
       Arden Fingerhut (lighting design, body of work)
       Michael Smuin, Donald McKayle, Henry LeTang (choreography, *Sophisticated Ladies*)
       Ted Talley (playwright, *Coming Attractions*)
       Special Citation: National Critics Institute at the O'Neill Theatre Center
       Special Citation: Elizabeth Taylor (*The Little Foxes*, most impressive debut)
       Geraldine Fitzgerald (outstanding new director)
       Brian Backer (*The Floating Light Bulb*, outstanding debut)
       Daniel Gerroll (*Knuckle* and *The Fly Boys*, outstanding debut)
       Bario Fo (*We Won't Pay! We Won't Pay!*, outstanding foreign play)
1979 *Children of a Lesser God* (Mark Medoff)
       Barnum
       Morning's at Seven (Maureen O'Sullivan, Kate Reid, Elizabeth Wilson, Lois de Banzie and Teresa Wright, for ensemble acting)
       Gerald Hiken (*Strider)*
       John Lee Beatty (designer, *Talley's Folly* and *Hide and Seek*)
       Tommy Tune (director and choreographer, *A Day in Hollywood / A Night in the Ukraine*)
       Phyllis Frelich (*Children of a Lesser God)*
       Ensemble Studio Theatre (director Curt Dempster)
       Samm-Art Williams (playwright, *Home)*
       Pat Carroll (*Gertrude Stein, Gertrude Stein, Gertrude Stein)*
       Paul Meyers (special award)
1978 *Elephant Man* (Bernard Pomerance)
       Sweeney Todd
       Carole Shelley (*The Elephant Man)*
       John Wulp (scenic design, *Crucifer of Blood*)
       Jack Hofsiss (director, *The Elephant Man*)
       Lucie Arnaz (*They're Playing Our Song)*
       Susan Kingsley (*Getting Out)*
       Café LaMama (for continuing contribution to the theatre)
       Gregory and Maurice Hines (*Eubie)*
       Brandt Organization (for return of the New Apollo Theatre)
1977 *Da* (Hugh Leonard)

Bernard Hughes *(Da)*
Melvin Bernhardt (director, *Da*)
Martin Balsam *(Cold Storage)*
John Wood *(Deathtrap)*
Vicki Frederick *(Dancin')*
Nancy Snyder *(5th of July)*
1976 *For Colored Girls* . . . (Ntozake Shange)
Annie
Liv Ullmann *(Anna Christie)*
Dorothy Loudon *(Annie)*
Andrea McCardle *(Annie)*
David Mitchell (scenic design, *Annie*)
John Gielgud *(No Man's Land)*
Ralph Richardson *(No Man's Land)*
Andrei Serban (director, *The Cherry Orchard*)
Santo Loquasto (scenic design, *The Cherry Orchard*)
Elizabeth Swados (music, *The Cherry Orchard, Agamemnon*)
Gordon Davidson (director, *Shadow Box, Savages*)
1975 Arts Council of Great Britain
Equus
Peter Shaffer (playwright, *Equus*)
Anthony Hopkins and Peter Firth *(Equus)*
Ellen Burstyn and Charles Grodin (for outstanding ensemble playing, *Same Time, Next Year*)
Maggie Smith *(Private Lives)*
Geraldine Page *(Absurd Person Singular)*
John Cullum and Chip Ford *(Shenandoah)*
Tovah Feldshuh *(Rodgers and Hart, Yentl, Dreyfus in Rehearsal)*
Leslie Lee (playwright, *First Breeze of Summer*)
Tom Jones and Harvey Schmidt (contribution to the musical theatre through the Portfolio Studio)
Long Wharf Theatre
1974 *A Moon for the Misbegotten*
Candide
Noel Coward in Two Keys
George Rose *(My Fat Friend)*
Doris Roberts *(Bad Habits)*
Janie Sell and Ann Reinking *(Over Here)*
Sammy Cahn
Patricia Birch (choreography)
Mark Medoff (playwright, *When You Coming Back, Red Ryder?*)
1973 Christopher Plummer *(Cyrano)*
Michele Lee *(Seesaw)*
Debbie Reynolds *(Irene)*
Ellis Rabb (direction, *A Streetcar Named Desire*)
Bob Fosse (direction, *Pippin*)
Julie Harris *(The Last of Mrs. Lincoln)*
The entire cast of *The Women* (for ensemble playing)
1972 *Sticks and Bones*
That Championship Season
Don't Bother Me, I Can't Cope
Chelsea Theatre Center and Equity Library Theatre (for distinctive contributions to the theatre)
Robert Morse *(Sugar)*
Brock Peters *(Lost in the Stars)*
Sada Thompson *(Twigs)*
Marlyn Criss *(Kaddish)*
Rosemary Harris *(Old Times)*
John Houseman (for a long-standing contribution to the theatre as writer and director)
1971 *Follies*

A Midsummer Night's Dream (Peter Brook)
No, No Nanette!
Joseph Papp (New York Shakespeare Festival)
Paul Sills *(Story Theatre)*
The Phoenix Theatre (for productions of *The School for Wives* and *The Trial of the Catonsville Nine*)
John Guare (playwright, *The House of Blue Leaves*)
Claire Bloom (*Hedda Gabler* and *A Doll's House*)
Anthony Quayle and Keith Baxter *(Sleuth)*
Susan Bloch (press agent)
1970 *Child's Play*
Company
The Last Sweet Days of Isaac
The White House Murder Case
Brian Bedford *(Private Lives)*
Sandy Duncan *(The Boy Friend)*
Bonnie Franklin *(Applause)*
Lewis J. Stadlen *(Minnie's Boys)*
Frank Grimes and Niall Toibin *(Borstal Boy)*
1969 Sherman Edwards (composer, lyricist, *1776*)
Edwin Sherin (direction, *The Great White Hope*)
Elaine May (direction and author of first part, *Adaptation/Next*)
Lonnie Elder III *(Ceremonies in Dark Old Men)*
Lorraine Serabian *(Zorba)*
Dames at Sea
The Front Page
Linda Lavin (*Little Murders* and *Cop-Out*)
Jules Feiffer *(Little Murders)*
Jean Rosenthal (for contributions to stage lighting)
David Hays (for work with the National Theatre of the Deaf)
1968 *Rosenkrantz and Guildenstern Are Dead*
The Price
George M!
Your Own Thing
Pearl Bailey and Cab Calloway *(Hello, Dolly!)*
Zoe Caldwell
Harold Gary *(The Price)*
Herman Shumlin (for his career as a director and for his playwriting debut with *Spofford*)
Mike Nichols (direction, *Plaza Suite*)
The Forum and the Public theatres (as important new forces in the American theatre)
Joel Grey *(George M!)*
Helen Hayes *(The Show-Off)*
Zena Jasper *(Saturday Night)*
1967 *Cabaret*
You're a Good Man, Charlie Brown
America Hurrah
You Know I Can't Hear You When the Water's Running
Martin Balsam *(You Know I Can't Hear You When the Water's Running)*
Alexander H. Cohen (for producing *The Homecoming* and *Black Comedy* and his work in revitalizing the Tony Awards)
Melina Mercouri *(Illya Darling)* and Leslie Uggams *(Hallelujah, Baby!)* (outstanding new personalities)
Joseph Hirsch (direction, *Galileo*)
Constance Towers (*The Sound of Music* revival)
Bill and Cora Baird (for establishing a permanent puppet theatre)
1966 *Man of La Mancha*
Wait a Minim!
Frank Loesser (for the revival of his work at City Center)
David Merrick (for his contribution to the season)

Institute for Advanced Studies in the Theatre Arts (for its revival of *Phaedre*)
Gwen Verdon *(Sweet Charity)*
Angela Lansbury and Beatrice Arthur *(Mame)*
David Donnelly and Patrick Bedford *(Philadelphia, Here I Come)*
Peter Brook (direction, *Marat/Sade*)
1965 City Center Light Opera Company (for consistent excellence)
Tartuffe
Oh, What a Lovely War!
Zero Mostell *(Fiddler on the Roof)*
Mike Nichols (for directing four hits)
Tommy Steele *(Half a Sixpence)*
Sol Hurok (for importing distinguished foreign attractions)
William Hanley (outstanding new playwright)
Association of Producing Artists (for continued progress in repertory)
1964 For "the inspiration it is giving other communites": Lincoln Center for the Performing
Arts
Outstanding revival (of a classic play): *The Trojan Women*
Outstanding revival (of a modern play): *The Lower Depths*
Outstanding new playwright: Frank D. Gilroy *(The Subject Was Roses)*
"For consistently fine achievement in the theatre": Beatrice Lillie *(High Spirits)*
Honoring her first Broadway appearance in an original Broadway production: Carol
Burnett *(Fade Out–Fade In)*
"For an outstanding performance in a musical": Inga Swenson *(110 in the Shade)*
"For an outstanding performance": Lee Allen *(Marathon '33)*
"Outstanding debut": Barbara Loden *(After the Fall)*
Posthumous award: Carol Haney, choreographer
1963 Outstanding American playwright of the season: Edward Albee
Outstanding staging: Alan Schneider *(Who's Afraid of Virginia Woolf?)*
Outstanding new playwright: Murray Schisgal *(The Tiger and the Typist)*
Achievement in staging: William Ball *(Six Characters in Search of an Author)*
Special citations: Alexander H. Cohen; Helen Hayes; Maurice Evans; *Oliver!* "Out-
standing creative production"
1962 Most overall creative contribution to the season: *No Strings;* George Abbott *(A Funny
Thing Happened on the Way to the Forum)*
Best revival: *Anything Goes*
For his contribution to *How to Succeed in Business* . . .: Rudy Vallee
Most original play and production: *Oh Dad, Poor Dad,* . . .
"For being the first American to play Eliza in *My Fair Lady*": Margot Moser
Special citations: George Freedley; National Repertory Theatre
1961 Most overall creative contribution to the season: *Rhinoceros*
Most effective and imaginative contribution to a stage production: Gower Champion
(Carnival!)
Best ensemble acting: *Big Fish, Little Fish*
Distinguished performance, musical: Don Tompkins *(Wildcat)*
Outstanding achievement in designing set: Oliver Smith *(Camelot)*
Special citation: American Shakespeare Festival Theatre and Academy
1960 Best play: *The Miracle Worker*
Best musical: *Bye Bye Birdie*
Distinguished performance, drama: Risa Schwartz *(The Tenth Man)*
Distinguished performance, musical: Cecil Kellaway *(Greenwillow)*
Special citation: National Phoenix Co. *(Mary Stuart* on tour)
1959 Best play: *The Visit*
Distinguished performance, drama: Diana Sands *(A Raisin in the Sun)*
Distinguished performance, musical: Tommy Rall *(Juno)*
Set design: Oliver Messel *(Rashomon)*
Special citation: Hal Holbrook *(Mark Twain Tonight)*
1958 Best play: *Look Homeward, Angel*
Best musical: *The Music Man*
Distinguished performance, drama: Henry Jones *(Sunrise at Campobello)*
Distinguished performance, musical: Jacquelyn McKeever *(Oh, Captain!)*

Best set designer: Rouben Terarutunian *(Who Was That Lady I Saw You With)*
Special award: Joe Papp
1957 Best play: *Long Day's Journey into Night*
Best musical: *My Fair Lady*
Distinguished performance, drama: Inga Swenson *(The First Gentleman)*
Distinguished performance, musical: Stubby Kaye *(Li'l Abner)*
Cited: New York City Center Light Opera Co.; Osbert Lancaster, designer *(Hotel Paradiso)*
1956 Best play: *Diary of Anne Frank*
Best musical: *My Fair Lady*
Distinguished performance: Anthony Franciosa *(Hatful of Rain)*
Cited: Alice Pearce *(Fallen Angels);* Peter Larkin, designer *(No Time for Sergeants)*
1955 Best play: *Inherit the Wind*
Best musical: *Three for Tonight*
Outstanding performances in supporting roles: Crahan Denton *(Bus Stop);* Gretchen Wyler *(Silk Stockings)*
1954 Best play: *The Caine Mutiny Court-Martial*
Best musical: *Kismet*
Best supporting performance, drama: Eva Marie Saint *(The Trip to Bountiful)*
Best supporting performance, musical: Bibi Osterwald *(The Golden Apple)*
1953 Best musical: *Wonderful Town*
1952 Best play: *Point of No Return*
1951 Best play: *Billy Budd*
Best musical: *Guys and Dolls*
Best supporting performance: Nomi Mitty *(A Tree Grows in Brooklyn)*
1950 Best play: *The Cocktail Party*
Best musical: *The Consul*
Outstanding performance in minor roles: Daniel Reed *(Come Back, Little Sheeba);* Sheila Guyse *(Lost in the Stars)*

PAGE ONE AWARDS

The Newspaper Guild of New York Awards in Theatre.

The Page One Award for theatrical achievement in the current season was made annually by a board of judges composed of New York journalists. First given in 1945, the awards were discontinued after 1965. During the course of its existence, winners were:

1965 *Fiddler on the Roof*
1964 Alec Guinness (for his performance in *Dylan*)
1963 No award because of newspaper strike
1962 *The Caretaker;* Margaret Leighton; Paul Scofield
1961 Circle in the Square; Joan Plowright; Tammy Grimes
1960 The Living Theatre
1959 John Gielgud; Elia Kazan; Geraldine Page
1958 New York Shakespeare Festival
1957 José Quintero
1956 Paul Muni
1955 Kim Stanley; Albert Salmi
1954 John Latouche and Jerome Moross *(The Golden Apple)*
1953 Victor Moore
1052 José Ferrer
1951 Shirley Booth
1950 Alec Guiness; Irene Worth; Maurice Evans
1949 *Death of a Salesman*
1947–48 Clarence Derwent, president of Actors Equity Association
1946 *Call Me Mister*
1945 Laurette Taylor; *Deep Are the Roots; On the Town*

THE PULITZER PRIZE FOR DRAMA

The Pulitzer Prize for Drama, worth $1,000, is one of the most prestigious of all awards. It is presented by the Columbia University Graduate School of Journalism, and administered by Prof. Richard T. Baker. The award is presented each spring along with the many Pulitzer Prizes in journalism.

1981 *Crimes of the Heart*, Beth Hanley
1980 *Talley's Folly*, Lanford Wilson
1979 *Buried Child*, Sam Shepard
1978 *The Gin Game*, D. L. Coburn
1977 *The Shadow Box*, Michael Cristofer
1976 *A Chorus Line*, Michael Bennett, Nicholas Dante, Marvin Hamlisch, James Kirkwood, Edward Kleban
1975 *Seascape*, Edward Albee
1974 No award
1973 *That Championship Season*, Jason Miller
1972 No award
1971 *The Effect of Gamma Rays on Man-in-the-Moon Marigolds*, Paul Zindel
1970 *No Place to Be Somebody*, Charles Gordone
1969 *The Great White Hope*, Howard Sackler
1968 No award
1967 *A Delicate Balance*, Edward Albee
1966 No award
1965 *The Subject Was Roses*, Frank D. Gilroy
1964 No award
1963 No award
1962 *How to Succeed in Business Without Really Trying*, Abe Burrows, Frank Loesser
1961 *All The Way Home*, Tad Mosel
1960 *Fiorello!*, George Abbott, Jerry Bock, Sheldon Harnick, Jerome Weidman
1959 *J.B.*, Archibald MacLeish
1958 *Look Homeward, Angel*, Ketti Frings
1957 *Long Day's Journey into Night*, Eugene O'Neill
1956 *Diary of Anne Frank*, Frances Goodrich, Albert Hackett
1955 *Cat on a Hot Tin Roof*, Tennessee Williams
1954 *Teahouse of the August Moon*, John Patrick
1953 *Picnic*, William Inge
1952 *The Shrike*, Joseph Kramm
1951 No award
1950 *South Pacific*, Richard Rodgers, Oscar Hammerstein 2nd, Joshua Logan
1949 *Death of a Salesman*, Arthur Miller
1948 *A Streetcar Named Desire*, Tennessee Williams
1947 No award
1946 *State of the Union*, Russel Crouse, Howard Lindsay
1945 *Harvey*, Mary Chase
1944 No award
1943 *The Skin of Our Teeth*, Thornton Wilder
1942 No award
1941 *There Shall Be No Night*, Robert E. Sherwood
1940 *The Time of Your Life*, William Saroyan
1939 *Abe Lincoln in Illinois*, Robert E. Sherwood
1938 *Our Town*, Thornton Wilder
1937 *You Can't Take It with You*, Moss Hart, George S. Kaufman
1936 *Idiot's Delight*, Robert E. Sherwood
1935 *The Old Maid*, Zoe Akins
1934 *Men in White*, Sidney Kingsley
1933 *Both Your Houses*, Maxwell Anderson
1932 *Of Thee I Sing*, Ira Gershwin, George S. Kaufman, Morrie Ryskind
1931 *Alison's House*, Susan Glaspell
1930 *The Green Pastures*, Marc Connelly
1929 *Street Scene*, Elmer Rice

1928 *Strange Interlude,* Eugene O'Neill
1927 *In Abraham's Bosom,* Paul Green
1926 *Craig's Wife,* George Kelly
1925 *They Knew What They Wanted,* Sidney Howard
1924 *Hell-Bent fer Heaven,* Hatcher Hughes
1923 *Icebound,* Owen Davis
1922 *Anna Christie,* Eugene O'Neill
1921 *Miss Lulu Bett,* Zona Gale
1920 *Beyond the Horizon,* Eugene O'Neill
1919 No award
1918 *Why Marry?,* Jesse Lynch Williams
1917 No award

THEATRE HALL OF FAME

When the Uris Theatre was built in 1971, a Theatre Hall of Fame was created to honor the men and women who attained distinction over 25 or more years in the theater. An executive committee (Roger L. Stevens, Joseph Papp, L. Arnold Weissberger, Nedda Logan, Brenden Gill, Anna Sosenko, Radie Harris, and Earl Blackwell) with the help of advisors make the nominations, which are voted on by drama critics and drama editors. Those so honored on the walls of the Uris lobby:

George Abbott	Bobby Clark	Tyrone Guthrie
Maude Adams	Harold Clurman	Oscar Hammerstein II
Viola Adams	George M. Cohan	Walter Hampden
Ira Aldridge	Constance Collier	Otto Harbach
Judith Anderson	Marc Connelly	Harrigan & Hart
Maxwell Anderson	Katharine Cornell	Julie Harris
Margaret Anglin	Sir Noel Coward	Sam H. Harris
Harold Arlen	Jane Cowl	Rex Harrison
George Arliss	Cheryl Crawford	Lorenz Hart
Boris Aronson	Hume Cronyn	Moss Hart
Fred & Adele Astaire	Russel Crouse	Helen Hayes
Brooks Atkinson	Charlotte Cushman	Lillian Hellman
Tallulah Bankhead	Augustin Daly	Katharine Hepburn
Philip Barry	Agnes DeMille	Victor Herbert
Ethel Barrymore	Dudley Digges	Raymond Hitchcock
John Barrymore	Marie Dressler	Arthur Hopkins
Lionel Barrymore	John Drew	De Wolfe Hopper
Nora Bayes	Eleanora Duse	John Houseman
S. N. Behrman	Jeanne Eagles	Willie and Eugene Howard
David Belasco	Florence Eldridge	Henry Hull
Norman Bel Geddes	Maurice Evans	Walter Huston
Richard Bennett	W. C. Fields	William Inge
Irving Berlin	Minnie Maddern Fiske	Elsie Janis
Sarah Bernhardt	Clyde Fitch	Joseph Jefferson
Leonard Bernstein	Henry Fonda	Al Jolson
Ray Bolger	Lynn Fontanne	Robert Edmond Jones
Edwin Booth	Edwin Forrest	Elia Kazan
Shirley Booth	Bob Fosse	George S. Kaufman
Alice Brady	Rudolph Friml	Jerome Kern
Fanny Brice	Charles Frohman	Bert Lahr
Billie Burke	Grace George	Lawrence Langner
Abe Burrows	George and Ira Gershwin	Lillie Langry
Mrs. Patrick Campbell	Sir John Gielgud	Gertrude Lawrence
Eddie Cantor	William Gillette	Eva Le Gallienne
Morris Carnovsky	Lillian Gish	Lotte Lenya
Mrs. Leslie Carter	John Golden	Alan Jay Lerner
Ruth Chatterton	Ruth Gordon	Beatrice Lillie
Ina Claire	Charlotte Greenwood	Howard Lindsay

Frank Loesser
Frederick Loewe
Joshua Logan
Pauline Lord
Alfred Lunt
Richard Mansfield
Robert B. Mantell
Fredric March
Julie Marlow
Mary Martin
Helen Menken
Ethel Merman
David Merrick
Jo Mielziner
Arthur Miller
Henry Miller
Marilyn Miller
Helene Modjeska
Ferenc Molnar
Victor Moore
Zero Mostel
Paul Muni
George Jean Nathan
Alla Nazimova
Clifford Odets
Lord Laurence Olivier
Eugene O'Neill
Geraldine Page
Cole Porter
José Quintero
Ada Rehan
Elmer Rice

Sir Ralph Richardson
Jason Robards
Jerome Robbins
Paul Robeson
Richard Rodgers
Sigmund Romberg
Lillian Russell
William Saroyan
Robert E. Sherwood
Lee and J. J. Shubert
Otis Skinner
E. A. Sothern
E. F. Sothern
Fred Stone
Jessica Tandy
Laurette Taylor
Ellen Terry
James and Lester Wallack
David Warfield
Ethel Waters
Clifton Webb
Margaret Webster
Weber & Fields
Kurt Weill
Orson Welles
Mae West
Thornton Wilder
Bert Williams
Tennessee Williams
P. G. Wodehouse
Peggy Wood
Irene Worth

Ed Wynn
Stark Young
Florenz Ziegfeld

1981
Winthrop Ames
Robert Anderson
Junius Brutus Booth
John Mason Brown
Carol Channing
Lee J. Cobb
Betty Comden
Colleen Dewhurst
Howard Dietz
Alfred Drake
José Ferrer
Adolph Green
Uta Hagen
Jed Harris
Leslie Howard
Sidney Howard
Michael Kidd
Rouben Mamoulian
Osgood Perkins
Molly Picon
Arthur Schwartz
Oliver Smith
Maurene Stapleton
Jule Styne
Margaret Sullavan
Gwen Verdon

THEATRE TERMINOLOGY

Act call   The stage manager's warning (usually relayed by his assistant) to warn everyone of the impending curtain.

Acting edition   A published script containing staging information.

Action   The physical movements of actors on the stage, as distinct from dialogue or singing. Also used to describe plot development.

Actor-proof   Of a particularly effective role, even if acted badly.

Advance   The tickets sold before a play opens.

Agitprop   Social protest drama of the 1930s, usually Marxist.

Alternate   An actor who switches parts with another actor, common in repertory companies.

Angel   A person who invests in a theatrical production.

Annie Oakley   Somewhat archaic term for a free pass. Probably named after the sharpshooter because passes have holes punched in them that suggest bullet holes.

ANTA   American National Theatre and Academy, a private group that has been working since 1935 to encourage "the best in theatre, both professional and non-professional."

Apron   The part of the stage in front of the curtain line.

Arena stage   A theatre in which the seats wholly or partially surround the acting area. Circle in the Square has an arena stage.

Aside   A short speech addressed, to the audience to reveal a character's thoughts or convey some bit of useful information.

At liberty   The nice way to say an actor's out of work.

Balcony   A seating area above the orchestra. Usually the first balcony is called the mezzanine.

Balloon   To forget one's lines.

Billing   The printed credits for a production: author, director, actors, etc. Specifically, where and how one's name is displayed.

Blackout   To darken the stage suddenly, to emphasize action or for a quick change of scenery. (A blackout skit is one in which the stage is darkened on the curtain line.)

Blow   Like *balloon,* to forget one's lines.

Book   Several meanings: to contract for a production, a theatre, an actor, or whatever. A synonym for the script. The libretto, without the lyrics, of a musical comedy.

Book show   A musical with a plot as contrasted to a revue.

Box office   In addition to being the place where you buy your tickets, it's used to refer to a show's financial performance. *42nd Street* does good box office, for example.

Break a leg   Theatre folk believe it's bad luck to be wished good luck, hence this phrase and some others that aren't printable.

Breakeven   The amount of business a production must do before profits begin. (In England the term is *get-out.*)

Bridging   The director in rehearsals will sometimes put in explanatory words in the script to make the meaning clear. This practice is called *bridging.*

Bring down the house   To get the audience clapping until the show comes to a temporary halt. Jim Dale does this in *Barnum.*

Burlesque   Once upon a time, a play parodying drama. Now a show that features scantily clad girls, risqué humor, songs, skits, and the like. A show like *Sugar Babies.*

Bus and truck company   A production, often scaled down, that tours extensively to colleges and smaller cities, the cast in the bus and the scenery in the truck.

Byplay   Stage action that's carried on aside from the main action.

Call board   A bulletin board backstage where notices and messages to the cast and staff are posted.

Cameo part   A small part with big potential; also a small part played by a well-known actor.

Catwalk   A narrow bridge above the stage that gives access to lights and scenery.

Center   Short for centerline of the stage, sometimes imaginary, sometimes marked, from which upstage, downstage, stage right, and stage left are cued. Stage right is to the actor's right as he faces the audience.

Character actor   One who specializes in parts with markedly different characteristics from his own.

Chew the scenery   Overacting. Hams chew the scenery.

Choreography   The composition and arrangement of dances for the stage.

Chorus   A group of singers or dancers that performs as a unit; hence, chorus boy, chorine, *A Chorus Line.*

Claptrap   Any overdone or cheap way of trying to get applause.

Classic drama   Greek and Roman drama, and later plays using the same forms.

Clear   What the stage manager yells to get everyone off the stage who shouldn't be there when the curtain goes up.

Closing notice   This goes up on the call board when a show is about to close.

Comedy of manners   Gay, witty, and sophisticated play, often involving high society. Noel Coward did these to perfection.

Comic relief   Technically, a humorous scene inserted in a tragedy to ease emotional tension temporarily.

Commedia dell'arte   Influential Italian comedy style of the 16th and 17th centuries in which actors wore masks and improvised from stock characters. The grandfather of modern improvisation.

Company   Everyone in or directly connected with a production.

Comp   Short for complimentary, a free ticket.

Count the box   Check the number of tickets sold; in the old days they would open the ticket box and count the stubs.

Count the house   If you're an actor, to stare at the audience when you're onstage; producers actually count.

Credit list   The small-type listing in the program giving the names of companies providing clothing, furniture, or whatever, that are seen on stage.

Cross   To move across the stage, particularly if you pass in front of another actor.

Cue   A signal to notify someone on or off stage that it's time to do something. (Sometimes the stage manager uses a cue light to do this.)

Curtain call   When the actors come out at the end of the performance to take a bow and acknowledge the applause.

Curtain time   (or *curtain*). When the performance is scheduled to begin.

Daddy   Stage managers are often called this.

Darling   Actresses are almost always called this by people in the theatre.

Dead area   Any portion of the stage that isn't lit.

Dead it   A term used to tell a stagehand to remove something from the stage.

Deadwood   When the box office closes, the unsold tickets for that performance.

Delivery   The manner in which an actor

speaks his lines.

Denounement   The action in a comedy after the climax that explains all the complications of the plot. (Correctly speaking, in a tragedy this action is called a catastrophe.)

Divertisement   A short entertainment between the acts of a play.

Doctor   To revise and, it is hoped, improve a script. A *play doctor* is called in to do this.

Double in brass   Once, to play in the orchestra as well as perform on stage; now to play two parts in one production.

Double take   A comic response: first one facial expression, then another when the character belatedly gets the meaning.

Do you recognize the profession?   An old-timey way of asking if professional actors are let in to the show free.

Dramatic irony   When the audience knows something the actors are unaware of: a bomb under the sofa, or that the mysterious stranger is really Gwenda's long-lost husband.

Dramatic unity   That much to be desired state where every element in writing and production contributes to a single, overall effect.

Dramaturgy   A classy word for playwriting.

Drame à clef   A play in which the characters can be identified with real persons.

Dress double   Put one costume on over another to facilitate a quick change.

Dresser   A person who helps actors get in and out of costume.

Dress the stage   To place the actors, furniture, and props in a pleasing arrangement.

Drop   Any curtain of canvas or other material that comes down from the flies to the stage, usually used for background.

Effect   The creation of a sight or sound (or even a smell) to enhance the production. A few years ago, *The Crucifer of Blood* had storm effects that stopped the show.

Encore   Strictly speaking, the repeat of a song or dance or the calling for same by the audience. *Encore* is French for "again," not "how about another one?"

Ensemble   The cast of characters, except for the principals.

Ensemble theatre   Actors working together for a series of productions.

Entr'acte   Intermission.

Entrance   An actor's entry on stage. To *make an entrance* means to appear in an impressive way.

Epilogue   A speech or scene following the main performance.

Equity   Short for *Actors' Equity Association,* the professional actors' union.

Fake   Another term for ad lib.

Farce   Comedy employs realism, but farce exaggeration and improbable situations.

Fat part   A good role with a good chance of success.

Feature   To give a actor billing second only to the star or stars. If his name is preceded by "with" he's being featured.

Feel the audience   To get the emotional impact and stimulation of playing before a good audience.

First money   A producer's guarantee that the theatre owner has first claim on the show's receipts.

First night list   The persons for whom free seats are reserved on opening nights, primarily critics.

Flat   A piece of scenery usually on a rectangular frame covered with painted canvas.

Flies   The space above the stage, out of view of the audience, where scenery is hoisted up and lights are placed.

Flop   Utter failure.

Fluff   To mishandle one's lines and commit other onstage blunders.

Footlights   A strip of lights on the floor across the front of the stage, shielded from the audience.

Four walls   If a producer rents a theatre for a fixed fee instead of a percentage of the profits, he's "four-walling it."

Front of house   The business operations of a theatre: box office, ushers, etc.

Front scene   A scene played downstage in front of a drop, permitting a change of scenery to take place.

Get the hook!   Vaudeville audiences used to shout this when they had tired of a performer.

Ghost   Slang for the company treasurer. If the ghost walks, you get paid.

Good house   To an actor, an appreciative audience; to a producer, a full house of paying customers.

Go to Cain's   Close the show. From 1886 to 1937, Cain's Warehouse here sold and rented scenery to road companies.

Grand Guignol   A short, sensational horror play, named after a French theatre famous for such plays.

Greasepaint   A waxy cosmetic used as makeup.

Greenroom   A backstage lounge where actors can relax or entertain.

Grid   A framework of beams or pipes above the stage on which lights are hung.

Guild Short for the Dramatists' Guild, an association of playwrights that has standardized contracts between playwrights and producers.

Ham To overact or act badly, or one who does.

Handcuffed What audiences who don't applaud are.

Heavy A very serious play is heavy. So is a bad guy.

High comedy The other end of the scale from broad comedy; more smiles and chuckles than belly laughs.

Histrionic Theatrical, overemotional.

Hokum Time-worn theatrical devices aimed at elicitating sentimental responses.

Hold the book Be the prompter.

Hold up the scenery What bit players are said to do.

House Can be a synonym for theatre ("the Shubert is a good house"), or audience ("it was a good house tonight").

I.A.T.S.E. The stagehands' union: International Alliance of Theatrical Stage Employees and Motion Picture Operators.

Ice A kickback or bribe to a box-office treasurer by a ticket agent for special consideration on tickets to hit shows.

In association with A phrase a producer uses in print to show that the responsibility or money (or blame) isn't all his.

Ingenue She's the sweet, pretty, naïve one.

Interior monologue A character's thoughts articulated by an actor but much more like stream of consciousness than asides or soliloquies.

Intermission That's what we call it. In Britain, it's an interval, in France, entr'acte, and in Italy, intermezzo.

Jump To omit some of one's lines through forgetfulness.

Juvenile lead If you're a boy, you're a juvenile lead. A girl is an *ingenue*.

Lampoon A satire involving ridicule of an individual.

Lay an egg Fail; particularly, tell a joke that doesn't get a laugh.

Lay 'em in the aisles The opposite of lay an egg; reduce them to helpless laughter.

Legitimate drama Plays presented by actors on a stage before an audience. Vaudeville, puppetry, musical comedy, pantomime, opera, television, movies—these are not legitimate.

Libretto The text of a musical comedy.

Limelight Actually, a spotlight shining on the front of the stage. That is the most desirable part of the stage for an actor to appear on, hence, the other meaning.

Living newspaper A popular form of play in the Depression that dramatized social and political events.

Marquee The projection over the entrance to a theatre, usually displaying the theatre's name and the production playing.

Melodrama A sensational, sentimental play with a happy ending. *East Lynne* is a melodrama.

Melpomene The Muse of Tragedy. The one who cries on the front of the Sardi's menu.

Mezzanine The seating area just above the orchestra.

Mike The currently widespread practice of amplifying the voice of an actor or a singer with microphones at the front of the stage or by cordless microphones on the body of the actor.

Milestone The 100th performance of a production.

Milk To work at a scene or routine to get as much audience response as possible.

Mixed reviews Some critics liked it, some didn't.

Momus The Greek god of ridicule.

Monologue A one-man recital or performance.

Mount a production To stage a presentation, more specifically, to provide most or all of the financing.

Nut The weekly cost of producing a show. To make the nut is to break even. The story goes that when an old-time player's troupe would come to town, the innkeeper would take the axle nut from their wagon and keep it until he was paid in full.

Off-stage character A character who is mentioned in a play but never seen or heard. Godot was an off-stage character.

Orchestra The main level seating area of a theatre.

Original cast The acting company that appeared in the initial production.

Paper A free ticket. To paper the house is to give out enough free tickets to fill it up. The show will look successful and the word of mouth may help.

Peep hole A small opening in the curtain through which the audience can be observed unseen.

Pepper's ghost A trick effect in which an inclined plate of clear glass reflects a ghostly image of an actor in the orchestra pit. Named for its inventor.

Plant To introduce an idea or object early in the play that will become important later on.

Platform stage A stage that extends into the audience without a proscenium.

Play of atmosphere   A play where a single emotion is dominant. *The Cherry Orchard* is such a play.

Play of character   A play in which the plot revolves around the flawed character of the principal. *Macbeth*, for instance.

Principal   An actor who has an important role in a play.

Producer   The person who arranges for the production, particularly the financing and management.

Prompt   To remind an actor what lines or action are required at a given time, particularly if he has forgotten.

Prompt book   A play script with all the production notes, including cues.

Proscenium arch   The framing arch throughwhich the audience views the stage.

Protagonist   The central figure in a drama, usually the hero.

Quick change   The rapid substitution of one costume for another; one who does this well is a *quick-change artist*.

Rake   The slope of the orchestra (or the stage) upward toward the rear of better visibility.

Read a play   To have actors read the various parts of a play without scenery or action.

Repertory   A group of plays which a company performs alternately; a company that so performs.

Reprise   The repetition of a song or dance.

Revue (or review)   A production of unrelated sketches or musical numbers.

Rialto   Old-timey name for the theatre district. (From the name of the business district in Venice.)

Run   The number of consecutive performances of a production.

Runway   A narrow projection from the stage into the audience. Al Jolson used to sing on one.

Scalper   A person who sells tickets to a hit show at an illegally high markup.

Scene   A self-contained unit of a play, shorter than an act.

Scrim   An open-weave drop, usually painted, that gives the effect, when lighted from behind, of mist or haze.

Second-run house   A theatre to which a production is transferred after its opening run.

Showcase   A production designed to display the talents of the actors, usually in the hope that they will be noticed and cast for other productions, or that the play will be picked up by a producer.

Sightline   An imaginary line from a seat in the audience to the stage; a good theatre has good sightlines from all areas.

Sit on one's hands   To give little or perfunctory applause.

Sleeper   An unexpected success. A show that has done badly in its out-of-town previews and is a hit on Broadway.

Sock   Ancient Greek and Roman comic actors wore low soft shoes called *succus*; hence, comic acting, a *sock* hit, *socko*.

Soubrette   Usually a friend of the heroine involved in the intrigue. In *All About Eve*, Celeste Holm was the soubrette.

Spelvin, George   A fictitious name used in theatre programs to conceal the identity of an actor playing two roles. In the more important role he would be listed under his proper name, as George Spelvin in the minor role. (In England, it's Walter Plinge.)

S.R.O.   Short for standing room only. Almost never seen here except in crossword puzzles. ("This performance is sold out" is what you usually see.)

Stage business   Or just *business*. An actor's minor physical actions on stage. Lighting a cigarette or setting a table, for example.

Stagehand   A person who sets the stage, moves the scenery, and does other physical jobs backstage.

Stage manager   Assists the director during rehearsals and, once the production opens, has complete charge of everything that happens backstage except the actual acting.

Stage whisper   What you in the audience can hear but the others actors pretend not to.

Stanslavski method   Or *the Method*. Theories and techniques designed to help an actor develop a naturalistic acting style by finding the "inner reality" of a part and by trying to feel and react as the character he is playing feels and reacts, often drawing on the actor's own experiences. Lee Strasberg at the Actors Studio is the leading American exponent of method acting.

Steal   To divert the audience's attention from what it should be watching. Children and animals are notorious scene-stealers, and W. C. Fields knew it.

Step on someone's laughs   Not to give the audience sufficient time to react before coming in. Bob Hope has made stepping on his own laughs an effective part of his comic style.

Stichomythia   In emotional scenes when actors deliver short, alternating lines. Also called *cat-and-mouse*, and *cut-and-par-*

ry. Remember *Who's Afraid of Virginia Wolfe?*

Subscription   To purchase tickets for a series of productions in a season at a particular theatre. This helps the theatre raise sufficient money for its operation.

Succes d'estime   The critics raved but it didn't go at the box office.

Tableau   When the actors are silent, motionless, and obviously posed at the end of an act or performance.

Telegraph   To signal the audience with a gesture or glance that something is about to happen.

Throw-away   To underplay one's lines or stage business, usually to pass quickly over a situation offering no opportunity for dramatic development.

Tin Pan Alley   Where the publishers of popular songs have their offices and where would-be songwriters converge. Originally, the area around 28th Street and Broadway, later 50th and Broadway.

Turkey   A production can fail for many reasons; a show that fails because it deserves to fail is a turkey.

Twofer   A card permitting the purchase of two tickets for the price of one. *Going on twofers* usually means a production is running out of steam.

Two weeks under, one week out   A contractual phrase meaning if a production's gross falls below an agreed-upon level two weeks in a row, the producer has one week to move it to another theatre or close the show.

Type   An actor suited to only one kind of role, hence *type casting.*

Understudy   An actor, almost always in a small role in the cast, who learns the role of a principal and can go on for him.

Up   To know one's part well, as in, "It's opening in a week and I'm not up on Act II yet."

Upstage   The back half of a stage. To *upstage* someone is to move to that area so that he must turn his back to the audience to address you.

Vamp   To improvise. Also to play, often repeatedly, the introductory music to a song or dance number, as in *vamp 'til ready.*

Variety   What we call vaudeville, the British call variety. Also the name of the trade newspaper of the theatre world.

Walk-on   A bit part without lines.

Walk through   Usually the first rehearsal in which stage action is added.

Week-to-week notice   A closing notice that can be extended on a week-to-week basis if business picks up.

Well-made play   The correct term for a play that is strongly plotted and builds intelligently to a conclusion.

Wings   The offstage areas to the sides of the stage.

INDEX

350

ABOUT THE AUTHOR

Chuck Lawliss has had a long career in newspaper and magazine journalism, and a longer career as an ardent devotee of the theatre. He has been a staff member of *The Associated Press, Collier's, Holiday Magazine,* the *New York Herald Tribune,* and *Art in America.* Mr. Lawliss lives in New York City and is currently working on his next book.

Photo: Jim Anderson